Fair Dealing and Clean Playing

Sports and Entertainment

Steven A. Riess, *Series Editor*

Other titles in Sports and Entertainment

Fair Dealing and Clean Playing

The Hilldale Club and the Development of Black Professional Baseball, 1910–1932

by **N e i l   L a n c t o t**

Syracuse University Press

In memory of Joy Kushner

Syracuse University Press, Syracuse, New York 13244–5160

Copyright © 1994 by Neil Lanctot

All Rights Reserved

First Syracuse University Press Edition 2007

07 08 09 10 11 12   6 5 4 3 2 1

This work was previously published by MacFarland & Company, Inc., Jefferson, North Carolina, in 1994.

A number of individuals have been particularly influential in the writing of this book. Special thanks go to John Holway, who hired me in 1988 as part of a research team compiling Negro League pitching and batting statistics for Macmillan's *Baseball Encyclopedia* and gave me my first introduction to Hilldale and the world of black baseball. Professor Allen Davis of Temple University in Philadelphia was helpful during the initial stages of this work and provided the impetus to attempt a book-length treatment of the subject. I would also like to thank Stan Arnold, the grandson of Hilldale's last owner, John Drew, for helping to lead me to the Lloyd Thompson–Bill Cash collection and the staff of the Philadelphia Afro-American Historical and Cultural Museum for granting me access to the Hilldale materials. Also, Dick Clark, co-chairman of the Negro League Committee of the Society of American Baseball Research, was extremely helpful throughout, as were fellow committee members Jerry Malloy, Bob Potts, Todd Bolton, Robert Eisen, and Jim Riley, who shared research or other materials with me. Finally, I would like to express my gratitude to Anne Douglas, who lent constant encouragement and emotional support during the writing of this book.

The paper used in this publication meets the minimum requirements of American National Standard for Information Sciences—Permanence of Paper for Printed Library Materials, ANSI Z39.48–1984.∞™

For a listing of books published and distributed by Syracuse University Press, visit our Web site at SyracuseUniversityPress.syr.edu.

ISBN-13: 978–0–8156–0865–3   ISBN-10: 0–8156–0865–9

Library of Congress Cataloging-in-Publication Data

Lanctot, Neil, 1966–

Fair dealing and clean playing : the Hilldale Club and the development of black professional baseball, 1910–1932 / by Neil Lanctot.—1st Syracuse University Press ed.

p. cm.—(Sports and entertainment)

Originally published: Jefferson, N.C. : McFarland, c1994.

Includes bibliographical references and index.

ISBN-13: 978–0–8156–0865–3 (pbk. : alk. paper)

ISBN-10: 0–8156–0865–9 (pbk. : alk. paper)

1. Hilldale Club (Baseball team)—History. 2. Negro leagues—History. I. Title.

GV875.H52L36 2007

796.357—dc22   2006101382

Manufactured in the United States of America

Contents

Introduction

Those were great players back then. But
nobody knows about us anymore. If you put all
these stories in the sporting pages, they could
read all about it and understand how it was. But
that's lost history, see? It's just past, that's all.
Nobody's going to dig it up.
  — *Crush Holloway recalling his days in black pro-*
  fessional baseball with the Indianapolis ABCs,
  Baltimore Black Sox, and Hilldale during the
  1920s. Holway, Voices, 69.

In recent years, studies of the evolution of black sport have provided
valuable insights into the symbolic meaning and value of athletics for urban black communities during the era of segregation. The formation of
all-black teams fostered community and racial pride, and participation in
sports allowed African Americans a rare opportunity to excel as well as
the chance to interact and compete with whites. Yet sport, particularly
baseball, reflects not only an important aspect of black social and cultural
history, but economic history as well. The successful organization of
black professional baseball teams and leagues, despite unfavorable conditions that plagued nearly all black business enterprises during segregation,
represented a significant achievement in black economic self-development.

Most historical accounts of Negro League baseball, however, have inadequately analyzed the economic factors that contributed to the success
or failure of black professional clubs, focusing instead upon player personalities and on-field occurrences. In addition, an overemphasis on the
impoverished nature of most teams has resulted in a somewhat distorted
view of the actual financial status of black professional baseball. In reality,
black baseball, from its earliest beginnings in the 1880s until its final collapse

1

in the 1950s, differed profoundly from city to city and decade to decade, with location, timing, local competition, business acumen, economic conditions, and white influence all determining a team's fate.

The history of the Philadelphia-based Hilldale Baseball Club from 1910 through 1932 reveals the complex internal and external factors integral to the success of black professional teams. Formed as an amateur club in the small town of Darby outside Philadelphia, Hilldale rose to prominence after World War I, reaping the benefits of a booming economy and a rapidly expanding local African American population increasingly capable of establishing and supporting its own business enterprises. Simultaneously, the team profited from the enormous popularity of semipro baseball in Philadelphia and the nearly constant bookings available for African American clubs, as well as a central location conducive to inexpensive travel to New York, Baltimore, and Atlantic City. Finally, the burning ambition and remarkable business skills of the team's African American president and part owner, Edward Bolden (1881–1950), enabled Hilldale to achieve two decades of prosperity and stability at a time when most black financed teams and enterprises were prone to failure.

This study examines Bolden's administrative role in the fascinating yet obscure history of Hilldale and utilizes the team's remarkably preserved financial records (housed at the Bill Cash–Lloyd Thompson Collection in the Philadelphia Afro-American Historical and Cultural Museum) and comparative analysis of other professional clubs to reveal how black baseball developed and prospered in the post–World War I era, faltered in the late 1920s, and eventually collapsed in the wake of the Depression. The economic significance of Hilldale's relationship with white semiprofessional teams, Organized Baseball clubs, and rival black professional franchises is also analyzed, as well as key factors affecting local African American support. In addition, Bolden's major involvement in the continued development of professional black baseball is considered, particularly his formation and operation of the Eastern Colored League and Hilldale's participation in the first black World Series in 1924.

Despite numerous accomplishments during his unprecedented 40-year active involvement in black professional baseball, Bolden has been largely overlooked by historians, perhaps because of his reserved manner and unspectacular employment as a postal worker. A recently published exhaustive biographical index of African Americans typically omitted Bolden despite the inclusion of several black baseball players and his daughter Hilda, a Washington, D.C., physician. By chronicling the forgotten story of Hilldale, this book attempts to grant him his rightful place in both baseball and African American history.

1

Beginnings: Baseball in Philadelphia, 1860–1916

> Since from the lots baseball stars must be
> recruited, there is abundant hope for the future
> of the national game in the increasing number
> of youngsters who engage in the sport.
> —Philadelphia North American, *May 15, 1910.*

The origins of Hilldale were profoundly shaped by developments in Philadelphia's baseball history. From baseball's earliest beginnings, Philadelphia was integral to the development of the sport as the game quickly became a local favorite of both blacks and whites. As early as the 1830s, "town ball," an antecedent of baseball, was played in Philadelphia by white teams like the Olympic Town Ball Club, and other bat-and-ball games such as cricket and rounders were also popular. Yet by 1860, the popularity of the New York game, developed by Alexander Cartwright of the Knickerbocker Club during the 1840s, had taken firm root in Philadelphia and other cities. Featuring nine players to a team, three outs per inning, and a diamond-shaped infield with bases 90 feet apart, the New York game was the prototype for modern baseball. In 1858, the Penn Tigers of Philadelphia began playing the Cartwright version of the game, and two years later the Olympic club switched from town ball to baseball.

Baseball reached new heights of popularity during the late 1850s and early 1860s as numerous teams were organized in Philadelphia and other northeastern cities. Growth continued during the Civil War. Soldiers of both Union and Confederate armies played baseball, and on the northern home front several teams operated successfully throughout the war with strong spectator support. In Philadelphia, the Athletic Baseball Club was

3

formed in 1860 and challenged the Olympic team for supremacy, finally emerging as the dominant local team by the war's end in 1865. While still technically amateur during this period, the Athletics and other strong clubs noted the growing attendance and potentially lucrative financial aspects of the game. Enclosed playing fields, allowing admission to be charged, would be built during the 1860s, with the Athletics field at 15th and Columbia among the first in the country. As early as 1865, the Athletics had even begun to pay salaries to certain players, and in 1869 the nation's first openly all-salaried team, the Cincinnati Red Stockings, appeared.

By 1871, the Athletics were salaried and joined the first professional baseball league, the National Association of Professional Base Ball Players, with teams in Chicago, Boston, Washington, New York, Troy (N.Y.), Fort Wayne, Cleveland, and Rockford (Ill.). The Athletics captured the association's first championship and would remain in the league until its demise in 1875. With the association's inclusion of two other Philadelphia teams (the White Stockings and the Centennials) and its disproportionate number of Philadelphia-born players, the city developed a well-deserved reputation as a baseball stronghold during the early 1870s. The Athletics, however, fared poorly in the first year of the newly organized National League of Professional Ball Clubs and were expelled after the 1876 season, along with the New York Mutuals, for failing to play scheduled games.

Philadelphia was without a professional team until 1882 when a new Athletic team joined the American Association, a second major league that lasted until 1891. Recognizing baseball's massive popularity in southeastern Pennsylvania, league organizers would never again overlook Philadelphia in the future. The following year, after a seven-year absence, the city finally gained a representative in the National League as the Philadelphia Phillies joined the circuit. In 1884, Philadelphia was the only city to be represented in all three major leagues with the Athletics in the American Association, the Phillies in the National League, and the Keystones of the short-lived Union Association. With the formation of the Players' League in 1890, baseball-crazed Philadelphians could again see three major league franchises in action, with three parks all located within a four-block area in North Philadelphia between 12th and Broad Streets and Dauphin and Lehigh Streets. Yet by the close of the 1890s, only the Phillies remained.[1]

Despite the rise of professionalism, amateur baseball flourished in Philadelphia and the surrounding area after the Civil War, sparked initially by professional clubs like the Athletics whose travels to small towns helped to stimulate interest. Dozens of neighborhood and town teams were formed as well as local "athletic clubs" that while modeled after the elite organizations of white-collar professionals, were usually composed of blue-collar workers who played only baseball. By the 1880s, several ballparks were located throughout the city, including Circus Park at B and Dauphin Streets, Jumbo Park at Broad and Dickinson Streets, Keystone Park at Broad and Moore, and Olympic Park at 18th and York Streets. Games were often scheduled in conjunction with a social event as several of the grounds had picnic and boating areas available for rental by amateur teams. The most notable nonprofessional club in the postwar years, the Shibe Club under Ben Shibe, who later owned the Philadelphia Athletics, operated from 1877 through 1881 in the absence of a professional team in Philadelphia.

Yet the postwar industrial surge provided the greatest impetus to the amateur game in Philadelphia and other northern cities as local businesses and industries began to sponsor and organize baseball teams as a means of improving relations with employees and an advertising device. In the larger industrial firms, employers were especially motivated by the idea of "welfare capitalism," which through the addition of company-sponsored athletics and recreation sought to improve worker morale and productivity while discouraging unionism and strikes. By 1900, department stores, hotels, insurance companies, newspapers, railroads, factories, mills, and other smaller business establishments regularly sponsored baseball teams and leagues, with games often scheduled during lunchtime or nonwork hours.

During this period, the line between "professional" and "amateur" teams became increasingly blurred. The strictly amateur teams became less common, as most were composed of younger players on neighborhood or small-town teams. Meanwhile, the more prevalent semiprofessional teams, or "semipros," earned money from playing ball either by passing the hat to cover expenses, charging admission, playing for a bet, or obtaining some form of sponsorship with a few players occasionally paid, usually the pitcher and catcher. Semipros, however, differed from professionals in that they did not derive their sole source of income from baseball. In contrast, the "independent" baseball team paid all its players, played baseball on a daily basis rather than weekly, and had home grounds or traveled. Unlike organized baseball (the major and minor leagues), however, independents had no reserve clause binding players to the clubs and were thus labeled semipro instead of professional.[2]

Between 1900 and 1910, the local baseball scene in Philadelphia exploded with activity. The *Philadelphia North American*, one of the more enthusiastic supporters of semipro ball, estimated that "on a Saturday in Philadelphia 50,000 men and boys either play or watch games" and noted that "people in Pennsylvania, New Jersey, Delaware and Maryland are inoculated with baseball virus, and every city, town, village, hamlet and corner lot has a team." The 1907 *Spalding Baseball Guide* reported that the Philadelphia area had more semipro leagues than ever before, and in 1908 the *Philadelphia Inquirer* sponsored its first amateur championship series.

Newly built trolley lines linking towns and neighborhoods heightened league formation in the city and suburbs. Delaware County, west of the city, formed its own league in 1908, and by 1911 other suburban leagues, including Montgomery County, Main Line, Interborough, North Penn, and Bucks County, were intact and flourishing. In Philadelphia the Knights of Columbus League, Philadelphia Independent League, Philadelphia Suburban League, Northeast Suburban League, and West Philadelphia League were but a few of the many organizations founded, and some, like the Philadelphia Suburban, lasted until the 1930s. Most leagues consisted of four to eight teams, played from May to October on Saturdays and holidays, and were usually semipro or amateur, although some circuits, especially the Delaware County League, eagerly hired skilled players for crucial games. Others followed the example of the Main Line League, which banned "professionals" from the league in 1912.[3]

The majority of teams, however, had no league affiliation and simply played ball on a casual basis, scheduling games against other teams of similar strength while hoping to build a local reputation and following. Newspaper publicity was important to any ambitious local club, and all the Philadelphia dailies gave generous coverage to semipro baseball, printing box scores, announcements, and challenges. In 1910, the *North American*'s annual "Roster of Local Amateurs" ranked nearly 300 teams into five classifications from ages 11 to 21 and provided a separate category of "First Class" clubs encompassing the finest teams in the city. The lower end of the hierarchy was occupied by the young boys' neighborhood teams, who often played without uniforms on open fields or sandlots yet gave many players their first exposure to baseball. Typically, local youngsters began their baseball careers on these teams and were recruited by stronger clubs if they showed promise. In 1913, for example, 16-year-old Jimmy Dykes started the season with his father's Penn Street Boys Club team, eventually jumped to a team in Ardmore on the Main Line for 50 cents a game plus carfare, and later joined yet another club when offered $1 a game. By 1916, Dykes was a regular in the Delaware County League and within two years he debuted in the major leagues with Connie Mack's Philadelphia Athletics.

With extensive backing and financial support, industrial and company teams dominated the semiprofessional scene nationally during the Progressive era. Facing increasingly hostile criticism from reformers and unions, industrialists responded by embracing welfare capitalism more eagerly than ever. The implementation of extensive industrial athletic and recreation programs helped silence critics by demonstrating concern for labor, but more importantly placated potentially dissatisfied workers, built company loyalty, and simultaneously suppressed unionism. Industrial recreation also provided an ideal opportunity for management to exert some control over employees' increasing leisure time resulting from a shorter workweek. By 1915, industrial sponsorship of sports was commonplace throughout the country, with baseball the most popular industrial sport.[4]

In Philadelphia several of the strongest semipro teams before World War I were corporate sponsored. In 1913, the nonunion Stetson Hat Company built a $100,000 baseball field at 4th and Berks with a seating capacity of 4,000 for its company team. Originally composed of employees, the Stetson team, like many other industrial teams, eventually included men hired by the company solely for their athletic ability. The Philadelphia-based Strawbridge and Clothier Department Store also featured an extensive athletic program and highly rated baseball team. With an attractive playing field at 63rd and Walnut Streets, the store had its own baseball league with various departments such as Credit, Retail, Clover, and White Sale represented, while the company's best players and imported "ringers" represented the "varsity" team.

As nationally renowned companies like Pullman, Ford, and General Electric began organizing entire athletic associations for their employees, local firms followed suit. With a membership of 1,200 employees, the Disston Saw Company's athletic association, organized in 1914, provided grounds for its soccer, baseball, football, basketball, tennis, and track teams at the interdepartmental and varsity level. Other large firms in the city—including the Philadelphia Electric Company, the United Gas and Improvement Company (UGI), Westinghouse Electric, Lit Brothers department store, Midvale Steel, E.G. Budd, and Pennsylvania Railroad—sponsored teams, leagues, and athletic associations. The continuing growth of industrial teams spurred further league development in Philadelphia, resulting in the formation of the Industrial League in 1913 and the Manufacturers League three years later, as well as the white-collar Bankers and Brokers League in 1914 and the Financial Mercantile League in 1915.

Corporate sponsorship was also integral to the formation of women's teams in Philadelphia. Though hardly encouraged, many young women were enthusiastic fans and played baseball when given the chance. As early as 1913, a baseball league for girls between the ages of eight and 15 was organized in the Germantown section of the city. Stetson and Disston both fielded women's baseball teams, and by 1921, other large companies in Philadelphia, including Fleisher Yarn, J. & J. Dobson, and Westinghouse Electric, sponsored teams for their female employees.[5]

Largely because of the impact of the national playground movement, municipal support for baseball became prevalent during the Progressive era. City governments began to view organized recreation and sports as effective antidotes to juvenile delinquency and a means of "Americanizing" immigrant children. The subsequent national increase in public parks and playgrounds available for ballplaying compensated for the rapidly declining sandlots victimized by subdivision. In addition, churches, citing the wholesome moral values of organized sport, increasingly sponsored athletics, with heavy Catholic involvement in Philadelphia resulting in the formation of several noteworthy teams, including the Shanahan, Nativity, Victrix, and Corley Catholic clubs. Political organizations also sponsored teams, ranging from the 36th Ward Republican Club in 1910 to the Socialist Baseball Club in 1911.[6]

With a multitude of unaffiliated teams and lack of a central authority to solve problems and arbitrate differences, chaos often prevailed in the ultracompetitive world of semiprofessional and amateur baseball. While some leagues had contracts and attempted to enforce a reserve clause, most semipro teams had virtually no control over their players, who freely jumped from team to team. Player personnel commonly fluctuated as some players appeared with as many as three clubs during the same week and entire teams were occasionally hired to double as another community's team.

Competition was especially fierce in securing public or private playing fields, and teams unable to obtain grounds and forced to travel found survival difficult. As prestige was crucial in scheduling games, clubs attempted to preserve or distort their won and lost record by any means possible. Some simply lied about their records; others recorded wins under one team's name and losses under another. Newspapers frequently complained of local clubs who sent in two vastly different summaries of the same game, each claiming victory. Team records, infrequently compiled, were rendered meaningless by constant player shifts and the diversity of competition, and outside an elimination tournament or series, no reliable method existed to determine the best team.

Umpiring, however, was the most insurmountable problem faced by semipro teams. Selected and hired by the home team, umpires were hardly impartial observers, and semipro clubs were often unbeatable on their home grounds. Despite frequent arguments and fights, umpires lacked sufficient authority or protection to control unruly players or enforce unpopular decisions, resulting in the common tactic of a team simply walking off the field if a decision displeased them. While organizations such as New York's Intercity Association were formed to regulate semiprofessional baseball, not until 1922 was a large-scale organization attempted in Philadelphia. Booking agents, however, such as Walter Schlichter locally and Nat Strong in New York, began to exercise greater control, arranging and scheduling semipro games for a fee of 5–10 percent of the gross gate receipts.[7]

Meanwhile, professional baseball continued to prosper in Philadelphia during the Progressive era, mainly because of a new team, the Athletics of the recently formed American League. During the late 1890s, Ban Johnson, president of the Western League, a minor league organization, had begun challenging the National League by signing players and placing franchises in large eastern cities. Renaming his circuit the American League in 1900, Johnson began a war with the National League that would last until 1903, finally resulting in a new National Agreement that created two separate but equal major leagues.

As part of his invasion of National League territory, Johnson had placed a franchise in Philadelphia in 1901 in direct competition with the Phillies. Managed by Connie Mack, a former National League catcher and manager, the Athletics soon eclipsed the Phillies in popularity. Under Mack, the team's manager through 1950, the Athletics enjoyed strong support at their home grounds, first at Columbia Park at 29th and Columbia until 1909 and later at newly built Shibe Park at 21st and Lehigh. Featuring pitchers such as Chief Bender, Eddie Plank, Rube Waddell, and Jack Coombs, and the "$100,000 infield" of Frank Baker, Jack Barry, Eddie Collins, and Stuffy McInnis, the Athletics achieved remarkable success between 1901 and 1914, winning the American League pennant six times and the World Series in 1910, 1911, and 1913. Meanwhile, the Phillies, generally mediocre, were outdrawn by the Athletics until 1915 when pitcher Grover Cleveland Alexander and slugging outfielder Gavvy Cravath led the team to its first World Series appearance (and its last until 1950).[8]

Minor league organizations such as the Tri-State League also attracted local supporters. Formed in 1904 as an "outlaw" league outside organized baseball, the Tri-State League eventually came under the protection of the major leagues in 1907 as a Class B minor league. Most of the larger towns in Pennsylvania, New Jersey, and Delaware were represented at various times during the league's existence from 1904 to 1914, including Wilmington in Delaware; Chester, Coatesville, Johnstown, Williamsport, Allentown, Harrisburg, Reading, York, and Lancaster in Pennsylvania; and Trenton, Camden, and Atlantic City in New Jersey. Yet despite the proximity of major and minor league baseball teams, sandlot and semipro ball remained extremely popular, especially among the working class. Working five and a half to six days a week, most laborers found it inconvenient or expensive to attend major league games played in the midafternoons during the week. With Sunday baseball illegal in Pennsylvania, the nearby Saturday semipro game was an attractive alternative for many local baseball fans.[9]

Major and minor league teams, however, remained in close contact with strong semiprofessional and independent clubs, often scheduling profitable exhibition games with them in spring training, on off days, and at the end of the season. Prohibited from playing Sunday ball in Philadelphia, the Phillies and Athletics as well as their opponents often scheduled games against strong Philadelphia area teams in communities where the Sunday ban was ignored or evaded. Major leaguers also realized that the caliber of local baseball was particularly strong in Philadelphia and that its amateur scene was a fertile breeding ground for future big leaguers. Connie Mack of the Athletics was never reluctant to try local players. Several key members of his championship teams between 1901 and 1914, including Amos Strunk, Monte Cross, Harry Davis, Danny Murphy, Jack Lapp, Herb Pennock, and Bris Lord, began their careers on the sandlots of Philadelphia or its suburbs. Other notable local players who went on to successful major league careers during this time included Wid Conroy, Roy Thomas, and Kid Gleason, manager of the infamous Chicago White Sox team implicated in the 1919 Black Sox scandal.

Aging major and minor league players often retired to the sandlots after their careers had declined. Vic Willis, an eight-time 20-game winner during his 13-year major league career, returned to his home state of Delaware in 1911 to pitch for the Newark team. In 1915, former Athletics third baseman Monte Cross appeared on the Media team at the age of 46 in the Delaware County League, and George Mullin, a 29-game winner with the Detroit Tigers in 1909, pitched for Chester. Occasionally, disgruntled players jumped their professional clubs to play for a strong semipro team, sometimes under assumed names, to the chagrin of organized baseball. While the National Commission, the three-man governing body of major league baseball until 1920, outlawed any semipro teams harboring ineligible players who were still legally the property of organized baseball, local teams and leagues, most notably the Delaware County League, remained a haven for professional ballplayers. Embroiled in a contract dispute with Connie Mack, Frank Baker refused to sign with the Athletics and spent the entire season with the Upland team of the Delaware County League in 1915. The Upland team, with backing by millionaire John P. Crozer, employed several other former and current major leaguers between 1915 and 1919, including Chief Bender, Bris Lord, and even Babe Ruth for a short time, and by 1919 the Delaware County League was declared an outlaw league by organized baseball.[10]

At the same time that baseball became popular among whites in Philadelphia, African Americans in the city also developed a keen appreciation of the sport. Free blacks had steadily settled in Philadelphia, thanks to its strategic location between the North and the South, and by 1860 more African Americans lived in Philadelphia than in any other northern city. Facing discrimination and segregation, the city's 22,000 black citizens responded by forming their own organizations and institutions. Like white Philadelphians, blacks enjoyed ball games during leisure time, playing town ball, and even formed cricket clubs during the 1850s, including the Olive, Metamora, and Diligente clubs, who played weekly games at Broad and Locust Streets.

By the end of the Civil War, baseball had eclipsed cricket in popularity among blacks in Philadelphia, symbolized by the formation of two amateur clubs, the Excelsiors and the Pythian Club. While the Excelsiors enjoyed early success, even traveling to Long Island for a "championship" game in October 1867, they were soon surpassed by the Pythians. Organized mainly by Octavius V. Catto, a teacher and principal at the Institute for Colored Youth, a Quaker-founded trade school, the Pythians, like early white amateur teams, functioned not only as a baseball club but also as a social club. A piniclike atmosphere prevailed at their games as spectators, including many women, enjoyed food and entertainment as part of the festivities. Relying on club membership dues and local contributions, the Pythians banqueted visiting black clubs and received the same treatment when traveling outside the area. With the increasing commercialization of baseball in the late 1860s and early 1870s, both white and black amateur teams would largely dispense with these elegant trappings. Yet baseball would remain an important part of any outdoor social occasion, and as late as 1920 holiday games between two Philadelphia-area black semipro teams still occasionally offered music, races, refreshments, and a picnic.

Like their white counterparts the Athletics, the Pythians faced local teams as well as regional opponents from Albany, Harrisburg, Washington, and Camden, even traveling to Washington in 1869 to play the Mutual Club. While the Pythians had some contact with the Athletics, renting their grounds on occasion and employing one of their players as an umpire, the two teams would never meet on the playing field. Some white clubs, including the Olympics and the City Items, did play the Pythians, but most chose to ignore the black team. The Pythians encountered more blatant discrimination in 1867 when two amateur organizations, the National Association of Base Ball Players (NABBP) and the Pennsylvania state amateur association, both rejected the team's application for membership. Noting that if "colored clubs were admitted there would be in all probability some division of feeling, whereas, by excluding them no injury could result to anybody and the possibility of any rupture being created on political bounds would be avoided," the NABBP's position began a policy of exclusion and segregation of African Americans that would continue with few exceptions in white professional baseball for the next 80 years.

The Pythians eventually disbanded in the early 1870s following the murder of Catto, an officer in a local black army brigade who was shot by Frank Kelly, a white man, while attempting to join his unit at the scene of the voting race riots in Philadelphia in October 1871. While Kelly was acquitted six years later, various incarnations of the Pythians would resurface in the future, some sponsored by the Knights of Pythias, a black fraternal organization.[11]

Despite lacking the widespread corporate and industrial sponsorship of white teams and being excluded from white semipro and professional leagues, black clubs, most notably the Mutuals and the Orions, continued to organize in Philadelphia during the 1870s and 1880s. Not surprisingly, Philadelphia's burgeoning black baseball scene contributed to the formation of the first black professional team, an event that would transform black baseball nationwide. In May 1885, Frank Thompson, a hotel worker, organized the Keystone Athletics, a black Philadelphia club. Relocating the team to the resort of Babylon, Long Island, in July, Thompson then merged his club with two other black teams, the Manhattans of Washington, D.C., and Philadelphia's Orions. Known as the Cuban Giants (supposedly because the team spoke a mock Spanish dialect attempting to pass as Cuban and for the popularity of the white New York Giants), the slick playing team provided entertainment for the wealthy patrons of the Argyle Hotel in Babylon while holding down positions at the hotel. Capitalizing on the novelty of an all-black baseball team, Thompson and S.K. Govern, the team's black manager, secured bookings and employment for the Giants in St. Augustine, Florida, at the Hotel Ponce de Leon during the winter, and in 1886, the team became established at Trenton, New Jersey, under the ownership of Walter Cook, a wealthy Trenton businessman, drawing salaries of $12 to $18 weekly.[12]

Featuring the best black players in the country, the Cuban Giants became the prototypical black independent professional team, traveling widely and playing year round against black and white semiprofessional and professional clubs, including the Philadelphia Athletics in 1885. Initially viewed as a circus or novelty act, the team soon attracted favorable notice from white sportswriters and players, and reportedly the Athletics were so impressed by first baseman Arthur Thomas of the Giants that he was offered a major league contract. While Thomas never appeared with the team, a handful of individual black players and teams did play in organized baseball between 1877 and 1899, mostly during the 1880s. Yet a nationwide resurgence in discrimination and hostility toward blacks, facilitated by Supreme Court decisions declaring the 1875 Civil Rights Act unconstitutional in 1883 and establishing the "separate but equal" doctrine for public accommodations in *Plessy v. Ferguson* (1896), doomed African American participation in organized baseball and would result in complete exclusion by 1900.[13]

The success of the Cuban Giants led to the formation of other independent black professional teams nationwide during the next decade, including the Pittsburgh Keystones, Cuban X-Giants (organized in 1896 by several former Cuban Giant players), Norfolk Red Stockings, St. Louis Black Stockings, New York Gorhams, Boston Resolutes, Chicago Unions, and Lincoln Giants (of Lincoln, Nebraska). Emphasizing showmanship as well as excellent ballplaying skills, black teams became increasingly attractive opponents for white professional and semiprofessional teams and sparked the continued growth of sandlot and amateur baseball among African Americans. In Philadelphia, as the city's black population continued to climb steadily, reinforced by a heavy southern migration during the 1890s, most black neighborhoods had amateur teams by 1900, although the city still lacked its own black professional team.

Local African Americans still had plenty of baseball to enjoy. Strong professional black teams made regular trips to Philadelphia, Camden, and Atlantic City to face both white and black competition, as the numerous white semiprofessional teams in Philadelphia and large black population made the city an especially attractive stop for barnstorming black clubs. In 1901 a heavily attended game at Columbia Park between the Cuban X-Giants and the fourth-place Philadelphia Athletics of the American League attracted the attention of H. Walter Schlichter, a white sportswriter for the *Philadelphia Item*. Sensing the possibilities of a strong black team in Philadelphia, Schlichter organized the Philadelphia Giants in 1902 with the help of Sol White, the captain of the Cuban X-Giants, and Harry Smith of the *Philadelphia Tribune*, the city's black newspaper. White, who had played in white organized baseball in the Ohio League in 1887 and with the finest black teams in the country, including the Cuban Giants, joined the team as manager and shortstop.

The *Item* proudly noted in April 1902, "For the first time in the history of base ball in this city a star team of colored ball players will wear a Philadelphia uniform. The Philadelphia Giants . . . is composed of some of the best players in America to-day, and were it not for the fact that their skin is black, some of them would to-day be drawing fancy salaries in one or the other of the big leagues." Spending most of their time on the road playing semipro teams in Pennsylvania, New Jersey, and New York, the team had a fine inaugural season in 1902 with an 81-43-2 record. Lacking their own grounds, the Giants were able to use the Philadelphia Athletics park at 29th and Columbia while the Athletics were away and played a hard-fought two-game series against the American League champion team at the season's conclusion. Despite losing both games, the Giants impressed the white major leaguers appearing in the series, especially slugging outfielder Buck Freeman of Boston, who struck out five times against Kid Carter of the Giants.[14]

Featuring stars such as pitchers Andrew "Rube" Foster (nicknamed for defeating the legendary Athletic pitcher Rube Waddell) and Danny McClellan, outfielder Pete Hill, and slugging shortstop Grant "Home Run" Johnson, the Philadelphia Giants enjoyed unparalleled success, winning 426 of 575 games played from 1903 to 1906, and defeated the Cuban X-Giants in 1904 in an unofficial world series of black baseball. In 1906 the Giants were named champions of the International League, a racially mixed Philadelphia league composed of black, white, and Cuban independent teams, after capturing the championship game at Phillies Park on Labor Day before a crowd estimated at 10,000 fans. Yet despite the team's numerous triumphs, salaries were low (supposedly $40 a month), and several players, especially Rube Foster, blamed the team's white booking agents, Schlichter and Nat Strong. Following the 1906 season, Foster, along with other dissatisfied players, jumped the Giants and joined the Chicago-based Leland Giants. The Philadelphia club continued to operate until player defections finally forced the team to disband during the 1911 season.[15]

Philadelphia Giants, 1905. Seated left to right: Danny McClellan, Pete Hill, Tom Washington, Mike Moore, Bill Monroe. Standing: Grant "Home Run" Johnson, Rube Foster, Emmett Bowman, H. Walter Schlichter, Sol White, Pete Booker, and Charlie Grant. Featuring a brilliant pitching staff of Foster, McClellan, and Bowman, the Giants posted an astounding 134-21-3 record during the 1905 season (National Baseball Library and Archive, Cooperstown, N.Y.).

Despite the collapse of the Giants, black Philadelphians could still attend dozens of semiprofessional and amateur games played in their neighborhoods on Saturdays and holidays. Restricted socially and economically, few of Philadelphia's 85,000 blacks had the opportunity or desire to attend major league games at Shibe Park or Phillies Park. As Rob Ruck noted in his study of black sport in Pittsburgh, blacks "were much more likely to watch or play on the sandlots of their own or a neighboring community, where admission was a contribution to the passing hat . . . and players were neighbors, workmates, and kin."

The Philadelphia area literally swarmed with black baseball clubs, all aspiring to reach the heights of the famous Philadelphia Giants. By 1914, the city was represented by the North Philadelphia Giants, West Philadelphia Giants, South Philadelphia Giants, East Philadelphia Giants, and East End Giants of Germantown. Outside the city, black teams in the nearby communities of Norristown, Ambler, LaMott, Chester, Camden (New Jersey), and Wilmington (Delaware) were similarly named. Other strong teams in the Philadelphia area included the Ideal Travelers, Evergreen Hall of southern New Jersey, Blue Ribbon Club of Germantown, Anchor Giants, Philadelphia Defiance, Bon Ton Field Club of Germantown, Ardmore Tigers, and Chester Stars.

While the sandlots continued to produce the majority of players and teams, increased sponsorship emerged both inside and outside the black community. Black redcaps (porters) at Broad Street Station sponsored a team, as did the black employees at the Central Post Office. Prominent African American organizations and businesses, including the *Philadelphia Tribune*, the 30th Ward Republican Club, and the Southwest branch of the YMCA, also organized teams after 1910, and black churches continued to make baseball part of social functions, occasionally sponsoring athletic events. Yet no organized league for black teams existed in the city, and most clubs, like many of their white counterparts, were relegated to a constant search for adequate opponents in hopes of gaining a reputation. Black teams also faced the additional difficulties of finding suitable playing fields as most playgrounds or parks were inaccessible, inadequate, or closed to blacks.[16]

In this environment, a group of young black men in the borough of Darby, an African American "satellite community" southwest of Philadelphia in Delaware County just across the city line, decided to form their own baseball team in the spring of 1910. Incorporated in 1853, Darby was originally part of Darby Township in Delaware County and was one of several communities partitioned from the original land area, including Upper Darby, Sharon Hill, Collingdale, Aldan, Colwyn, Yeadon, Glenolden, and Folcroft. Seeking to escape the congestion of the city, a handful of black families had moved into Darby, and by 1910 nearly 700 blacks lived in the conveniently located borough, only a 45-minute, five-cent ride from downtown Philadelphia. Comprising 10 percent of the town's population by 1910, blacks nonetheless were restricted to living "up on the Hill," as white realtors refused to make housing available in any other section of Darby.[17]

Naming themselves Hilldale, perhaps after a local thoroughfare, the team hardly differed from any of the dozens of black or white amateur teams that formed, folded, and disappeared during the season. Consequently, the following notice buried within the *Philadelphia Sunday Item*'s "Amateur Base Ball Notes!" of May 29, 1910, probably did not attract much attention: "Hilldale A.C. would like to arrange games with all 14 and 15-year old traveling teams. Pay half expenses. Address Manager A.D. Thompson No. 329 Marks Avenue, Darby, Pa."[18]

The team's first manager was 19-year-old Austin Devere Thompson, and his younger brother Lloyd was the team's 14-year-old second base-man. Ranging from ages 14 to 17, most of the players were young work-men from Darby and nearby communities who, like most African American men, held unskilled or semiskilled jobs. One of the early Hill-dale players, Mark Studevan, was a soap maker; the team's catcher, Thomas Jenkins, was a bricklayer who after working a half day on Satur-day would rush home to put on his uniform in time for an afternoon game.[19] The team played in an open clearing in Darby at 10th and Sum-mit Streets and took up a collection after each game to meet expenses.

Little is known about Hilldale's first year. The earliest documented game was played on June 11, 1910, as the "Hilldale Field Club" suffered a 10–5 defeat at the hands of Lansdowne.[20] Before the team's first season ended, A.D. Thompson had left the team and was replaced by Ed Bolden, a Philadelphia postal clerk who, like Thompson, lived on Marks Avenue in Darby. Bolden had been asked to keep score of one of Hilldale's games and was subsequently invited to assume control of the undisciplined young team. Born on January 17, 1881, in Concordville, Pennsylvania, 15 miles from Darby, Bolden at 29 was older and more firmly established than most of the players with a stable, prestigious job, a wife, Nellie, and a three-year-old daughter, Hilda. Yet he was a rabid baseball fan, and the prospect of managing a local team clearly intrigued him.

The diminutive Bolden, barely 5-7 and 145 pounds, was not a baseball player but had been employed in the Central Post Office in Philadelphia since 1904 after working as a butler for three years. With nearly impeccable work habits, he was said to possess "an efficiency record for case examination and floor-work unsurpassed and seldom equalled" at the post office.[21] Quiet yet ambitious, Bolden immediately began to make changes in the club's operation. As Lloyd Thompson remembered, "Bolden had a head for business and right off we began pooling our earn-ings, even though they didn't amount to much."[22]

Bolden led his team to a 23-6 record in 1911, yet the club was virtually indistinguishable from the dozens of other black teams in the Delaware County and Philadelphia area, most unknown outside of their own com-munities. Publicity was difficult to obtain as black teams were generally ignored by the white press in Philadelphia and other cities. While the *North American*, for example, offered extensive coverage of white semipro-fessional clubs in Pennsylvania, New Jersey, Delaware, and Maryland, "giving the latest gossip" as well as "amateur notes," black teams were seldom mentioned unless they faced a white opponent. The tendency of the white press to refer to black players and teams as "duskies" further discouraged contribution.[23]

HILLDALE DOWNED

Hit and Run Game Won by Lansdowne F. C., 10 to 5

The Lansdowne F. C. defeated Hilldale by the score of 10 to 5, the features being the pitching of Dowd and the all-around playing of Lansdowne.

LANSDOWNE	r.	h.	o.	a.	e.	HILLDALE F. C.	r.	h.	o.	a.	e.
F.M'G'e,1b	1	1	9	0	1	Scott, cf.	0	0	0	0	1
Craw'd,ss..	2	2	0	2	0	J.Wi'n, rf	1	2	0	0	0
Tinney,3b..	1	1	0	2	1	Stud't, 1b	1	0	6	0	1
J.M'G'e,2b.	0	1	2	0	0	Balw'n, 3b	0	1	1	1	2
Carroll,lf..	1	1	0	0	0	Jones, cf	1	0	0	0	0
Brenn'e,c.	1	2	0	8	1	F.Wi'n, ss	1	0	0	2	0
Lawler,rf..	0	0	0	0	0	Huhns, c	0	2	2	0	0
Devine,lf..	1	0	0	0	0	Kemp, p	1	1	0	2	1
Totals..	10	8	11	10	3	Totals	5	7	9	5	5

Lansdowne F. C.. 5 0 1 0 1 2 1 0 0—10
Hilldale F. C... 0 4 0 0 0 0 1 00— 5

Box score of Hilldale's earliest known game (*Philadelphia Inquirer*, June 12, 1910).

Seeking to expand the team's prestige and reputation, Bolden turned to the African American press for publicity and began a campaign on the pages of Philadelphia's leading black weekly, the *Philadelphia Tribune*. The *Tribune*, founded in 1884, offered a single page of sports coverage and acted as a forum for local black semiprofessional teams to air grievances, make announcements, or simply promote themselves. Bolden bombarded the newspaper with constant press releases from March to October 1912. Declaring that "we have good grounds, and give a good guarantee for a good attraction," Bolden asked to hear from "all good, fast colored uniformed teams" in the area.[24]

While organized professional baseball in the early twentieth century attempted to curb "rowdyism" among its players to attract the patronage of the "better classes" and women to its games, working-class community and neighborhood-supported amateur teams in Philadelphia and other cities were less affected by this movement. Frequent fights between players or among spectators, especially when bets had been placed, often required police to restore order, and "near riots" involving umpires continued to be a common occurrence.[25] In contrast, Bolden attempted to

Hilldale, 1911. The young team won 23 of 29 games in its first full season under Bolden's management. Bolden is standing fourth from the left (Cash-Thompson Collection, courtesy Afro-American Historical and Cultural Museum, Philadelphia, Pennsylvania).

bring a sense of orderliness to the somewhat chaotic local world of amateur and semipro baseball. Consistently emphasizing the need for "clean baseball," Bolden warned managers that if they failed to "caution their men from using profane language and interrupting the games, their teams will be barred from our grounds." In 1913, a catcher for the Ardmore Tigers who had purposely knocked a Hilldale player unconscious was banned from the field as Bolden announced that he would "take this stand against dirty ball players." To Bolden, "clean baseball" meant the difference between success and failure, and he requested that his players be "gentlemen in uniform as well as off the ballfield."[26]

Impressed by Bolden's efforts, the crowds began to increase for Hilldale's games. Crowds of 1,000 to 3,000 were reported in 1912 and 1913 for holiday games (Decoration Day, July 4, Labor Day) and contests with the South Philadelphia Giants, who dominated press coverage in the *Tribune*. Noting the growth in attendance, Bolden moved the team to a new playing field at 9th and Cedar Avenue in Darby that would popularly become known as Hilldale Park. The team opened its grounds on May 16, 1914, and drew 3,000 fans for a Decoration Day game two weeks later.

Hilldale, 1912. Back row left to right: Bill Anderson, Lloyd Thompson, Devere Thompson, Mark Studevan, Ed Bolden, Charles Gaskins, Hubert "Lefty" Jackson, Sam Anderson, Leon Brice. Front row: Hulett Strothers, Raymond Garner, Billy Hill, Frank "Chink" Wilson, George Kemp, Hugh "Scrappy" Mason, Clarence Porter (peeking in: Alice Robinson, Marian Caulk, Clara Ivory, Helen Barrett, Mary Ricketts, Grace Ricketts) (Cash-Thompson Collection, courtesy Afro-American Historical and Cultural Museum, Philadelphia, Pennsylvania).

Philadelphia's black men and women were increasingly motivated to take the short trolley ride to watch the young team in action. The *Philadelphia Tribune* noted that at the Decoration Day game, "many of Philadelphia's professional men mixed with the large crowd that packed the Hilldale grounds until the overflow crowd had to go to deep center field."[27]

Large crowds, however, did not necessarily bring huge profits. Admission, if charged, was probably 10 cents, and may have been even less. In 1914 gate receipts from the grandstand at Hilldale Park ranged from $20 to $40 a game, with a high of $57.59 for July 4. Collections added another $3 to $6, and refreshments contributed $5 to $15. With club expenses such as uniforms ($3.75 apiece), a steamroller for the field ($12), baseballs (two for $1.68), an umpire ($50 per season), park rent ($50 semiannually), and the visiting team's share of the receipts, Hilldale's

Hilldale, 1913. Left to right: Billy Hill, unidentified, unidentified, Hubert "Lefty" Jackson, Lloyd Thompson, unidentified, unidentified, unidentified, unidentified, unidentified, Chink Wilson, Mark Studevan, Ed Bolden, Bill Anderson, unidentified. Anderson, Thompson, and Studevan later became members of the Hilldale corporation (Cash-Thompson Collection, courtesy Afro-American Historical and Cultural Museum, Philadelphia, Pennsylvania).

profits were not overwhelming. To raise additional money for the team, Bolden held a raffle, offering a ton of coal as first prize, $5 in gold for second prize, and $2.50 in gold for third. His fund-raising efforts paid off as Hilldale ended the 1914 season with $217.89 in its account, and finished the following year with a balance of $620.32.[28]

The black baseball scene in Philadelphia was teeming with several would-be champions and continued to grow after the birth of Hilldale. J. Arthur Norris, manager of the South Philadelphia Giants, noted the increase in competition in 1913, stating that "in the past five years, there has been an increase of colored clubs in and around Philadelphia." With the proliferation of teams, the *Tribune* suggested that local black teams should form a league with a definite schedule instead of issuing challenges through the newspaper, "which as a rule does not bring any results. Let us hope that our local managers will wake up." Any local black league, however, faced the common dilemma of obtaining home grounds for its teams as only four of the 15 leading black clubs in the Philadelphia area in 1913 had grounds. In addition, the few playing fields available to blacks were generally inferior, with one park at 26th and Allegheny located in the midst of a "veritable forest of trees" featuring "wooden blocks for bases."[29]

Bolden's control of conveniently located, well-maintained Hilldale Park gave his club a unique advantage. As Hilldale's prestige grew, the club became more attractive to traveling white teams lacking their own playing fields. In 1914, Hilldale scheduled three games against white clubs and faced Deegan, a minor league pitcher owned by Connie Mack's Philadelphia Athletics, who was making an appearance for a local semi-professional club. The same year, Hilldale defeated Three Links, the champions of the Interborough League, for the championship of Darby. Favoring neither black nor white teams, Bolden paid visiting teams a guarantee of $7 to $15, noting, "We cannot give visiting teams 50 percent; that is unreasonable but we bar no one."[30]

While Hilldale steadily climbed to the top of the black baseball hierarchy in Philadelphia, Bolden hardly rested on his success. Attempting further to improve his club, he began to recruit players from other sandlot teams in the area. Following the pattern of other local managers, the Hilldale leader used the pages of the *Tribune* to attract the attention of a desired player: "If Jackson, the left hand boy who pitched against Hilldale for the Bon Tons is idle, it will be to his advantage to communicate with Hilldale's manager."[31]

Bolden acquired several new players in this fashion and began to rebuild the local team of "small boys" to a more substantial and powerful club. During the next few seasons, he would obtain players from the Morton Republican Club, the Evergreen Hall team of Woodbury, New Jersey, the Ardmore Tigers, and other clubs in Camden and Philadelphia.

In 1915, pitcher Doug Sheffey, an 18-year-old graduate of Southern High in Philadelphia, joined the club. Born in Huntsville, Alabama, the light-complected Sheffey pitched for Hilldale for two years and later attended the University of Pennsylvania where he starred for the school's varsity baseball team for three years. While two African American newspapers mentioned that Sheffey, a black man, was pitching for the University of Pennsylvania team, evidence suggests that Sheffey may have passed for white while at Penn, as the white press made no apparent mention of his color despite the relative rarity of black college athletes in white schools at the time. Sheffey would later shed his black identity entirely. A notation in the University of Pennsylvania archives states that upon graduation from the Dental School in 1923, he changed his name, "moved to the coal region and became a white man."[32]

In 1915, Bolden guided Hilldale to another successful season as the club won 20, lost eight, and tied two. The team had continued to prosper and began to receive preferential treatment on the sports pages of the *Philadelphia Tribune*. Box scores were printed for the first time in 1914, and in September 1915, the club received its own column, "Hilldale Pickups." Bolden, however, realized that his team was still mainly a local phenomenon. Games were seldom scheduled outside of Darby, and although white teams were increasingly booked at Hilldale Park, most games were against black sandlot teams of a similar level of skill.

During the winter prior to the 1916 season, Bolden held nearly weekly meetings with his players at his home in Darby and made plans for substantial changes in the team's operation. The grounds were improved, new blue-gray uniforms were ordered, and a new grandstand was built, with admission fixed at 20 cents. More significantly, Bolden implemented a stern new set of rules for the 1916 season. Absence from games, except for unavoidable reasons, was punishable by a $5 fine unless a three-day notice was given. Players were expected to attend practices twice a week in addition to a 30-minute practice before games.[33] Insubordination was warned against, as was the use of alcohol: "No player shall indulge in any intoxicating liquor before the game nor at any time during his sojourn upon the field, nor on his way to or from the field. Neither shall he come upon the field under the influence of, or smelling of alcoholic liquors."[34]

Under stricter control in 1916, Hilldale continued its success. Always aware of the value of publicity, Bolden posted placards, mailed postcards, and began to place advertisements of the team's upcoming games in the *Tribune*. Large crowds flocked to the ballpark, and by May 1916, Philadelphia Rapid Transit began to run extra cars on No. 13, Walnut Street Line all the way to Hilldale Park. As a press release to the *Tribune* noted, "Progress is the watch word of the hour and the local crowds augmented by large crowds of respectable fans from Philadelphia helps [sic] us to have a real live organization in a live town. Follow the Hilldale Flag."[35]

In Chicago and New York large crowds of less than "respectable" fans had caused numerous problems at black baseball parks. Adequate park security was often lacking, and intoxicated spectators were especially uncontrollable. At Schorling Park, the home of the Chicago American Giants, one observer witnessed fans buying whiskey in rest rooms, noting that the "actions of women in the ladies' rest room . . . is not fit to put into print."[36] In Baltimore, patrons at Maryland Park were known to offer the players alcohol during the game. The black press constantly chastised

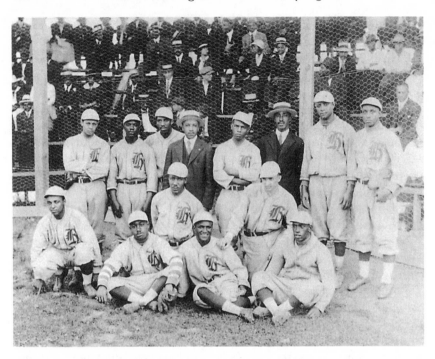

Base Ball

HILLDALE vs. R. G. DUNN
3 P. M., April 22
HILLDALE PARK
4-8 6m   Darby, Pa.

Top: Hilldale, 1916. Identifiable players include Lloyd Thompson (first row squatting), Fred Pinder (sitting adjacent to Thompson), George Mayo (standing third from left), Ed Bolden (standing fourth from left), Bill Anderson (standing third from right), Mark Studevan (standing second from right), and Doug Sheffey (kneeling far right). Hilldale finished with a 19-9-2 record in 1916, the team's last season before ascending to professional status in 1917 (Cash-Thompson Collection, courtesy Afro-American Historical and Cultural Museum, Philadelphia, Pennsylvania). *Bottom:* Always realizing the value of publicity, Bolden began advertising Hilldale games in 1916. The first Hilldale newspaper advertisement appeared in the April 15, 1916, *Philadelphia Tribune,* announcing the season opener against R.G. Dunn of the Main Line League.

fans for drinking, betting, vulgar language, fighting, and cushion throwing and urged them to remain seated during on-the-field arguments.[37] Editorials in the *New York Amsterdam News* and *Chicago Defender* typically condemned fan conduct:

> The way the men fans at the Giants park act is not only disgusting, but it is a fright. Sunday one threw a cushion into the box seats next to where I sat and it knocked a woman's hat off. Too bad that some people never know how to act.

> Last Sunday I went to the ball game at Protectory Oval in the Bronx and was disgusted by a member of my race, drunk with "home-made" gin from Harlem making himself odious with the use of vulgar language and by standing in the aisle, cutting the view of many spectators.[38]

In contrast, Bolden attempted to provide a comfortable and orderly environment for patrons of Hilldale Park. In 1916, after several fans caused a disturbance at a game, Bolden swore out warrants on four of the men, who were eventually prosecuted and fined. Attempts by park management to eliminate gambling were less successful. While public betting was banned in 1917, gamblers were again a familiar sight at Hilldale Park by 1923, even offering money to pitchers if they won their games. Finally, after a particularly violent fight between two gamblers resulted in the injury of a park policeman, Bolden quickly acted to increase security, and several bettors, gamblers, and bookies were arrested.[39]

Bolden also continued to insist upon disciplined behavior from his players. Through his weekly press releases and special meetings at his home, the Hilldale manager encouraged and scolded his "boys" in enthusiastic fashion, urging them to "get plenty of practice and get right in the game to beat the big fellows on your schedule. Systematize, that's all."[40] Following their most successful season to date, the 13 Hilldale players expressed their gratitude to their manager for his fatherly leadership and inspiration by presenting him with a $100 diamond ring, purchased after the profits for 1916 had been divided (⅔ to players, ⅓ to club). Bolden, however, was not through reorganizing and rebuilding the team. He pooled his share of the club's profits together with several of the "old fellows" who had been with the team since its inception and incorporated the team in November 1916 as the Hilldale Baseball and Exhibition Company in hopes of building a stable, permanent organization.[41]

At the end of 1916, Bolden had exceeded the dreams of most sandlot managers. Taking control of an inexperienced amateur boys' team, Bolden had built the club into a success. His team had achieved a solid local following, controlled its own park, had no trouble finding opponents, and was able to earn a small profit. Refusing to stand pat, however, Bolden looked toward the future by incorporating his team, the first of a series of calculated moves that would place Hilldale squarely in the center of the volatile world of black professional baseball.

2

Professional Black Baseball Takes Off, 1895–1917

> Of the players of to-day with the same prospects
> for a future as the white players there would
> be a score or more colored ball players cavort-
> ing around the National or American League
> diamonds at the present time.
> — *Sol White, 1907.*

As Hilldale prepared to jump to professional status in 1917, prospects for newly organized African American teams were hardly encouraging. While black baseball had developed significantly during the prior two decades, the few established salaried clubs monopolized players and opponents and left newer teams at a severe disadvantage. Even seemingly well-financed clubs found the competition stiff, exemplified by the collapse of the white-sponsored Philadelphia Giants in 1911. In May 1917, as Hilldale prepared to begin its landmark season, Dave Wyatt of the *Chicago Defender* pessimistically noted that the average black professional team with grounds was lucky to last three years.

Thirty years earlier, in 1887, the future of black professional baseball had seemed more promising. The Cuban Giants had become nationally known, and a dozen black players appeared in organized baseball, including seven in the International League. Increasingly hostile racial attitudes in the early 1890s, however, would spell the end of integrated major and minor league baseball and threatened the already fragile stability of black professional teams. Several strong clubs, including the Big Gorhams of New York and the Lincoln Giants of Lincoln, Nebraska, were forced to disband within a season or two after formation after experiencing greater difficulty finding white opponents and securing travel accommodations. In the South, the enforcement of segregation laws

27

during the 1890s ended interracial baseball, severely limiting the earning capacity of black teams, and retarded the development of professional clubs in the region for years. By 1894, according to Sol White, the Cuban Giants were once again the only professional black team in existence, nearly ten years after their formation.

The increasing tide of national racism would eventually provide the impetus for the revival of professional black baseball in the late 1890s. Economic and social conditions especially declined for southern blacks, and a steady stream migrated to northern industrial cities, resulting in the development of sizable African American communities in Chicago (44,000), New York (92,000), and Philadelphia (85,000) by 1910. With race relations worsening in the North as well, most urban blacks found Booker T. Washington's "accommodationist" philosophy advocating the establishment of separate, self-reliant, racially cooperative black communities a practical and more realistic alternative to political agitation and militancy. The growing urban black population allowed the establishment of separate hospitals, banks, self-help organizations, publications, and businesses in the black "metropolises" of the Northeast and Midwest, with the expansion and development of black professional baseball an invariable part of the trend. By 1906 there were nine professional black teams operating within 100 miles of Philadelphia.

Yet as historian Kenneth Kusmer has noted, blacks lacked adequate financial resources and "were frequently unable to establish separate race institutions without at least some white assistance." Baseball was no exception. Urban African American communities were still too small and economically oppressed to support a professional team more than one day a week (usually Sunday). Earning the bulk of their income from games against white teams played before white fans, eastern-based black professional clubs, faced with sure discrimination, often turned to influential white promoters to obtain bookings and to lease available parks. As Lester Walton of the *New York Age* ironically noted, while black teams in the East were "the strongest drawing cards and always bring out hundreds of admirers, white and colored," their finances were largely overseen by white men. By 1906 white promoters controlled three of the four major teams in the East: the Cuban X-Giants under E.B. Lamar, the Philadelphia Giants under Walter Schlichter, and the "Original" or "Genuine" Cuban Giants under John Bright. Only the Brooklyn Royal Giants, formed in 1904 and named for owner John W. Connors's Royal Cafe in Brooklyn, were black owned.[1]

At a time when few black investors were willing or able to risk capital in an unpredictable venture like a professional baseball team, white sponsorship proved initially beneficial. White owners provided more opportunities for black players by increasing the number of professional teams and were especially invaluable in facilitating profitable relationships with organized baseball. The Cuban Giants entered the Middle States League, a white minor league organization, in 1889 with the help of their white owner, John Bright, and Walter Schlichter's influence helped clinch the Philadelphia Giants' use of the Athletics' Columbia Park in 1902. Yet the early reliance on white owners and business managers, however necessary, would ultimately prove counterproductive for eastern black baseball, as aspiring black owners would find white sponsored teams difficult to dislodge, once in place. Lacking racial awareness and driven solely by profit, most white owners had little interest in the progress of black baseball or the welfare of its players. In addition, whites were less willing to employ blacks except on the playing field and typically refrained from hiring African American umpires or park personnel. Rube Foster, later a successful black owner and promoter, complained that white owners seldom let blacks "count a ticket [or] learn anything about the business."[2]

While Walter Schlichter of the Philadelphia Giants was the "ideal of an owner of a colored baseball team" according to Sol White, other white promoters like Nat Strong were exploitive at best. Born in 1874 in New York City, Strong, a sporting goods salesman, had become involved in the booking and promoting business in the late 1890s with the Cuban X-Giants and Cuban Giants. By the early 1900s, Strong controlled a number of white semipro parks in the metropolitan New York area. Arranging games for white, black, and Cuban clubs for 10 percent of the gate receipts, Strong built a booking empire that would eventually include much of the East and Midwest. Black teams seeking lucrative Sunday games in New York were forced to deal with Strong, who refused to share gate receipts regardless of the paid attendance. Typically, professional black teams received only flat guarantees, which reportedly amounted to $100 and two 15-cent meals for a Sunday doubleheader.[3]

Despite the preponderance of white ownership, black ballplayers managed to remain somewhat autonomous. With salaries fairly modest, ranging from about $50 to $100 monthly in the 1900s, professionals were quick to leave their team if offered more lucrative pay elsewhere. Attempting to curb this trend, in 1905 Nat Strong and several eastern owners formed the National Association of Colored Professional Clubs of the United States and Cuba. With Strong as secretary and business manager and Walter Schlichter as president, the organization handled bookings for the Philadelphia Giants, Brooklyn Royal Giants, Cuban X-Giants,

Nat Strong (courtesy of Dr. Bennett Rosner).

Original Cuban Giants, and Cuban Stars of Havana, later absorbing other eastern and Cuban teams. Acting in collusion, owners in the white-dominated organization tightened control over black players by imposing salary limits and denying bookings to uncooperative teams or managers. In 1909, the association temporarily outlawed Sol White for leaving the Philadelphia Giants to form a new team based in Camden, New Jersey. Two years later, the association's only black owner, John Connors, defied the organization by booking outlaw teams and obtaining his own park, Harlem Oval, at 142nd and Lenox. Connors's Royal Giants found subsequent bookings scarce, however, and the once profitable team began to lose money. By 1913, the team had fallen into the hands of Strong.[4]

The development of professional clubs in the Midwest eventually undermined Strong's efforts to control eastern black baseball. While Strong's booking empire would eventually extend westward to Chicago and Detroit, his influence in the Midwest was far less pronounced. Less dependent on Strong than the eastern clubs, midwestern black professional teams ignored the threats of the association and offered a safe haven to dissatisfied or outlawed eastern players. Rube Foster's successful jump to the Chicago Leland Giants in 1907 with several other players revealed the inherent weakness of the association and helped stimulate the growth of midwestern professional teams.

Professional black baseball had developed more slowly in the Midwest as the less populous and more dispersed black communities of the region were initially unable to support or finance a professional club on even a weekly basis. In 1890, the combined African American population of Chicago, Cincinnati, Cleveland, Detroit, Milwaukee, and Minneapolis totaled only 34,115, less than Philadelphia's black population of nearly 40,000. Except for the short-lived Lincoln Giants of Lincoln, Nebraska, in 1891, no major professional team appeared in the Midwest until the formation of the white-sponsored Page Fence Giants of Adrian, Michigan, in 1895. Financed by the Page Woven Wire Fence Company of Adrian and a New England bicycle company, the Page Fence Giants featured Bud Fowler, the first black player to play in white organized baseball, as well as star shortstop Grant "Home Run" Johnson. Traveling throughout the Midwest in its own private railroad car, the team was an instant success and defeated the Cuban X-Giants in a championship series in 1896.

Like many of the early black professional teams, the Page Fence Giants played mostly white semipro teams before predominantly white audiences that expected entertainment from traveling black clubs. Clowning or performing comedy while on the field was encouraged, and as Sol White noted, "Every man on a team would do a funny stunt during a game." The Page Fence Giants' gimmick of parading into towns on bicycles in full uniform initially delighted fans and attracted interest but occasionally overshadowed the team's superior ballplaying skills. By 1899 the team had faltered financially, lost its white backing, and relocated to Chicago, where several of the players became part of the new Columbia Giants sponsored by the Columbia Club of Chicago, a black business organization.[5]

Chicago became the center of black baseball in the Midwest after 1900, sparked by the enormous popularity of semipro baseball in the Chicago area and its rapidly expanding black community. According to the *Indianapolis Freeman*, four times as many people attended semipro games in Chicago than professional games, and by 1909 the city reportedly had 50 baseball leagues in operation, including the all-black Presbyterian League. Simultaneously, the city's African American population continued to grow, doubling to 30,000 between 1890 and 1900 and reaching 44,000 by 1910.

In 1899-1900, the newly formed Columbia Giants vied for local supremacy with another professional black team, the Chicago Unions. Formed as an amateur team in the late 1870s, the Unions turned professional in 1896 under the management of W.S. Peters and Frank C. Leland, a black man who later became a local deputy sheriff. Both the Unions and Columbia Giants enjoyed success on the playing field and participated in championship contests with the two leading New York–based teams, the Genuine Cuban Giants and the Cuban X-Giants. Financial setbacks, however, resulted in the collapse of the black-financed Columbia Giants by 1901, and the team was absorbed by the Unions, who became known as the Union Giants.

In 1905, Leland left the Union Giants to form a new club, the Leland Giants. Leland hardly fared better than his predecessors, and in the winter of 1906 the debt-ridden team was purchased by the Leland Giants Baseball and Amusement Company, a stock company consisting of several black leaders of Chicago, including Major R.R. Jackson, a successful businessman and future state representative, and Beauregard Mosely, an attorney. In return for retaining the name Leland Giants, Leland was given part of the club by its new owners and continued to handle bookings through 1909.[6]

The addition of Foster and several eastern stars in 1907 transformed the Leland Giants into a nearly unbeatable team. Now under Foster's control, the club traveled extensively throughout the Midwest, defeating both black and white teams with ease. The Lelands became a local favorite as well, and drew large crowds at Auburn Park, their home grounds located at 79th and Wentworth Streets. In 1908, the Lelands joined the Chicago City League, a highly competitive organization featuring several major and minor leaguers that was recognized by organized baseball. Hardly fazed by the stronger competition, the team was undefeated at the time of the league's collapse and reportedly finished the season with an overall record of 108-18. Financially lucrative as well, the Lelands traveled by private Pullman car and were one of the first black professional clubs to tour the South successfully.

The Lelands' remarkable success was mainly attributable to Rube Foster, whose masterful pitching and managing skills were nearly surpassed by his highly developed business sense. With the team's finances overseen by Foster, the Lelands became a solvent, stable enterprise capable of paying higher salaries than the eastern teams. Frank Leland, however, privately chafed over his diminishing lack of influence with the Giants. In October 1909 he resigned from the organization and organized a new Leland Giants team in 1910 with the support of one of the Lelands' financial backers, Major R.R. Jackson. Meanwhile, Foster and Beauregard Mosely joined forces to block Leland, instigating a legal battle over the right to the Leland Giants' name.

While Leland eventually lost the courtroom fight, his new team, known as the Chicago Giants, retained the lease at Auburn Park and seized several players from the original Leland Giant team. Leland received an additional boost from the powerful Chicago City League, which invited his team to join its organization while expelling Foster's club. Hardly threatened by Leland's challenge, Foster and Mosely promptly leased Normal Park at 69th and Halstead in Chicago and strengthened their team by raiding the eastern clubs once again. Featuring eastern stars, including catcher Bruce Petway, John Henry Lloyd, and Grant "Home Run" Johnson, the Lelands soon dwarfed the Chicago Giants in popularity and finished the 1910 season with an astounding record of 109-9. Foster concluded the season with a triumphant eastern tour on which the team reportedly won 18 straight games despite Nat Strong's attempt to block their bookings.

In the span of only four years, Rube Foster had revolutionized black baseball in the Midwest. Born in 1879 in Calvert, Texas, the son of a minister, Foster worked on his father's farm and attended school until the eighth grade. He pitched for several local teams before attracting the notice of Frank Leland, who asked him to try out for the Union Giants in 1902. After a brief stint in Chicago, Foster, along with his teammate Dave Wyatt, left to join a white semipro team in Otsego, Michigan. Foster subsequently jumped to the East and remained there for the next four years, pitching for E.B. Lamar's Cuban X-Giants in 1903 and Walter Schlichter's Philadelphia Giants from 1904 through 1906. Nearly unbeatable in the East, Foster's most brilliant pitching occurred in the two championship series held in 1903 and 1904 between the Cuban X and Philadelphia Giants. In 1903 the Cuban X-Giants, backed by Foster's four wins, beat Sol White's club five games to two to win the championship. A year later the Philadelphians took the series two games to one as Foster won both games over his old team, striking out 18 men in one game. By the time of his signing with the Leland Giants in 1907, Foster was probably one of the best pitchers in the country, white or black, and had even authored "How to Pitch" in Sol White's *Official Base Ball Guide.*

Foster's celebrity status rose even higher in Chicago as the white press, usually oblivious to African American sports, began to take notice and constantly noted that only his skin color kept him out of the major leagues. In 1907, after Foster and the Leland Giants took four of six games against major leaguer Mike Donlin's All-Stars, the *Chicago Inter-Ocean* hailed him as "the greatest pitcher" in the world. Foster's sensational pitching career, however, would be cut short by a broken leg and weight gain, which limited his effectiveness after 1909. While Foster would continue to pitch sporadically through 1918, he increasingly concentrated on managerial duties and the financial operation of his teams.

Like most managers during baseball's dead ball era, Foster emphasized speed, pitching, and the extensive use of the bunt. He attributed his team's successes, however, to his carefully devised "system," which involved tiring the opposing team's pitcher by forcing him to field bunts, run the bases, and throw more pitches than usual. A firm believer in disciplined teamwork, Foster expected his men to function as part of his carefully constructed system and allowed little room for individual decision making on the playing field, even calling pitches for his catchers. Rather than relying on a few stars, he instead attempted to utilize each player's unique skills as part of the team's overall strategy. Never reluctant to bend the rules slightly to his team's advantage, Foster often froze baseballs before games, wet down the infield to slow ground balls, and built ridges along the baselines to keep bunts from rolling into foul territory.

Though a strict disciplinarian and hard loser, Foster was a generous man who wanted the best for himself and his players. Well equipped and well paid, Foster's teams, along with boxer Jack Johnson, were a source of pride for the nation's African Americans before World War I. In addition, his successful resistance to Nat Strong's National Association conclusively proved that black professional teams could function and flourish without direct white ownership. Championed by the African American press, especially the *Chicago Defender*, Foster was increasingly perceived as the savior of black baseball who had singlehandedly stopped the domination of white promoters. As his prestige and fame mounted, Foster emerged as black baseball's dominant spokesman and began to exercise greater control over its operation in the Midwest.[7]

Foster's success, compounded by the continued growth of African American communities in the Midwest and upper South, spurred the formation of several notable clubs that would soon challenge the Lelands' hegemony in the region. In Missouri, the St. Louis Giants began in 1907 as a sandlot team that like Hilldale eventually reached professional status. Managed by Charles Mills, a local black saloonkeeper, the team was mostly composed of youngsters who wore cheap unmatching uniforms and earned less than 60 cents a game, playing before crowds that seldom exceeded 100 fans. In 1909, the Giants leased Kuebler's Park at 6100 North Broadway in St. Louis and began playing mostly white teams at home on Saturdays and Sundays. The Giants soon outdrew the local white trolley league and attracted a crowd of 3,000 fans, including 1,000 whites, for a 1910 game against the Chicago Giants. In 1911, after receiving backing from local black businessmen, the St. Louis team leaped into full professional status by signing several well-known players and traveled east to face the powerful Lincoln Giants.[8]

In Indiana, the Indianapolis ABCs were originally sponsored by the American Brewery Company in the 1890s. By 1908, the team, now owned by Ran Butler, a local black saloon owner and political leader, had its own grounds at Northwestern Park in Indianapolis and received regular coverage in the *Indianapolis Freeman*. In the Indiana communities of West Baden and French Lick, resort hotels sponsored black baseball teams to entertain their wealthy patrons, continuing a precedent begun 20 years earlier by the Cuban Giants. Both clubs, the French Lick Plutos and West Baden Sprudels, enjoyed success for several years before returning to amateur status. Strong teams also developed in Kansas (Topeka Giants, Kansas City Giants), Minnesota (St. Paul Gophers, Minneapolis Keystones), Missouri (Kansas City Monarchs, Kansas City Royal Giants), Iowa (Buxton Wonders), and Ohio (Dayton Marcos).[9]

Cuban teams, at first mixed and later predominantly black, also provided formidable competition. The popularity of baseball in Cuba resulted in the formation of numerous teams of both blacks and whites, and by 1900 Cuban teams began making trips to the United States to barnstorm against professional and semiprofessional teams. While lighter skinned Cuban ballplayers were eventually accepted into the major leagues in 1911, black Cubans continued to be barred and were relegated to the same plight as African Americans. Usually lacking home grounds, Cuban teams, usually known simply as the Cubans or Cuban Stars, traveled constantly and were underpaid by the standards of other black teams. Two Cuban promoters, Abel Linares in the Midwest and Manuel Camp in the East, operated teams, relying heavily on Nat Strong and Rube Foster for booking arrangements.[10]

With the more gradual development of professional black baseball in the Midwest, white promoters had been slow to invest in black teams, and African American sponsors quickly stepped in. While few individual black investors had the necessary capital available to finance their own team, a number of clubs, including the Leland Giants, Dayton Marcos, and Louisville Giants, incorporated and sold stock to avoid white ownership and obtain home grounds. By 1910 the Kansas City Royal Giants, Kansas City Giants of Kansas, St. Louis Giants, Oklahoma Monarchs, Bluff City Tigers of Memphis, Dayton Marcos, and Indianapolis ABCs had acquired their own parks, several conveniently located near trolley lines. Most black baseball parks, however, could only be leased from year to year and were owned by whites, including Auburn Park, the home of the Leland Giants and Chicago Giants until 1910, and the St. Louis Giants park.

Like eastern teams, black midwestern clubs derived much of their income from games with white semiprofessional teams. Located in cities separated by greater distances than the eastern clubs, western teams especially relied on games with whites while making long trips to face a rival African American club. In addition, with midwestern black communities still fairly small except for Chicago and St. Louis, games with whites often offered greater profits and commonly drew more fans than contests featuring two black teams. In August 1908 the *Indianapolis Freeman* reported that the Lelands had played only three other black or Cuban teams through their first 57 games of their season. Similarly, in a 1909 press release to the *Freeman*, Charles Mills apologetically noted that his St. Louis Giants were in such demand by whites that they had only played two black teams.[11]

The significant disparity in team strength also limited competition among black clubs. Despite achieving "professional" status, the majority of black teams still remained underfinanced and inadequately supported by small communities with limited resources. Weaker teams often lost their best players to the wealthier Chicago and eastern based clubs, who traveled by train, were well equipped, and were paid monthly salaries. Smaller teams, in contrast, still relied upon the cooperative or "co-op" plan, dividing gate receipts between the players and the club after each game. Others, like the Indianapolis ABCs, were still traveling by a farm wagon in 1908 clad in worn dirty uniforms. Of the handful of strong black clubs formed in the Midwest and upper South before 1910, only the Dayton Marcos, St. Louis Giants, Indianapolis ABCs, Chicago Union Giants, and Rube Foster's Leland Giants (later the American Giants) would continue to develop and prosper significantly beyond World War I, the remainder disbanding or returning to amateur ball.

In the South, black teams were similarly victimized by the stronger professional clubs after 1900. Faced with arduous social conditions and prohibited from playing whites until the Depression, southern teams lacked the necessary resources to compete and were unable to retain their most promising players. Professional black teams viewed the South as a major source of player development and typically recruited talented sandlot players and even entire teams to bring north. Black colleges in the South, especially Morehouse, Clark, and Morris Brown in Atlanta, also produced a number of well-known players, including C.I. Taylor.

Born in Anderson, South Carolina, Taylor attended Biddle and Clark universities and was a Spanish-American War veteran. In the early 1900s, Taylor with his three brothers (Ben, "Candy" Jim, and "Steel Arm" John) organized the Birmingham Giants in Alabama and enjoyed success barnstorming throughout the South. Relocating to West Baden in 1910, Taylor merged his team with the Sprudels, took control of the team's management, and built the club into a solid organization. In 1914, he left West Baden to assume the management of the Indianapolis ABCs, where he would soon challenge Rube Foster for midwestern dominance.[12]

Recognizing the possibilities offered by black baseball in the Midwest, white promoters became more actively involved after 1910. The Indianapolis ABCs were purchased by Tom Bowser, a white man, in 1912, while whites backed the newly formed Louisville White Sox in 1913. Whites continued to monopolize park rentals as well, and as Dave Wyatt noted in 1910, not one of Chicago's 30 or more semiprofessional parks was owned by a black team. While Rube Foster, the acknowledged leader of baseball in the Midwest, scorned white sponsorship, he realized that black park ownership was not forthcoming in the near future. In 1911 white backing would enable Foster to obtain the finest black baseball park in the country.

Faced with a rent increase, Charles Comiskey, owner of the Chicago White Sox, vacated South Side Park at 39th and Wentworth after his 10-year lease expired in 1910. Comiskey's brother-in-law John Schorling, a local semipro promoter and park owner who had previously leased Auburn Park to the Leland and Chicago Giants, expressed interest in obtaining the grounds but needed a strong attraction to recoup his potential investment. In 1911, Schorling approached Foster, promising to purchase the property and rebuild the grandstand and bleachers if Foster agreed to organize a new team to play at South Side Park. After obtaining the permission of Beauregard Mosely, the major backer of the Leland Giants, Foster accepted Schorling's offer and formed a new club, the Chicago American Giants, with home grounds at newly named Schorling Park. Made of wood with a capacity of about 18,000, the park's convenient location in Chicago's Black Belt ensured the team's instant success. Foster's alliance with Schorling, however, occasionally engendered considerable criticism, and as early as 1912, the *Chicago Broad Ax* noted that the white promoter was unfairly profiting on money that "should be received by the Race to whom the patrons of the game belong." Foster subsequently masked Schorling's financial involvement, and within a few years many black fans believed that Foster, not Schorling, owned the park.[13]

Following in the footsteps of the Lelands, the American Giants would dominate black baseball in the Midwest for the next decade. Foster's expert managing, superior baseball knowledge, and business skill enabled the team to build a huge personal following in Chicago, often outdrawing the Cubs and White Sox on Sundays. As lucrative Sunday games at Schorling Park soon became a main financial support for midwestern black teams, Foster's already substantial influence leaped considerably. By 1917, he booked several midwestern clubs, including the Chicago Giants, Cuban Stars, and Havana Cubans, and was closely involved with the activities of several others. Some managers, however, resented Foster's fame and control of the Midwest as well as his tendency toward self-promotion. As early as 1909, a former Leland Giant player accused Foster of attempting to "belittle" the accomplishments of other black teams to advance his own successes. Sol White, meanwhile, believed that Foster's fame had unfairly overshadowed the accomplishments of others and asked what Foster had done "to merit the adulation and homage he seeks and craves."[14]

Despite criticism, Foster remained virtually unchallenged until the ascendancy of C.I. Taylor, who became manager and part owner of the ABCs with Tom Bowser after leaving the West Baden Sprudels in 1914. An astute judge of talent, Taylor utilized several southern and local players to develop a strong team to rival Foster's American Giants. Matching Foster's every move, Taylor placed the ABCs on full salary in 1915 and leased Washington Park, used by the Indianapolis Hoosiers of the Federal League. Within a year, Taylor had ousted white owner Tom Bowser and gained full control of the ABCs and the park lease. Unlike the affable, gregarious Foster, Taylor was a serious, quiet man who shied from the public spotlight. Both managers, however, were shrewd businessmen who treated their players well. The ABCs and American Giants traveled in Pullman cars, and as Dave Malarcher, who played for both Foster and Taylor, noted, conditions were "high class. I got my money every first and fifteenth of the month." Several future black baseball stars of the 1920s, including Oscar Charleston, Frank Warfield, and Otto Briggs, would develop under Taylor's tutelage.

The proud Foster, meanwhile, used to having his own way in the Midwest, did not react well to the rise of the ABCs and ominously threatened to destroy Taylor's baseball career. Seeking to discredit the ABCs' manager, Foster claimed that Taylor had ruined baseball in West Baden, was disliked by his own players, and had succeeded only because of Foster's assistance. Taylor denied the charges and denounced Foster as a publicity hound who insisted on receiving all the credit, adding that "no one will deny that he has done a great deal for baseball, but he has not worked single handed." While Taylor and Foster continued to feud for several years, Foster's popularity hardly diminished and the American Giants eventually withstood the challenge of the ABCs.[15]

While Rube Foster and his teams prospered in the Midwest, eastern black baseball had remained largely stagnant, still controlled by Strong's increasingly impotent National Association. Already demoralized by Foster's raids and the Leland Giants' undefeated tour through the region in 1910, the association received its final death blow with the formation of the New York–based Lincoln Giants in 1911. Named for the Lincoln, Nebraska, professional team of 20 years earlier, the club was owned by two local white sports promoters, Roderick "Jess" McMahon and his brother Ed, and organized with the help of Sol White. Ignoring Strong and his organization, the McMahons proceeded to raid association teams, including the Philadelphia Giants, who were forced to disband in July after several players, including catcher Louis Santop and pitcher Dick Redding, jumped to Lincoln. Other clubs such as John Bright's Genuine Cuban Giants and Ed Lamar's Cuban X-Giants, soon faded from the scene as well, and the once powerful National Association of Colored Professional Clubs of the United States and Cuba ceased to exist.

Despite white ownership, the Lincoln Giants achieved immediate success in New York as the McMahons treated their players fairly and paid competitive salaries comparable to Foster's teams. Playing each Sunday at their ideally located home grounds, Olympic Field, at 136th Street and Fifth Avenue in the heart of Harlem, Lincoln took full advantage of New York's burgeoning African American population that had reached nearly 92,000 by 1910. With commercial Sunday baseball illegal in New York until 1919, the Giants, like other semipro teams in the area, used various devices to avoid prosecution, admitting fans free, then charging for programs. Heavily supported by whites as well, the Giants became the foremost eastern team and eventually defeated the American Giants in an unofficial world series of black baseball in 1913.

The McMahons' success was short-lived, however, as financial setbacks in their other business ventures, notably boxing, resulted in the loss of Olympic Field. By 1914 the Giants had been split into two teams with local sports promoters James Keenan and Charles Harvey obtaining control of the Giants and Olympic Field. The McMahons continued with a new team, the Lincoln Stars, at Lenox Oval at 145th Street and Lenox Avenue until 1917 and then dropped out of baseball altogether, becoming heavily involved in the New York basketball and boxing scenes.[16]

Despite the collapse of the National Association, the almost complete exclusion of black business management continued in the East. After Nat Strong gained control of the Brooklyn Royal Giants from John Connors in 1913, no major professional team in the East would be black owned until Hilldale's leap to professional status in 1917. The Royal Giants provided the strongest competition to the Lincolns but were handicapped by Strong's refusal to obtain home grounds for the team, despite his control of several parks in the New York area. While failing to build a local following comparable to the American Giants or Lincoln, the Royals remained a profitable traveling team and ranked among the best clubs in the country until the early 1920s.

Following the Lincoln Giants, three more white-owned teams were formed: Coogan's Smart Sets of Paterson, New Jersey, in 1912; the Mohawk Giants of Schenectady, New York, in 1913; and the Bacharach Giants of Atlantic City, New Jersey, in 1916. While the Smart Sets and Mohawk Giants faded within a few seasons, the Bacharach Giants would become one of the leading eastern teams for the next 15 years. Organized by two Atlantic City politicians, Tom Jackson and Henry Tucker, the Bacharachs were mostly composed of former members of the Jacksonville (Florida) Giants, who were recruited and brought north by Tucker, a Jacksonville native. The team was named in honor of Mayor Harry Bacharach of Atlantic City, who supported the club at the urging of Jackson and Tucker. Fashioning a 93-14 record in 1916, the team quickly achieved success in Atlantic City at Inlet Park and would soon compete with Hilldale for bookings in the Midatlantic region.[17]

Despite significant national growth during the prior 20 years, black professional baseball still faced financial problems on the eve of World War I. Sunday continued to be the best-paying day for black baseball as most African Americans, mainly restricted to low-paying unskilled laboring positions, were unable to attend weekday afternoon games. Rube Foster, however, warned of an overreliance on Sunday games and noted that three rainy Sundays with low attendance could force a team into debt. Dave Wyatt agreed that "base ball can not live or thrive upon the attendance of colored only" and predicted failure for teams unable to secure weekday road games with whites. Several clubs, despite obtaining regular bookings, were overwhelmed additionally by the increasing cost of salaries, park rentals, and travel expenses. By 1914, financial setbacks forced the Smart Sets, St. Louis Giants, Chicago Giants, and Mohawk Giants to abandon monthly salaries and return to the "co-op" plan.

Wyatt and other newspapermen suggested that improved public relations and better use of publicity would heighten interest and solve some of the financial problems faced by black teams. Encouraged by the success of Rube Foster and boxer Jack Johnson, the black press had expanded its coverage of sports after 1910, with a corresponding increase in circulation. Yet black weekly newspapers, relying mainly upon press releases, were continually frustrated by uncooperative teams that failed to report game results and news, especially when negative. The more successful clubs, with the exception of Nat Strong's Brooklyn Royal Giants, recognized the necessity of cultivating a mutually rewarding relationship with the local black press. Rube Foster, like Bolden, never passed up an opportunity to publicize his team. He gave season passes to Schorling Park to black sportswriters, took a regular correspondent on all trips away from home, and presented Frank Young of the *Defender* with the same championship belt awarded to other members of the American Giants. C.I. Taylor, however, felt that sportswriters' friendly relations with Foster undermined all claims to objectivity and especially disliked Dave Wyatt's loyalty to his "Big Boss" Foster.[18]

Black professional teams, like white semipros, operated independently and lacked a central organization to administer problems affecting individual players or teams. As player jumps reached epidemic proportions by 1913, the absence of a reserve clause seemed especially burdensome. Several professional teams became particularly leery of certain owners, including Rube Foster and the McMahon brothers, for fear of losing players. In 1912, Lester Walton of the *New York Age* advocated an agreement not to "kidnap," noting that "the policy of making players jump teams is a very bad one, for no manager is given protection but can have his players taken away from him without any redress." After a key game between the American Giants and the Lincoln Giants was canceled because of a dispute over ineligible players, Walton observed that "the sooner the managers of the colored teams get together and agree upon a working basis for their baseball protection the better." Player raids continued to be the main source of friction among eastern and western owners and undermined any cooperative venture for several years.

Umpiring continued to be a problem. Hired by the home team,

umpires lacked the authority to punish unruly players or enforce unpopular decisions and required police protection at times. In 1914 several members of the Brooklyn Royal Giants nearly beat up an umpire in Chicago after a questionable call, and a controversial decision by an American Giants umpire precipitated a near riot at Schorling Park a year later. With umpire violence common, most owners insisted on using one or two white umpires, believing that black players were more likely to accept the decision of a supposedly impartial white arbiter without argument. In addition, few black umpires were available, as the continued reliance on whites had prevented blacks from gaining experience. As white umpires proved no more successful in controlling the excessive rowdiness and lack of discipline on the playing field, black fans and sportswriters began to clamor for African American umpires. In 1912 Lester Walton advocated the use of two black umpires when two black teams were playing at the Lincoln Giants' Olympic Field: "This may seem a bit idiotic to the management but it is good wholesome advice, which will be found out sooner or later." The use of white umpires continued to be a controversial issue for black owners and managers, caught between a desire to please their fans and a reluctance to employ inexperienced black umpires.[19]

Race prejudice and discrimination posed a threat to all black teams, especially while barnstorming. Accommodations were particularly poor in predominantly white areas, with stalls and jails sometimes used. Racial attitudes, however, varied considerably and were often unpredictable. In Otsego, Michigan, a town supposedly friendly to blacks, Rube Foster found himself advertised as a "coon" on a poster and was greeted on the street by a child saying, "There's a big nigger." In Glens Falls, New York, in 1910, several fans taunted the New York Black Sox with insults of "nigger," "dinge," and "smoke." While on the West Coast in 1914, Foster found the color line drawn and had difficulty booking games with whites.[20]

While a few white fans and newspapermen recognized professional black baseball as equal to the caliber of organized baseball, most continued to view African American teams as semipro at best and at worst, little more than vaudeville entertainers. Once a mainstay among black teams, clowning had become increasingly frowned upon as demeaning and deferential to white audiences, yet its legacy and lingering practice consistently distorted white perceptions of black baseball. While Sol White optimistically predicted that the "funny man in colored base ball is becoming extinct," some clubs continued to believe that clowning was necessary to attract white interest. In 1908 the *Indianapolis Freeman* chased players on the Louisville Giants who felt that they had to "act a monkey and cut a lot of capers before 'de white folks' to get cheers." While black baseball would continue to be noted for its showmanship, a more serious style of play gradually evolved, with the hope that greater respect from whites might lead to the eventual integration of organized baseball.[21]

As blacks became increasingly more segregated in urban communities, the baseball diamond became one of the few places for the two races to meet. Suppressed interracial hostility sometimes erupted, caused by seemingly minor disagreements. In 1911 a dispute over the size of a player's glove resulted in a brawl between two Harlem teams, with several players injured. In 1917 two whites and two blacks were injured in a shooting incident in Cleveland after a black man supposedly stepped on a white man's foot at a sandlot game. In addition, the presence of white policemen, hired to provide security at black baseball parks, often precipitated violence. On July 18, 1915, at Washington Park in Indianapolis, a white policeman reportedly pulled a gun on one of Rube Foster's players who disputed a umpire's decision and cursed and threatened Foster the next day if he caused any trouble. While the incident was cited by Foster as a clear case of police brutality, Afro-Americans had little legal recourse, and similar episodes would occur in the future.[22]

Over a 20-year period, the steady migration of southern blacks into northern cities had resulted in the establishment of substantial African American communities increasingly capable of supporting their own professional baseball teams. The onset of World War I would accelerate the growth of the northern black population. Facing mounting production demands and a dwindling supply of immigrant labor, northern industries actively began to recruit southern blacks in 1916, some railroads initially even providing free transportation. With economic and social conditions in the South at their nadir, an unprecedented number of African Americans migrated north, buoyed by the promises of higher wages and greater freedom. The Great Migration of 1916–19 would result in a significant national growth of black business enterprises, with baseball transformed as well.

In Philadelphia, heavy migration began in the spring and summer of 1916 as area industries — including the Pennsylvania Railroad, Midvale Steel, Atlantic Refining Company, Franklin Sugar Company, Keystone Paving and Construction Co., Westinghouse, Eddystone Munitions, and Disston Saw — began employing large numbers of blacks. With thousands of migrants swarming into the city, conditions were ideal for launching a new black-sponsored professional team. In addition to Hilldale's incorporation in December 1916, a second African American–sponsored team, the Peerless American Giants, was organized with similar professional aspirations. The new team openly challenged Hilldale by obtaining grounds at Delaware County Park, directly across the street from Hilldale Park at the southwest corner of 9th and Cedar in Darby.[23]

Bolden, the new corporation's president, refused to be intimidated, and in February he hinted to the press that the team would be "bigger and better" in 1917. One month later, Hilldale's transformation began with the signing of left-handed-hitting outfielder Otto Briggs, the team's first professional player. A native of Kings Mountain, North Carolina, Briggs had been taken north by C.I. Taylor in 1914 and played with several leading midwestern clubs, including the ABCs, West Baden Sprudels, and Dayton Marcos, before permanently relocating to Philadelphia in 1916. A fan favorite for his steady play, Briggs was named the team's captain in 1917 and would remain with Hilldale for most of the next 13 years, with time out for military service in World War I. He was later employed at the *Philadelphia Tribune* as circulation manager and married Beatrice Perry, daughter of Chris Perry, the founder of the *Tribune*.[24]

After signing Briggs, Bolden made no other radical personnel changes before the season began. The team's April 21, 1917, opening-day lineup was largely intact from 1916, featuring veterans and Hilldale corporation members George Mayo and Charles Freeman. With the club struggling early in the season, however, Bolden promised fans in his weekly press release of May 12, 1917, that the team was "going through a form of evolution, [and] each game will bring rapid changes until in the near future we produce the real Hilldale team." Within a week, Bolden signed his second professional player, Frank "Doc" Sykes, a 25-year-old pitcher from Decatur, Georgia. Before joining Hilldale, Sykes had previously pitched for several eastern teams, including the Lincoln Giants, Lincoln Stars, and Brooklyn Royal Giants while attending Morehouse and dental school at Howard University. Sykes threw shutouts in his first two starts and stabilized the team's previously shaky pitching.

Attracted by the team's large crowds, stable finances, and African American management, several other veterans of New York and midwestern professional teams joined Hilldale by late July, including infielder McKinley "Bunny" Downs, outfielder Spottswood Poles, and catcher–first baseman Bill Pettus. In addition, Bolden acquired pitcher Dan "Shang" Johnson and second baseman William Fuller from the Atlantic City Bacharach Giants and hired the legendary Joe Williams to pitch a single game on loan. Since Hilldale continued to play only home games on Saturdays and occasional weekdays, most of the newly signed professional players continued to appear with other clubs during the week.

Hilldale, 1917. Standing left to right: Harris, Frank Ford, John Taylor, Ed Bolden, George Mayo, Otto Briggs, Frank "Doc" Sykes. Kneeling: William Fuller, Tom Jenkins, Triplett, Fred Pinder. Front: Neal Rhoades, Louis Burgee. By midseason, the team had been virtually transformed by the addition of Spottswood Poles, Bill Pettus, McKinley Downs and other eastern professional players (Cash-Thompson Collection, courtesy of Afro-American Historical and Cultural Museum, Philadelphia, Pennsylvania).

Within a year, the "old fellows" had been relegated to full-time corporation duties, and no local semiprofessional players remained. The expensive talent imported by Bolden resulted in a corresponding five-cent increase in ticket prices at Hilldale Park beginning in August 1917, yet attendance did not diminish.[25]

With a vastly strengthened lineup, Hilldale began attracting nationwide attention. The leading black teams in the East, including the Lincoln Giants, Brooklyn Royal Giants, Atlantic City Bacharach Giants, and Cuban Stars, all debuted at Hilldale Park in 1917, Hilldale managing to win three of eight games. The team also received its first coverage in the *Chicago Defender* and *Indianapolis Freeman*. While touring the East as correspondent with Rube Foster's American Giants, Dave Wyatt noted, "We learned that a club known as the Hillsdales [*sic*] at Philadelphia, operated by a bunch of post office employees, is a real money-maker. They are located in a suburb known as Darby, and are said to pull from three thousand to nine thousand bugs out to the contests." In October,

Outfielder Otto Briggs, the team's first professional player, was signed by Bolden in 1917 and was named the team's captain. Briggs missed the 1918 season because of military service but rejoined Hilldale after World War I (Cash-Thompson Collection, courtesy Afro-American Historical and Cultural Museum, Philadelphia, Pennsylvania).

Wyatt again acknowledged that he had heard "a lot of babble about this Hillsdale [*sic*] club" during his recent trip to the East.[26]

Foster, however, ignored Hilldale while in Philadelphia and instead played Bolden's competitors, the Peerless American Giants, at Point Breeze Park at 22nd and Point Breeze. Within a year, the two teams would finally meet in a three-game series touted in the black press as "brains against brains." While Hilldale managed to take one of the three games, the western press was less than respectful. Wyatt blamed the American Giants' loss to the "Hill-billies" on "umpirical robbery, hostility of the police force and wrathfulness of the crowd — who seemed unusually inhumane." Foster, however, was impressed by the financial returns, noting in a letter that "they paid me $2154.50 for three week days — its [*sic*] must be to life, as you know what Phila. was."[27]

Whites began to pay attention as well. After defeating Media, the 1916 champion of the strong Delaware County League, Hilldale was praised by the *Philadelphia North American* as the "crack colored team of this city" and became increasingly in demand by local white teams. Tensions occasionally ran high during interracial games, yet Bolden, still insisting on "clean baseball," managed to maintain constant control over his players, as epitomized by the following account:

HILLDALE A CLUB OF CULTURE

Any one who attended the game on Saturday and witnessed the actions of the Fairhill players (white) and the Hilldale players (colored) cannot help but admire the colored boys for their *gentlemanly* conduct. It is true the umpire gave raw decisions on both sides, but the Hilldale boys did not open their mouths, they let their manager adjust matters. But that "beef trust" fry of the Fairhills kicked harder than a mule with seven pairs of shoes on each foot. The score was 3–2 in favor of the white team, but the colored boys proved themselves to be gentlemen, which was a greater victory.[28]

At the close of the 1917 season, Bolden had seemingly realized his ambition of building a powerful, disciplined, professional organization both on and off the field. While Hilldale had beaten the leading black teams from New York as well as strong local white clubs, it had yet to encounter one last opponent — white major league players. Games between major league teams and black clubs had been annual events in New York and other cities for years, and black teams had always held their own in the competition. As recently as 1915, the Lincoln Giants behind the pitching of Joe Williams had beaten the National League champion Philadelphia Phillies and had defeated their ace pitcher, Grover Cleveland Alexander, in 1913.[29]

Bolden, now ready to put his club to the ultimate test, scheduled three games for successive Saturdays at Hilldale Park against the "All-Americans," a team composed of several members of the Philadelphia Athletics and other American League clubs. Taking no chances, Bolden supplemented his already strengthened lineup by adding catcher Louis Santop of the Brooklyn Royal Giants; Dick Lundy of the Bacharachs; and Jess Kimbro, Jules Thomas, Joe Williams, and Pearl "Speck" Webster of the Lincoln Giants. On October 6, 1917, before an "immense" crowd of 8,000 fans, Hilldale defeated the All-Americans 6–2 behind the pitching of Joe Williams. The climactic play of the game occurred in the eighth inning. With the bases loaded and no outs, Wally Schang of the All-Stars hit a sinking line drive grabbed by center fielder Spottswood Poles, who then threw to catcher Louis Santop. Santop fired to first base, catching George Burns off the base for a double play to end the threat, preserving the 6–2 lead. Although Hilldale would lose the following two games, the victory placed the team in the national black sports spotlight and represented the pinnacle of Bolden's career to 1917.[30] G. Grant Williams, managing editor of the *Tribune*, expressed the prevailing mood and praised Bolden for his publicity use:

> There are but few, if any, athletic associations in this vicinity that have made the success of the Hilldale Baseball Club at Darby. Just a few years ago they were playing in an open field. . . . Several years ago they rented their present grounds and put in a few seats and a small grandstand. This year they extended the grandstand and today they have a park second to none of its class . . . Manager Bolden and his associates deserve unstinted praise for their business-like methods in handling the large crowds . . . and for everything they have accomplished.[31]

The victory offered a glimmer of hope to Philadelphia's black population, still reeling from the effects of race riots in nearby Chester, and proved conclusively that black players, if given the chance, could excel in the major leagues.[32]

3

Hilldale and the Philadelphia
Semipro Baseball Boom, 1918–1923

> A twilight game between white and colored
> teams is a daily thing in this city [Philadelphia].
> Around six o'clock the playgrounds in various
> sections are crowded with people. All mak-
> ing wages on their boys. Color does not enter
> into the life of the spectators as they mingle
> together jibing each other.
> — Baltimore Afro-American, *August 4, 1928.*

The United States' entry into World War I in April 1917 immediately transformed semiprofessional baseball in Philadelphia and other cities. Faced with increased wartime production demands, industries embraced welfare capitalism more fervently than ever to maintain control over labor. Corporate sponsorship of athletic programs, especially baseball, significantly expanded during the war and provided organized competition for thousands of workers. The war's devastating effect on organized baseball provided semiprofessional ball with an additional boost. Secretary of War Newton Baker's "work or fight" order on May 23, 1918, and the government's subsequent assessment of organized baseball as nonessential employment sent dozens of major and minor league players to jobs in mills and shipyards, "particularly mills and shipyards that happened to have fast semipro baseball teams." While most of organized baseball was forced to suspend operations early in 1918, semiprofessional baseball thrived as never before, largely due to the increased presence of professional players. The *Chicago Defender* remarked in 1918, "There are a greater number of high class clubs at present than ever was known, owing principally [to] . . . many big and minor leaguers . . . seeking work considered essential employment," and noted the attendance boost at semiprofessional games throughout the country.

In the Philadelphia area, numerous major and minor leaguers joined shipyard and industrial teams, lured by promises of high salaries and undemanding positions. In Wilmington, the Harlan and Hollingsworth team featured Joe Jackson, Lefty Williams, and Byrd Lynn of the Chicago White Sox as well as several other professional players and won the championship of the Delaware River Shipbuilding League in 1918. In Chester, the Chester Shipyards team managed to obtain Scott Perry, a 20-game winner for Connie Mack in 1918, and nearly acquired Boston Red Sox pitcher Babe Ruth after he became involved in a dispute with his manager, Ed Barrow. The massive Hog Island shipbuilding complex in southwest Philadelphia employed several organized baseball players, including Hans Lobert, Chief Bender, Erskine Mayer, and Joe O'Rourke, and featured a new athletic park at 94th and Tinicum Road built at a cost of $90,000. Regular shipyard employees, however, were sometimes alienated by the presence of highly paid professionals. At Cramp's Shipyard in the Kensington section of Philadelphia, workers went on strike in protest against ballplayer-employees, including Sherry Magee, Joe Bush, and Mule Watson, who apparently did little except play baseball for the company team. Facing similar employee complaints, the Hog Island facility discontinued the use of professional players on its sports teams in October 1918.[1]

With the proliferation of white teams during the war, the stronger African American clubs found themselves in demand by a greater array of available opponents. In 1918 Hilldale scheduled 48 games, its highest total to date, against mostly white industrial teams, and in Chicago, one observer noted that he would not be surprised if the American Giants soon "depended on the other race altogether" for games. Hilldale also benefited from the war's profound effect upon Philadelphia's black inhabitants. By 1920, the Great Migration had swelled Philadelphia's black population to 134,229 in 1920, a 58.9 percent increase from 1910. (In Darby Borough, the black population leaped 64.9 percent, from 676 to 1,114.) As baseball had been popular among southern blacks and the majority of black professional players were southern born, many of the new migrants soon became regular patrons at black baseball parks in Philadelphia and other northern cities. In addition to Hilldale, the Great Migration spurred the growth of numerous black enterprises in Philadelphia, including the Brown and Stevens Bank, the Dunbar Theater, the Hotel Dale, and three new black newspapers — the *Philadelphia Defender*, the *Philadelphia American*, and the *Public Journal*.[2]

While World War I stimulated the growth and development of Hilldale and other semiprofessional teams, some black teams suffered temporary setbacks. Ticket prices were raised as a result of a national 10 percent war tax. Wartime limits on building materials prevented park improvements, and restrictions on sporting goods made equipment replacement difficult. Coverage of black baseball was drastically reduced as well, resulting from a severe newsprint shortage that would last until 1920. The draft, adopted by Congress in May 1917, weakened several black teams by 1918, especially Rube Foster's American Giants, who would lose eight players. Hilldale was also hit hard, as four players (Otto Briggs, Jess Kimbro, Speck Webster, and Spottswood Poles) were drafted and eventually served in the armed forces in France. Like white major league players, many black professional players took "essential" factory jobs to avoid the draft and managed to continue to play baseball.[3]

Despite war-related problems, Hilldale continued to prosper financially under Bolden's management, bolstered by an expanded base of support and greater range of opponents. The corporation abandoned the cooperative plan during 1918 and became one of a handful of black teams to pay salaries. Contracts typically extended from May through September, with pay ranging from $100 to $500 a month (roughly comparable to salaries paid in the minor leagues at the time). In 1918, the corporation paid $6,699.05 in player salaries, nearly 35 percent of its total expenses of $19,056.79, yet still realized a net profit of $1,576.22 for a 48-game season. Despite Hilldale's success, the team still traveled rarely in 1918, venturing only to Paterson, Atlantic City, and Penns Grove in New Jersey; and Parkesburg, Reading, and Pottstown in Pennsylvania. Limited to twice-weekly games at Darby, most Hilldale players continued to freelance with the Lincoln Giants, Brooklyn Royal Giants, and the Bacharach Giants during off days.[4]

While Bolden added several key players in 1918, including shortstop Dick Lundy, pitcher Tom Williams, and outfielder Pearl Webster, four other acquisitions would play especially significant roles in Hilldale's subsequent development. Left-handed-hitting catcher Louis Santop (Loftin) from Texas joined Hilldale in 1918 after appearing with the team in the 1917 postseason series against the All-Americans. Known like Babe Ruth for his home-run prowess and prodigious appetite, Santop began his eastern career with the Philadelphia Giants and later starred for the Lincoln Giants and Brooklyn Royal Giants. A fan favorite, especially among whites, Santop would become Hilldale's best-known player in the postwar period and even received a "Santop Day" at Hilldale Park in 1918. Bolden would later remember Santop as "the greatest star and best drawing card we ever had" and eventually paid him a salary of $450 a month in the 1920s.[5]

The additions of outfielder George Johnson, pitcher Phil Cockrell (Williams), and infielder William Julius Johnson in 1918 also contributed substantially to Hilldale's remarkable rise in the early 1920s. A native of Texas, George Johnson was signed by Bolden at the behest of his fellow Texan, Louis Santop. While Johnson broke his leg in July 1918 and missed most of the season, he would return in 1919 and developed into an outstanding outfielder and home-run threat for Hilldale for several years. Cockrell, a Georgia native, began his career with the Havana Red Sox of Watertown, New York, and was eventually acquired by the Lincoln Giants in 1918. After a brilliant performance against the Brooklyn Royal Giants on May 12, Cockrell was obtained by Hilldale and soon became the team's best pitcher. The spitballing Cockrell would anchor Hilldale's pitching staff for much of the next 14 years and pitched six no-hitters during his lengthy career.

Local sandlot product William Julius Johnson was born in Snow Hill, Maryland, in 1899, but moved to Wilmington, Delaware, as a child. The 18-year-old rookie third baseman debuted with Hilldale late in 1918, receiving $5 a game. Overmatched and inexperienced, he failed to make the team in 1919, but was reacquired by Bolden in 1921. Nicknamed "Judy" for his resemblance to veteran outfielder Judy Gans, Johnson would remain with the club for most of the next 10 years and became one of the legends of black baseball for his fielding excellence and superior hitting. Johnson's remarkable career culminated with his election to the Baseball Hall of Fame in 1975.[6]

With an all-professional lineup in 1918, Hilldale finished the season with a 41-7 record, winning nearly 20 more games than in 1917. While the team occasionally struggled against stronger black professional clubs, Hilldale was virtually unbeatable against white semipros, despite the occasional presence of major league players. The team defeated two former major league pitchers, Chief Bender and Jack Powell, and narrowly missed defeating the All-Americans, who featured seven organized baseball players. For the second consecutive season, Bolden once again brought a barnstorming major league team to Hilldale Park. On September 14, 1918, a team advertised as the World Champion Boston Red Sox (actually consisting of only four Red Sox players, one Philadelphia Athletic, one Detroit Tiger, one Cincinnati Red, and two unknown players) forfeited a game to Hilldale after its pitcher, Joe Bush, attempting to hold a slim 4–3 lead in the ninth inning, used his spikes to rip the baseball and then refused to accept a new ball from the umpire. The *Tribune* noted that "the game was for blood, each team striving their utmost to down the other" and marveled at the "frenzied baseball between two crack teams."

During the next two seasons, Hilldale would play seven more post-season games against major leaguers, including a two-game series at Hilldale Park in 1919 and five games at Phillies Park in 1920. While Hilldale would manage only a single victory and a tie in seven attempts, the team had the chance to compete against some of the major leagues' best players, including Herb Pennock (16-8, 2.71 ERA) and Bob Shawkey (20-11, 2.72) in 1919 as well as Casey Stengel (.292 batting average), Carl Mays (26-11, 3.06), and Babe Ruth (.376, 54 home runs, 137 RBI) in 1920. The 1920 series was marked by the competition between the two great sluggers, Babe Ruth and Louis Santop. While Santop failed to homer, the *Philadelphia Record* reported that Ruth "cast one of 'Lefty' Starks' fast ones into Broad Street. The ball sailed far above the concrete barrier."[7]

The unprecedented interest in sports, especially baseball, continued unabated in the postwar period. The extensive sports programs launched in army training camps had exposed thousands of Americans to organized athletics for the first time, resulting, as historian John Betts noted, in a "more truly national appreciation of sport" during the 1920s. Simultaneously, the general postwar prosperity and further reductions in the workweek allowed many workers to enjoy greater income and more leisure time than ever before. As organized baseball's attendance dramatically leaped in 1919, the *New York Times* suggested the entire nation was "plunging into sport" to forget its wartime miseries of recent years.[8]

Semipro ball also continued to flourish after the war despite the return of most professional players to organized baseball. Seeking to control workers' increased leisure time while simultaneously discouraging unionism, corporate sponsorship of athletics, especially baseball, would peak in the early 1920s. In the Philadelphia area, industrial backing spearheaded the postwar semipro boom, resulting in a number of powerful independent teams that bordered on professional status. Large manufacturing and textile firms, including Aberfoyle, Disston Saw, J. & J. Dobson, Stetson Hat, Campbell's Soup, Crane Ice Cream, Westinghouse Electric, Fleisher Yarn, Paterson Silk, and Parkesburg Iron, sponsored notable clubs, as did department and sporting goods stores such as Lit Brothers, Marshall E. Smith, Gimbel's, and Strawbridge and Clothier. Industrial sponsorship of women's baseball also continued as Fleisher, Westinghouse, Aberfoyle, Dobson, Stetson, and Disston featured female employee teams.

Overmatched in his debut with Hilldale in 1918, Judy Johnson returned to the team in 1921 and developed into an outstanding third baseman and clutch hitter. By 1924, the veteran Ben Taylor pronounced him "as good as we have in the game today" (Cash-Thompson Collection, courtesy Afro-American Historical and Cultural Museum, Philadelphia, Pennsylvania).

Industrial backing, while extensive, did not displace all other forms of sponsorship. A number of independent clubs, notably North Philadelphia, South Philadelphia, Trenton, Camden, and Chester, were community or individually owned. Religious backing also remained important as several Catholic teams in Philadelphia, including Nativity, Shanahan, and Ascension, enjoyed success in the early 1920s. In 1923,

Ascension would draw one of the largest crowds in local semipro history for a benefit game highlighted by the appearance of Babe Ruth in Ascension's lineup. Meanwhile, the South Philadelphia Hebrew Association sponsored strong baseball and basketball teams, both managed by Ed Gottlieb, who would later become a leading sports promoter in the Philadelphia area.

Numerous amateur leagues, both community and industrial, were formed or reorganized after the war, including the Commercial, Bankers and Stock Brokers, Philadelphia Optical, Bell Telephone, Pennsylvania Railroad, and Philadelphia Rapid Transit leagues. In addition, older organizations like the Delaware County, Main Line, and Philadelphia Suburban leagues continued to operate during the 1920s. After 1920, however, local amateur baseball was increasingly overshadowed by white and black independent professional teams that traveled extensively, drew large crowds, played daily baseball, and attracted players of organized baseball caliber.[9]

Much of the growth of the independent baseball scene was due to the advent and popularity of twilight baseball. With the passage in 1917 of the wartime bill authorizing daylight savings time, early evening or twilight baseball was made possible for the first time, attracting hundreds of fans previously unable to attend afternoon games. As James Isaminger of the *North American* noted, twilight baseball quickly became "the biggest kind of hit in Philadelphia," appealing heavily to working class fans because of its convenient starting time (6:00 to 6:30 P.M.) and easily accessible locations. By 1922 the "Old Sport" of the *Philadelphia Inquirer* observed that twilight baseball had "developed into one of the biggest sport propositions" in the city. Several teams even petitioned municipal officials to start daylight savings in April instead of June to get in more games. The *North American*, meanwhile, devoted a weekly column, "Evening Stars Twinkle Everywhere," to the local twilight baseball scene.[10]

The enormous popularity of semiprofessional baseball in Philadelphia after World War I partially stemmed from the sagging fortunes of the city's two professional teams. After losing the 1914 World Series, Connie Mack began dismantling his pennant-winning club. Between December 1914 and January 1918, Mack unloaded Stuffy McInnis, Jack Barry, Joe Bush, Wally Schang, and Amos Strunk to the Boston Red Sox; Eddie Collins and Eddie Murphy to the Chicago White Sox; Frank Baker and Bob Shawkey to the New York Yankees; and pitchers Eddie Plank and Chief Bender to the newly formed Federal League, receiving only cash or inferior players in return. The Athletics won only 43 games in 1915, falling to last place, where they would remain until 1922. The

Phillies, meanwhile, temporarily surpassed the Athletics in popularity after winning the National League pennant in 1915 and finishing second in 1916 and 1917. The team's fortunes, however, began to decline after the trade of 30-game winner Grover Cleveland Alexander to the Chicago Cubs for two mediocre players and $55,000 in December 1917. By 1922, the Athletics and Phillies had both finished last three consecutive seasons, and neither team would draw more than 400,000 fans between 1917 and 1921.

Local fans sensed that the best baseball could be seen not at Shibe Park at 21st and Lehigh or Phillies Park at Broad and Huntington but at semiprofessional diamonds throughout the city. In March 1920 Louis Steele of the *Philadelphia Tribune* commented on this trend, noting that "the strides made by the industrial and semi-professional baseball teams in all big cities during the past season has [*sic*] thrown a harpoon into the attendance figures of the big leagues." Receiving generous press coverage and fan support, a group of 15 to 20 powerful independent clubs in the tristate area (southeast Pennsylvania, southern New Jersey, and Delaware) largely supplanted the hapless Phillies and Athletics in importance and successfully rented their ball parks on occasion. On July 25, 1921, both of Philadelphia's major league parks were simultaneously occupied by independent clubs, with three-team doubleheaders scheduled at Shibe Park (Bridesburg, J. & J. Dobson, and the Irish Giants) and Phillies Park (Hilldale, Stetson, and Fleisher).[11]

The increased interest in amateur and semipro baseball sparked a flurry of park construction in Philadelphia. Park enclosure, allowing admission to be charged, became increasingly common and ensured higher profits than soliciting donations from spectators. Between 1920 and 1923, parks were built or remodeled at numerous locations throughout the city, including Broad and Bigler (South Phillies), 26th and Reed (Fleisher Yarn), and 25th and Snyder (Forty-Eighth Ward) in South Philadelphia; Tioga and B (Marshall E. Smith), Frankford and Pratt (Frankford Athletic Association), and I and Tioga (Harrowgate and later Ascension) in Northeast Philadelphia; 48th and Spruce (Lit Brothers, later used by the Elks and Passon teams) in West Philadelphia, and 54th and Elmwood (Bartram Park) in the southwest section. Enclosed parks, however, still remained at a premium in the city and were often obtained only after heated bidding or the intervention of a local ward leader.[12]

With park enclosure resulting in higher earnings and salaries for independent clubs, the participation of professional players accelerated as well. Hilldale, for example, faced numerous pitchers with recent major league experience between 1919 and 1922, including Jeff Tesreau (Tesreau's

Bears, South Phillies), Lefty Weinert (Millville, Upland), John "Mule" Watson (E.G. Budd, Nativity, Earl Mack's Merchant Shipbuilding), Jing Johnson (Norristown Professionals), Scott Perry (Maury's Professionals), Erskine Mayer (Marshall E. Smith), Ad Swigler (Aberfoyle), Ed Gerner (Fleisher Yarn), and Lefty George (American Chain). Several players considered too old for organized baseball, including Bris Lord of Chester, Moose McCormick of Donovan-Armstrong, Wid Conroy of Crane Ice Cream, Howard Ehmke (Eighth Ward) and Chief Bender (Wentz-Olney), also found a haven in the prosperous Philadelphia baseball scene and continued to compete at the semiprofessional level after their professional careers ended. Other professionals, notably Howard Lohr, Herb Steen, and Buck Lai of the South Phillies, were marginal major leaguers or career minor league players who preferred stardom and financial security in independent ball to toiling in uncertain obscurity in the minors. Risking severe penalty, a number of players currently under contract in organized baseball, including Frank Baker, Scott Perry, and Stan Baumgartner, also jumped to local independent clubs yet still later managed to return to the major leagues.

The strong caliber of the local baseball scene contributed to the development of a number of young players eventually signed by major league teams. During the early 1920s, the close relationship between professional and semiprofessional baseball continued, and numerous sandlot players were given chances in organized baseball. Three former members of the Nativity Catholic Club—John Chapman, Ernie Padgett, and Bill Hockenbury—were signed by organized baseball teams, with Chapman and Padgett eventually reaching the major leagues. Lefty Stiely, Vic Keen, and Mike Wilson of the Bridesburg team also played major league ball, as did Ray Steineder of the Norristown Professionals, Bill Warwick of Vineland, Clay Touchstone of Parkesburg Iron, and Milt Gaston of the Paterson Silk Sox. Other more notable local players included catcher Jimmy Wilson of the Kensington section of Philadelphia, who spent 18 seasons in the National League, and pitcher George Earnshaw of the 1919 Strawbridge and Clothier team, later a three-time 20-game winner with the Philadelphia Athletics.[13]

For young players in the 1920s and in later decades, success against a strong professional black team like Hilldale often foreshadowed careers in organized baseball. As Gene Benson, a black baseball star of the 1930s and 1940s observed, "If you could play well against a colored team, you could go to the major leagues." During 1921, impressive performances by three local pitchers against Hilldale helped attract the attention of major league scouts. Within a year after shutting down the powerful Hilldale lineup without a hit in September 1921, former Nativity pitcher Tom Carrigan was pitching with New Haven of the Eastern League. Rube McKenty of Fleisher was signed by the Chicago Cubs soon after defeating Hilldale in July. In September, Bridesburg pitcher Vic Keen joined the Chicago Cubs a month after compiling a 34-1 record against local clubs, his only loss to Hilldale. In eight major league seasons, Keen compiled a 42-44 record with a 4.11 earned run average.[14]

The postwar semipro boom dramatically expanded the local black baseball scene as dozens of amateur and semipro teams were formed. By 1920 the *Tribune* noted nearly 30 area black teams, including the Bryn Mawr Browns, North Philadelphia Tigers, Sharon Hill Giants, Burlington Giants, West Philadelphia All-Stars, and many others. In addition, the Colored Tri-State League, a black amateur organization formed in 1919, operated locally with six teams. While most clubs continued to be formed along neighborhood or geographical lines, the increased presence of blacks in Philadelphia industries produced some corporate-sponsored teams. Several firms, including George B. Newton Coal, United Gas and Improvement, Strawbridge and Clothier, and Keystone Brick, sponsored separate teams for their black employees during the 1920s.

Interracial games continued to be extremely popular, especially among white fans, and as Rollo Wilson of the *Pittsburgh Courier* observed, "Good colored teams are very much in demand in the Quaker district." As the leading black team in the area, Hilldale was able to obtain bookings easily due to the dozens of newly formed white semipro clubs, all looking for a good attraction for weeknight twilight games. In 1919, as Hilldale began playing regular away games for the first time, several local teams, including Hess-Bright of the Philadelphia Manufacturing League and Stetson Hat, chose "the fast negro aggregation" as their first twilight attraction. Typically, the team received a guarantee of $100 to $500, with an option of receiving 40–50 percent of the game's receipts. If the game was arranged through a booking agency, a promoter might take an additional 5–10 percent of the gross. Hilldale had no trouble filling its schedule, and the *Tribune* noted that "the managers of independent teams in and around Philadelphia reported record breaking crowds when Ed Bolden had his charges on exhibition at their parks." The Nativity Catholic Club of Kensington reportedly drew between 10,000 and 12,000 fans for games with Hilldale in 1919, while games against Marshall Smith (Tioga and B Streets) and Shanahan (48th and Brown) drew equivalent numbers. The huge crowds, spilling onto the playing field after all available seats were taken, often made ground rules necessary, and routine pop flies falling into the crowd became ground rule doubles.[15]

Firmly entrenched as the dominant black team in Philadelphia, Hilldale still faced constant challenges from newly formed local clubs aspiring to professional status. While earlier attempts by the Peerless American Giants and a reorganized Philadelphia Giants team had failed in 1917 and 1918, the Madison Stars presented a more serious threat in 1920. Partially financed by John Gibson, a wealthy black theater magnate, the Madisons featured a new park at 34th and Reed Streets as well as the endorsement of Rube Foster. Appealing to the racial pride of Philadelphia blacks, the team asked for strong local backing to "give us a chance to rise like our white brothers." Despite the management of former Philadelphia Giant star Danny McClellan and the presence of Otto Briggs, the Madison Stars never seriously endangered Hilldale's high-ranking status. By August 1920, the team had lost its grounds, and Briggs had returned to Hilldale.

The Madison Stars would function more significantly as a "farm team" for Hilldale in the early 1920s. Several promising prospects, not quite ready to join Hilldale, were sent to the Madisons to gain more experience under Danny McClellan's guidance. Judy Johnson, for example, had failed to impress Bolden in his first stint with the club in 1918 but was reacquired in July 1921 after a stint with the Madison Stars. Other future Hilldale stars, including Frank Dallard and Webster McDonald, also began their careers with the Madisons. In John Holway's *Voices from the Great Black Baseball Leagues*, Webster McDonald recalled how he became involved with the Madison Stars:

> The best colored team in the East then was Hilldale in Philadelphia. But they had so many good pitchers.... I couldn't break in with them. We were sort of Hilldale's farm club. Hilldale wouldn't play some of those teams around there. They wanted the big part of the meat, and we took the little end.[16]

While Hilldale would retain an almost impenetrable monopoly over bookings with local white teams, Philadelphia's burgeoning semipro scene was still attractive to other eastern-based black professional clubs. The Baltimore Black Sox, Richmond Giants, Norfolk Stars, Harrisburg Giants, Cuban Stars, Bacharach Giants, Lincoln Giants, and Brooklyn Royal Giants were but a few of the many clubs who relied heavily on the Philadelphia area for weekday or Saturday twilight games away from their own home grounds. On several occasions in the early 1920s, no fewer than five different professional black teams simultaneously appeared in the Philadelphia vicinity against white semipro clubs. The overabundance of local semipro teams gave Hilldale and other eastern professional clubs a distinct advantage over their western counterparts. Extensive barnstorming trips were unnecessary, and as Judy Johnson recalled, Hilldale "didn't travel too much, because around Philadelphia there were so many teams — white clubs and leagues." While travel was necessary on Sundays to circumvent the local ban on commercialized baseball, Hilldale profited greatly by the city's central location, traveling with relative ease to eastern cities at minimal expense. After 1919, the team made regular Sunday trips to New York, Brooklyn, Baltimore, Washington, Atlantic City, and Newark or scheduled games in surrounding Pennsylvania communities (Allentown, Harrisburg, and Bristol) where the ban was laxly enforced.[17]

At Hilldale Park attendance reached new highs in the early 1920s, and the team began regularly drawing between 6,000 and 8,000 fans for Saturday and holiday games. Described by black Illinois congressman Oscar DePriest as the "finest semipro park in America," Hilldale Park was an odd wooden structure with a seating capacity of about 8,000. Until 1920, the outfield was dotted with several trees and stumps. Center field was an especially hazardous spot, featuring a "depression or hollow that dropped off abruptly about thirty feet inside the fence line" as well as a spring that trickled under the boards of the outfield fence. The corporation continually financed improvements to the field, covering the grandstand roof and removing the tree stumps in 1920. In 1924, the park was enlarged, 56 box seats were built, and the center-field ditch was filled in. Judy Johnson recalled that the infield was particularly well kept by Hilldale's corps of groundskeepers:

> We had the best infield that the big league players had ever played on — that's what they told us. The dirt — I don't know what it was, but it shone something like silver. . . . A ball would very seldom take a bad hop unless someone dug a hole with his spikes.[18]

Admission to Hilldale Park after World War I remained low enough to ensure the steady patronage of Philadelphia's largely working class black community. Prices ranged from 25 cents to 55 cents between 1918 and 1921, considerably less than the typical 1920 major league prices of 50 cents for bleachers, $1.00 for grandstand, $1.25 for reserved seats, and $1.65 for box seats. Cigars, soda, cigarettes, peanuts, and occasionally ice cream were sold at the park. Games began at 3:30 each Thursday and

Saturday, with lineups announced by megaphone. From 1920 through 1923, the team also leased a park in nearby Camden, New Jersey, at 3rd and Erie for Wednesday games. Like other black teams, Hilldale's weekday home games drew smaller crowds since few workers were able to attend, and a second game, usually a twilight affair away from home, was often scheduled as well.[19]

The team drew its largest home crowds for morning-afternoon doubleheaders on Memorial Day, July 4, and Labor Day. On Memorial Day in 1920, a massive crowd of 20,000 became so uncontrollable that the umpire was forced to suspend the game in the eighth inning with Hilldale at bat. In the future, huge crowds were roped off or were restrained by mounted policemen. Opening games at Hilldale Park, marked by band concerts and flag raising exercises, were also popular, and commonly attracted "beautifully gowned ladies" and Philadelphia's "professional men," the elite of black society. Local black celebrities, including Andrew Stevens Jr. of Brown and Stevens Bank; E. Washington Rhodes, an attorney and later editor of the *Tribune*; and G. Grant Williams, city editor until 1922, were typically chosen to throw out the first ball of the new season.[20]

Declaring that "the best is none too good for Hilldale fans," Bolden was able to build an exceptionally loyal group of supporters. Observers from other cities, like Rollo Wilson of the *Pittsburgh Courier*, were astounded at the sight of Hilldale fans eagerly waiting to buy tickets for the afternoon game of a doubleheader minutes after the morning game had ended. Hilldale players were equally amazed that the team's fanatical followers would chance "losing their jobs to see Hilldale play a tight game or series" during the week. Some fans, like the members of the Hilldale Loyal Rooters Club, presented gifts to Hilldale players, while others were known to accompany the team on out of town trips. In 1926 the wife of a Baltimore Black Sox player suggested that Hilldale's fiercely loyal fans had contributed to the team's success:

> Take Hilldale. The fans in Philly stick with their club regardless how bad they play or how many games they lose. That club belongs to them and they never knock it.
> That is why they have always led. The fans are with them and will fight you if you speak ill words against them.[21]

White fans as well as blacks were attracted by the superior brand of baseball played at Hilldale Park. Judy Johnson recalled that "in the later years of the Hilldales we had to put in an extra row of box seats for the whites," and pitcher Scrip Lee also noted the presence of "quite a few" white fans at the games. Since the majority of Hilldale's games after World War I would be played outside Darby against local white semipro teams, white fans were still more likely to see Hilldale in action at their own teams' playing fields. In 1921, for instance, Hilldale played 93 of its 149 games (62.4 percent) against whites and only 56 against black teams. In addition, the team played 47 home games at Hilldale Park, 36 games in New Jersey, two in Washington, four in Wilmington, 12 in New York and Brooklyn, and the remainder in Philadelphia and other Pennsylvania communities. Two years later, the team would schedule an astounding 186 games, with 124 (66.6 percent) against white teams.[22]

As with all black professional teams, playing conditions varied substantially. A Hilldale player might find himself in a major league park one day and on an open field during the next game (which led Judy Johnson to relate to James Bankes that he kept two pairs of baseball shoes, "one for good fields and one for bad ones"). While Hilldale booked games with other black teams at major league parks, including Ebbets Field in Brooklyn, Phillies Park (Baker Field) in Philadelphia, and American League Park in Washington during 1920 and 1921, the team continued to schedule games at odd locations, including a recently plowed field in Norristown and an open playground in Wilmington. Accommodations were occasionally harsh as well, especially when white teams restricted access to dressing rooms. In Bloomfield, New Jersey, players lacked even chairs to sit on and were forced to change sitting on empty bottle crates, while Jake Stephens, the team's shortstop, remembered using a stable in Norristown as a dressing room. As late as 1950, black baseball players were still prohibited from staying in hotels in Wilmington and Trenton.[23]

Hilldale's semipro opponents differed widely in quality. Some, like the Brooklyn Bushwicks, featured former major leaguers, excellent home grounds, and thousands of loyal fans. Formed in 1913, the team was named and later became one of the finest semiprofessional teams in the country in the 1920s under the ownership of Max Rosner and Nat Strong. With lavish home grounds at Dexter Park in Brooklyn, featuring a hotel, dance hall, carousel, swings, bowling alleys, and a shooting gallery, the Bushwicks were a regular Sunday opponent for Hilldale and other eastern black professional teams for years. Despite high attendance (reportedly outdrawing the Brooklyn Dodgers on occasion) and profits, Strong continued to offer only flat guarantees (usually $500 to $600), and refused to pay visiting white or black teams on a percentage basis.

Like the Bushwicks, the Paterson Silk Sox were a popular rival of

Hilldale and other eastern black teams in the 1920s. Sponsored by silk-mill owners Harry and Frank Doherty, the Silk Sox began as an employee team in 1915 and later merged with the Jersey City Red Sox, a strong semipro club. By the early 1920s, the Silk Sox had built a powerful organization and regularly drew large crowds at Doherty Oval, their magnificent home grounds in Clifton, New Jersey, near the silk mills. Featuring Milt Gaston, who would later pitch 11 years in the major leagues, the team won 10 of 13 games against major league competition in 1923. The Silk Sox would lose their park at Doherty Oval in the late 1920s but continued to provide formidable competition for black teams as a traveling team. Like the Bushwicks, the Silk Sox enjoyed remarkable longevity, and both teams would survive until 1951.[24]

Other semipro clubs simply lacked the player personnel to compete with Hilldale and were beaten with little effort. In 1921 Hilldale won nearly 75 percent of its games against white teams, finishing with an impressive 68-23-2 record, compiling a 37-18-1 mark against blacks. While some white semipro teams like Fleisher, Bridesburg, and Chester managed to beat Hilldale three times apiece in 1921, others, like the North Phillies, struggled even to score a run. Yet nearly every community, factory, church, and business had its own team, and Hilldale was willing to play them. In the future, as the competitive gap widened between professional black and semipro teams, Hilldale began to ease up in games against weaker white teams to ensure continued bookings. Judy Johnson recalled that Hilldale especially tended to "fool around a lot" against small-town teams. At the conclusion of infield practice, the team's shortstop sat on second base and caught a perfect throw from catcher Louis Santop, who then proceeded to fire the ball over the outfield fence. On other occasions, Hilldale players shifted to unfamiliar positions to give weaker teams a chance. By the mid–1920s, Black Sox manager Ben Taylor would observe that interest in interracial games had declined, as "white people in the little towns see so many colored clubs and half the time the white clubs win the games because our boys refuse to take the game seriously."[25]

Racial incidents were surprisingly few, although some white teams and fans could not accept being beaten by a black team, even if the black club was obviously superior. A Hilldale fan remarked, "It is a bitter dose for white teams to be beaten by colored clubs. Watch the expression on some of the white fans' faces when their club is losing." Some white teams used a variety of tactics to ensure victory. During twilight games, managers were known to instruct umpires to call the game on account of darkness as soon as the white team had taken the lead. Otto Briggs noted that if the umpire "fails to help and a close game is lost, they are called all kinds of names by the losing players and managers after the game . . . [and are] told they are N____lovers."

Stalling techniques were also a common device, especially when rain was imminent. In a 1922 game, the Pyotts, clinging to a slim lead in the late innings and sensing a thunderstorm, began calling for time to "adjust" their gloves and other equipment. When rain began to fall soon after, the game was immediately called despite the protests of Bolden and his players. On other occasions, Bolden pulled his team off the field when the umpire seemed to be trying to give the game to the "white lads."[26]

Some local teams, like Strawbridge and Clothier, simply refused to book games with black teams, while others attempted to cheat them out of their proper share of the gate receipts. Donn Rogosin's *Invisible Men* includes Judy Johnson's recollection of an especially ugly racial incident:

> Hilldale encountered a home umpire who happened to double as the local sheriff. "The ball'd be over your head and if there were two strikes, you'd be out," recalled Johnson. . . . "And Santop went out to the pitcher and said, 'Throw a hard one, and I'll let it go by and hit him,'" Sure enough, the ball hit the umpire — in the groin. "He couldn't breathe and was choking; it broke up the game," remembered Johnson. "We had to get in the car with our baseball clothes and they chased us six miles down the road. I was really scared."[27]

The Midatlantic region was hardly a haven from race prejudice. Jess Hubbard, who played with eastern clubs during the 1920s, noted that "in Jersey, Pennsylvania, Delaware, Maryland, shoot, I'd just as soon be down in Georgia." Locally, Hilldale faced some of its worst racial hostility at Shettsline Field, home of the powerful South Phillies during the 1920s. For Judy Johnson, South Philadelphia was like "playing in the middle of Mississippi. They used to buy those little cushions you sit on and if their team lost, they'd throw them at you. To get out of the park, you had to go between the two stands, like walking through a tunnel, and they'd hang out over the sides and toss stuff at you — bottles, garbage, whatever was handy — and call you all sorts of names."[28]

With the increasing residential segregation in northern cities during the 1920s, interracial baseball, despite reinforcing the color line, did present a rare opportunity for the two races to mingle and forced whites to acknowledge the presence of the usually ignored African American community. The *Baltimore Afro-American* enthusiastically noted that interracial games provided "some of the strongest lessons in inter-racial good will that it will ever be your lot to see" and felt the competition contributed to "better inter-racial contacts." Other observers, like Ben Taylor, felt the

Ed Bolden (National Baseball Library and Archive, Cooperstown, N.Y.).

professional black teams needed to curtail their reliance on white opponents.

Bolden, however, had no qualms about dealing with whites, and realized that Hilldale's financial success was inextricably linked to their involvement. As Hilldale's drawing power grew, Bolden formed valuable alliances with leading white baseball promoters in Philadelphia, enabling the team to monopolize the more lucrative bookings with white teams. Like Rube Foster (who once stated that while he preferred black umpires, "I cannot allow my preference to run away with my business judgment"), the Hilldale leader was a businessman first and a "race man" second. Bolden summed up his philosophy in 1925: "Close analysis will prove that only where the color-line fades and co-operation instituted are our business advances gratified. Segregation in any form, including self-imposed is not the solution."[29]

Despite his outwardly congenial relations with whites, Bolden never abandoned the black community. He participated in several black fraternal organizations as an Elk, a thirty-second-degree Mason, and a Shriner, and was a member of the Citizen's Republican Club, a local black business and professional group. Despite his lifelong reputation as a "dour and taciturn" man, Bolden was an eloquent speaker who spoke publicly on a variety of subjects, including a "forceful" speech, "The American Negro, Immigration, and Race Consciousness," delivered before the Commonwealth Club of the YMCA in 1924. The Hilldale corporation gave generously to black causes, and the team took part in annual benefit and charity games for hospitals, churches, and war veterans. In addition, Hilldale continued to be linked to Philadelphia's most potent black voice, the *Tribune*. Bolden advertised Hilldale's games each week in the *Tribune* and faithfully sent in press releases, game results, and box scores. The *Tribune*, realizing the selling value of Hilldale, gave the team favorable coverage and staunchly defended Bolden from his occasional critics.

Like any other black citizen of this era, Bolden was not immune to racial prejudice. In one incident, he was forced to use a freight elevator while attending a meeting of the Philadelphia Baseball Association in the early 1920s. Later, whites in Darby reacted with hostility and prejudice when his daughter Hilda was named valedictorian of Darby High School in 1924. Despite the gains made by blacks during World War I, Bolden and his team often were confronted by discrimination during the 1920s in Philadelphia, still "a Jim Crow town, segregated in its restaurants, theaters, and hotels."[30]

Encouraged by the overwhelming popularity of semipro baseball in

Base Ball! **HILLDALE** Base Ball!

AT PHILLIES BALL PARK

BROAD AND HUNTINGTON STREETS

TWO SOLID WEEKS OF BASEBALL THAT "THRILLS."

Monday, Oct. 4th, to Saturday, Oct. 16th, Inclusive

Monday, October 4th, 3 p m.	Tues., & Wed., Oct. 5th & 6th,
AMER. LEAGUE ALL★STARS	**CASEY STENGEL'S**
All Athletic's Line-Up	National-American All Stars—3 p. m.

Thursday & Friday, 7th & 8th, 3 p. m. **Babe Ruth & Carl Mays** All Stars

Saturday, Oct. 9, (Two games for one Ad-mission; 1st game at 1:45) Big Double Header

PARKESBURG VS. J. J. DOBSON; WINNER VS. HILLDALE

This game is to play off a triple tie.

WORLD SERIES WILL BE SHOWN ON PHILLIES SCORE BOARD

Advertisement in the *Philadelphia Tribune*, October 2, 1920.

the Philadelphia area after World War I, Bolden and other local promoters began to challenge the city's archaic blue laws prohibiting commercialized baseball on Sunday. While most eastern cities had relaxed or abandoned Sunday blue laws by 1920, Pennsylvania's rural-dominated state legislature had continued to favor strict observance of an American sabbath. Connie Mack, however, maintained that the loss of lucrative Sunday home games severely limited the ability of the Athletics to compete financially with other American League clubs. While at home on Sunday, the Athletics and the Phillies were forced to remain idle or schedule exhibition games against semipro clubs in communities where the ban was loosely enforced.

Encouraged by a recent court decision allowing noncommercial Sunday baseball games at Fairmount Park in Philadelphia, several clubs, including Marshall Smith, Nativity, and the Madison Stars, began scheduling local Sunday games in July 1920. By August, Sunday ball in Philadelphia had achieved widespread success, especially among working class men and women, with nearly 20 games scheduled each week. While some independent clubs, including Hilldale, continued to be arrested and fined for participating in commercialized Sunday games, local enforcement became increasingly sporadic as a result of the general acceptance and popularity of Sunday baseball. In May 1921, however, local public opinion abruptly shifted after a policeman's attempt to break up a Sunday game at Ann and Almond Streets in Northeast Philadelphia caused a riot and the shooting death of a fan. Philadelphia's mayor, J. Hampton Moore, quickly ordered a general crackdown on all Sunday games charging admission or taking collection, as well as noncommercial games near houses of worship or residential districts.[31]

Despite Moore's attempts, a number of local teams continued to schedule Sunday games and employed various methods to avoid detection and prosecution. Some teams sold tickets during the week for Sunday games or charged admission at a safe distance from the park. At 4th and Wingohocking, fans of the North Phillies were charged higher prices for Saturday games but were issued a blue ticket stub good for admission on Sunday. The Bridesburg team at Richmond and Orthodox Streets instructed fans to drop money in an old ice cream barrel, a ruse eventually detected by Philadelphia police. As prosecution escalated during the summer of 1921, fans reacted with increasing hostility to police or others sent to disperse a Sunday game. In July a pastor was struck on the head with a brick while attempting to break up a game in East Germantown.

With tensions mounting, the city's leading semipro teams joined to form the Allied Athletic Association, with plans to raise money for a legal challenge to the Sunday baseball ban. On Sunday, August 28, 1921, a test game was played at 48th and Brown Street between the Shanahan Catholic Club and Belfield. Despite the protests of an angry crowd, police promptly stopped the game after one inning of play and arrested 23 players from both teams. Three days later, the two teams were acquitted and discharged to the cheers of a packed courtroom. Mayor Moore, however, refused to discontinue his enforcement of the Sunday baseball ban and noted that only the state legislature could repeal the law. While personally in favor of a more lenient interpretation, Moore nevertheless announced that "commercialized baseball must go, even if it is necessary to station a policeman on each base to prevent the game from being played." Moore's crusade was largely successful, and the ban continued to be enforced in Philadelphia until its repeal in November 1933. Like Hilldale, the leading semipro teams turned to New York, Brooklyn, Baltimore, and Newark for Sunday dates as well as nearby towns in New Jersey and Pennsylvania that were lax in enforcement or where Sunday ball was legal.[32]

Despite its Sunday baseball defeat, the Allied Athletic Association did not disband but instead gave birth to a new cooperative organization, the Philadelphia Baseball Association (PBA) in February 1922. Headquartered at the Hotel Walton at 1524 Chestnut Street, the PBA represented an attempt to regulate the fast-growing local twilight baseball scene by organizing clubs into a single association that would afford protection to all members. The PBA planned to resolve the inevitable problems faced by semipro teams, including player jumps, poor umpiring, lack of discipline, and gambling. To prevent jumping, players would be required to sign "contracts," and tampering by clubs was made punishable by a $100 fine. The home umpire system was abolished among member clubs, replaced by rotating umpires under PBA control. An elimination tournament was also planned, with 10 percent of the receipts allocated to the organization.

By May, more than 60 local teams had joined the PBA, including Hilldale. As manager of one of the area's most powerful and profitable clubs, Bolden could not be left out of the new organization despite his racial status. Bolden would serve a prominent role in its administration and was elected to the PBA Board of Governors, along with Ed Gottlieb, Art Summers, and other leading promoters. While the PBA did admit a number of other black teams, including at least 10 local sandlot teams and several out-of-state professional organizations that barnstormed regularly in the Philadelphia area, the white-dominated organization hardly encouraged racial integration. For the proposed elimination tournament, teams were classified into three divisions: A for white teams in Philadelphia, B for white teams outside Philadelphia, and C for all area "colored" teams. Despite their separate status, the presence of black teams in the PBA still dissuaded some local clubs like Strawbridge and Clothier from joining the new organization. Some blacks criticized Bolden for his participation in a white-dominated organization featuring "northern, southern and Jim Crow sections."

The PBA's attempt to provide a central authority to administer the local baseball scene proved unsuccessful as the new organization was unable to enforce its ambitious program. Player violence and contract jumping continued as the PBA's constitution was "evaded ... at pleasure." The organization's attempt to secure impartial officiating was thwarted as well. The majority of local umpires, dissatisfied by the PBA's proposed pay scale, refused to join. Financial obligations also proved problematic as a number of less financially stable teams were unable to pay the 5 percent booking fee per game and the $150 minimum guarantee required for games between member clubs. In July, after 26 PBA members had been suspended for nonpayment of debts, several stronger teams, including Hilldale, Nativity, Bridesburg, Chester, J. & J. Dobson, Fleisher, North Phillies, and South Phillies, discussed forming a separate league within the PBA but rejected the plan. The PBA would continue to struggle as little more than a booking agency until finally collapsing after the 1923 season.[33]

With the failure of the PBA, the local semiprofessional baseball scene began a slow decline. The popularity of radio and motion pictures reduced attendance at twilight games, as did gains made by other sports, including football, basketball, boxing, tennis, and golf. Simultaneously, a lengthy recession in Philadelphia commencing mid-decade drastically reduced the industrial sponsorship that had sparked the postwar growth. By 1928, a number of once powerful industrial teams, including Lit Brothers, Strawbridge and Clothier, Fleisher Yarn, and Stetson Hat, had disbanded or returned to amateur status. In the late 1920s and early 1930s, amateur baseball continued to flourish under renewed Catholic and American Legion involvement and received an additional boost from the participation of thousands of unemployed men and women during the Great Depression. Only a handful of independent professional teams, however, managed to maintain their earning capacity of the early 1920s, and profits and salaries remained a far cry from the postwar era.[34]

Local interest increasingly shifted to professional baseball, sparked by the renaissance of Connie Mack's Athletics. With the addition of outfielder Al Simmons, catcher Mickey Cochrane, pitcher Lefty Grove, and first baseman Jimmy Foxx in 1924 and 1925, the Athletics became instant pennant contenders for the first time since 1914. Attendance at Shibe Park rose from 225,209 in 1919 to 531,992 in 1924 as improvements in public transportation and increased automobile use allowed working-class fans easier access to the city's major league parks. In 1925, after leading the American League for much of the season, the second place Athletics drew nearly 870,000 fans, an attendance figure unsurpassed by any Philadelphia team until 1946. While the team won 83, 91, and 98 games over the next three seasons, the Athletics were unable to overtake the powerful New York Yankees, finishing third in 1926 and second in 1927 and 1928. In 1929, the Athletics surpassed the Yankees and defeated the Chicago Cubs in the World Series to give Philadelphia its first world champion since 1913. The hapless Phillies, weakened by poor finances and a decaying park, drew only 281,200 fans in 1929 but made modest gains by the end of the decade. Led by sluggers Lefty O'Doul (.398 average) and Chuck Klein (43 home runs), the team rose to fifth place in 1929, its highest finish since 1917.

The rising fortunes of the Athletics and the corresponding decline of the local semipro scene adversely affected Hilldale and other regional black professional teams. At Hilldale Park, the once substantial white patronage fell off to a trickle by the late 1920s. In addition, while Hilldale and other black professional teams remained in continuous demand by white clubs, the competition became increasingly one-sided. In 1926, the Inter-State League, a newly formed racially balanced semipro organization, was forced to disband because of the poor showing of the three white clubs against Hilldale and the league's other two black members. Despite weaker white competition, interracial games still remained profitable, and some black teams still found them more lucrative than games against other African American clubs.[35]

Despite its eventual collapse, the postwar semipro boom from 1919 through 1922 raised Hilldale's prestige and financial stability to new heights. Obtaining nearly constant bookings after 1919, the team played more than 500 games over a four-year period and defeated the best black and white independent teams in the East. Using the local African American and white press, Bolden had kept the team's name constantly before the public, even sponsoring a Hilldale uniform display at Marshall E. Smith's sporting goods store in downtown Philadelphia in 1921. By 1922, the *North American* would note that "the colored championship of the city to date rests with Hilldale," an assertion that few would dispute.

The ill-fated PBA, meanwhile, provided invaluable training for Bolden's future league-forming endeavors and prepared him for the inevitable problems and challenges faced by a cooperative baseball organization. In addition, Bolden's presence as the only African American on the Philadelphia Baseball Association's Board of Governors demonstrated his unquestioned domination of the local black baseball scene. In 1923, the Philadelphia Giants, a new black professional team under Danny McClellan, attempted to compete with Hilldale for local bookings but soon inexplicably lost several dates through last-minute cancellations, and was subsequently barred from the PBA's elimination tournament after Bolden threatened to withdraw. In the future, other black clubs attempting to defy Bolden would face similar retribution. Despite his perception as little more than a "short, chunky brown-skinned man who seemingly always had a half smile on his moon face," Bolden could also be ruthless, a fact that Rube Foster and other managers would soon discover.[36]

4

Foster, Bolden, and the NNL, 1919–1922

We cannot get along without organization.
— *Rube Foster, January 1920.*

Hilldale's remarkable postwar growth coincided with similar developments in black professional teams in other cities. By 1919 the African American population of the three major centers of black professional baseball (New York, Philadelphia, and Chicago) exceeded 100,000, and Detroit, Indianapolis, Cleveland, Cincinnati, St. Louis, Kansas City, and other areas had experienced dramatic growth since 1916. The economic gains engendered by World War I and the Great Migration, however slight, gave blacks greater discretionary income and leisure time than ever before, and national interest in semiprofessional baseball was at a fever pitch. Black baseball would reach its "absolute zenith" during the postwar period, with several communities in the Northeast, Midwest, and upper South able to support successful professional teams, often under African American ownership.

Like most black teams, Rube Foster's Chicago American Giants optimistically looked toward the 1919 season. Lured by promises of industrial employment, thousands of southern blacks had migrated to Chicago during the war, doubling the city's African American population from 44,000 in 1910 to nearly 110,000 by 1920. In addition, local semiprofessional baseball had continued to flourish with over 600 teams in operation in 1918 and nearly 1,000 predicted for 1919. In February, one American Giant player accurately observed that "semi-pro ball will be a big success this season and we will do the work. It has been reduced to a business enterprise like the major leagues and many games will be played during the week days, baseball will be in such demand."

Other black teams in the Midwest had not weathered the war as successfully as the American Giants and were slow to return to their prewar status. Suffering financial losses and threatened by Foster's attempts to absorb his team in 1918, C.I. Taylor decided not to reorganize the Indianapolis ABCs in 1919. Meanwhile, J.L. Wilkinson's barnstorming All Nations club, a multiracial team of blacks, Cubans, Mexicans, American Indians, and Asians formed in 1912, had disbanded in 1917 and would not be revived until late in 1919.[1] Foster, however, realized the necessity of bringing strong attractions to face the American Giants at Schorling Park and noted that "to have the best ball club in the world and no one able to compete with it will lose more money on the season than those that are evenly matched."

Deprived of his traditional rivalry with the ABCs, Foster instead looked toward Detroit, whose once modest black community had rapidly expanded during the Great Migration and would reach 40,000 by 1920. In the spring of 1919 Foster transferred several players from his team to help organize the Detroit Stars, placing John "Tenny" Blount at the helm. Initially depicted by the black press as a legitimate businessman, Blount was heavily involved in gambling enterprises in Detroit and was one of several black vice leaders increasingly connected with the promotion and financing of black baseball.[2]

While Sol White condemned Foster's division of the American Giants as a "hard, cold, calculating, money-grabbing, baseball-destroying transaction" unfair to Chicago fans, the Detroit Stars were an immediate success in 1919, finishing with a 62-18 record. The team drew 16,666 fans to its home games at Mack Park, owned by John Roesink, a white pants store owner and baseball promoter, and would realize a net profit of close to $30,000 in 1920. Foster, however, exercised considerable influence over the team, receiving 10 percent of the gross receipts at Mack Park and handling the team's bookings there.[3]

In the East, the increased entrepreneurial opportunities afforded by the Great Migration had allowed Hilldale and other black-owned teams to mount the first serious African American threat to Nat Strong since John Connors's ownership of the Brooklyn Royal Giants from 1904 through 1912. In 1918, Strong, warily noting Hilldale's financial success, had offered to "amalgamate" with the team and proposed that Walter Schlichter, the former owner of the Philadelphia Giants, handle local bookings. Despite the considerable influence of the two white promoters, Bolden refused to be intimidated and responded in an open letter published in the *Philadelphia Tribune*:

I succeeded in getting the Directors together and laid before them your, or rather Mr. Strong's proposition to amalgamate our Corporation with him. The result was as I contemplated and coincided with my feelings. The success, good name and reputation of our Hilldale Company has been acquired by nine years of untiring effort to give to our race an institution that we have finally perfected.

The race people of Philadelphia and vicinity are proud to proclaim Hilldale the biggest thing in the baseball world owned, fostered and controlled by race men and in return we are modestly proud to be in a position to give them the most beautiful park in Delaware County, a team that is second to none and playing the best attractions obtainable.

That others propose to enter similar business in [an] adjacent neighborhood is not our affair.

To affiliate ourselves with other than race men would be a mark against our name that could never be eradicated.

We are personally responsible for the fame and success of Hilldale, to place it in jeopardy would be absurd.

With due consideration for your intentions and efforts as an amalgamator I remain

Yours truly,

Edward W. Bolden, Manager
Hilldale Exhibition and Baseball Co., Inc.[4]

Strong retaliated by reviving the old Philadelphia Giants, using several of his players, and placed the team in Darby at Delaware County Athletic Park, directly across the street from Hilldale Park. Interest was minimal, however, perhaps due to Strong's unpopularity among blacks. In a letter to the *Tribune*, Claude Miller of South Philadelphia expressed the attitude of most local African American fans: "I feel quite sure that Mr. Bolden will give us just as good if not better entertainment than Mr. Schlichter. Mr. Bolden being a gentleman of color and an honest promoter. I believe our race will support him. Hilldale for mine, first and last."

Thwarted by Bolden, Strong turned his attention to another black-owned club, the Grand Central Red Cap team of New York. After signing several of Strong's players in 1918, Grand Central struggled to obtain decent bookings and suspected that Strong had ordered a general boycott of the team. As Lester Walton of the *Age* noted, it was "not the first accusation" of this kind against Strong, and "no colored baseball manager has been very much of a success in these parts for several years," largely because of the desire of white promoters to maintain their monopoly over the New York area. Walton, however, additionally blamed New York's black citizens, who failed to patronize African American enterprises as extensively as blacks in Chicago and other cities.[5]

While Strong weathered the challenge of the Grand Central team, the unexpected return of John Connors would provide a more serious threat. The former Brooklyn Royal Giants owner, out of baseball since 1912, revived the near bankrupt Atlantic City Bacharachs with the help of Baron Wilkins, the notorious leader of Harlem's underworld and owner of the Exclusive Club cabaret, and Henry Tucker, one of the original founders of the team. Wilkins had backed various baseball clubs including the short-lived New York Black Sox and boxer Jack Johnson and was said to have to have won $250,000 on Johnson's July 4, 1910, championship fight against James Jeffries. Offering higher salaries than either James Keenan or Nat Strong, the new Bacharach owners enticed several players from the Brooklyn Royal Giants and Lincoln Giants and temporarily broke the white hold on black baseball in New York. Strong, simultaneously accused of stating that no black player was worth more than $65 a month, was hit especially hard, losing Bill Gatewood, Dick Redding, John Henry Lloyd, Jesse Hubbard, and Johnny Pugh to the Bacharachs. In desperation, Strong attempted to lead a boycott against the Bacharachs and supposedly accused Wilkins and Connors of undermining his business by offering "coons" more money. By June 1919, however, the Bacharach owners' powerful contacts with white major league players and officials (including first baseman and notorious gambler Hal Chase of the New York Giants and owner Charles Ebbets of the Brooklyn Dodgers) as well as the support of other eastern white promoters and park owners forced Strong to concede defeat.[6]

The successful return of John Connors coupled with Tenny Blount's astounding success in Detroit reflected the growing economic power and more aggressive entrepreneurial spirit of blacks as a result of the Great Migration. William White, an eastern based columnist for the *Chicago Defender*, noted the trend: "The East is lining up with the West in not allowing white men to own, manage and do as they feel like doing in the semi-pro ranks with underhand methods, etc." In addition, the temporary defeat of Strong, who had "leashed and throttled" black baseball for years, provided a rare opportunity for African Americans to enjoy a racial victory during the troubled summer of 1919. While race riots, triggered by white hostility to the increasing presence of blacks competing for jobs and housing, had occurred in several communities, including Chester, Philadelphia, and East St. Louis during the war, the most violent episode erupted in Chicago in July 1919, resulting in 38 dead and over 400 wounded. Returning home to Chicago after the riot for a

Hilldale, 1919. Left to right: Jim York, Willis "Pud" Flournoy, Dick Lundy, Toussaint Allen, George Johnson, Ed Bolden, Tom Williams, Chick Meade, Phil Cockrell, Yank Deas, Lefty Starks, John Reese, Elihu Roberts, McKinley Downs. The team debuted in Detroit and New York during 1919, but the Chicago race riot forced cancellation of a series at Schorling Park against Rube Foster's American Giants (Cash-Thompson Collection, courtesy Afro-American Historical and Cultural Museum, Philadelphia, Pennsylvania).

scheduled game against the Bacharach Giants, Rube Foster and his American Giants found Schorling Park occupied by soldiers. The team was forced to cancel its home games for nearly a month, including a long anticipated meeting at Schorling Park with Hilldale, in the midst of their first trip west. Undaunted, Foster took the American Giants on a lengthy tour highlighted by the team's first New York appearance in five years and a return trip to Darby where his team split a two game series with Hilldale.[7]

Despite exacerbated racial tensions, the 1919 season proved extraordinarily profitable for the majority of black professional teams. As C.I. Taylor noted, several clubs had made a "remarkable 'come back'" in 1919 and "shared in the general prosperity along with the whites." In the West, the Cuban Stars, Dayton Marcos, Cleveland Tate Stars, and Joe Green's Chicago Giants enjoyed successful years, while Charles Mills's St. Louis Giants, who had dissolved in 1917, also returned to form. Meanwhile, a

Rube Foster (National Baseball Library and Archive, Cooperstown, N.Y.).

fierce rivalry between Hilldale and the revived Bacharach Giants heightened eastern interest. On September 8, 1919, the ninth and deciding game of a series between the two teams was played before 5,000 fans at Shibe Park, marking the first simultaneous appearance of two black teams at the Athletics' grounds.

For Rube Foster, now booking several midwestern clubs in addition to controlling the American Giants, the season far exceeded all preseason expectations. By July, Foster marveled to a friend that "colored base ball has at last come to the front—you would be surprised at the way the western clubs are doing, and from what I gleam [sic] from the East, they are also doing nicely." At Schorling Park, Foster noted that "we are drawing double of any year here, even adding 2300 Boxes, cannot accommodate the people." By the season's close, Foster had reportedly realized a profit of nearly $15,000, a far cry from his $1,000 earnings in 1907, his first year in Chicago, and was consistently lauded as "genius" by the *Chicago Defender*.[8]

Less established teams, however, still remained at a distinct disadvantage. While a handful of black semipro clubs, including the Baltimore Black Sox, Homestead Grays, Cleveland Tate Stars, and Harrisburg Giants, made initial tentative steps toward professionalism in 1919, the majority of newly formed teams continued to be plagued by insufficient financial resources, an inability to secure adequate playing grounds, and competition from the professional organizations. Since most individual black investors lacked the necessary capital to undertake a business venture on their own, incorporation became an increasingly popular means for African Americans to finance their clubs and avoid white ownership. Black fans, however, possessing only limited discretionary income, had little patience with the struggles faced by new franchises and refused to support teams that did not instantly achieve success.

The unforeseen success of Detroit proved elusive to other communities that typically lacked the experience, organizational skills, and finances of Rube Foster and Tenny Blount. As Dave Wyatt noted, increasingly high expenses and a limited supply of "first-class players" inevitably frustrated the efforts of aspiring black baseball entrepreneurs, and "so long as this condition exists it is going to be a very hard job for new and untried cities to break in." An attempt to place a professional team in Pittsburgh, home of nearly 38,000 blacks by 1920, failed in 1919. In Washington, Rube Foster expressed interest in organizing a team with S.H. Dudley, a noted black theatrical magnate, but eventually abandoned the idea. Despite boasting the nation's third largest black population by 1920 as well as legalized Sunday baseball, Washington, like other border cities, was handicapped by an intolerant local attitude toward interracial competition. In the impoverished South, black teams in Birmingham, Memphis, and other cities were similarly restricted from playing white opponents until the Depression and simply lacked the resources to compete financially with the established eastern and midwestern organizations, often losing their best men to these clubs.

Despite the successful ascendancy of black-owned clubs in several communities during 1919, white capital continued to be an important support of black baseball. Regardless of their success, no black teams were immune to what Donn Rogosin called the "structural problem" of black baseball: its reliance upon a relatively small, economically oppressed population base with little leisure time or discretionary income. With African American fans still unable to support a professional team on a day-to-day basis, most successful promoters, including Foster and Bolden, realized that some financial involvement with white promoters, park owners, and teams was still necessary for survival.[9]

Nevertheless, Foster realized that conditions were at their most favorable for black baseball and began to advocate the formation of a professional league patterned after the white major leagues. Since the formation of the Cuban Giants in 1885, several unsuccessful attempts had been made to organize leagues. In 1886, a group of black amateur and semipro teams representing Memphis, Atlanta, Savannah, Memphis, Charleston, Jacksonville, and New Orleans organized the short-lived Southern League of Colored Base Ballists. A more promising circuit, the League of Colored Base Ball Clubs, was formed in 1887 by Walter Brown, a Pittsburgh newsstand manager, with franchises based in Boston, New York, Philadelphia, Baltimore, Pittsburgh, Washington, Louisville, and Cincinnati. While reportedly protected by the same National Agreement that governed organized baseball, the new league soon collapsed, victimized by high travel expenses and the conspicuous absence of the nation's best black team, the Cuban Giants, who wisely realized that barnstorming against white teams offered greater profits.

For the next 20 years no serious attempt was made to organize black teams, except for Nat Strong's National Association of Colored Professional Clubs of the United States and Cuba. While functioning more as a booking agency than a league, the association did serve as a governing body for several eastern teams and awarded a pennant to the organization's championship team. Black teams also held various unofficial championship contests in an attempt to determine the nation's best team. In 1888 a four-team tournament in New York was won by the Cuban Giants and received favorable comment from the white press. By 1905 championship series featuring regional or intersectional rivals were annual events in the East and Midwest. The enormous success of the 1903 and 1904 series featuring the Cuban X-Giants and Philadelphia Giants once again raised hopes among black baseball fans for the formation of a league. In November 1904 Bud Fowler, former captain of the Page Fence Giants and a minor leaguer, optimistically predicted that "[one] of these days . . . a few people with nerve enough to take the chance will form a colored league of about eight cities and pull off a barrel of money."

Within three years, the general prosperity enjoyed by western clubs after Foster's arrival in Chicago encouraged several promoters to consider a league based in the Midwest and upper South. In December 1907 Frank Leland held a meeting for a proposed eight-team National Colored League of Professional Ball Clubs with franchises to include the Leland Giants and other midwestern clubs. While the project was supported by Rube Foster and even attracted the attention of Nat Strong, Leland's plan was eventually abandoned, although a small regional league, eventually known as the Ohio State Colored League, later evolved from the attempt. Three years later, Leland Giants promoter Beauregard Mosely organized the Negro National Base Ball League with the help of Rube Foster. Despite ambitious plans for a half black umpiring staff and a reserve clause designed to "put Negro baseball on par with the National and American League clubs," Beauregard's attempt also ended unsuccessfully.[10]

While the movement for organization was a failure among the stronger black professional teams, several regional amateur leagues had developed since 1900, including the Ohio State Colored League, Missouri-Illinois League, Presbyterian Baseball League of Chicago, Greater Boston Colored League, New England Colored League, Colored Texas League, and the District of Columbia League, composed of black federal employees. Though limited in scope and ambition, these leagues did stimulate local interest in baseball and helped develop skilled players. In addition, white semipro leagues occasionally allowed one or more black teams to participate. The Philadelphia Giants and other eastern black clubs joined the Philadelphia-based International League in 1906, while the Leland Giants, Chicago Giants, and Atlantic City Bacharachs competed in local city leagues. Most African American teams, however, remained unaffiliated with any league, and several organizations, including local municipal leagues in Kansas City and St. Louis, formally excluded African American teams.[11]

With the marked expansion of black baseball in the teens, discussion of a proposed league once again resumed. C.I. Taylor heartily endorsed the idea of organization as a means to curb player jumps, and Rube Foster, despite his own raiding tendencies, also supported league formation, especially after the success of the Lincoln Giants and Chicago American Giants intersectional series in 1913. Lester Walton of the *New York Age* remained skeptical, however, and perceptively predicted the potential problems of black professional baseball, including an overreliance on Sunday baseball, the financial weakness of franchises outside Chicago and New York, and the disparity in strength among league teams. Other observers noted that high railroad expenses had cut into the profits of black theatrical performers and warned that a similar fate awaited league teams separated by great distances.

While the draft and other wartime difficulties temporarily suspended league discussion, the tremendous profits enjoyed by the American Giants and other clubs rekindled interest in the subject during 1919. By July, Foster was confident enough to predict that "we will have the circuit at last" in 1920, and in October an article by Cary Lewis of the *Chicago Defender* announced that a black baseball league backed by Foster was planned for the following season. Foster, however, realized that he could not act without the support of his fellow owners, several of whom had been alienated by his occasionally heavy-handed tactics. In addition, he recognized that the lucrative financial returns from 1919 had temporarily blinded many promoters to the problems still present in black baseball. To gather support for his proposal, Foster wrote a series of weekly articles entitled "The Pitfalls of Baseball" that appeared in the *Chicago Defender* from November 29, 1919, through January 17, 1920, cogently explaining why a league was the only solution to the chronic difficulties of black baseball.[12]

In Foster's view, black baseball was still in a financially precipitous position despite its recent success. While ticket prices had remained relatively low, park rentals, player salaries, and travel expenses had dramatically increased. Yet as Foster noted, most black teams continued to draw successfully on only one day per week (Saturday or Sunday), and few clubs could "show a profit of $1,000 per season for their time, trouble, money or investment." In addition, most teams lacked long-term financial security, possessing no tangible assets or personal property other than their players. Meanwhile, investment in new ballparks continued to be nearly impossible for black teams because of expenses and the objections of nearby white property owners.

Foster, however, perceived contract jumping as the "root of all the trouble" in black baseball, with much of the problem caused by players who had been advanced salaries but left owing their old team money. As a result, victimized owners typically retaliated with costly player raids and boycotts that constantly undermined the progress of professional black baseball. Refusing to blame players, Foster instead criticized the poor business management and selfishness of owners, especially those who offered higher salaries than they were able to pay, and argued that a cooperative organization "open to all" that respected contracts was necessary to ensure continued prosperity. Foster also believed that a successful league would create sufficient interest among black teams to reduce the dependency upon white opponents and booking agents and would perhaps even gain the attention and respect of organized baseball and its fans, leading to possible integration of the major leagues.

Despite Foster's claim that there were "thousands of dollars waiting for such an organization" and his prediction that a league would be supported better than the American Association, response to his offer was initially lukewarm. Eastern clubs, grappling with their own difficulties, were hardly receptive to the idea of a midwestern league controlled by Foster, and several western owners feared that a league would solidify Foster's domination of the region. Some observers doubted that a true "cooperative" organization could exist and cited Foster's massive ego and contemptuous attitude toward his fellow owners, exemplified by the following:

> They forget that I have been a player, whose intellect and brains of the game have drawn more comment from leading baseball critics than all the other colored players combined, and that I am a student of the game. They do not know, as I do, that there are not five players nor three owners who know the playing rules.[13]

In the January and February 1920 issues of *The Competitor*, two veteran observers of the black baseball scene, C.I. Taylor and Dave Wyatt, offered cautious support of Foster's proposal. Taylor, despite an ongoing feud with Foster, acknowledged that the business of black baseball was indeed in "chaotic condition" and revealed that the ABCs had barely managed to break even during their three most successful seasons (1915–1917). While he agreed that a contract-respecting organization was necessary "if we are to make anything out of baseball for the black Americans," Taylor found it ironic that "the very men who ... stood in the way of such an organization" were now its staunchest advocates. As Taylor noted, Foster had declined his suggestion to form a league as recently as 1916 and cited Foster's pessimistic view that black players "as a whole are a lot of ingrates — that they are enemies to their best friends, and would do anything to defeat the honest efforts of those who are rightly the leaders and promoters of their best interests."

Wyatt, while more encouraging, warned that the disproportionate financial strength and patronage of black teams would undermine the effectiveness of a reserve clause, noting that "to induce first-class players to remain in Kansas City, Indianapolis or even St. Louis is a difficult assignment for any baseball manager so long as there remains a possibility of the player securing a berth in Chicago or in the East." In addition, Wyatt believed that with the "demand for first-class players . . . greater than the supply," black baseball still lacked the talent necessary to support a balanced eight team professional circuit.[14]

While discussions continued in the black press during January and February 1920, Foster negotiated with reluctant western owners in two secret sessions held in Detroit and Chicago. Foster made peace with C.I. Taylor, who agreed to reorganize the Indianapolis ABCs as a member of the new league, and attempted to find suitable backing for a new Kansas City franchise. Although Foster considered proposals from black investors, he eventually turned to J.L. Wilkinson, a local white promoter, who had access to the minor league park used by the American Association's Kansas City Blues and had recently reorganized his All-Nations club. Wilkinson's new team, the Kansas City Monarchs (named for an earlier Kansas City team), was subsequently formed from the remnants of the All-Nations club and the baseball team of the black 25th Infantry regiment. While Wilkinson's inclusion in the new league would engender some criticism, the Kansas City owner would prove perhaps the most honest and generous promoter in black baseball.[15]

On February 13 and 14, the long-anticipated league organizational meeting was held in Kansas City, with Foster, Taylor, Blount, Wilkinson, Joe Green (manager of the Chicago Giants), W.A. Kelly of Washington, D.C., and L.S. Cobb (secretary of St. Louis Giants) in attendance. Dayton Marcos owner John Matthews, though unable to attend, also sent his support, and the western Cuban Stars were represented at the meeting by Foster. Realizing the importance of press support, several newspapermen, including Elwood Knox of the *Indianapolis Freeman*, Charles Marshall of the *Indianapolis Ledger*, Cary Lewis of the *Chicago Defender*, and Dave Wyatt of the *Indianapolis Ledger*, were invited to the meeting and encouraged to participate in the proceedings. Wyatt, along with attorney Elisha Scott of Topeka, wrote much of the constitution and bylaws of the new organization, which became known as the National Association of Colored Professional Base Ball Clubs (usually referred to as the Negro National League, or NNL). League members, which included the Chicago American Giants, Indianapolis ABCs, Detroit Stars, Chicago Giants, St. Louis Giants, Dayton Marcos, Cuban Stars, and Kansas City Monarchs, paid a $500 deposit and agreed to respect player contracts and to play a schedule of games to determine a league champion each season.

In an unprecedented display of cooperation, several players, including several former contract jumpers, were transferred to league clubs in an attempt to maintain competitive balance throughout the new circuit. To show his own impartiality, Foster, the league's newly elected president and treasurer, sent back the American Giants' Oscar Charleston to the newly reorganized ABCs, Sam Crawford to the Kansas City Monarchs, and Dick Whitworth to the Detroit Stars. The Stars were forced to return former All-Nations players Jose Mendez and John Donaldson to J.L. Wilkinson, but received Jimmy Lyons of the St. Louis Giants. While official league play was not scheduled to begin until 1921 or until each team owned or leased a park, the circuit opened in May 1920 despite the inclusion of two traveling teams, the Cuban Stars and the Chicago Giants. With Foster administering the league's finances and scheduling, the Negro National League had a successful inaugural season in 1920, the American Giants capturing the first pennant.[16]

Despite high expectations, the league failed to resolve the problems that had faced black teams in the past and would continue to haunt all professional black leagues for the next 30 years. As anticipated, the "top-heavy" aspect of black baseball was soon apparent in the NNL. Despite Foster's attempts at player distribution, the American Giants quickly dominated, winning 32 of their first 37 league games, and by July Dave Wyatt admitted that the "fans are tiring of a one-team league." Meanwhile, weaker NNL members, including the Chicago Giants and Dayton Marcos, were unable to sustain fan support and became less desirable opponents for the more powerful teams. By late August the last-place Chicago Giants had played only 35 league games, while the Kansas City Monarchs had already played 64. Scheduling was a constant problem as well, especially in Indianapolis and Kansas City where home games could only be arranged when the grounds were not in use by the local American Association teams (Indianapolis Indians, Kansas City Blues). In addition, with most league teams playing from two to four games per week, weekday games against white semipro teams remained a significant source of income.[17]

Fans, as well as the black press, were especially disappointed by the new league's lack of reliable player statistics, box scores, and team standings. In July 1920, the *Competitor* noted that several league teams failed to wire box scores to newspapers for publication and claimed that "with two full playing months past, not one box of official standing of the clubs has appeared in any of the papers published in league cities." The press also criticized the NNL for failing to hire umpires able to discipline and control unruly and argumentative players. On July 31, 1920, at Kansas City, a particularly violent episode involving John Donaldson of the Monarchs and Leroy Grant of the American Giants touched off a near riot that required "pistol packing" officers to control. Yet as Foster noted, the league could not be expected initially to function as effectively as the white major leagues whose owners were "rich men." Despite Foster's expectation of advancement, the NNL would never adequately resolve its recurrent difficulties with poor umpiring, inaccurate statistics, and unbalanced schedules.

Like Ban Johnson of the American League, Foster's "czar-like" rule came under harsh attack by league owners, who objected to his dual role as team owner and NNL president. W.E. Ferance, an official with the St. Louis Giants, revealed the inherent unfairness of the league's hierarchy, noting that a complaint against manager Foster would be mailed to league secretary Foster, then ruled on by President Foster! Meanwhile, C.I. Taylor and Charles Mills bitterly opposed the league's financial arrangements, which allocated 10 percent of the gross receipts from each league game (5 percent from each team) to Foster to finance the league's operation. The Detroit Stars' Tenny Blount felt that with 20 percent of the gross already reserved for park owners, the additional 10 percent required by Foster was especially destructive to league teams struggling to make a profit.[18]

The NNL's relationship with eastern promoters was equally stormy in the league's first season. While Nat Strong reportedly sent a supportive letter to the league "stating that he was ready to do anything that would promote the best interests of baseball all over the country," Hilldale and other eastern clubs eventually rejected Foster's organization, and a meeting for a proposed eastern based league was never held. In response, Foster accused the eastern clubs of encouraging contract jumping by creating dissension and dissatisfaction among players and subsequently forbade any NNL team from scheduling games with Hilldale, the Bacharach Giants, Lincoln Giants, and Brooklyn Royal Giants.

Foster was especially incensed by Bolden's signing after the 1919 season of three American Giant players (outfielder Jess Barbour, third baseman Bill Francis, and pitcher Dick Whitworth) and his near acquisition of Oscar Charleston, the team's star center fielder. Seeking revenge, in April 1920, Foster traveled east where rumors circulated that the NNL planned to raid Hilldale. Foster, however, avoided open warfare, and instead attempted to jeopardize Hilldale's standing in Philadelphia by supporting and offering protection to the newly formed Madison Stars. As a further slap at Bolden, Foster negotiated a settlement to bring NNL teams to Dyckman Oval in New York while attempting to block Hilldale from appearing in the area. Finally, Foster induced the Bacharach Giants to join his new organization as an associate member, which allowed the team to play NNL clubs traveling east or visit league teams in the West. The Bacharachs, now protected by Foster, promptly grabbed catcher Yank Deas, shortstop Dick Lundy, and outfielder Jess Barbour from Hilldale.[19]

Forced to respond, Bolden published an open letter to Foster in the August 21, 1920, *Philadelphia Tribune*. While calling for cooperation between the East and West, Bolden claimed that the NNL leader had a "belligerent attitude toward our club" and "sought to place us in disfavor" in the East. Defending his controversial acquisition of Francis, Whitworth, and Barbour, Bolden noted that since the NNL's reserve clause binding players to their current team did not take effect until February 1920, the players had been free agents when signed by Hilldale in November 1919. While indifferent to Foster's organization, Bolden warned that if the NNL and its affiliates chose to boycott Hilldale Park, they would only be hurting themselves financially.[20]

By the end of the 1920 season, Bolden's attitude toward the new league had begun to waver. The NNL showed evidence of stability, reportedly drawing 616,000 fans in 1920, all eight clubs finishing with a profit. Fearing that his own players might be vulnerable to contract offers from raiding NNL teams, Bolden opted for the protection of the league and joined as an associate member at the December 1920 annual meeting of the league in Indianapolis, paying a $1,000 deposit. As the *Chicago Defender* noted, Bolden's first meeting with the NNL was surprisingly amicable as "the magnates acted more than fair and treated Bolden as if he had been a member all the time." Hilldale lost no major players and was even allowed to keep Dick Whitworth and Bill Francis. In addition, Bolden and Bacharach owner John Connors ended their lengthy dispute over player raids and became friends during the meeting.

While slightly marred by continued disagreement over the league's 10 percent share of gross receipts, the Indianapolis meeting represented the league at its cooperative peak. The owners, determined to resolve the NNL's first-year difficulties, reelected Foster as president and secretary and ratified a new constitution that called for stiffer punishments and fines for rowdy players, made the reserve clause a standard part of every league

Veteran third baseman Bill Francis left Foster's American Giants to sign with Hilldale in 1920 and served as team captain through 1922 (Cash-Thompson Collection, courtesy Afro-American Historical and Cultural Museum, Philadelphia, Pennsylvania).

contract, and raised the required team deposit from $500 to $1,000. The league also continued its progression into eastern territory with its addition of Hilldale, the Pittsburgh Keystones, and Cleveland Tate Stars as associate members. With the subsequent defection of John Henry Lloyd and several other Brooklyn Royal Giants to the NNL in early 1921, the East seemed all but ready to fall into Foster's hands. Once denounced as

Hilldale, 1921. Top row, left to right: Ed Bolden, George Johnson, Chaney White, Dick Whitworth, Jim York, Connie Rector, Louis Santop, Pud Flournoy, Toussaint Allen, James Byrd (treasurer). Bottom: Otto Briggs, McKinley Downs, Jake Stephens, Flammer, Nat Dobbins, Bill Francis, Chance Cummings, Phil Cockrell. The team finished with an outstanding 105-41-3 record and defeated the American Giants in a postseason series (Cash-Thompson Collection, courtesy Afro-American Historical and Cultural Museum, Philadelphia, Pennsylvania).

ludicrous, Foster's ambitious dream of organized colored baseball composed of black major and minor leagues seemed almost possible in 1921.[21]

For Hilldale, now an associate NNL member, the 1921 season would prove its most successful to date as the team topped 100 wins for the second consecutive year. While most strategy and field decisions were now overseen by captain and third baseman Bill Francis, Bolden continued to administer the team's finances and exercised complete control over player personnel. Always able to recognize talent, Bolden had used a variety of sources to assemble his championship-caliber club. Paul "Country Jake" Stephens of York, Pennsylvania, sent Bolden a barrage of anonymous letters touting his abilities at shortstop, leading Bolden to give the youngster a tryout in 1921. The slick fielding Stephens quickly earned a spot on the team and became Hilldale's regular shortstop for most of the next 10 years. In July, Bolden recognized the promising ability of another local sandlot player, Judy Johnson, and reacquired him from the Madison Stars. Like Stephens, Johnson soon blossomed into a star with Hilldale and emerged as one of the team's most well regarded players.

Since 1917, Bolden had taken advantage of the vast talent pool

Featuring a strong throwing arm and remarkable range at shortstop, Paul "Country Jake" Stephens became one of the most popular Hilldale players during the 1920s (Cash-Thompson Collection, courtesy Afro-American Historical and Cultural Museum, Philadelphia, Pennsylvania).

available in the South, often relying on Hilldale veterans such as Louis Santop and McKinley Downs for leads on promising players. By 1921, Hilldale featured several outstanding players recently recruited from the South, including pitcher Connie Rector, outfielder George Johnson, and outfielder Chaney White of Texas as well as first baseman Toussaint Allen and pitcher "Pud" Flournoy of Georgia. Trading, while comparatively rare, was also employed by Bolden as a four player deal was completed with the Norfolk Stars in 1920. Finally, like other professional clubs, Bolden had obtained players by raiding rival clubs, epitomized by Hilldale's controversial signing of three American Giants in 1919.[22]

Bolstered by Bolden's masterful acquisitions, Hilldale overwhelmed its competition in 1921 as the team won its first 15 home games, compiled two 10-game winning streaks, and finished with a respectable 22-16-1 record against other clubs affiliated with Foster's extremely competitive Negro National League. The season's numerous

Louis Santop (with glove) and pitcher Dick Whitworth. After jumping to Hilldale from the Chicago American Giants in 1920, Whitworth enjoyed two fine seasons but returned to the American Giants after the 1921 season (Cash-Thompson Collection, courtesy Afro-American Historical and Cultural Museum, Philadelphia, Pennsylvania).

highlights included Louis Santop's mammoth home run against the New York Bacharach Giants at Ebbets Field in June, Phil Cockrell's no-hitter of the Detroit Stars in September, and a brilliant pitching staff featuring four 20-game winners — Connie Rector, Dick Whitworth, Pud Flournoy, and Phil Cockrell.

Hilldale's phenomenal year culminated in October with a dramatic six game series with Rube Foster's NNL champion American Giants. In game 1, played at the Philadelphia Phillies' Baker Field on October 4, the American Giants stole 10 bases on Hilldale's hapless catcher, Jim York, and won easily 5–2. Hilldale quickly recovered with a win in game 2 and led by Phil Cockrell's two victories, eventually claimed the six game series with three wins, two losses, and one tie. Most black baseball observers were shocked by the defeat of the seemingly invincible American Giants, who had not lost a series of games all season. As Lloyd Thompson noted, "No person who is an authority on Negro baseball, would grant Ed Bolden a place in the sun with Rube Foster, when it comes to generalship on the diamond, but when Bolden's Boulders struck Foster's scientific craft amidship, the next job was for the salvagers." Foster, meanwhile, blamed the American Giants' defeat on poor umpiring during the series and the idiosyncratic playing conditions at Hilldale Park where the final two games were played. The Chicago manager argued that the presence of a center-field ditch and tree stumps necessitated ground rules and complained that "it is impossible to get Hilldale to play according to the playing rules."[23]

The American Giants' humiliating loss to Hilldale was but one of several setbacks for Foster in 1921, including the death of his daughter and his arrest in Atlanta for supposedly failing to pay his players. In addition, a combination of high travel expenses, bad weather, and the postwar recession resulted in a disappointing second year for the NNL. While the American Giants managed to increase attendance, Foster admitted that several NNL teams had lost money, and the league reportedly suffered a 25 percent drop in gate receipts. More ominously, the circuit, as predicted, seemed unable to sustain eight financially stable franchises. By the end of 1921, two clubs, the Dayton Marcos and their replacement, the Columbus Buckeyes, had already failed, while the St. Louis Stars, backed by Richard Kent and Sam Shephard, supplanted Charles Mills's St. Louis Giants. In 1922, Foster was forced to replace the Buckeyes and Joe Green's Chicago Giants with two former associate clubs, the Pittsburgh Keystones and Cleveland Tate Stars, both of whom collapsed by the following season. While Chicago, Kansas City, Indianapolis, St. Louis, and Detroit would remain profitable cities throughout the NNL's existence, other midwestern communities, including Milwaukee, Toledo, Dayton, and Cleveland, consistently proved unsuitable as franchise locations.[24]

Foster and several black sportswriters attributed much of the league's financial problems to poor management and "slack business records" of franchise owners and attempted to increase the involvement and investment of experienced black businessmen. Most prosperous black entrepreneurs, however, were reluctant to participate in such a financially risky venture that typically required a $1,000 deposit, 10 percent of the gross receipts from each game, and an additional 20–25 percent to a white park owner. In addition, few teams were able to draw on weekdays, and the NNL continued to rely on Sunday games, especially in Chicago at Schorling Park.

Foster's controversial involvement with John Schorling continued to annoy several league owners, who accused Foster of attempting to recoup his substantial rental costs by arranging the schedule so that Schorling Park was occupied each Sunday. Ollie Womack of the *Kansas City Call* claimed that the American Giants remained home nearly every Sunday and "make one trip around the league circuit while several other clubs, especially the Monarchs, make from two to five." Tenny Blount alleged that while league owners struggled to meet their finances, "Foster and Schorling got theirs and looked wise." Foster, however, denied that Schorling had any input into league affairs and depicted the Chicago promoter as an honorable and fair landlord. In addition, he defended the American Giants' schedule, accurately noting that Sunday games in Chicago were consistently lucrative for both the American Giants and their opponents and offered more than any other league location.[25]

Bolden, like other NNL owners, soon grew disenchanted with Foster's once unquestioned leadership. While Hilldale was protected from player raids by its associate membership, the team had also lost lucrative dates against outlawed eastern clubs, including the Brooklyn Royal Giants and Lincoln Giants. In early 1922 Bolden requested a return of his $1,000 deposit and prepared to withdraw from the league with plans to raid NNL teams. Foster, however, quickly retaliated with a threat to sign away Hilldale players, and as the pro–Foster *Chicago Defender* warned, "Unless Manager Bolden comes into the fold he may find his club wrecked." Facing the loss of several players, Bolden capitulated and remained in the league for a second season, to the glee of the *Defender*: "This means that Hilldale has decided to remain in baseball. . . . No one wanted to see a great ball club like Bolden had built up wrecked. . . . Bolden was far-sighted enough to see his mistake." Foster, however, seized pitcher Dick Whitworth from Hilldale before allowing Bolden to return as "the league directors decided it would be best for the morale of the league not to return him to the Philadelphia club."

The 1922 season proved disappointing for Hilldale as Bolden, unable to sign NNL players, was forced to rely on veterans Louis Santop, Bill Francis, and McKinley Downs. While easily defeating most white semipro teams, Hilldale finished with a losing record against black professional clubs, facing increasingly stiff competition from several newcomers to the professional black baseball scene, including the Harrisburg Giants, Richmond Giants, Baltimore Black Sox, and Chappie Johnson's Philadelphia Royal Stars. The team managed only a 10-17-1 record against NNL affiliates and won only three of nine games against the American Giants and Detroit Stars during a western trip in August, all three victories earned by Phil Cockrell. The season's major highlight was the consistently brilliant pitching of Cockrell, who no-hit the Paterson Silk Sox in June, a week after they had defeated the Chicago Cubs, and duplicated the feat in August against the American Giants in Chicago.[26]

While Bolden and Foster continued their uneasy alliance through 1922, a break seemed inevitable. With Foster firmly in control, Bolden had no authority in league affairs, and the misspelling of Hilldale ("Hildale") on the league stationery hardly conveyed a positive attitude toward the team. Despite paying $1,000 for an associate membership, only four western teams had visited Hilldale Park during 1921 and 1922, while Hilldale had made a single costly western trip during 1922. Annoyed by high western travel expenses, Bolden noted in disgust that "we have received more money for a twilight engagement in Philadelphia, where the players could walk to the park, than a Sunday game in the West, with over a thousand miles' railroad fare to cover!" and continued to chafe over the loss of lucrative games against outlawed eastern clubs. Finally, with Hilldale showing signs of decline in 1922, Bolden viewed the NNL's reserve clause restriction on player raids as a hindrance to the team's continued success.

Citing the "decided disadvantage of membership," Bolden submitted his resignation from the NNL in early December 1922 and demanded the return of his $1,000 deposit. While accepting Hilldale's withdrawal, Foster refused to refund Bolden's money, citing a recent amendment to the NNL constitution forbidding its return, and stated his awareness of Bolden's plans to raid NNL teams. Threatening a "legal shakedown," Bolden claimed that he had not been informed of the rule governing his $1,000 deposit or been present when it was enacted.

On December 16, 1922, at the Southwest YMCA building at 1724 Christian Street in Philadelphia, Bolden struck back at Foster by forming a rival organization, the Mutual Association of Eastern Colored Baseball Clubs (or Eastern Colored League), with Hilldale, the Baltimore Black Sox, Brooklyn Royal Giants, Lincoln Giants, Cuban Stars, and the Original Atlantic City Bacharachs as members. Unlike the NNL, the new league had no president but was governed by six commissioners representing each team as well as a chairman and secretary-treasurer. Bolden was elected the league's first chairman, with James Keenan of the Lincoln Giants as secretary-treasurer.[27]

Reaction from the West was predictably hostile as the NNL refused to recognize the new league and criticized its preponderance of white owners. Bolden's alliance with Nat Strong was seen as especially objectionable, and the *Chicago Defender* claimed that "colored baseball in the East has gone back a decade when Nat Strong offered ball clubs $100 flat and two 15-cent meals for a Sunday game."

Bolden, however, viewed the new league as a necessary step to free Hilldale and other eastern clubs from Rube Foster's iron rule. Participation in Foster's western league was an expensive proposition that offered Hilldale "no benefits, no protection," while an eastern based circuit with easily accessible cities and lower travel costs would be far more profitable. Bolden explained his league forming activity to the *Tribune* in 1923: "The fans have loyally supported the club and there is little doubt that they will continue doing so, but I think they are entitled to better competition among our own clubs; and the best way to secure it is through an organized circuit."

The formation of the Eastern Colored League was an inevitable reaction to Foster's domination of the Midwest, revealing conclusively that black baseball had grown beyond the control of one man. With his league threatened by the prospect of an almost certain player war with Hilldale and other eastern clubs, Rube Foster bitterly noted, "There can be no peace in baseball."[28]

5

The Eastern Colored League at Its Peak, 1923-1924

> Colored baseball in the East has grown and developed into the biggest sport proposition in recent years. It brings to the cities baseball of a splendid excellence, and gives cosmopolitan crowds a chance to indulge the favorite sport under ideal conditions.
> — *Ed Bolden, March 1923.*

The formation of the Eastern Colored League (ECL) effectively crushed Rube Foster's dream of a national black baseball league. Although the East had once seemed ripe for NNL development after the ascendancy of two black-owned clubs, the Bacharach Giants and Hilldale, and their subsequent incorporation into the league, Foster had drastically underestimated two factors: the still considerable influence of Nat Strong and the ambition of Ed Bolden.

Bolden's break with Foster and alliance with Strong was inevitable, as the NNL had little to offer Hilldale except protection from player raids. Strong's nearly exclusive control of lucrative Sunday bookings with white teams in the metropolitan New York area appealed heavily to Bolden, especially with Sunday ball still prohibited in Philadelphia. Meanwhile, Strong, while never an enthusiastic league supporter, realized that his participation in an eastern-based circuit would ensure lucrative dates at Hilldale Park for his Brooklyn Royal Giants and the Cuban Stars, whose bookings he controlled. In addition, Strong and his partner Max Rosner had recently purchased Dexter Park, the home of the Brooklyn Bushwicks, for $200,000 and were eager to book Hilldale there for the first time since 1920.

Bolden's affiliation with Strong, the "Hebrew menace in colored

baseball," and his severing of ties with the NNL shook the entire foundation of black baseball. John Connors's New York Bacharach Giants, once
an eastern ally of Hilldale against Strong, were raided and lost John
Henry Lloyd, their captain and shortstop, to Hilldale. To Foster, Bolden's action represented racial treachery at its worst and demonstrated
that Hilldale had "at last fallen in line" with Strong. By April 1923 Connors dissolved the Bacharachs, leaving Foster without an eastern representative. Most of Connors' players were absorbed by the "Original
Bacharach Giants" who had operated under original founders Tom
Jackson and Henry Tucker in 1922 in Atlantic City and Wilmington and
had recently joined the ECL.[1]

    The increasingly frustrated Foster unleashed the first of a series of
attacks on Bolden in January 1923 with a scathing press release that denounced Bolden's role in organizing a league that seemed little more than
a booking agency for Nat Strong. To Foster, Bolden's fear of Strong had
led him to bolt the NNL, organize the ECL, and sign Lloyd away from
the Bacharachs. In contrast, Foster cited his defiance of Strong, noting
that he had even refused Strong's offer of support in exchange for John
Connors's exclusion from the NNL. While obviously embittered, Foster
decided against immediate retribution and instead challenged Bolden to
a debate before newsmen on the "merits and demerits of the two leagues."
Scorning Bolden's leadership of the ECL, Foster declared, "May God
help his tongue and guide his faculties . . . [or] he will do the game such
harm that centuries will not erase his mistakes." Further, he warned that
"at the proper time, I will drive a blow that will strike at the very vitals
of this treachery."

    Refusing to retreat before Foster's attack, Bolden readily accepted
the offer to debate and suggested that Foster take part of Bolden's $1,000
deposit, rent the Academy of Music in Philadelphia, and hold the event
before fans, using the proceeds to help disabled ballplayers like Dick Whitworth. While no face-to-face debate was ever held, the two men continued
to snipe at one another on the pages of the African American press. In
a widely circulated article published in several black eastern newspapers,
Bolden dismissed Foster's charges of race abandonment and decried
Foster's use of the "poison pen" to advance his own agenda. The NNL,
Bolden noted, had "a few skeletons lurking in the closet," with respect to
white influence in league affairs, and cited J.L. Wilkinson's position as
league secretary and John Schorling's continued ownership of the
American Giants' park. In addition, Bolden observed that most NNL
teams played in parks "where they give from twenty to twenty-five per
cent of gross receipts to white men." In defense of his relationship with

Nat Strong, Bolden noted that Foster had been equally eager to enlist his assistance, citing two letters in November 1921 and January 1922 that invited Strong to join the NNL. Bolden felt that Foster's depiction of the ECL as a booking agency was particularly unfair, especially in view of Foster's administrative role in the NNL, and questioned whether the NNL "can run on the level with one meeting a year, one man to make up a schedule for ten clubs and juggle it to suit his own interests, [and] one man heading an organization and holding the strings of its purse?"

Asserting their independence from Foster, Bolden and other ECL owners began openly luring NNL players to the East. By April 1923, Hilldale's already powerful lineup was strengthened by the addition of several western stars, including outfielder Clint Thomas and second baseman Frank Warfield from the Detroit Stars, catcher Raleigh "Biz" Mackey from the Indianapolis ABCs, and utility man George Carr from the Kansas City Monarchs. Meanwhile, an attempt by Foster to lure Hilldale pitcher Phil Cockrell to the NNL was unsuccessful. By March 1924, the *Baltimore Afro-American* reported that a total of 30 NNL players had jumped to the more prosperous eastern-based teams, whose lower travel expenses and cheaper park rentals enabled them to offer higher salaries than the West. The increasingly chaotic state of NNL affairs acted as a further inducement to contract jumping as league owners, demoralized by declining gate receipts and the recent defection of Hilldale, began to quarrel incessantly among themselves and particularly with Foster. The *Chicago Whip* reported that during the December 1922 league meeting Foster had faced more opposition than ever before, with one owner suggesting that Foster should give up control of his team if he wished to remain league president.[2]

The death of C.I. Taylor in March 1922 had seriously undermined the cooperation that had characterized the NNL during its first two seasons. Taylor, while never more than an uneasy ally of Foster, was nevertheless a devoted league advocate whose considerable experience and business acumen ensured the continued stability of the ABCs. Following Taylor's death, the once proud Indianapolis franchise enjoyed one final successful season and then began a slow decline, hastened by a struggle between Taylor's widow and his brother Ben, the team captain, for control of the club. Despite Ben Taylor's claim that his brother had promised him controlling interest in the team on his deathbed, the wife of C.I. Taylor instead assumed ownership of the team. Foster, though sympathetic to Taylor's claim, refused to involve himself in the struggle, instead hoping that Mrs. Taylor would eventually turn the team over to her brother-in-law. Meanwhile, Foster attempted to appease the disgruntled Taylor with an offer of a new NNL franchise in Cincinnati. After the club failed to materialize, Taylor defected to the East with several ABCs in January 1923 with plans to organize a new team in Washington.[3]

While understandably bitter at the loss of Taylor and other NNL players, Foster largely absolved the players from blame and instead attributed "the influence of older heads who are disgruntled and seek to wreck an institution that they have never contributed one cent or one ounce of effort toward its building." Foster, however, was disturbed by the ingratitude of ballplayers who had been brought north and given a chance yet were now deserting him for eastern teams, such as pitcher Dave Brown of the American Giants, who had once been arrested for assault and battery but had been paroled by Foster. Nevertheless, he offered all contract jumpers a chance to return to the NNL before the season started, but after receiving no response, he rescinded the offer and banned all contract jumpers "forever" in April 1923. With the future options of contract jumpers now limited to the ECL, Foster gambled that eastern teams would eventually cut their salaries, discouraging further NNL defections.

Foster, refusing to accept his role in the formation of the ECL, continued to perceive the circuit as little more than an attempt to destroy both the NNL and its leader. To Foster, the ECL had rejected his leadership because "they know if I play where money is, I must share equally in it, so it's good reason that they don't care to have me." Yet league rumors had circulated since 1920, and most observers realized that with the growth of professional black baseball in the East, an organization with or without Foster's support was inevitable. As business manager Charles Spedden of the Baltimore Black Sox noted, eastern black baseball could no longer be run in the "haphazard" manner that it had in the past, and organization offered the best way to increase profits and interest regionally. In addition, Spedden claimed that Foster's name was never once mentioned during the December organizational meeting of the ECL and argued that NNL players had come east on their own volition rather than as a result of eastern tampering.

While each league continued to hurl accusations at the other, Bolden turned to the monumental task of building a functional organization. Bolden's participation in the PBA and NNL, though limited, had given him valuable firsthand experience, and he was determined to avoid the obstacles that had marred both organizations. Despite receiving applications from other eastern teams, including the LeDroit Tigers of Washington, D.C., Bolden held league membership at six teams, at least temporarily, hoping that a compact circuit would prevent the recurrent franchise failures that had plagued the NNL. The ECL received a tempting offer from Ben Taylor, whose new Washington-based club, the Potomacs, had received backing from George W. Robinson, a successful African American entrepreneur who owned the Roadside Hotel and a flourishing catering business in Philadelphia. Though rejecting the proposal, the ECL promised encouragement to Taylor and consideration for a future league franchise.[4]

As league chairman, Bolden soon discovered the difficulty of establishing positive working relationships among six fiercely independent owners mutually suspicious of one another. James Keenan of the Lincoln Giants and Nat Strong of the Brooklyn Royal Giants, longtime adversaries in New York, found themselves uncomfortably allied in the new circuit, both motivated by the declining interest in black baseball in the area. Keenan's Lincoln Giants had been hit especially hard in recent years and had been forced to vacate their grounds at Olympic Field in Harlem to make room for a new parking garage in 1920. Their new home, the Catholic Protectory Oval, located at an orphanage in the Bronx at East Tremont Avenue near 180th, was miles away from Olympic Field and inaccessible to many black fans who had followed the team religiously in the 1910s. While white fans continued to support the Lincoln Giants, interest in New York waned among blacks, as one observer would note:

> To see a good baseball game in which colored men engage you now have to travel miles out of the district. In the days when the McMahons operated at Olympic Field ... thousands of colored fans looked forward to the weekend with pleasurable anticipation. Now it takes a dyed-in-the-wood [*sic*] fan to make up his mind to trail all the way up to the Catholic Protectory Oval.[5]

Like Keenan, the white owners of the Baltimore Black Sox hoped the league would increase local interest by ensuring the regular appearance of strong attractions at their home park. Still unproven as a major black baseball power, the Black Sox were also eager to demonstrate their ability to compete with Hilldale and other major professional eastern teams. Formed in 1910, the Black Sox, like Hilldale, rose from the sandlots, eventually obtained their own playing field (Westport Park) about 1917, and slowly built a reputation as a strong team. Originally owned by Charles Spedden, a white clerk employed by the Baltimore and Ohio Railroad, the club was eventually sold to George Rossiter, a local white tavern owner, with Spedden remaining with the team as business manager. The Black Sox were incorporated in 1921, moved to a new park (Maryland

Park at Bush and Russell Streets), and began paying salaries and attracting professional players during the following year, adding future black
superstar Jud Wilson in 1922. Like Hilldale, the team had a significant
white following in the early 1920s (reportedly outdrawing the International League's powerful Baltimore Orioles on occasion), but the enthusiasm and support typical of Philadelphia's black fans were lacking in
Baltimore. As the *Baltimore Afro-American* noted, the city had a reputation
as a "poor sports town" and had "never been on the colored baseball 'map'
to the extent that its location and colored population justified."

While less exploitive than Nat Strong, the white management of the
Black Sox contributed to the apathy of many Black Sox fans. Their insen-
sitive policies alienated many of their black patrons, who constantly complained of the wretched condition of Maryland Park, the home of the
Black Sox during the 1920s. The seats were said to be dirty, the roof full
of holes, the grandstand unpainted and foul smelling, the infield rough,
and the outfield full of weeds with uncut grass. The lack of black park
employees also discouraged greater patronage. The Black Sox owners
claimed the "experiment" of black employment in the box office had been
abandoned because they had "not found them satisfactory in the rapid
handling of change" and were "most always short when the count up is
made." While more black employees were eventually hired by the Black
Sox management, owner George Rossiter faced constant criticism from
the black press for a variety of abuses, including offering "special reserva-
tions" for whites.[6]

The league's controversial inclusion of Rossiter and three other white
owners (Strong, Keenan, and Thomas Jackson of the Atlantic City
Bacharachs) was a disappointment to many eastern fans, who had hoped
for greater involvement of African American businessmen. Meanwhile,
Foster and his supporters in the western press claimed that viable black-
owned franchises, including the Richmond Giants and Harrisburg Giants,
had been excluded from the league because of their nonaffiliation with
Strong. Bolden, however, had little choice but to admit white-owned
teams since eastern black baseball had been dominated by whites since its
inception and few adequate black-owned replacements of equal caliber
were available. Most eastern sportswriters acknowledged the league was
"not an out-and-out Race affair" yet urged public support of the endeavor
with the hope that no more white owners would be involved in the future
and would eventually be replaced by African Americans.

The six league owners met regularly during early 1923 to prepare for
the ECL's first season. While perceived as the league's head, Bolden's
position as chairman granted him far less authority than Foster enjoyed

in the NNL. In response to Foster's virtual one man rule in the NNL, the ECL had adopted a commission form of government that provided each owner or commissioner with an equal say in league affairs. Most league policies were subject to the approval of all six commissioners with Bolden allowed to cast the deciding vote if a consensus could not be reached.

Surprisingly, the usually contentious eastern owners worked harmoniously to formulate an organization that paralleled the NNL but incorporated several unique features. With eastern black baseball still profiting heavily from games with white semipro opponents, only 50 league games were scheduled per team to allow flexibility for other bookings. Weekday league games, a financial disaster to the NNL, were also kept at a minimum. In contrast to the NNL, which continued to allocate 10 percent of gross receipts to the league, 40 percent to the visiting team, and 50 percent to the home club, the ECL retained the traditional financial arrangements of independent baseball, with visiting teams assured of a guarantee ranging from $150 to $300 or an option of 40 percent of the gross receipts. Yet the ECL, like its western counterpart, was determined to transcend independent baseball as league statistics and standings were to be compiled and issued at regular intervals and the official league schedule was to be published before the season's outset in late April.

Despite the attempts of Bolden and other commissioners, the ECL proved unable to develop a balanced schedule. With black baseball parks able to draw only one or two days a week, league games were mostly limited to Wednesdays at Camden (where Hilldale would continue to lease grounds through 1923), Thursdays and Saturdays at Hilldale Park, and Sundays at Baltimore, New York, and Atlantic City. The presence of two traveling teams, the Cuban Stars and the Brooklyn Royal Giants, further undermined any attempts at a balanced schedule, and several observers questioned Nat Strong's steadfast refusal to obtain grounds for either club despite his control of Dexter Park. The anticipated schedule never appeared, and an explanation offered by the league foreshadowed future difficulties:

> Due to petty differences between commissioners of several league clubs, the schedule has not been balanced properly, although all of the commissioners agreed upon a fifty-game layout for each team, because of it being the first venture in organized ball, a portion of the schedule being left open for the benefit of a couple of teams. For this reason it was impossible to publish the schedule prior to the season's opening.[7]

While no league team managed to complete its schedule, Hilldale came closest, playing 49 of 50 league games. The team's popularity at home and on the road discouraged cancellations, and Hilldale, like the American Giants in the NNL, soon became the financial backbone of the league. Other league teams were less than cooperative; the Baltimore Black Sox, for example, refused to play weekday league games at home late in the season. Yet by far the worst offenders were Nat Strong's Brooklyn Royal Giants, who seemingly participated only when convenient, ignored many scheduled games, and did not play a single league game during the month of June. By mid–July, Hilldale had played 30 league games, the Royal Giants only 10. Bolden and other league officials began to sense the disadvantages of Strong's membership, and as Rollo Wilson of the *Pittsburgh Courier* quipped, "Several of the commissioners . . . would like to see Mr. Nat Strong taken up to the 'L' tracks on the Brooklyn Bridge and dumped into the East River."

Though busy with league affairs, Bolden remained actively involved in Hilldale's management. The team had been successfully overhauled during the winter with a series of key personnel changes, including the signing of Thomas, Warfield, Mackey, Carr, and Lloyd and the subsequent release of veterans Bunny Downs, Bill Francis, and outfielder Chaney White. To strengthen the team's mediocre pitching staff, Bolden had added two Washington, D.C., natives: submarine-balling Holsey "Scrip" Lee, formerly of Chappie Johnson's Philadelphia Royal Stars, and Jesse "Nip" Winters, a brilliant young left-handed pitcher who had starred for several eastern clubs since 1920.

To no one's surprise, Hilldale took a quick lead in the ECL pennant race, reeled off 17 consecutive victories in June, and eventually captured the pennant with a 32-17 record in official league games and a 137-43-6 overall record. Virtually without a perceptible weakness, the club featured a brilliant pitching rotation of Lee, Cockrell, Winters, and recent acquisition Red Ryan that shut out opponents 18 times, and a powerful hitting attack that averaged nearly seven runs a game. In addition, the club possessed remarkable bench strength, with the versatile George Carr filling in at first base, outfield, and catcher; Jake Stephens backing up the veteran John Henry Lloyd at shortstop; and the still dangerous Louis Santop available for pinch-hitting duty. Notably, the influx of several highly salaried newcomers had no effect on the team's disciplined style of play. As Jake Stephens recalled, Hilldale "played like a team. There was so much cooperation; everybody knew his job. The main thing was to win ball games, regardless of how you did it."

New captain and shortstop John Henry Lloyd would prove the team's biggest disappointment. While perhaps one of the greatest African American players of his generation, the future Hall-of-Famer seldom endeared himself to management during his lengthy career and in 1923 was with his fourth team in as many years. At 39, Lloyd had slowed down in the field but was still a fearsome hitter and seemed initially worthy of the hefty salary that had lured him from the Bacharachs. Yet Lloyd's handling of the team quickly alienated several Hilldale players, particularly Clint Thomas, whose salary increase was blocked by Lloyd despite prior approval by Bolden. In addition, Lloyd was forced out of the lineup in July after a sliding injury, resulting in a shift of catcher Biz Mackey to shortstop and Louis Santop back to regular duty behind the plate.

Though Lloyd eventually returned to the starting lineup, his injury, high salary, and unpopularity among most Hilldale players forced Bolden to release him in late September. As a replacement, Bolden selected second baseman Frank Warfield, who was thrust into the unenviable position of assuming control of Hilldale prior to the team's appearance in the PBA tournament and postseason series against a pair of barnstorming major league clubs. Determined to avoid negative publicity at all costs, Bolden refused to divulge the specific details of the incident, simply noting that "the change has been effected for the good of the team." Scrip Lee, however, felt that Lloyd's salary considerations weighed most heavily in the decision, claiming that Bolden "figured he could halve Lloyd's salary and give it to Warfield to be manager and player."[8]

After tuning up with an easy defeat of Chester in the PBA tournament, Hilldale was ready to face its first major league competition since 1920, a barnstorming team featuring Wid Matthews, Jimmy Dykes, Fred Heimach, Bing Miller, Cy Perkins, and Curly Ogden of the sixth-place Philadelphia Athletics. The series began on Tuesday, October 9, 1923, at Shettsline Field in South Philadelphia. Hilldale, supplemented by shortstop Dick Lundy of the Bacharach Giants, took the opener 3–0 behind a brilliant one-hit shutout performance by Phil Cockrell. In game 2 at Smedley Field in Chester on October 10, the major leaguers were once again stymied by Hilldale pitching, managing only seven hits against Nip Winters, while Hilldale ripped nine off Fred Heimach of the A's (6-12, 4.32 ERA) to take a 3–2 decision. A ninth-inning rally gave Hilldale a series sweep on Thursday, October 11, with a 3–2 win over Curly Ogden (1-2, 5.63) at Shettsline.

On October 12 Hilldale returned to Shettsline Park to face a second barnstorming group of Athletics led by pitcher Eddie Rommel (18-19, 3.27), featuring the team's starting first baseman Joe Hauser (16 HR, 94 RBI, .307), right fielder Frank Welch (.297), and shortstop Chick Galloway (.278). Rommel, ranked in the top 10 in the American League

Though known for his catching prowess and powerful throwing arm, the versatile Raleigh "Biz" Mackey saw considerable duty at shortstop and third base during the 1923 and 1924 seasons. The switch-hitting Mackey was also a fine hitter and like Louis Santop, became a favorite of both white and black fans (National Baseball Library and Archive, Cooperstown, N.Y.).

in games, innings pitched, and ERA in 1923, allowed 10 hits and six runs but coasted to an easy 11–6 win in game 1. On Saturday, October 13, the series shifted to Hilldale Park where the largest crowd in Hilldale history, estimated at 20,000, watched Phil Cockrell outduel Robert Hasty (13-15, 4.44) for a 3–1 Hilldale victory. The series ended a week later as Hilldale, minus Warfield, Mackey, and Thomas, crushed Rommel 9–4 at Darby.

Hilldale's five victories against two barnstorming clubs provided a stunning climax to an amazing season and placed the club at the forefront of black baseball. The team had convincingly demonstrated its superiority in all competition by winning the ECL championship, PBA tournament, and the two postseason series against major league teams. The *Washington Tribune* hailed Hilldale as "unquestionably the best in the east and quite possibly the country," and the *Philadelphia Inquirer*, typically unappreciative of the achievements of African Americans, complimented the team's

Outfielder Clint Thomas jumped to Hilldale in 1923 after a stint with Tenny Blount's Detroit Stars. Thomas led Hilldale with 28 home runs in 1924 and followed up with 18 in 1925 along with 32 stolen bases (National Baseball Library and Archive, Cooperstown, N.Y.).

"million dollar outfield" of George Johnson, Otto Briggs, and Clint Thomas.

For Bolden, the 1923 season represented the second peak of his career. Bolden had not only assembled one of the best black teams in the country but had established the club as an unusually stable and prosperous business enterprise. The team continued to draw massive crowds at home and received almost constant bookings locally with white teams, causing one sportswriter to observe that "few teams can boast the wealth of the Hilldale club." The annual Hilldale banquet held at the Hotel Attucks in October 1923 was an especially lavish affair featuring an eight-course meal and a presentation of gold belt buckles to the players. With a new influx of southern black migrants swelling the Philadelphia population during 1922 and 1923 and the semipro boom still in full swing, future prospects indeed looked bright for the Hilldale corporation and the ECL, which had also enjoyed increased attendance and now seemed financially secure enough to resist any potential retribution from the NNL.[9]

Foster, confronted by declining gate receipts and two more franchise failures (Toledo and Milwaukee), had chosen mostly to ignore the ECL after his series of preseason attacks on Bolden. With the apparent success of the ECL, however, fans from both regions had begun to clamor for an East-West World Series to decide the true champion of black baseball. Several league officials from both regions expressed support of the idea, as well as a number of black sportswriters. William Ready of the *Baltimore Afro-American* observed that it would "make the white world series resemble a game of ping pong" and would succeed in placing both leagues "on the baseball map with both feet," perhaps even leading to a series with the white World Series champions. Still bitter over eastern raids, Foster, however, scorned the ECL as a "booking agency" and maintained that a series was impossible until the East agreed to respect player contracts.

Foster's refusal to negotiate with the ECL was based upon an optimistic belief that the eastern league could not maintain its current salary structure and would eventually collapse. Yet in contrast to the NNL, the ECL had managed to survive its first year without a single franchise failure and even added two new teams, the Harrisburg Giants and Washington Potomacs, at its annual meeting in December 1923. To counteract its public perception as a white-dominated organization, both new clubs were financed by African Americans: C.W. Strothers, a former city patrolman and local entrepreneur, heading the well-established Harrisburg club at Island Park and George W. Robinson and Ben Taylor beginning their second year at Washington. With the addition of two franchises, the season was extended from 50 to 70 games, each team to play 10 games against the others. In March 1924 the league published its first season schedule, proudly noting that the West had yet to publish a full-season schedule in its four-year existence.[10]

Eastern owners, brimming with confidence after a financially successful first year, resumed their raids on the West. Once again, the dissension-ridden Indianapolis ABCs were easily victimized, losing most of their remaining players to eastern teams. The ABCs suffered a particularly devastating blow with the defection of superstar Oscar Charleston, who signed with the Harrisburg Giants at a reported salary of $400 a month. Although the NNL considered legal action against eastern teams, the league soon abandoned the idea in the face of prohibitive expense and was forced to watch helplessly the exodus to the East. As Crush Holloway, who left the ABCs to join the Baltimore Black Sox, explained, the team was "getting $150–175 out there, came out here and got $350–375. Man, you know we were going to come here!"[11]

Unable to stop the contract jumping, the proud Foster instead attempted to denigrate the ECL in a series of widely published articles in early 1924. To Foster, the East's "drunken orgy" of player raiding clearly confirmed indifference to a peaceful settlement between the two leagues and simultaneously revealed a failure to develop skilled players, "hence [the East] must steal them after they are developed." As usual, Foster expressed his contempt for the ECL's relationship with Nat Strong: "You tolerate conditions there that you should pass up. Have stood for Nat Strong to collect 10 per cent from the revenue of colored clubs for 30 years, yet . . . run your league with a club in it, and do not allow them at his own park. When allowed they play for nothing." Foster's attacks elicited little reaction and failed to damper the enthusiasm of league officials, particularly Charles Spedden of the Baltimore Black Sox, who predicted "everyday baseball" in the ECL within 10 years.

Bolden, reelected chairman of the Board of Commissioners, was more cautious in his expectations and realized that the league's greatest chance for success lay in continued cooperation by the league's eight franchises. Yet the second season of the ECL proved frustrating as a number of controversies came dangerously close to shattering the fragile coalition of league owners. Although the ECL since its inception had promised the use of independent "rotating" umpires under league control, the much maligned home umpire system used in independent baseball continued to be employed, contributing to a disturbing escalation in on-field violence toward umpires. On July 19, 1924, in Harrisburg, a called third strike provoked a riot, eventually culminating in assault charges against two Cuban Star players by the two umpires, Nick Stroup and Art Fields.

A similarly violent episode occurred earlier in the season in Baltimore after an umpire forfeited a game to Hilldale. While the league implemented a system of fines ranging from $25 for umpire baiting to $100 for umpire assault, Bolden and the Board of Commissioners proved unable to enforce penalties or provide umpires with adequate authority to discipline players.[12]

Once again the league schedule, carefully designed to provide 70 games per team, was followed only haphazardly, resulting in a significant disparity of league games played by each team. While the press blamed Bolden and other league officials for seemingly creating an unbalanced schedule, the majority of canceled or unplayed league games were the result of the lukewarm participation of several league teams, particularly the Brooklyn Royal Giants. As in 1923, Strong selectively followed the schedule, often passing up league games for more lucrative dates with white semipro teams and was more than willing to sacrifice the league temporarily for a tour of New England. In addition, Strong's briefly suppressed feud with James Keenan had once again erupted, resulting in the cancellation of all games between Lincoln and Brooklyn.

Tired of Strong's lack of interest, the commissioners took the unprecedented step of voting the Royal Giants out of the ECL on May 24, 1924. The expulsion, however, lasted only two days as Strong agreed to play all scheduled games in the future. While Strong's league participation increased somewhat, the Royal Giants would play only 42 of 70 league games during 1924, and as Ben Taylor, manager of the Washington Potomacs, noted, the team "did not care whether they won or lost." Nevertheless, Strong's ousting symbolically demonstrated to skeptics the league's autonomy as well as Strong's reliance on the financial support of ECL teams.

Other problems caused disruptions in the league schedule. The Lincoln Giants refused to leave their home grounds on Sunday to play scheduled games in Baltimore without high guarantees, and the increasing unprofitability of Atlantic City resulted in canceled dates. Meanwhile, the Washington Potomacs, crippled by lukewarm local interest and the high cost of renting the Washington Senators' Griffith Stadium, were forced to cancel a number of league games, eventually rescheduling several to Wilmington, Delaware, where they would relocate to in 1925. By September, with only first-place Hilldale close to completing the 70-game schedule, the ECL decided that no league games would be played after September 30. Fans of the second-place Baltimore Black Sox, who had played nearly 20 games fewer than Hilldale, angrily protested the ruling, and the *Baltimore Afro-American* complained that "the league bosses refuse to take chances on the Black Sox winning the pennant, as it seemed to be cut and dried that Hilldale must be given the bunting at all costs."[13]

While facing strong challenges from Baltimore, Lincoln, and the Harrisburg Giants, Hilldale had once again proved to be the class of the league, and as Potomacs manager Ben Taylor noted, "The best team won the pennant." After the substantial changes made in 1923, the team's roster remained basically intact during 1924 as Bolden did not actively participate in the preseason raids except to sign pitcher Rube Currie from the Kansas City Monarchs. In addition, the club acquired catcher Joe Lewis from Baltimore, shifted Biz Mackey to shortstop, and placed short-stop Jake Stephens with Danny McClellan's New England–based Phila-delphia Giants to obtain more seasoning and experience. The slick-fielding Stephens became the regular shortstop after his recall in July and formed half of a great double-play combination with team captain Frank "Weasel" Warfield that would remain intact through 1928. Strangely, relations between the two men were stormy as Warfield rarely spoke to Stephens and was sometimes uncooperative on the playing field. According to Jake Stephens, Warfield, who reportedly carried a knife, threatened him on one occasion. Stephens' response was a promise to "get a shotgun and kill you."

With the pugnacious Warfield in his first full season at the helm, Hilldale won 47 of 69 league games and finished with a 112-51-9 overall record. Warfield, a brilliant base runner and fine defensive second base-man, strongly emphasized speed to force opponents' mistakes, and nearly every Hilldale player, even big men like Clint Thomas, George Johnson, and George Carr, were running threats. While newcomer Rube Currie was hampered by a shoulder injury, the team's pitching staff remained formidable as well, thanks to its remarkable diversity. As Nip Winters remembered, "We had everything on it. Red Ryan threw a fork ball, Phil Cockrell had a spitter, I threw a left-handed curve, and Scrip Lee was an underhander." Winters, who fashioned a 19-5 record against league teams (according to recent SABR calculations), would replace veteran Phil Cockrell as the staff ace in 1924 and pitched the league's first no-hitter in September against Harrisburg.[14]

Once again, fans and sportswriters from both leagues began to dis-cuss the idea of a World Series that would feature Hilldale and the Kansas City Monarchs, the NNL pennant winner. In August, Ollie Womack of the *Kansas City Call* predicted that a black World Series would draw at least 160,000 fans and urged the leagues to settle their differences. While the ECL remained silent, Foster, after watching the NNL suffer continued financial setbacks, realized that an agreement between the two leagues was needed. Travel expenses had cut heavily into league profits, especially with the inclusion of two new southern franchises, the Birmingham Black Barons and the Memphis Red Sox, who replaced the debt-ridden ABCs at midseason. With all NNL teams reportedly failing to profit in 1924, Foster recognized that another off-season of eastern raiding could seriously place the existence of the league in jeopardy.

In late August, Foster publicly announced his willingness to arrange an East-West series, provided the ECL agreed to respect NNL contracts, and suggested a seven game series with three in Chicago, three in Philadelphia, and one at a neutral location. In response, Bolden indicated that the East would not stand in the way of a series as the "fans must be respected at all times" and even agreed to compromise on the $1,000 deposit that Foster had refused to return to him in 1922. Meanwhile, rumors began circulating that Judge Kenesaw Mountain Landis, the commissioner of organized baseball, had offered to arbitrate the two leagues' differences and draw up a working agreement to govern their mutual operation. Lloyd Thompson, however, considered the idea "farfetched," and even Nat Strong, never a friend of Foster's, expressed a preference for Foster's judgment.

In early September, Foster traveled to New York for a meeting with Bolden and other ECL members. With both sides in a spirit of compromise, the two leagues quickly reached a settlement, agreeing to "respect the sanctity of their inter-relationship" and honor player contracts issued in either league. To prevent interleague jumping and raids, a reserve clause (previously adopted by both circuits) would now bind all NNL and ECL players who had signed contracts or received advance pay to their current team until release. Some observers, noting the relative ease with which the controversial contract-jumping issue had been resolved, felt the extent of the problem had been exaggerated by the NNL. As Rollo Wilson of the *Pittsburgh Courier* noted, "Most of this talk about ball players not respecting contracts is blah, blah. In most instances the players who jumped east or west were either free agents or the property of clubs which had not paid their salaries." Indeed, the NNL's numerous difficulties, especially Mrs. C.I. Taylor's weak finances and Tenny Blount's reputation as a hard loser, were at least partially to blame for the player jumps.[15]

With the contract-jumping issue resolved, the two leagues agreed to stage a World Series between the two pennant winners, the Kansas City Monarchs and Hilldale. A four-man National Commission, Bolden and George Robinson (later replaced by Alex Pompez and Charles Spedden) from the ECL and Rube Foster and Tenny Blount from the NNL, was organized to oversee the financial arrangements of the series, which would be a best-of-nine affair with games scheduled in Philadelphia, Baltimore, Kansas City, and Chicago. Ticket prices were fixed at major league levels of $1.00 to $1.65, substantially higher than typical league prices of 35 to 85 cents. While the commission originally decided to adopt the major leagues' division of gate receipts, which allowed the leagues to share in only the receipts of the first four World Series games, the idea was abandoned as impracticable, as neither league had the reserves available to cover series expenses. Eventually, the commission decided upon an arrangement that allocated 10 percent of the profits to the National Commission (5 percent to each league), 35 percent to the players (split 60-40 between winners and losers), 35 percent to the club owners (split 60-40), and 20 percent to the second- (60 percent) and third-place (40 percent) teams in the respective leagues.

The sorry state of umpiring in black baseball was reflected by the plan to use white major league umpires in the series. With both leagues wary of partial decisions by regular league umpires, the commission felt that a "disinterested third party" would prevent losing clubs from blaming defeats on umpiring. Some fans were disappointed by the absence of African American umpires, especially since the NNL had made extensive use of black umpires since 1923, while several ECL clubs, including Hilldale and Baltimore, maintained mixed umpiring crews. Charles Spedden, however, claimed that the commission had decided to choose major league umpires after failing to agree upon a choice of African Americans. Eventually, four umpires from the International League, Southern League, and American Association were hired for the Philadelphia and Baltimore dates at $50 per game plus expenses, with the West to employ umpires from organized baseball for the games in Kansas City and Chicago.[16]

While the commission made its final preparation for black baseball's first official World Series, sportswriters and fans assessed the relative strengths of the two teams. Despite Hilldale's remarkable season, most observers, including the veteran Pete Hill of the Black Sox, predicted victory for J.L. Wilkinson's powerful Kansas City Monarchs, who seemed superior "on paper." Managed by the legendary Cuban pitcher Jose Mendez, the Monarchs featured Bullet Joe Rogan, a brilliant hitter and pitcher who led the NNL in victories in 1924, and slugging outfielder Oscar "Heavy" Johnson, who reportedly smashed 60 home runs during the season. The team was particularly strong defensively, as catcher Frank Duncan, second baseman Newt Allen, and shortstop Walter "Dobie" Moore were all standouts. In contrast, Hilldale was entering the series handicapped by the loss of Jake Stephens, who had broken his ankle two weeks earlier in a game against the Brooklyn Bushwicks. While the crafty Warfield shifted Judy Johnson to shortstop, catcher Biz Mackey to third base, and asked Louis Santop and Joe Lewis to handle catching chores, the team's normally stellar defense was now questionable and was certain to be exploited by the Monarchs.[17]

On Sunday, September 28, 1924, Hilldale played its final tune-up games in preparation for the series, defeating the Meadowbrook club of Newark and the Doherty Silk Sox of Clifton, New Jersey. With the first two series games scheduled in Philadelphia at Phillies Park, the team then took a much needed rest and awaited the Monarchs, who arrived by train on Wednesday and boarded at George Robinson's Roadside Hotel. On Friday, October 3, the series began at 2:00 P.M., with the Monarch ace Joe Rogan pitted against Phil Cockrell. As a good weekday crowd of 5,366 fans watched anxiously, the game remained scoreless until the sixth inning, when a series of Hilldale defensive lapses, including three errors by Cockrell, allowed Kansas City to score five unearned runs. The Monarchs added another unearned run in the ninth inning on errors by Mackey and Cockrell and survived a ninth-inning rally by Hilldale to take the first game of the series 6–2. Joe Rogan allowed only eight hits for the victory.

Despite a shaky performance by Hilldale in game 1, local fans turned out eagerly for Saturday's game as a crowd of 8,661 packed Phillies Park hoping to see the home team tie up the series. Hilldale jumped out to a quick 5–0 lead in the first inning and cruised to an easy 11–0 victory, ripping 15 hits off four Monarch pitchers. Starter Nip Winters, meanwhile, dominated Kansas City, allowing only four hits in a masterful shutout performance. Dizzy Dismukes, covering the series for the West for the *Pittsburgh Courier*, marveled at the team's confidence during the game and noted that the Hilldale infield, perhaps influenced by Bolden, consistently showed the "college spirit. . . . Each play was appreciated by a slap on the back by the comrades of the player making the play."[18]

The series then shifted to Baltimore for Sunday's game. As early as 7:00 A.M., African American fans from the entire region began heading towards Maryland Park awaiting the opening of ticket windows at 9:00 A.M. Prior to the start of the game, the crowd of 5,503 fans witnessed the formal end of nearly two years of feuding between Foster and Bolden as the two men publicly shook hands to the sound of cheers. While the two leaders of black baseball watched, the Monarchs took an early lead after battering Hilldale starter Red Ryan for four quick runs. Hilldale quickly recovered and a key two run double by Joe Lewis in the fifth inning tied the score at 4–4. After the Monarchs pushed a run home in the ninth to take a 5–4 lead, Hilldale launched a dramatic comeback in the bottom of the inning, manufacturing the tying run on a Warfield walk, a Mackey bunt misplayed by Monarch third baseman Newt Joseph, and a throwing error by first baseman Lemuel Hawkins. In the twelfth, the Monarchs regained the lead for the third time after Newt Allen doubled and scored on Rogan's single. Refusing to fold, Hilldale loaded the bases with one out in the twelfth and tied the score on pinch hitter George Carr's walk. With Judy Johnson on third base, Otto Briggs, the next hitter, lofted a fly ball to left fielder Hurley McNair, who fired home to nab Johnson attempting to score after the catch. One inning later, the game ended in a frustrating 6–6 tie, called on account of darkness.

With most fans returning home or to work on Monday, October 6, a mere 584 fans watched Hilldale take a 2–1 edge in the series by defeating the Monarchs 4–3. For the second consecutive game, Warfield started Red Ryan, who was again ineffective and was replaced by former Monarch Rube Currie. Currie, a disappointment in his first year with Hilldale because of injuries, pitched brilliantly in relief allowing no runs in nearly seven innings as Hilldale battled back from a 3–0 deficit and finally won the game in the bottom of the ninth on a bases-loaded throwing error by Newt Allen. Both Baltimore games had been marked by crucial defensive lapses by the usually sure-handed Monarchs and the inability of Monarch starting pitchers to shut down Hilldale's offensive attack in the late innings. Meanwhile, Hilldale relief pitching had been excellent, as Lee and Currie had allowed only two runs in nearly 16 innings in games 3 and 4.[19]

After Monday's game, both teams boarded a train for Kansas City, the series to resume on Saturday, October 11, at Muehlebach Park, the recently built home of the American Association's Kansas City Blues leased by the Monarchs. Although the eastern games had been relatively free of controversy, two incidents would interfere with the start of game 5, both symbolic of the financial problems in black baseball. While Muehlebach Park was one of the most impressive grounds regularly in use by a black professional team, the Monarchs were but one of a number of tenants, and the first game in Kansas City was nearly delayed by a high school football game that ended only 30 minutes before game time. Meanwhile, fans purchasing a scorecard received a Blues program with Hilldale and Monarch names taped over it. In addition, the management of the Monarchs objected to the expense of hiring four umpires but finally yielded after Bolden's insistence. To the East's chagrin, one of the umpires selected was Ed Goeckel, who had officiated in the West at Schorling Park for years.

Despite the pregame controversies, the game began as scheduled at 2:00 P.M. as 3,891 Kansas City fans prepared for their first look at the eastern champions. Trailing two games to one, Mendez sent out Joe Rogan, who had stopped Hilldale in game 1, while Warfield countered with his ace, Nip Winters. For the third consecutive game, Kansas City jumped out to an early lead and held a 2–1 advantage as Hilldale came to bat in the top of the ninth inning. Once again Hilldale launched a heroic ninth-inning comeback, culminating in Judy Johnson's third hit of the day against Rogan, an inside-the-park home run that drove in Mackey and Joe Lewis. Winters set down the Monarchs in the bottom of the ninth, giving Hilldale a 5–2 win and a 3–1 lead in the series.

On Sunday, October 12, 8,885 fans, the largest crowd of the series, jammed Muehlebach to watch Hilldale veteran Phil Cockrell face William Bell of the Monarchs. The usually reliable Cockrell, suffering from a boil under his arm, failed to last an inning and was replaced by Scrip Lee, who had relieved so brilliantly in game 3. While Lee allowed only two runs in his 7.1 innings of work, George Sweatt's run-scoring triple in the eighth inning broke a 5–5 tie and gave the Monarchs a hard-fought 6–5 victory.

The postponement of game 7 on Monday because of a benefit game for a local white hospital once again revealed the problems faced by black professional teams who leased parks with limited availability. While Frank Young of the *Chicago Defender*, covering the series for the NNL, had scoffed at Maryland Park in Baltimore as one of the "poorest diamonds imaginable," the eastern correspondent Lloyd Thompson noted, "It is far better to dwell in an unencumbered cottage that you have absolute authority to manage to your own liking, than to live in a palatial mansion and be subjected to the wishes of your superiors."

After a one-day layoff, the series resumed at Muehlebach on Tuesday, October 14. With a chance to tie the series at three wins apiece, the Monarchs sent Cliff Bell against Nip Winters, who had stopped the Monarchs in games 2 and 5. Winters, pitching on only two days' rest, held the Monarchs to three runs but found himself trailing 3–2 in the ninth inning. Once again "the old Darby fight" appeared as Hilldale mounted a comeback led by key hits by Judy Johnson and Warfield and tied the score at 3–3. With Hilldale threatening to take the lead, manager Jose Mendez replaced Monarch pitcher Bill Drake and promptly quelled the rally. In

Opposite: **Pregame ceremonies, game 5 of the 1924 World Series, October 11, 1924, at Muehlebach Park in Kansas City. In the first World Series game in the West, Hilldale defeated the Monarchs 5–2 and took a 3–1 lead in the series (National Baseball Library and Archive, Cooperstown, N.Y.).**

the twelfth inning, George Sweatt smashed a key triple for the second consecutive game and pinch runner William Bell then scored on Joe Rogan's single to give Mendez and the Monarchs a crucial 4–3 victory, tying the series at three games apiece.[20]

A four-day layoff followed as the teams traveled to Chicago for games 8, 9, and 10 at Schorling Park. Some observers, such as Ollie Womack of the *Kansas City Call*, objected to the Chicago games and asked, "Why let Mr. Schorling, who has not driven a nail in his park for fifteen years, cut in on something that Chicago has not won." Chicago, however, as the black baseball capital of the Midwest and perhaps the country, could not be bypassed, and both leagues expected heavy attendance. On Saturday, October 18, a modest crowd of 2,608 fans watched a pitcher's duel unfold between former Monarch Rube Currie and Joe Rogan. Currie, who had relieved in games 3 and 4 without allowing a run in 7.2 innings, sailed along with a 2–0 shutout until the ninth inning when the makeshift Hilldale defensive arrangement that had performed adequately through the first seven games finally collapsed.

With one out in the ninth inning, Joe Rogan beat out an infield hit to third baseman Mackey, who was playing too deep to throw out the speedy Rogan. Currie, refusing to become rattled, then retired Newt Joseph for the second out and was now one out from a shutout. The inning was kept alive, however, by Dobie Moore's single off the glove of shortstop Judy Johnson, McNair's run scoring single, and a hit-by-pitch of Oscar "Heavy" Johnson. With the bases loaded, two out, and the score still in Hilldale's favor 2–1, Currie induced light hitting catcher Frank Duncan to loft a pop up behind home plate. To Currie's horror, catcher Louis Santop, whose age and injuries had relegated him to pinch-hitting and reserve duty much of the season, dropped the seemingly harmless foul ball. Given another life, Duncan bounced a grounder through the legs of Mackey, which allowed both runners to score and ended the game in a shocking 3–2 victory for the Monarchs.

After the game, the stunned Hilldale players retreated to the dressing room where Rube Currie and Santop both broke down in tears. Hilldale, which had once led the series by a 3–1 margin, now trailed 4–3 after three consecutive games won by Kansas City in their last at-bat. Meanwhile, Santop was unfairly cast as the scapegoat, while Mackey's equally crucial misplay of Duncan's grounder was largely forgotten. Hilldale outfielder Clint Thomas recalled that after the fiery Warfield screamed at the tearful Santop and called him "all kinds of so-and-so . . . I said, 'Santop, pick him up and throw him out the door; throw him in the street.'" In reality, the fielding lapses by Mackey and Santop had resulted from Warfield's

Louis Santop's costly error in game 8 of the 1924 World Series tarnished an otherwise fine career that spanned nearly two decades (National Baseball Library and Archive, Cooperstown, N.Y.).

revamped defensive alignment, which proved unequal to the task of replacing Jake Stephens. Mackey, an adequate infielder at best, had only limited experience at third base, and Santop, no longer capable of catching against stronger teams, had already been replaced in the sixth inning of game 6 after the Monarchs had stolen four bases in seven tries.

Nevertheless, Warfield did not change his lineup for the following day's game as Santop was once more behind the plate. With his team on the brink of elimination, Nip Winters again rose to the occasion, pitching Hilldale to a 5–3 victory before 6,271 fans at Schorling. Winters stopped the Monarchs on nine hits for his third win of the series in four starts, and the Hilldale offense banged out 13 hits against three Kansas City pitchers. Meanwhile, Santop played errorless ball and contributed two hits to the cause. The series was now down to its final game, scheduled for Monday, October 20, at Schorling Park.

With neither Rogan nor Winters available for the crucial series finale, both managers faced difficult pitching decisions. For Hilldale, Phil Cockrell and Red Ryan were well-rested, although both had been ineffective in their prior series starts. Warfield also had the young spitballer Bill "Bullet" Campbell, whom the Monarchs had yet to face in the series. Warfield finally decided upon the submarine-baller Scrip Lee, who had pitched impressively in relief in games 3 and 6, allowing only four runs in 15.1 innings. For the Monarchs, Cliff Bell, the starter in games 4 and 7 was available, but the 37-year-old Mendez, who had shut out Hilldale in his last two relief appearances, designated himself as the starter.

The small crowd, 1,549 because of inclement weather, watched intently as Lee and Mendez hooked up in a classic pitcher's duel. While the Monarchs managed only a single off Lee through seven innings, Hilldale once again was unable to solve Mendez. In the eighth, Lee finally weakened, allowing five hits and five runs as Hilldale watched their world-championship dreams turn to ashes. Mendez finished his brilliant shutout performance by retiring Hilldale in the ninth inning, and after 10 hard-fought games, the Monarchs were now undisputed champions of the black baseball world.

The somber Hilldale players arrived home in Philadelphia at Broad Street Station on Tuesday, October 21, to a hero's welcome for their valiant effort in the series. As the *Pittsburgh Courier* reported, a number of faithful fans greeted the team and "ushered the players into waiting motors," forming an "impromptu parade" down Broad Street that eventually disbanded at George Robinson's New Roadside at the 500 block of South 15th Street. While Bolden had kept a low profile during the series, Robinson had heartily supported the team, buying the players

Chosen by Frank Warfield to start the deciding game of the 1924 World Series, submarine-baller Holsey "Scrip" Lee held the Kansas City Monarchs scoreless for seven innings. Lee, however, surrendered five runs in the eighth to give the Monarchs the game and the series (National Baseball Library and Archive, Cooperstown, N.Y.).

cigars and cigarettes for their train ride west, and even traveled to Chicago during the series to offer encouragement. On Friday a banquet honoring the team, largely organized by Robinson, was held at the Hotel Brotherhood at 1529 Bainbridge Street in South Philadelphia, with over 300 in attendance. The Hilldale players, prodded to speak, mostly remained silent, and as Otto Briggs observed, "While the boys were smiling, deep in their hearts they did not mean it."

Despite defeat, Hilldale had little to be ashamed of. Both teams had played a magnificent series, as each of the final seven games was decided in the last two innings of play. Hilldale had particularly distinguished itself against a fine Monarch pitching staff, outhitting the westerners .251 to .225 and outscoring them by a 43–38 margin, with Judy Johnson leading both teams with 15 hits. Hilldale pitching, despite weak defense, had performed capably as well, Nip Winters, Scrip Lee, and Rube Currie combining to allow only 21 runs in 78.1 innings. While Hilldale was handicapped by the absence of Stephens except for one game and a disappointing series by Cockrell, the heroics of Joe Rogan and Jose Mendez eventually swung the championship to the Monarchs. Rogan appeared in all 10 games as a pitcher and outfielder, led the Monarchs with 13 hits, and beat Hilldale in two of his three starts, while Mendez won two games, allowing only three earned runs in 19 innings.[21]

While Bolden remained silent on the series, Foster expressed enthusiasm, noting that while he had seen most of the World Series played during the last 20 years, "never did any of them have anything on our colored series" and termed the final eight games as "eight of the best played games of ball I have ever witnessed." Yet officials in both leagues, particularly Monarchs owner J.L. Wilkinson, expressed disappointment at the modest financial returns. Although the 10 games drew 45,857 fans, weekday attendance was weak except for the opener in Philadelphia. In a letter to Tenny Blount, Wilkinson noted that only good weather had prevented a complete financial failure, as "the returns from the series was [sic] nothing for the chances taken and the dates lost." Most observers agreed that the series had lasted too long to sustain interest, causing Rollo Wilson to quip, "It seemed once that we would not be able to get the boys out of the diamond in time for Thanksgiving."

Gross receipts for the 10 games totaled $52,113.90, with $23,463.44 remaining to be disbursed after deductions for park rent, room and board, railroad expenses, publicity, umpires salary, and miscellaneous items. Each of the 16 Monarch players received $307.96; Hilldale's 17 men earned $193.22 apiece. While supposedly no player earned less than his normal daily salary for the 17-day series, some players felt that postseason barnstorming with major leaguers was more lucrative. Others, like Hilldale's George Johnson, felt that the players deserved a greater share of the receipts, especially since the owners and managers had the "best rooms in the hotels while the players fare like hoboes."[22]

While less profitable than anticipated, the 1924 World Series significantly helped to focus national attention on the phenomenon of professional black baseball. Noteworthy events such as postseason barnstorming games with organized baseball teams and the formation of the NNL and ECL had previously failed to attract the notice of most white Americans. The 1924 series, however, acknowledged by the white daily press in a number of cities, demonstrated to many surprised white baseball fans the existence of two fully functioning African American professional leagues whose organizations in many ways resembled organized baseball's. As the *Chicago Defender* noted, the series was the "biggest move in the history of colored baseball" and had done "more to gain the fans' attention in the national pastime as regards to our group, than anything that has been done in recent years." The *Kansas City Call* was even more enthusiastic, arguing that "Negro sport has done what Negro churches, Negro lodges, Negro business could not do." The series had "shown that a Negro can get attention for a good deed well done, and that publicity is no longer the exclusive mark of our criminals."

With the league wars resolved and the series over, both the NNL and ECL looked toward a future of mutually cooperative growth and expansion. Neither league realized that the 1924 World Series would represent the pinnacle of professional black baseball in the 1920s and that the economic status of African Americans had peaked for the decade. While the first half of the 1920s had been marked by revolutionary developments, the remainder of the decade would bring about a series of frustrating setbacks that would threaten the existence of both leagues.[23]

6

Economic Downswing and a World Championship, 1925

Hilldale — Alphabetically Speaking
H — stands for Home runs, we don't care how
  many
I — stands for It, it's the pennant we mean
L — stands for Liquor, but we don't want any
L — stands for Luck too, the best ever seen
D — stands for Dollars, we hope they come
  pouring
A — stands for Action, we give it you know
L — stands for Ladies, the kind we're adoring
E — stands for Everything good, so let's go!
    —*John Howe,* Philadelphia Tribune, *April
    1924.*

With the formation of the ECL and the gradual decline of the semi-pro boom by mid-decade, Hilldale's continued growth and expansion was now more than ever inextricably tied to the fragile economic fortunes of the local African American community. While 70 percent of the team's bookings had once been with white semipro clubs, close to 50 percent of Hilldale's 172 games in 1924 were played against black teams before predominantly African American audiences. With ticket prices at Hilldale Park still reasonably priced at 35 cents to 85 cents, the team had continued to draw well during the season, yet Bolden, as an astute businessman aware of the volatility of black business enterprises, had reason to be cautious regarding his team's and the league's future.

Although the city of Philadelphia enjoyed unprecedented prosperity during the early 1920s, most local African Americans failed to share in the flourishing postwar economic environment. In the six decades following the Civil War, Philadelphia's African American population had evolved

122

from a small enclave of less than 25,000 people to a substantial community of over 165,000 by the mid-1920s, largely as a result of three distinct phases of black southern migration in the years 1890–1910, 1916–1919 and 1922–1923. While the population expansion accelerated the development of separate black enterprises such as Hilldale, discrimination continued to limit African American social and economic advancement.

Despite Philadelphia's reputation for tolerance, the city did not escape the national escalation in racial discrimination during the late nineteenth century. As early as the 1890s, the city's 40,000 black citizens were already increasingly segregated into a single area in South Philadelphia, shut out from economic opportunities and denied full access to restaurants, hotels, and other public establishments. With many whites unwilling to hire or work with blacks, the majority of African Americans were relegated to the lowest-paying and least desirable jobs in the area. By 1900 nearly 75 percent of black workers in Philadelphia were employed in unskilled labor despite their proximity to nearby manufacturing jobs. While local manufacturers such as Midvale Steel and Penncoyd Steel hired some African Americans by 1910, most blacks would remain excluded until World War I from Philadelphia's leading industrial mainstays, including textiles, clothing manufacture, machine shops, hardware, and printing and publishing. The majority of black workers obtained domestic or personal service positions as butlers, janitors, hotel doormen, cooks, chauffeurs, and stewards or were hired to perform unskilled manual labor such as trash collection, street repair or construction, street cleaning, or loading and unloading.[1]

For blacks seeking higher status jobs and income, limited clerical opportunities were available, especially in merit-based civil service positions where overt discrimination was less rampant. By 1911, 185 African Americans held post office positions, including Bolden, who earned a comfortable annual salary of $1,200. Yet chances for advancement were marginal, and Bolden, despite an excellent work record, would never advance beyond the position of "special clerk" during his 42 years at the post office. While the professions offered another avenue to advancement, most blacks lacked the necessary training, education, and encouragement to secure such positions. Despite an 1881 law outlawing separate schools in Philadelphia, residential segregation forced most black children to be educated apart from whites in inferior schools, and some nearby communities such as Chester openly segregated black students until high school. Nevertheless, a small elite corps of black professionals managed to develop by 1911 as the city featured 50 African American doctors, 11 lawyers, and 100 public school teachers.[2]

The continued expansion and segregation of the local African American community during the 1900s increased available entrepreneurial opportunities, providing another option to blacks aspiring to middle-class status. By 1913, the city featured over 1,000 black-owned businesses, a growth of nearly 700 since 1896, although the majority were small establishments such as barber shops, caterers, or cafes that grossed between $1,000 to $3,000 a year. Hampered by inefficiency, inexperienced management, and difficulties obtaining capital, black businesses were particularly susceptible to failure, especially since African Americans, with limited discretionary income, often chose to patronize the more reliable and stable white-owned establishments. On South Street in the heart of the South Philadelphia black community, Jewish business ownership especially predominated, causing local African American leader R.R. Wright to observe, "As a rule, the business of Negroes is done by whites."

The dispersed settlement pattern of the African American community also discouraged the development of black businesses. While many newly arrived southern migrants settled in the African American community in South Philadelphia, several black neighborhoods developed in other sections of the city, including West Philadelphia, Frankford, Germantown, Holmesburg, Manayunk, Wissahickon, and Roxborough. Other blacks, seeking to avoid the city's congestion, established communities in nearby suburbs and towns surrounding the city, including Darby, Chester, West Chester, Coatesville, and Norristown, as well as nearby Camden in southern New Jersey. Despite the evolution of four business sections by 1910 (West Philadelphia, South Philadelphia, Germantown, and North Philadelphia), the lack of a central black business district comparable to those in Chicago or New York constantly retarded entrepreneurial development.

Black businesses faced the additional disadvantage of operating in an increasingly hostile environment as local whites, influenced by the resurgence in racism in the South in the late 1890s and early 1900s, began expressing their resentment toward the expanded African American presence. In 1911, the town of Coatesville in nearby Chester County was the scene of the brutal lynching of Zachariah Walker, a black man accused of murder. To the outrage of the nation's African Americans, not a single participant in the lynching was convicted or punished. For blacks who had fled the South hoping to escape similar injustices, the entire incident revealed that the North was equally capable of blatantly disregarding African American civil rights. Meanwhile, the *Philadelphia Tribune* blamed the episode on the deteriorating local racial climate:

What other results are to be expected from a population that is daily edu-
cated to be prejudiced to colored people? When people are taught that a colored boy or girl cannot work in the same factory or mill, cannot attend the
same public school . . . is it not natural that . . . their children's children
should grow up with embittered feelings against, and disrespect for, the class
ostracized? [3]

Despite outrage over the Coatesville lynching, race relations continued to stagnate as a number of legal and social barriers were erected
to enforce segregation in the Philadelphia region. In 1915 a court ruling
upheld the decision to exclude black children from attending a new school
in nearby Morton, home of several original Hilldale players, including
George Mayo. Meanwhile, local authorities in the borough of Colwyn in
Delaware County attempted to pass a segregation ordinance similar to
Baltimore's that provided, "No colored persons may permanently occupy
any property . . . in a 'white block'." Some whites resorted to intimidation
to prevent integrated neighborhoods. In 1914, a black chauffeur and his
family attempting to move into a home at 61st and Spruce Streets in West
Philadelphia were harassed by whites who threw rocks through the windows and demanded their departure. Four years later, whites attacked
two black families residing on the 2500 block of Pine Street in central
Philadelphia, burning the belongings of one household. Noting the local
exacerbation in racial tensions, one contemporary observer accurately
noted that the "days of a benevolent feudalism toward the Negro" were
now over in Philadelphia. [4]

Beginning in 1916, the Great Migration substantially transformed
the African American community in Philadelphia, as nearly 40,000
blacks, motivated by worsening social and economic conditions in the
South and increased industrial opportunities in the North, settled in the
city by 1919. As a result of wartime demands and a concurrent shortage
of immigrant labor, blacks obtained industrial employment with several
large local firms, including Midvale Steel, Atlantic Refining Co., Franklin Sugar Co., Keystone Paving and Construction Co., Westinghouse,
Eddystone Munitions, Disston Saw, Hog Island, United Gas and Improvement, and Philadelphia Rapid Transit. While the entrance into industrial work represented a significant economic breakthrough for blacks,
the majority of employment opportunities remained in unskilled labor. A
1919 study by Sadie Mossell of 100 migrant families in the previously white
Twenty-Ninth Ward in North Philadelphia revealed that 134 of the 161
wage earners surveyed held unskilled or domestic positions, and more

than a third of the 100 families were unable to earn enough to maintain a "fair standard of living."

In addition, the sudden influx of thousands of southern migrants created an unparalleled housing problem as few employers, despite a heavy demand for black labor, provided adequate homes for the newly arrived migrants. Despite assistance from local black churches and social welfare organizations such as the Armstrong Association, most migrants struggled to secure housing in the already congested black communities in the Philadelphia area. By 1917, the *Public Ledger* noted the presence of 32 persons in a five-room house on Kenilworth Street and 36 in a seven-room house on Lombard, and Mossell reported "single dwellings of twelve and fourteen rooms sublet to as many as sixteen different families or individuals." Meanwhile, African Americans continued to be prevented from obtaining housing in white neighborhoods. In Lansdowne black families found it nearly impossible to rent except from blacks, while in Swarthmore as well as Darby blacks were constrained from buying or renting housing, with the exception of one "colored" section.[5]

The increased presence of African Americans at previously all-white worksites and neighborhoods aggravated existing racial tension and occasionally precipitated racial violence. In July 1917 the hostile white reaction to blacks recruited for war work at Baldwin Locomotive and Sun Shipbuilding triggered a minor race riot in Chester, 35 miles south of Philadelphia. With the migration at its peak in 1918, a more serious episode erupted in Philadelphia. On July 26, 1918, a mob of angry whites surrounded the home of a black woman living on the 2900 block of Ellsworth Street in South Philadelphia, and a rock was thrown through her window. The incident touched off three days of racial violence throughout the city, with some blacks randomly attacked on the street or getting out of streetcars. Not surprisingly, African Americans were blamed for the disturbances and received typically unfair legal treatment, with 60 blacks eventually arrested but only three whites.

A new racial pride emerged during the riot however, as reflected by the formation of the Colored Protective Association and the subsequent accelerated establishment of separate "colored" institutions after World War I. The rapid growth in the population and collective income of the increasingly segregated black community gave Bolden and other entrepreneurs unprecedented business opportunities, resulting in the development of the Hotel Dale, Dunbar Theater, and the Brown and Stevens Bank. Numerous black business associations and cooperative enterprises were organized, including the Citizens Republican Club, an elite organization of local professionals and businessmen that included Bolden.[6]

The trend toward racial solidarity and cooperation continued during the early 1920s as a reaction to the persistent and blatant discrimination experienced by black Philadelphians. In 1921 the *Philadelphia Tribune* reported that most restaurants in downtown Philadelphia would not serve blacks and noted that one establishment even featured a sign, *Colored Customers Not Wanted Here.* The YMCA, YWCA, and hotels refused accommodations to blacks during the 1920s, and in 1921 the visiting president of Liberia, the only black head of state in the world, was forced to stay at the black-owned Hotel Dale after being turned away at the Bellevue Stratford. Although J.C. Asbury and Andrew Stevens, the first African Americans from Philadelphia elected to the Pennsylvania legislature, introduced an equal rights bill in 1921, the legislation failed to pass until 1935 as a result of aggressive lobbying by theater, restaurant, and hotel owners who claimed desegregation would drive white patronage away.[7]

Local newspaper coverage of African Americans helped inflame the already racist attitudes of most white Philadelphians. While the Democratic *Record* was usually praised by blacks for its lack of bias and capitalization of the word "Negro," the *Inquirer*, *Public Ledger*, *Evening Bulletin*, and *Daily News* typically ignored blacks or focused exclusively on their involvement in criminal activities. The sports section, as the *Philadelphia Tribune* and Bolden were always quick to observe, was one of the few places where blacks received any positive publicity, although some newspapers continued to use racial stereotypes in descriptions of black athletes, especially boxers. Surprisingly, an unusually sympathetic editorial appeared in the *Public Ledger* in 1922; "A Square Deal Denied" asked, "How can we look for good citizenship among the Negroes . . . if at every step the individual colored man or woman is repressed and discriminated against, denied the training that would fit them for the higher service of humanity?"[8]

While continued discrimination and a brief postwar recession temporarily dampened the enthusiasm engendered by the Great Migration, the subsequent recovery in 1922 and 1923 revived the optimistic outlook of the black community. Spurred by the postwar industrial boom, continued deterioration of conditions in the South, and the availability of jobs due to the declining pool of white immigrants, a second wave of the Great Migration occurred during 1922 and 1923 as another 500,000 blacks left the South to relocate in northern cities. Between July 1, 1922, and June 30, 1923, 10,500 blacks migrated to Philadelphia, many once again forced into the overcrowded predominantly black neighborhoods in South and West Philadelphia. While a large number settled in North Philadelphia, increasingly abandoned by whites fearing black encroachment, other areas such as Northeast Philadelphia and certain Irish neighborhoods in South and West Philadelphia remained mostly inaccessible. The severe congestion would result in an epidemic of smallpox and other infectious diseases, and by 1925 Philadelphia would be the second most congested black city in the country, behind only New York.

Like their predecessors, many new migrants obtained industrial employment with large firms such as Westinghouse, Atlantic Refining, and Lukens Steel. While discriminatory hiring practices continued to relegate most migrants to unskilled positions, the *Public Ledger*, like others, justified this apparent inequity by stating, "Negroes for the most part do not like to work in mills and factories." In 1923, a Migration Committee Report noted that 77.1 percent of the 7,313 African Americans employed by 10 major companies occupied unskilled positions. A survey of 142 new migrant households by the Philadelphia Housing Association similarly reported that more than 75 percent were employed in unskilled jobs, service labor, or domestic positions, with more than half the households headed by a male unskilled laborer earning about $3.90 a day.[9]

Blacks seeking nonindustrial employment also faced widespread discrimination. Bell Telephone, Western Union, and other local companies refused to hire blacks; others, like Philadelphia Rapid Transit, excluded them from higher-paying positions. Meanwhile, most black women continued to be restricted to low-paying ($10-$15 weekly) domestic or personal service work and were unable to obtain jobs that involved public interaction. Despite modest incomes, black families were additionally victimized by high rents due to the shortage of available "Negro" housing. During 1922 and 1923, rents increased 27.5 percent for blacks in Philadelphia but only 17.8 percent for whites. In addition, less than 12 percent of blacks owned homes, compared to almost 45 percent of whites.

With the onset of a mid-decade recession in Philadelphia, prospects for continued economic growth of the African American community became increasingly bleak. Facing diminishing production demands, the once vibrant industrial economy began reducing its unskilled labor force, resulting in fewer opportunities for blacks. Local African American entrepreneurs, already facing high rents and competition from whites, were now forced to contend with the potentially devastating effects of the black community's declining discretionary income. The once promising black business community suffered several disheartening setbacks, including the collapse of the Brown and Stevens Bank in February 1925, and looked uncertainly to an insecure future. Bolden, meanwhile, was confronted with the additional dilemma of providing a service considered by some especially nonessential during times of economic hardship.[10]

In addition to an unfavorable economic climate, Hilldale faced dozens of new competitors for the African American entertainment dollar. With the sudden increase in the discretionary income and leisure time of southern migrants, commercialized amusements catering exclusively to African Americans had become particularly significant after the Great Migration, offering new social and entertainment alternatives to the fraternal orders, social clubs, and church functions that had once predominated. Access to white commercial recreation, meanwhile, remained severely restricted as most local theaters and movie houses continued to feature segregated seating, and amusement parks such as Willow Grove Park and Woodside Park accepted black patronage but denied access to swimming pools.

During the early 1920s, the Palace Hall, Palais Royal, the Strand, and Olympia Gardens dance halls offered a variety of amusements "for the Colored People," including roller skating, racing, and an orchestra at prices ranging from 25 cents to 50 cents. In addition, eight theaters provided movies and vaudeville to the city's black citizens. Two were black owned: the Dunbar at Broad and Lombard (financed by Brown and Stevens) and John Gibson's Standard at Twelfth and South. While the Standard featured vaudeville, the Dunbar offered more sophisticated productions, with admission ranging from 35 cents to $1.00 for matinees and 50 cents to $1.50 for evening shows. [11]

The Dunbar's failure in 1921 and eventual sale to white owners raised serious questions about the black community's ability to support commercial amusements. As seen with black professional baseball teams, white patronage and backing was often integral to the success of other entertainment ventures. Black Philadelphia, hindered by the city's proximity to more prominent venues in New York and Atlantic City and the conservative attitudes of native born "Old Philadelphians," failed to develop a flourishing nightclub and cabaret scene, and the city's few black-and-tan nightclubs relied heavily on white ownership and patronage to survive. By the late 1930s, not one cabaret or theater was owned by blacks in Philadelphia. Similarly, the city's commercial vice district, located in the heart of the black theater and entertainment district in South Philadelphia, was dominated by whites and failed to offer income opportunities to blacks as in other cities like Chicago or New York.

Despite local entrepreneurial setbacks, Hilldale Park, along with the black church and Gibson's Standard Theater, still occupied a particularly favorable position in the African American community as one of the few public places where all blacks, regardless of social status, could comfortably congregate without the possible interference, discrimination, or ownership of whites. With black Philadelphia still proud to support the Hilldale corporation as a true "race institution," Bolden at mid-decade had reason to believe that the team would endure despite the economic downturn and simultaneous semipro decline.[12]

Despite disappointing financial returns from the 1924 World Series and gradual signs of economic decline among African Americans, the NNL and the ECL looked toward the 1925 season with renewed optimism, hoping that the current sectional harmony would continue and lead to greater success in the future. In December 1924 the two leagues had met in a joint session in Chicago and agreed that ECL territory should encompass the East Coast as far west as Buffalo, Pittsburgh, and Atlanta, the remaining western territory granted to the NNL. In addition, a formal National Agreement, written mostly by Bolden, was ratified by the two leagues as well as standard player contracts and a reserve clause. Relations between Bolden and Foster were surprisingly amicable, and Bolden even nominated the NNL leader as chairman of the joint session.

While Foster's eastern troubles were seemingly resolved, he became embroiled in another controversy, this time with Detroit Stars owner Tenny Blount. Forced to pay 10 percent of gross receipts to Foster and 20 percent to the park owner, Blount had suffered mounting financial losses at Mack Park in Detroit and objected to the unprofitable and expensive road trips required by the NNL. At the close of the 1924 season in mid–September, Blount announced to his players that he was terminating his involvement with the club and granted them permission to play on the cooperative plan for the remainder of the season. The Detroit players, however, protested to Foster that Blount still owed them two weeks' salary, as league contracts were still in effect to October 1. The matter remained unsettled until the league's annual meeting in December. In a strategic ploy designed to marshal support and uphold his authority, Foster vacated the president's chair, returned all franchise deposits, and offered to resign and open the league's books for examination. Refusing to accept Foster's resignation, the league owners instead reelected him president, while Blount was unseated as vice president and abruptly departed the meeting soon after.

Blount, at one time a dedicated league supporter, bitterly launched a series of attacks on Foster denouncing his control of league scheduling and finances. In response to charges of cheating his players, Blount noted, "I will state that I was never put in jail for not paying a ball player as was done to Rube Foster." Meanwhile, Foster, who had cosigned Blount's lease at Mack Park, assumed control of the Stars and turned the team over to new ownership in time for the 1925 season.

Blount's eviction from the NNL reinforced Foster's authority but also revealed the magnitude of financial problems even among the league's most stable and financially successful franchises, which had reportedly lost money in 1924. While supporting Foster's stand against Blount, Ira Lewis of the *Pittsburgh Courier* noted that the "league has been a nightmare for everybody but the railroads." Meanwhile, J.L. Wilkinson, owner of the world champion Monarchs, reportedly lost money in 1924 and agreed with Blount that railroad mileage was too high, especially with franchises in Memphis and Birmingham. Foster, however, blamed uncooperative and incompetent owners for league difficulties, observing that the NNL was "sick from causes of both ignorance and finance." To ensure greater cooperation and prevent franchise withdrawals, the franchise fee was raised from $1,000 to $5,000. In addition, the Cleveland franchise was replaced by a new Indianapolis ABC team owned by Warner Jewell, who had operated his own ABC club since 1917, and a new split season was instituted with 50 games each half to sustain league interest.[13]

While largely immune to high travel expenses, the ECL still faced a number of frustrating difficulties as it prepared to begin its third year in 1925. Complaints over scheduling had mounted during 1924, and Bolden, sensitive to the charge that the schedule had favored Hilldale, was determined to make changes. Although 70 games were planned for each team in 1925, the published league schedule was deliberately left incomplete to allow teams greater flexibility to schedule lucrative games with white semipro teams without forcing cancellation of league games. To further facilitate scheduling, extra parks were leased, including Roosevelt Field in Norristown for Hilldale, J. & J. Dobson's park at 35th and Queen Lane in Philadelphia for Wilmington, Rossemere Park in Lancaster, Pennsylvania, for the Harrisburg Giants, and the Jersey City International League Park for the Cubans and Brooklyn Royal Giants. Remaining league games would be arranged at these parks by team owners or managers with a 72-hour notice necessary for league approval. In addition, only the first 10 games between two teams would count in the league standings.

After revising the schedule, the league made a second bold stroke with its decision to abolish the home umpire system and hire "rotating" umpires subject to league authority. While Bolden had witnessed the PBA's failed attempt to employ rotating umpires, he had continued to be a tireless advocate of the system since the ECL's formation but had been unable to marshal necessary support from other league commissioners. The home umpire system, a fixture in semipro ball, seemed anachronistic in the ECL, and as J.M. Howe of the *Philadelphia Tribune* noted, "In most cases the home umpire system means that the visiting team must utterly outclass the home team in order to win." Bolden hoped that league-controlled umpires, no longer subject to reprisals from individual owners, would provide more impartial decision making and enforce discipline more effectively.[14]

The decision to rotate umpires was well received until Bolden announced the hiring of Bill Dallas, a local white semipro league official and sportswriter with the *Philadelphia Public Ledger,* as the league's umpire supervisor at a salary of $50 per month. For black sportswriters, who had supported and publicized the league for two years, Dallas' hiring was particularly offensive and puzzling. Rollo Wilson of the *Courier,* unsuccessfully nominated for the position by Potomacs owner George W. Robinson, ironically quipped, "Yes, this is the Mutual Association of Eastern COLORED Clubs." Meanwhile, John Howe of the *Tribune* felt that since the league was "of . . . for . . . and by Negroes," it had no right to "bring in Caucasians on the salaried jobs." Howe also ran a controversial cartoon in the *Tribune* depicting the ECL as an Uncle Tom attempting to curry the white man's favor.

Bolden, always an advocate of racial cooperation, reacted angrily to Howe's criticism. To Bolden, the league's interracial composition allowed rare collaboration between blacks and whites and had "gone further to break down race prejudice than any like organization." Defending Dallas as a "good mixer," Bolden also insisted that all eight commissioners had unanimously voted for Dallas. In reality, Bolden's unquestioned support of Dallas was typical of his pragmatic attitude toward race relations that he would exhibit throughout his career. Driven by ambition, he was willing to sacrifice racial purity if necessary to achieve his immediate goals. The hiring of Dallas, a sportswriter with a major metropolitan daily newspaper, offered the league a greater chance for more publicity as well as the opportunity to regain the attention of local white fans, who had increasingly abandoned semipro and black professional baseball.

To Bolden's disappointment, the use of rotating umpires offered little improvement over the home umpire system, and much of the blame was attributable to Dallas's indifferent performance as supervisor. Black sportswriters accused Dallas of replacing African American umpires with white officials and noted that league umpires were frequently as poor as those previously employed by the teams. In addition, the anticipated increase in white press coverage failed to materialize. Although some local

Philadelphia newspapers occasionally published the league standings or Hilldale statistics, the majority continued to regard the ECL and NNL as little more than "booking agencies."[15]

Dallas's umpiring corps proved unable to stop the escalation of violence on the field, especially toward umpires, and as Rollo Wilson would note, "Rowdy baseball is becoming the rule in the Eastern League." During July, John Beckwith of the Baltimore Black Sox attacked an umpire after a game, and an umpire at Hilldale Park had sand thrown in his face after calling a runner out. Although Beckwith was fined $100 and suspended, other players such as notorious umpire baiter Oscar Charleston of the Harrisburg Giants escaped punishment through the intervention of their team's owners.

Charleston's Harrisburg Giants were involved in several incidents during July, and violence even reached Hilldale Park on July 25. After Clint Thomas attempted to intervene in an altercation between Dick Jackson of the Giants and Hilldale's Frank Warfield, Oscar Charleston pushed Thomas away. Jackson then hit Warfield, and a full-scale brawl followed. In the aftermath, Bolden noted that he did "not encourage fighting" on his team and condemned Charleston's "poison tongue and foul tactics." By 1926 the rotating umpire system would be discontinued and replaced by the much maligned home umpires. Player discipline, however, would remain a serious problem in the ECL and NNL, and neither league was consistently able to enforce penalties.[16]

The league's attempt to improve scheduling also resulted in failure. The schedule was disrupted by the collapse of the Wilmington Potomacs in July as well as constant confusion over league and exhibition games. While the additional parks allowed more league games to be played, a number of games did not count in the final standings simply because they were not originally on the schedule, had been added without league permission, or exceeded the 10-game-per-opponent limit. As Oscar Charleston observed, players were often unaware of the status of a particular game until its conclusion. The hapless Brooklyn Royals, for example, beat Hilldale for the first time all season on August 31, 1925, only to learn afterwards that the game was an exhibition.

Bolden faced a steady torrent of criticism over the league schedule, especially with the continued success of Hilldale during 1925. Garland Mackey of the *Baltimore Afro-American* denounced the schedule as little more than a "scrap of paper," adding, "When Hilldale wins it's a league game, when they lose it's an exhibition. That's the way it looks." In August, Bill Nunn of the *Pittsburgh Courier* demanded an investigation into the league standings, claiming that the second-place Harrisburg Giants had been slighted in favor of Hilldale. Yet a careful analysis by Lloyd Thompson, the ECL's statistician and publicity agent, revealed that the standings were indeed correct, temporarily quelling the controversy. In a letter to Nunn, Thompson admitted that the ECL schedule was seriously flawed but explained that "just as many of our weekly papers are printed on leased presses, so are our ball clubs forced to play in leased parks and try to arrange schedules in a manner to show a financial return." Nunn, impressed by Thompson's frank reply, was forced to admit that the ECL was actually "run on a thoroughly business like basis, as much as was possible, under the conditions which prevail in organized colored baseball."[17]

As league statistician, Thompson was particularly aware of the ECL's numerous administrative problems. Statistics and standings had appeared fairly regularly in 1923 but became less common in ensuing seasons. In many cases, league standings and statistics were incomplete or inaccurate, largely because of uncooperative teams such as Atlantic City, Harrisburg, Brooklyn, and the Cuban Stars that consistently failed to send in results to the league office. A.D. Williams, the NNL's league secretary and statistician during the mid–1920s, faced similar problems. While NNL teams were threatened with fines for noncompliance, a number of clubs continued to withhold game results, especially if unfavorable.

Unable to solve the league's recurrent difficulties with scheduling, umpires, and statistics, Bolden became an increasingly popular target of criticism from owners, players, fans, and sportswriters in 1925. In a widely published press release, Oscar Charleston denounced the league as a "farce," and Bacharachs manager John Henry Lloyd noted the league "will not be worth a picayune . . . until men that know baseball are in charge." The most devastating attack came from George W. Robinson, the owner of the recently disbanded Washington and Wilmington Potomacs. Disillusioned with Bolden and his relationship with Strong, Robinson refused to sell any of his players to Hilldale or Brooklyn and subsequently blasted the ECL as the "poorest operated business proposition I have ever known." Robinson claimed that the schedule was unfairly designed to favor Hilldale and other clubs and particularly objected to the awarding of the lucrative July 4 date at Hilldale Park to Lincoln three years in a row. Bolden, however, had given Robinson the equally profitable Labor Day doubleheader at Hilldale Park and had scheduled Hilldale as the attraction for Wilmington's opening game that had been rained out.

Alienated by Bolden's "taciturn and unapproachable" nature and restricted access to league meetings, several black sportswriters began advocating his replacement as league commissioner. In August, the *Washington Tribune* labeled Bolden as a "pigmy" [*sic*] compared to Rube Foster and called for his dismissal. Even John Howe of the *Philadelphia Tribune* noted that it was "fundamentally wrong" for an owner of a league team to be president of a league, especially since weaker teams, aware of Bolden and Strong's control of bookings with white teams, were reluctant to resist stronger clubs in league affairs. Although public support of Bolden and the ECL was clearly eroding, he offered little response except to state, "As long as I can get six teams to work for and back up the organization we shall have a league."[18]

Despite the controversy surrounding Bolden throughout the season, Hilldale quietly put together another brilliant year. Once again Bolden made few changes in the club except for the addition of two utility infielders, Namon Washington and Bill Robinson, and the release of Toussaint Allen, who had been with the team since 1919. George Carr, who had filled in at several different positions in 1924, replaced Allen at first base and enjoyed a fine season; published Hilldale figures credited him with 20 home runs, 20 triples, 70 doubles, and a .409 batting average in 177 games played against white and black opponents. The team continued to emphasize speed and stole over 200 bases, led by Warfield with 35, Carr with 34, and Thomas and Briggs with 32 each. The pitching staff excelled too, as Nip Winters, Phil Cockrell, and Rube Currie combined for nearly 50 victories in games against league opponents.

In 1925 Oscar Charleston's powerful Harrisburg Giants provided Hilldale with its first serious challenge. In June the Giants beat Hilldale three straight games and took sole possession of first place. Local fans reacted with shock and disbelief to the news, which was reported on the front page of the June 20, 1925, *Philadelphia Tribune*. The *Tribune* defended the team, noting that "attacks upon the management are both fruitless and unfair when they come from the fans. Bolden has run the club quite awhile and if he deems changes necessary, he will make them." Bolden remained patient and the club soon caught fire to recapture first place and eventually finished comfortably ahead of Harrisburg. As Garland Mackey admiringly observed, the 1925 Hilldale team was "one of the most perfect baseball machines . . . every man working in perfect unison, the main object being to win." In addition, Mackey credited the team's continued success to its stable player personnel and lack of "squabbling or petty grievance" that plagued other clubs.[19]

With the Kansas City Monarchs once again capturing the NNL pennant, fans eagerly anticipated a rematch of the 1924 World Series. The

Hilldale, 1925. Back row, left to right: Red Ryan, Judy Johnson, George Johnson, unidentified (possibly Joe Lewis), Louis Santop, Ed Bolden, George Carr, unidentified (possibly Rube Currie), Raleigh "Biz" Mackey, Bill Campbell, Clint Thomas. Front row: Phil Cockrell, Bill Robinson, Scrip Lee, Namon Washington, Frank Warfield, Rocky Ellis (mascot), Jake Stephens, Otto Briggs, Nip Winters (Cash-Thompson Collection, courtesy Afro-American Historical and Cultural Museum, Philadelphia, Pennsylvania).

Monarchs would be forced to face Hilldale's regular lineup intact with a healthy Jake Stephens at shortstop, Biz Mackey behind the plate, and Judy Johnson at third base. The absence of superstar outfielder-pitcher Joe Rogan, who had accidentally stuck a needle in his knee and would be sidelined for the entire series, gave Hilldale another advantage, as well as an injury to Monarchs outfielder Dink Mothel. While the series was to be played under the same financial conditions as 1924, both leagues were eager to cut expenses. Only two umpires, once again from the minor leagues, were hired for each game, and funds for league officials were reduced. In addition, no games were scheduled at Chicago or Baltimore to avoid the length and travel expense of the previous year's series.

After winning two of three games against a team of International League All-Stars, a confident and relaxed Hilldale left Philadelphia for

Kansas City on Monday, September 28, and arrived in Kansas City two days later. The series opened on Thursday, October 1, at Muehlebach Park with Kansas City native Rube Currie matched against Cliff Bell of the Monarchs. Before a slim crowd of 2,065 because of cool weather, the two evenly matched teams resumed their struggle of the prior season and once again were deadlocked after nine innings of play. With the score tied 2–2, Hilldale scored three runs in the twelfth inning on three singles and a hit batsman and held on to take the opener 5–2. Rube Currie, avenging his bitter defeat in game 8 of 1924, allowed only two runs in 12 innings of work to gain credit for the victory.

On Friday, October 2, in Kansas City, manager Jose Mendez sent Nelson Dean to the mound to face Phil Cockrell, who had been ineffective in the 1924 series. With Cockrell's spitball baffling the Kansas City hitters, the score remained tied at 2–2 until the eighth inning when two key fielding lapses by the usually reliable Jake Stephens allowed Kansas City to take a 5–2 lead. Hilldale's rally in the ninth inning fell two runs short as relief pitcher William Bell, facing Judy Johnson with the bases loaded, induced the Hilldale third baseman to fly out to end the game in a 5–3 victory for Kansas City before a disappointing crowd of only 1,519 fans.

With the series tied at one game apiece, Warfield turned to Scrip Lee for game 3 on Saturday and Mendez countered with William Bell. Lee had pitched well despite being defeated twice by the Monarchs in 1924 and once again proved a puzzle, striking out eight and allowing only one run. Hilldale, however, was able to do little better against Bell and found themselves trailing 1–0 as they came to bat in the eighth inning. After loading the bases with no outs, Bell was replaced by Hilldale's 1924 nemesis, Jose Mendez. The crafty veteran promptly forced Carr out at the plate on a Clint Thomas grounder to shortstop, then induced pinch hitter Louis Santop to bounce into a double play, extending his scoreless streak against Hilldale to 16 innings. It was to be Mendez's last hurrah as Hilldale tied the score in the ninth and sent the game into extra innings. While Kansas City was unable to score off Hilldale relief pitcher Red Ryan, run-scoring hits by reserves Namon Washington and Bill Robinson in the tenth inning would give Hilldale a 3–1 victory over Mendez and a 2–1 lead in the series.

Although Saturday's crowd had been disappointing at 1,880, 7,208 fans packed Muehlebach Park on Sunday, October 4, to watch the matchup between Nip Winters and Bill Drake. For the second consecutive day, the Monarchs were unable to stop Hilldale's hitting attack in the late innings. Trailing 3–2 in the ninth inning, the Monarchs allowed four runs in the ninth inning, led by a key two-run triple by Frank Warfield, and suffered a 7–3 defeat. Nip Winters beat the Monarchs for the fourth time in two years, scattering eight hits and fanning eight hitters. Following the game, the Hilldale players, now leading the series three games to one, boarded a Pullman train bound for Philadelphia and indulged in relaxed horseplay during the trip. A sleeping Joe Lewis was doused with a pitcher of water, and notorious drinker Nip Winters was fooled into sipping from a gin bottle filled with water. Meanwhile, Biz Mackey accidentally put his hand through a window while trying to demonstrate his strength but was not seriously injured.

The series resumed on Thursday, October 8, at Phillies Park at Broad and Huntington with Rube Currie facing the Monarchs' Cliff Bell for the second time in the series. The game remained scoreless until the fourth inning when a homer by George Carr and doubles by Biz Mackey and Clint Thomas gave Hilldale a 2–0 lead. In the fifth Bell was replaced by Dean after allowing successive singles by Stephens and Currie. While Dean would hold Hilldale scoreless for the remainder of the game, the Monarchs once again were handcuffed by Currie, who allowed only one run on seven hits to give Hilldale an exciting 2–1 victory before 4,049.

With Hilldale leading the series four games to one and needing only a single victory for the championship, the Philadelphia area was suddenly hit with a stretch of inclement weather. Rain forced cancellation of Friday's game, and the temperature at game time on Saturday was an unseasonably chilly 30 degrees. As in game 2, William Bell of the Monarchs faced the veteran Phil Cockrell, who had yet to beat the Monarchs in three starts during the prior two seasons. Hilldale jumped out to a 1–0 lead in the fourth inning on a double by Clint Thomas, followed by George Johnson's run scoring single. In the fifth Biz Mackey doubled home Frank Warfield, who had reached on an error by Dobie Moore, to give Hilldale a 2–0 lead. Another Monarch error helped set up two more Hilldale runs in the sixth inning, and the Monarchs, unable to solve the pitches of Phil Cockrell, found themselves trailing 4–0. Kansas City finally managed to score off Cockrell in the seventh, but Hilldale quickly regained the run on Mackey's home run off Bell in the seventh. In the ninth the Monarchs added another run and loaded the bases with one out, and the score 5–2. As the shivering crowd of 1,121 nervously watched, Cockrell bore down, fanning a pinch hitter and retiring William Bell on a flyout to give Hilldale the world championship. A seventh game, scheduled for Sunday, October 11, at the Jersey City International League Park, was played as an exhibition. Youngster Chet Brewer, a future star with the Monarchs, defeated Hilldale 6–1 before a crowd of 2,225 that included Foster and Bolden.

Brooklyn native Red Ryan was hit hard in his two starts in the 1924 World Series but bounced back to win game 3 of the 1925 rematch against the Monarchs (National Baseball Library and Archive, Cooperstown, N.Y.).

Superior pitching, improved defense, and the Monarchs' devastating loss of Joe Rogan gave Hilldale the World Series victory. The Monarchs were unable to mount a serious offensive attack, with only 46 hits and 14 runs in six official series games. Meanwhile, Hilldale rapped out 65 hits, led by Otto Briggs with 12, Biz Mackey with nine, and George Carr with eight. The true hero of the series, however, was Rube Currie, who recovered from his gut-wrenching defeat of 1924 to win two games against his former teammates, allowing only three runs in 21 innings of work.[20]

Despite an exciting, well-played series, financial returns were once again disappointing. Attendance for the six series games totaled only 17,842, less than 3,000 per game.While bad weather and reduced press coverage had affected attendance, the declining gate receipts also reflected the gradually deteriorating economic fortunes of the national African American community, particularly in Philadelphia.

Attendance would continue to decline in future series. The 1926 series between the Bacharach Giants and Chicago American Giants lasted 11 games but drew only half as many fans as the 1924 series between Hilldale and Kansas City, and the 1927 series featuring the same two clubs barely attracted notice in the black press. Facing dwindling support, both leagues attempted to reduce publicity and umpiring expenses, and by 1927, second- and third-place teams were no longer allowed to share in the net profits of the series. With the exception of the 1924 series, most players received less than $100 for their participation, far less than what might have been earned in postseason barnstorming games with major league players. In 1926, Rollo Wilson would accurately note, "There's no getting away from it—these colored world series games have not been worth a nickel, financially to date."[21]

Hilldale's championship, however, helped revitalize the sagging morale and self-esteem of black Philadelphia, now struggling with increasing economic difficulties, continued discrimination, and the recent disruptive presence of the Ku Klux Klan. During 1925, black politician Ed Henry had bemoaned the disturbing passivity of local blacks, noting that some had even become afraid to read the *Philadelphia Tribune* publicly for fear of white reprisals or attended "Jim Crow" theaters with segregated seating yet "seem to like it." In contrast, loyal Hilldale fans, filled with racial pride, openly basked in the glory of their team's World Series victory and even pooled their limited resources to honor the club. On October 14, 1925, a banquet was held at the Hotel Brotherhood at 1529 Bainbridge where gold baseballs were awarded to the players. The evening featured speeches, dancing, and singing, with some selections performed by the "Hilldale Quartet" of Scrip Lee, George Carr, Clint Thomas, and Jake Stephens.

Despite the banquet, Henry expressed disappointment over the perceived lack of fan support among whites and blacks during the series and its aftermath:

> Hilldale won the championship! This does not seem to mean much to the community although the Hilldale ball club is really an asset to Philadelphia. While the club is housed in Darby and plays there Darby is nothing if not a suburb of this city. Most of the players live here and spend their money here. Particularly do newspapers, cafes, hotels and the P.R.T. profit by Hilldale's games and so does the community generally yet we pay but scant attention to these colored champions of the great American game. . . . The Hilldale ball club is honored everywhere but here. The baseball fans throughout the country know Manager Bolden and the Hilldale team better than we in Philadelphia know them.

Bolden, however, received considerable accolades for his part in Hilldale's victory and was singled out by the *Philadelphia Tribune* for his "ability and . . . sportsmanship" which had "done a great deal to cement the friendliness of the two racial groups in this section." With Hilldale's World Series victory, Bolden had finally realized his ambition of building the finest black baseball team in the country, yet he would enjoy his triumph for only a short time, as the declining economic status of African Americans had already begun to affect profits. The Hilldale corporation had borrowed to begin the 1925 season and would be forced to do so again in 1926. The always precipitous foundation of black baseball had begun to totter, with no recovery in sight.[22]

7

The End of
a Dream, 1926–1928

> Lack of co-operation, which is essential to
> any organization, is tearing the vitals from the
> Eastern Colored League.
> — *Ed Bolden, March 1928*

From the end of World War I through the mid–1920s, black professional baseball had enjoyed significant expansion as a result of the Great
Migration's dramatic impact on the size, income, and available leisure
time of the northern African American population. By 1926, however,
profits had begun to decline as attendance and ticket prices had failed to
keep pace with the corresponding increases in salaries, park rentals, and
railroad expenses. Both leagues could no longer ignore the stagnating
economic status of most blacks, who according to one labor historian,
would already be in the midst of the "Great Depression of the 1930s . . .
by the end of 1926."

The reduced attendance at the 1925 World Series culminated a
season described by the *Pittsburgh Courier* as "one of the most disastrous
years for black teams in the last ten." James Keenan's Lincoln Giants
reportedly lost $13,000 in 1925, and Baltimore Black Sox owner George
Rossiter, hit hard by financial setbacks, was sued by Spalding Company
for nonpayment of a bill for sporting goods. To reduce expenses, the two
leagues agreed to a monthly salary cap of $3,000 per team at the second
annual joint session of the ECL and NNL held in Philadelphia at the
Christian Street YMCA in January 1926. In subsequent months the NNL
would attempt to cut travel costs by replacing its two southern franchises,
Memphis and Birmingham, with teams more centrally located, in Cleveland and Dayton. Meanwhile, the ECL reduced its guarantees for

142

weekend games from $350 to $250, and ticket prices were lowered at Hilldale Park from 85 cents to 75 cents for box seats and 55 cents to 50 cents for general admission.

Eastern teams, still reliant upon twilight games with white semipros to "take care of the overhead," were also faced with the increasing difficulty in obtaining lucrative bookings. With the waning interest in independent ball in Philadelphia, the rising fortunes of the Philadelphia A's, and the increasingly one-sided nature of interracial competition, black professional teams were no longer as much in demand. While Ben Taylor, manager of the Black Sox, suggested that the ECL should emulate the NNL and schedule more weekday league games "without asking a big guarantee," Foster himself realized that weekday league games were seldom profitable.[1]

One eastern team, the western Pennsylvania based Homestead Grays under Cumberland "Cum" Posey, had seemingly been immune to the financial woes afflicting the ECL and NNL. Posey, the son of a successful black businessman, first achieved national stature as a star basketball player-coach with the Loendi Club of Pittsburgh. In the 1910s he began his baseball career as an outfielder with the Grays, a Pittsburgh area sandlot team, became captain soon after, and by World War I had assumed full control of the team's promotion and finances.

Posey, along with Bolden and Foster, was among the most successful black baseball entrepreneurs during the 1920s. Like Bolden, Posey strengthened his team by gradually importing professional players and similarly exerted considerable influence in the local booking scene in Pittsburgh. While Posey and Bolden both built powerful and financially successful organizations, their personalities and behaviors differed markedly. In stark contrast to the quiet and sportsmanlike Bolden, Posey was short tempered, argumentative, and considered by many a poor loser obsessed with winning at all costs. Posey's relentless raiding tendencies also alarmed numerous observers, including Romeo Dougherty of the *New York Amsterdam News*, who offered a particularly damning indictment of Posey and his tactics:

> They say he spends half of his time copping or trying to cop players from other teams to help strengthen the Grays. Well, that same tendency gave Posey his world-beating basketball team. Posey has been a menace to sport ever since the day the bug of being a big promoter entered his brain.[2]

Posey, hardly fazed by criticism, continued to pursue the best players aggressively regardless of their team affiliation and had acquired several ECL and NNL players, including legendary pitcher Smokey Joe

Williams and power-hitting John Beckwith. In 1924 Posey even attempted to raid Hilldale, offering contracts to Biz Mackey and Nip Winters. To Posey's chagrin, Mackey and Winters reneged on a deal to join the Grays despite having already accepted advance salary.

By the mid–1920s, the Grays were the equal of any of the established black teams in the East or West and had played several games against the Kansas City Monarchs, Chicago American Giants, Detroit Stars, and Baltimore Black Sox. Aware of the increasing power of Posey, the NNL and ECL expressed interest in adding the Grays as an associate or full league member and invited Posey to the joint session in January 1926 to discuss an agreement to respect contracts. No formal action was taken at the league meeting as Foster refused to consider any agreement with Posey unless the Grays became an associate member of the NNL. Posey, however, had no interest in joining the NNL, citing the previous failures of league franchises in Pittsburgh and Cleveland. The Grays continued to operate as an independent club, traveling through western Pennsylvania and scheduling occasional home games at Forbes Field, the home of the Pittsburgh Pirates. While Homestead remained outside of organized black baseball until 1929, the team continued to attract attention and would soon challenge Hilldale for eastern supremacy.[3]

Unable to add Homestead, the ECL selected the Newark Stars to replace the disbanded Wilmington Potomacs. Launched with the assistance of Sol White, the Stars had also received backing from Charles Davids, owner of the International League's Newark Bears, and planned to use the Bears' recently built park, Davids Stadium. With eight teams in place, the ECL prepared for a 70-game season for 1926 but once again designed a flexible schedule, leasing parks at Wilmington and Germantown for additional games if necessary.

The ECL's recurrent scheduling difficulties would reach their nadir during the 1926 season. Unusually rainy weather and continued poor attendance at most weekday league games resulted in numerous cancellations. In addition, the league schedule was disrupted again by the midseason failure of an expansion team. The Newark franchise was a disaster, compiling a 1–10 record, and was dropped from the league in July, as Davids was reportedly heavily in debt and unable to pay bills. Realizing that newly organized teams had little hope of success in the current economic environment, the ECL finally decided to halt further expansion in August 1926. As in 1925, the league agreed that all games played against disbanded clubs would count in the final standings, a decision perceived as unfair by some league teams who had yet to play the now defunct Stars and had missed the opportunity to secure easy victories.

As usual, the indifferent participation of Nat Strong's Brooklyn Royal Giants was ruinous to the league schedule. By August the Royals had played only 14 league games and would finish the season with only 27. Meanwhile, Lincoln Giants owner James Keenan, objecting to the failure of the Royals or the Cuban Stars to secure home grounds, refused to list either team in scoresheets or standings and canceled scheduled games with both clubs. Realizing the liability of traveling teams, Bolden and other league owners began to consider the possibility of a six team league for 1927, the Cubans and Royals to be excluded. Strong, however, still exerted considerable influence in league affairs as owner of the Royals, booking agent for the Cubans, and co-owner of Dexter Park where Hilldale and other ECL teams were regular attractions. As Rollo Wilson would insightfully note, Strong would "get out only when it suits Nat Strong to do so."[4]

The marked increase in rowdyism noted in 1925 continued in 1926, affected little by the return of the home umpire system. On June 27, Rev Cannady of Harrisburg attacked an umpire at the Lincoln Giants' Catholic Protectory Oval after being called out trying to stretch a single into a double. A near riot ensued with only the intervention of park security and Lincoln manager John Henry Lloyd preventing a more serious incident. A month later, on July 29, Cannady smashed an umpire's car window with his bat after a Harrisburg defeat at Hilldale Park. Frank Dallard of the Black Sox was also involved in a series of incidents during the season, including an assault on two umpires after the conclusion of a game. With the escalation in violence, a number of black sportswriters questioned why white organized baseball had managed to suppress most umpire assaults with fines and suspensions while the ECL seemed unable to enforce its penalties. Yet the failure of most league owners to support disciplinary measures undermined attempts to curb rowdyism, and as Bolden would admit, the ECL had been "very lax in meting out punishment to belligerent players who seek to intimidate umpires."

In contrast to other league officials, Bolden remained a dedicated advocate of "clean baseball" and refused to tolerate transgressions by his players. On August 8, 1926, at Atlantic City, Hilldale pitcher Phil Cockrell attacked an umpire for reversing a decision. While many observers were angered by the harsh response of white park security, who hauled Cockrell from the field and struck him with a blackjack, Bolden insisted that Cockrell was at fault for assaulting the umpire: "The attack was unwarranted and it is the policy of the Hilldale Club to always discourage rowdy tactics and will not tolerate them on our ball club." As Bolden noted, umpiring difficulties should be handled by the commissioners rather than player intimidation, and Cockrell received a five-day suspension and a $100 fine.

Although Bolden's unbiased handling of the Cockrell incident won him support, he faced an unrelenting flow of criticism from both fans and sportswriters. One disgruntled fan noted in a letter to the *Baltimore Afro-American* during 1926 that the ECL had "remained on the same level" for four years, and unfairly blamed Bolden for the league's recurrent problems with erratic umpiring, unbalanced schedules, inaccurate statistics, poor publicity, and uncooperative owners. In August, Bolden attempted to clarify his actual limited role as league chairman, once again explaining that league affairs were determined by the majority vote of the commissioners. Even the usually subdued Cuban Stars owner, Alex Pompez, publicly defended the Hilldale leader, noting that the much criticized schedule was "not made by Mr. Bolden" and had been a joint effort of all the commissioners.[5]

For the first time, however, Bolden faced criticism from the usually supportive local African American community, which reacted angrily to Hilldale's disappointing follow-up to its 1925 championship season. In contrast to recent years, Bolden had refused to stand pat in the off-season and orchestrated a number of surprising player moves. Veteran George Johnson, who had been with the club since 1918, was sold to the Lincoln Giants with catcher Joe Lewis, and Rube Currie, the hero of the 1925 World Series, returned to the NNL after a salary dispute. Although Bill Campbell proved an adequate replacement for Currie, Bolden struggled to find a successor to the hard-hitting Johnson, and no fewer than three outfield recruits (Dewey Rivers, Rudolph Ash, and Melvin Sykes) were tried during the season and released. Bolden's much renowned ability for discovering and developing the talents of sandlot players such as Judy Johnson or Jake Stephens had largely deserted him by 1926, and the team increasingly would be forced to rely upon trades to strengthen itself.

The team began the season with four consecutive defeats to white teams but soon recovered and stood atop the ECL with a 10-6 record by June. Weakened by the loss of Johnson, Hilldale's usual powerful hitting attack abruptly collapsed as the club dropped 10 of 12 games to ECL opponents between June 9 and June 21 and fell to fifth place by July. Dubbed the "hitless wonders" by the *Philadelphia Inquirer*, Hilldale even temporarily struggled against white semipro clubs. On July 25 the Farmers became the first team to hold Hilldale scoreless in both games of a doubleheader, Charlie See, a former Cincinnati Red, hurling one of the shutouts. Later in the season, Hilldale committed nine errors in a doubleheader sweep by the Brooklyn Bushwicks at Dexter Park. As John Howe noted, the team was in a "spiritual slump. The old punch is missing." Although local observers were increasingly vocal in their protests as the team continued its difficulties, Bolden made relatively few changes, but the veteran Louis Santop was finally released in July. Led by Carr, Mackey, and Judy Johnson, the team's hitting eventually returned, but Hilldale was unable to overtake the Atlantic City Bacharach Giants and finished in third place with a 34-24 record in league games.

The season was salvaged in October as Hilldale, appearing in its first postseason series against barnstorming major leaguers in three years, won five of six games played at Wilmington, Hilldale Park, and Blooms-burg, Pennsylvania. Despite the presence of Jimmy Dykes of the Phila-delphia Athletics (.287), American League batting champion Heinie Manush of the Detroit Tigers (.378), and George Burns of the Cleveland Indians (.358, 114 RBI), the All-Stars managed only eight runs against Hilldale pitching and were shut out by Phil Cockrell in the fourth game. As the major leaguers struggled against Cockrell, Winters, Lee, and Ryan, a Hilldale fan taunted Manush: "You'd never hit .385 in this league." Meanwhile, Hilldale, supplemented by sluggers John Beckwith and Oscar Charleston of Harrisburg, defeated Philadelphia Athletic pitcher Lefty Grove (13-13, league leading 2.51 ERA) in both his starts, and the Athletics' Jack Quinn (10-11, 3.41), Rube Walberg (12-10, 2.80), and Fred Heimach of the Red Sox (3-9, 4.98). The series was reportedly a financial success as a result of heavy white patronage in Bloomsburg with players surpassing their previous World Series earnings. The two games played at Hilldale Park drew disappointing crowds, however, with only 3,102 fans in attendance.

As anticipated, profits continued to decline for both leagues during 1926, a year marked by poor World Series attendance; franchise failures in Cleveland, Dayton, and Newark; and diminishing interest in several league cities. The season was also notable for the sudden end to Rube Foster's reign as NNL president. In May 1925 Foster had nearly died of gas poisoning but had continued his dual duties as league president and owner of the American Giants. By July 1926, Foster's mental and physical health had seriously deteriorated, perhaps exacerbated by overwork and league pressures, leaving him increasingly unable to deal with league affairs. Finally, in August Foster suffered a mental collapse from which he would never recover and spent the remaining four years of his life in a mental institution, a sad end to the remarkable career of a man who had nearly single-handedly revolutionized black baseball.[6]

During Foster's nearly 30 years as player, owner, and administrator, professional black baseball had developed into a legitimate business enterprise with corresponding increases in attendance, salaries, and press coverage. While conditions had significantly improved for professional players, the world of black baseball in the 1920s was still a far cry from the white major and minor leagues despite possessing players of equivalent or superior skills. Even after several years of organized league ball, black baseball still closely paralleled semiprofessional baseball in its manner of operation, and as Bolden admitted, "It will be many years before we can even get in sight of the major leagues."

Young players had a particularly difficult time breaking into the "colored majors." Unlike organized baseball, no prolonged spring training season existed where young players could be leisurely evaluated. Hilldale's preseason, for example, usually consisted of a few brief workouts at the local YMCA, and other clubs sometimes barnstormed in the southern states, usually scheduling games against black college teams. Although some youngsters were given tryouts, most teams felt pressured to sign veterans to contracts in the off-season and had little roster space for rookies in the spring. In many cases, young players, particularly pitchers, were given greater opportunities to break in during the regular season, especially teams decimated by injuries. In 1925 a severe shortage of pitchers forced the Lincoln Giants to place an advertisement: "Any local pitcher who thinks he can make the team will be given a tryout by reporting to Mr. Keenan at the grounds or writing him at his home, 505 W. 135th Street."

As in the past, most young players developed from the sandlots. Black amateur baseball continued to flourish during the 1920s with leagues organized in several cities, including St. Louis, Pittsburgh, Kansas City, Harrisburg, Baltimore, and Chicago. Locally, the Penn-Jersey Colored League, formed in 1926, was touted as the "minor league of eastern baseball," and featured several players who would later appear with professional teams, including pitcher Porter Charleston of the Swarthmore Giants. After pitching brilliantly in a 4–3 loss to Hilldale on July 28, 1927, Charleston was signed by Bolden within three weeks and became an outstanding pitcher for several seasons. Meanwhile, Billy Yancey, Jim Thorpe, Wilbur Pritchett, Obie Lackey, Ted Waters, and Neck Stanley were some of the Philadelphia area sandlot products to appear in a Hilldale uniform during the mid- to late-1920s.[7]

Independent professional teams also provided prospects as well as functioning as a crude version of the minor leagues. During the 1920s, nonaffiliated clubs such as Danny McClellan's New England–based

Philadelphia Giants, Chappie Johnson's teams in Schenectady and later Montreal, the Pennsylvania Red Caps of New York, and Louis Santop's Broncos in Philadelphia provided valuable experience to unproven rookies while allowing aging veterans a chance to extend their playing careers. Although Hilldale and other league teams occasionally formed loose agreements with independent clubs like the Philadelphia Giants, most received little or no compensation for the loss of a player. After outfielder Dewey Rivers defected to Hilldale in 1926, the Brooklyn Cuban Giants complained that the team had discovered Rivers in the South, developed his playing skills, but had received nothing in return.

Despite Rube Foster's belief that college players were "the hardest kind to keep straight," a number of players were also recruited from white and African American schools. Earl Brown was signed by the Lincoln Giants soon after graduating from Harvard in 1924, and Hilldale signed former University of Michigan star Rudolph Ash in 1926. The Atlantic City Bacharach Giants featured several college pitchers from African American institutions, including Red Grier of A&T College, George Lockhart of Talladega, and Jimmy Shields of Howard. Laymon Yokely of the Baltimore Black Sox, despite achieving professional status, continued to pitch for his Livingston College team.[8]

The few young players who managed to join league clubs each season often faced the wrath of openly hostile veterans fearful of losing their jobs. In 1927 rookie George Giles of the Kansas City Monarchs was unable to drink from the team's water supply because of intimidation of veterans. Future Hall-of-Famer Cool Papa Bell experienced similar difficulties while breaking in with the St. Louis Stars in the early 1920s: "See, we all dressed in the same clubhouse with Charleston and those guys. They'd say, 'Where'd you get this new boy from?' They would push me out from under the shower, spit on me, step on me. They used to do that, see, just to try to get your goat." With Hilldale, Jake Stephens and Judy Johnson were forced to carry veteran Louis Santop's equipment during their early years with the club. Years later, Stephens recalled Santop's taunting words: "'Heh, boy' — he called me boy — 'take my bag. . . . You ain't gonna be on this ball club but just so long.'"

The cutthroat competition for roster spots contributed to the aggressive, exciting, yet occasionally violent brand of baseball seen in both leagues. As Newt Allen of the Monarchs noted, "We used every trick in the book to win a ball game. All kinds of good tricks and nasty ones. In fact, there were more nasty ones than there were good. Caused many a ballplayer to get hurt." In the ECL, John Beckwith, Rev Cannady, Jud Wilson, Oscar Charleston, George Britt, Charlie Smith, and Frank

Dallard were notorious "bad boys" involved in numerous scrapes with umpires and opposing players. Spiking was a favorite tactic, and several ECL players, including Julian Rojo, Dick Lundy, and Crush Holloway, were notorious for filing spikes. On July 8, 1926, Holloway spiked Judy Johnson so badly that the usually even-tempered Johnson threatened him with a bat. Five years later, on July 25, 1931, fans swarmed on the field after Holloway once again almost "cut the pants off" Johnson while sliding into third base. Years later, Judy Johnson recalled, "We had more trouble with violence in the Negro Leagues than playing with white boys. My leg's all cut up."

With rosters usually limited to 14 to 16 players as in the low minor leagues, injury to a single individual could be devastating. Unless hurt severely, players were expected to continue at their position or risk possible release. While Hilldale occasionally employed players such as Namon Washington in predominantly reserve roles, most teams functioned with little bench strength and versatile players such as Biz Mackey, Martin Dihigo, John Beckwith, and George Britt were particularly valuable. Mackey, for example, played nearly every position for Hilldale during his nine years with the club and even pitched occasionally against weaker semipro teams. Good-hitting pitchers capable of playing additional positions were also highly regarded. When not on the mound, Joe Rogan played outfield for the Monarchs, and Nip Winters pinch-hit regularly and sometimes filled in at first base for Hilldale.[9]

Players typically had few off days during the season. Hilldale and other eastern teams typically played 2–4 league games weekly with twilight games scheduled daily whenever possible. As in organized baseball, travel occupied a considerable part of every player's life, even in the more compact ECL. During the 1920s, most black teams used special rail cars for long trips and public transportation or automobiles for shorter distances. With expenses mounting by mid-decade, several eastern teams, including the Baltimore Black Sox, Atlantic City Bacharachs, and Washington Potomacs, switched to buses in 1924, and the Kansas City Monarchs followed suit in 1926. Other clubs, like Alex Pompez's Cuban Stars, traveled in two seven-passenger Packard cars and Hilldale began using Cadillacs in addition to rail travel in the late 1920s. With the eventual advent of night baseball and skyrocketing transportation expenses, buses would become the primary mode of transportation in the 1930s, to the chagrin of the players. For Jake Stephens, black baseball during the Depression with its long bus rides was "no longer a pleasure."

With franchises mostly located in urban areas with a widespread black vice district nearby, players were susceptible to numerous temptations off the field. Despite Prohibition, alcohol was easily obtainable. In 1923 the Baltimore Black Sox were noted to have a recurrent problem with too much "moonshine," exacerbated by fans who sometimes gave players liquor between games of a doubleheader. Several Hilldale players, including Nip Winters, Joe Lewis, Biz Mackey, and Porter Charleston, had reputations as hard drinkers. Bolden, usually unwilling to tolerate improper behavior on his teams, largely overlooked training transgressions if player performance was not obviously affected. Joe Lewis, however, would be released in 1926 for his drinking, and Winters would later wear out his welcome with the team. The popularity of gambling establishments also concerned owners, particularly Rube Foster, who refused to pay his men in Detroit for fear they would patronize Tenny Blount's gambling houses. Later in the decade, several Hilldale and Bacharach players were arrested in a raid in Philadelphia at a gambling establishment at 1616 South Street.[10]

Some players paid a severe price for their involvement in vice-related activities. In 1923 Hilton Kimbro, a former Bacharach Giant, was murdered in a moonshine saloon, and veteran pitcher Darknight Smith was shot during a gambling argument. Three years later, Dobie Moore and a Kansas City Monarch teammate were wounded by women in separate shooting incidents, resulting in the abrupt end of Moore's promising career. In the East, former Hilldale catcher Jim York lost an eye in a fight with a South Philadelphia bootlegger in 1927, and Henry Jordan of the Harrisburg Giants was killed by gunfire in 1928. Other players, notably Bunny Downs, Dave Brown, Frank Wickware, and Oliver Marcelle, were implicated in murder cases, though apparently never prosecuted. Jimmy Moss, however, a former Chicago American Giant, was executed in Georgia in 1928 for murder.

Realizing the brief length of most baseball careers and the unpredictable financial situation in both leagues, other professionals shunned hard drinking, self-destructive lifestyles and prepared for the inevitable life after baseball. Praised as one of the "cleanest livers in black baseball," Otto Briggs married Beatrice Perry, the daughter of *Philadelphia Tribune* founder Chris Perry, and began a successful career as circulation manager while active with Hilldale. Other players quit baseball to accept full time employment. Luther Farrell left the Bacharachs after obtaining a position with the Atlantic City police in 1929. Meanwhile, Pennsylvania Station in New York lured a number of players, including Jules Thomas and Bill Lindsay of the Lincoln Giants, with offers of year-round employment and a chance to play for the company's highly regarded black baseball team, the Pennsylvania Red Caps.

With contracts extending only through September, seasonal employment was necessary for many players. Hilldale's Joe Lewis worked as a
riveter in Philadelphia during the winter, and the Bacharachs' Milt
Lewis, a native of West Philadelphia, was a shipper for the Pennsylvania
Railroad. Ben Taylor of the Black Sox operated a newsstand and shoe
shine during the off-season, as his brother C.I. had done in Indianapolis
a decade earlier, and several Detroit Stars painted cars for Briggs Manufacturing. Some players switched to basketball during the winter, as Fats
Jenkins, Bill Yancey, George Fiall appeared with the legendary Renaissance Five and Scrappy Brown with the Baltimore Athenians.[11]

For most players, however, baseball remained the most attractive
option in the off-season. In Palm Beach, the Royal Poinciana and Break-
ers hotels continued to sponsor black baseball teams as entertainment for
their white patrons through the 1920s, both clubs comprised of professional players employed by the hotels for the winter. The Cuban leagues
were lucrative as well, offering the opportunity to earn as much as $400
to $500 a month. The California Winter League, usually with one black
team and three white, attracted professional players of both races. With
several eastern players in the lineup, the league's major black team was
known as the Philadelphia Royal Giants, and a later edition was renamed
the Philadelphia Hilldale Giants.

Despite the tenuous financial status of black professional baseball,
player income typically exceeded the normal earnings of African Americans. The minimum monthly salary (about $100) was at least equal to the
typical pay of an unskilled worker. Others, like Oscar Charleston, earned
over $400 per month and lived in a "pretty three story front porch home"
in Harrisburg. Several Hilldale players were able to purchase new cars,
as was Jud Wilson of the Black Sox, who sported a Buick Roadster. In
contrast, Ed Henry, Philadelphia's highest-paid black official, earned less
than $500 monthly in the 1920s. While neither the NNL nor the ECL had
achieved the stability that Foster had hoped for, their very existence, as
John Howe observed, had provided "a medium through which men who
possess a peculiar ability that spells fortune and glory for men of another
race may find an outlet for their skill and receive monetary remuneration
as well."[12]

The future of professional black baseball appeared increasingly
uncertain during the winter of 1926–1927. The NNL, now without Foster's dynamic leadership and administrative skills, found itself confronted
with the prospect of finding eight viable franchises for the 1927 season, as
only Detroit, Kansas City, and St. Louis appeared financially solvent.

Ten years after his first stint as Hilldale's captain, Otto Briggs once again was named to the position in June 1927. In 1928 one local fan wrote admiringly of Briggs: "Who is the most valuable man to the Hilldale team? Why, Otto Briggs, of course. Yes, Jake Stevens and 'Biz' Mackey played very good ball. But as a steady fielder, hitter and field general, Otto Briggs was the peer of them all, and hence the most valuable player" (Cash-Thompson Collection, courtesy Afro-American Historical and Cultural Museum, Philadelphia, Pennsylvania).

In addition, the fate of Foster's American Giants remained undecided as John Schorling had become embroiled in a struggle with Foster's wife over the club's ownership. Meanwhile, the ECL had been dealt a serious blow in December 1926 when James Keenan, angered by the proposed schedule for 1927 and the continued influence of his rival Nat Strong, abruptly walked out of a league meeting and subsequently announced his withdrawal. In a foreshadowing of subsequent events, Keenan noted that independent baseball offered the Lincoln Giants financial incentives equal to or greater than those of league baseball.

As 1926 drew to a close, a *Pittsburgh Courier* article by Cum Posey of the Grays offered a harsh assessment of the ruling powers of organized black baseball. In a discussion of the now disabled Rube Foster and the NNL, Posey noted that Foster's national popularity and influence had steadily declined since 1920 and denounced Foster's tendency to blame the league's numerous franchise failures on lack of business acumen. Analyzing the East, Posey recognized that the league was "far from a booking agency" but nevertheless objected to the Strong-Bolden alliance's disproportionate control of league affairs at the expense of dedicated yet less powerful owners like Alex Pompez and C.W. Strothers. While Posey grudgingly admitted that Bolden "means alright and is for the best interests of the league," he chided the ECL chairman for lacking the "guts" to enforce league rules and scornfully noted that he would rather schedule the Grays against a white team down south than play some of the rowdier ECL clubs. Finally, Posey suggested that the ECL would be in far better financial condition if Strong would only secure home grounds for the Royal Giants and Cuban Stars.[13]

Posey's analysis was hardly debatable, and both leagues now realized that sweeping administrative and financial changes were necessary for survival. In response to the numerous critics of Bolden's dual role as league owner and chairman, the ECL in early 1927 decided to appoint a league president unaffiliated with the organization. Although local black politician Ed Henry and former Pennsylvania Boxing Commission member Charles Fred White were considered, the league eventually chose Isaac Nutter, an African American attorney from Atlantic City previously involved with John Connors's Bacharach Giants. The NNL quickly followed suit and selected William Hueston, a black municipal judge from Gary, Indiana, as the new league head at their meeting in late January 1927. In addition, both leagues, aware of the deteriorating economic climate of blacks, continued their attempts to reduce operating expenses and for the second consecutive year cut monthly salary limits from $3,000 to $2,700. The East slashed its minimum guarantee for weekday games from $150 to $125, and the NNL abandoned the controversial practice of allocating 10 percent of gross gate receipts to the league. The NNL also began discussing a plan for sharing travel expenses equally among the owners as well as ways to schedule more exhibition games during long road trips to increase profitability.

With some maneuvering, both leagues managed to enter the season with full quotas of teams. The NNL continued its franchise shuffle, returning to the South to add the Memphis Red Sox and Birmingham Black Barons as replacements for the short-lived Dayton and Cleveland teams. In addition, the once venerable Indianapolis ABCs were transferred to Cleveland where new owners prepared to launch the Hornets, the fourth NNL franchise based in Cleveland. Meanwhile, the ECL lured the tempestuous James Keenan back into the fold and subsequently reelected him as secretary-treasurer.

Player morale, however, had sunk to an all-time low as a result of the continued salary reductions. The NNL and ECL, realizing the players might be easily lured by contract offers from the Homestead Grays and other independent teams, jointly announced a five-year ban on any contract-jumping player, severely limiting their future options. The ban initially appeared a success as Oscar Charleston, despite announcing his intention to sign with Homestead in March 1927, eventually decided to return to Harrisburg after considering the financial repercussions of a five-year exile from league baseball. Yet four highly regarded players from both leagues, Rap Dixon of Harrisburg, Biz Mackey of Hilldale, Frank Duncan of Kansas City, and Andy Cooper of Detroit, quickly tested the five-year ban by failing to report to their clubs, choosing to embark on a four-month barnstorming tour of Hawaii and Japan with Lonnie Goodwin's Philadelphia Royal Giants of the California Winter League.[14]

Presented with their first substantial challenge, the two league presidents proved unable or unwilling to enforce the five-year ban. Nutter, who reportedly believed the rule excessive, suspended Mackey and Dixon for less than two weeks upon their return in July, and Duncan and Cooper received 30-day suspensions and $200 fines from Hueston. Other contract jumpers similarly avoided punishment, including Nip Winters and Red Ryan, who joined the Homestead Grays in late summer. While Ryan elected to remain with Homestead, Winters abruptly returned to Hilldale after a few days and received no disciplinary action. As John Howe of the *Philadelphia Tribune* would note: "Of course there are laws to cover this sort of thing but what are laws that have no teeth in them. . . . It's very apparent that a good man can jump as he pleases and judge of his own importance by the manner in which the laws are sliced in order that he may be forgiven and taken back into the fold."

Nutter and Hueston would be faced with another substantial challenge in an interleague dispute involving Alonzo Montalvo of the Lincoln Giants. Montalvo, a former member of the western Cuban Stars, had sat out the 1926 season after being denied a pay raise and subsequently signed with the Lincoln Giants in 1927. The NNL, however, claimed that Montalvo was still the property of the Cubans, citing the crude version of organized baseball's reserve clause enacted by the two leagues that bound players to their current club unless officially released. A potentially explosive situation loomed as Keenan refused to return Montalvo, insisting that his omission from the Cuban Stars' reserve list automatically had made him a free agent.

Other ECL owners, including Alex Pompez and Bolden, realized that Montalvo's omission from the reserve list had been an oversight and agreed that he was still technically the property of the Cuban Stars. On May 1, 1927, Bolden, realizing that the controversy might initiate a resumption of hostilities with the NNL, refused to play Lincoln unless Montalvo was removed from the lineup. While Keenan yielded to Bolden's request, he suggested that the matter should be decided by Judge Landis, the commissioner of organized baseball, illustrating his lack of faith in the authority of either league. Keenan, however, subsequently agreed not to play Montalvo until the two league presidents reached a decision. After the case was decided in favor of the West, Keenan abruptly resigned from the league for the second time in seven months on June 22, 1927. While Keenan claimed Strong and Pompez had engineered the decision, the Montalvo case actually provided Keenan, an increasingly ambivalent league member in recent years, with a convenient opportunity to withdraw from the troubled circuit.[15]

The withdrawal of the Lincoln Giants in June frustrated the league's revamped schedule, which had been expanded to 120 games to help offset the continued loss of lucrative dates with white semipros. While the ECL, following the NNL's lead, had adopted a split season with the winner of each 60-game half to play for the pennant, the league was forced to reduce the second half to 40 games after Lincoln's departure. The schedule was additionally marred by numerous rainouts as well as the abrupt cancellation of a series of league games at Bradley Beach, New Jersey. Commenting on the ECL's schedule woes, Bolden faulted the league's "internal dissension and a willful club owner" as several teams, particularly the Brooklyn Royal Giants, had continued their reluctance to play less profitable weekday league games. Meanwhile, the ECL's innovative attempt to attract new black fans by leasing neutral parks in previously unexplored markets failed, as league games played in Richmond and Norfolk, despite the presence of large African American populations that lacked professional black teams, drew poorly.

The increasingly unstable ownership of several franchises exacerbated the league's internal difficulties. Despite a pennant winning season in 1926, the Atlantic City Bacharachs were reportedly $30,000 in debt at the season's outset. Although the team's park annual rent of $1,000 was paid by Congressman Isaac Bacharach, the Bacharachs were unable to pay even the taxes required by their lease agreement. On June 21, 1927, Bacharach ordered the park locked, forcing cancellation of a scheduled game with Hilldale. After a shakeup of the Bacharach ownership group, Bacharach agreed to lease the park back to the beleaguered franchise.

In Baltimore the Black Sox were rocked by a scandal involving longtime business manager Charles Spedden. Spedden, a member of the interleague committee handling finances for the 1926 World Series, was ousted by owner George Rossiter after the ECL's $385 share was reported missing. In August the Black Sox suffered another mishap as several players were injured in a car accident near Aberdeen, Maryland. Meanwhile, local support of the club dwindled during 1927, causing an observer to note: "What's the matter with the fans? They don't turn out like they used to."

To the shock of local fans, Hilldale (or the Darby Daisies as they were increasingly called) appeared similarly unstable as the club was hampered by a continuous series of disturbing developments during 1927.[16] With star catcher Biz Mackey touring overseas and Clint Thomas sidelined with a fractured rib, the team got off to a slow start, dropping five consecutive league games in early May, and fell to sixth place after losing four straight games to the Cuban Stars in June. Team morale began to sink, and in June, Nip Winters, George Carr, and Namon Washington were suspended by Bolden for "lack of discipline and indifferent playing." Fan reaction to the team's difficulties was predictably irate, as revealed by a letter to the *Pittsburgh Courier* from a "A Hilldale Ball Fan":

> We want to know what is the matter with the Hilldale Club. It used to be "Hilldale wins another," now it is "Hilldale Loses Another." . . . We want to see the home team win, and if the manager and stockholders of the Hilldale club can't produce a winner, we'll join the list of falling off patrons and go where our money will be appreciated.

In late June, with the team still struggling with a 13-22 league record, Bolden was finally forced to make a change and named Otto Briggs to replace Frank Warfield as captain. While Hilldale finished the first half in fifth place with a dismal record of 17-28, the club would improve remarkably in the second half under Briggs despite the disruptive contract jumping of Winters and Ryan. In July, Bolden began a general overhaul

Opening Game Eastern Colored League, Mayo Island Park, Richmond, V., May 9–1927

of the club, re-signing George Johnson after his release from the Lincoln Giants, then completed a blockbuster trade sending Nip Winters and Clint Thomas to the Harrisburg Giants in exchange for slugging out-fielder Oscar Charleston. Although the deal was announced on the front page of the *Philadelphia Tribune*, the trade was subsequently canceled after Harrisburg fans petitioned for the popular Charleston's return. Never-theless, Hilldale improved to 19-17 and third place in the second half, thanks to impressive debuts by local sandlot products Porter Charleston and Billy Yancey, the return of Biz Mackey, and an outstanding year by Jake Stephens, who had continued to blossom defensively.[17]

Yet the declining fortunes of Hilldale, erosion of fan support, and the league's continuing instability took their toll on the 46-year-old Bolden in 1927. In addition, Bolden still maintained his full-time post office position and had been forced to take several periods of unpaid leave from his job to attend to team and league matters. In late September while preparing to leave for the World Series between Chicago and Atlantic City, Bolden finally broke from the pressure and suffered a nervous breakdown, only 13 months after his old adversary Rube Foster's mental collapse. While the specific nature of Bolden's condition is unknown, he would remain out of both team and league affairs for several months. Acting quickly, the Hilldale corporation chose Vice President Charles Freeman to replace Bolden as president. Other changes followed in Bolden's absence, includ-ing the return of veterans Dick Whitworth and Chance Cummings and the rehiring of Bill Francis, the team's captain from 1920 through 1922, as a nonplaying manager.

Bolden's collapse culminated a disastrous season for the ECL marked by the withdrawal of Lincoln, the bankruptcy of the Bacharachs, and the usual problems of player discipline, umpires, uncooperative owners, and scheduling that Nutter, like Bolden, had been unable to solve. Several owners seemed resigned to the league's fate, particularly Nat Strong and Colonel Strothers, who ignored a meeting to arrange the 1927 World Series. Meanwhile, Strothers, rumored to be the next owner to withdraw, failed to attend a hearing to discuss his team's challenge to the Bacharachs' first-place finish in the second half. Citing the league's "glaring lack of discipline, the unwise moves of the men at the helms of the various teams

Opposite: **With patronage falling off in league cities by 1927, the ECL scheduled games in Richmond and Norfolk, hoping to attract local black fans hungry for professional baseball. In the league's opening game in Richmond on May 9, 1927, the Cuban Stars trounced Hilldale 12–7, sparked by Martin Dihigo, who drove in nine runs on two grand slams and a solo home run (National Baseball Library and Archive, Cooperstown, N.Y.).**

and the general disorder that seems to characterize the whole business," the *Tribune*'s Howe predicted that "the beloved league is a very fragile thing."[18]

Despite the nearly endemic financial problems of both leagues and widespread unemployment among African Americans, the NNL and ECL decided to hold their annual joint session as usual, scheduling a two-day meeting in February 1928 at the Southwest YMCA in Philadelphia. While numerous issues were discussed, including interleague play, World Series expenses, and rotating umpires, the most significant development during the meetings was the return of James Keenan to the ECL after agreeing to surrender Montalvo to the Cuban Stars. At Keenan's insistence, however, the leagues' waiver rules were clarified and amended to prevent similar misunderstandings in the future. In general, the joint session, attended by the press for the first time, avoided frank discussions of the current status of organized black baseball, and most owners were reported as still expecting "highly successful" seasons in 1928.

Yet prospects for the ECL seemed particularly bleak. The Harrisburg Giants had already withdrawn from the league prior to the joint session. Although Harrisburg had been burdened with several high-salaried players, including John Beckwith, Oscar Charleston, Fats Jenkins, and Rap Dixon, owner C.W. Strothers had particularly objected to the league's schedule, the refusal of the Bacharachs to play league games in Harrisburg, and his team's disputed second-place finish in the second half of the 1927 season. In early March 1928, the league received another blow as Nat Strong, apparently deciding that he had milked the league dry, also dropped out, leaving the ECL with only five intact franchises.[19]

Meanwhile, Bolden, fully recovered from his physical and mental difficulties, had gradually renewed his involvement in league affairs. In February, Bolden was reelected secretary-treasurer of the ECL and later attended the joint session in Philadelphia. In addition, he issued a statement to the *Philadelphia Tribune* that blamed the league's problems on the "narrow minds and selfish motives of some of the Commissioners" and suggested that the press and players be allowed to attend league meetings to "curb underhand work" of the owners. By March, Bolden, though still subordinate to current Hilldale president Charles Freeman, had regained the confidence and support of other corporation members and was now prepared to launch a fight to reclaim control. On March 8, 1928, Freeman and his major ally, Secretary Lloyd Thompson, were ousted at a corporation meeting as Bolden returned as president with George Mayo as vice president, Mark Studevan treasurer and Thomas Jenkins secretary. A week later, the *Philadelphia Tribune* reported the startling news that Hilldale, like Harrisburg and Brooklyn, had withdrawn from the ECL and would operate as an independent team in 1928.

Despite expectations, Hilldale had profited little from its participation in the Eastern Colored League. The corporation had been forced to borrow in 1925, 1926, and 1927 to open the season and lost $21,500 in 1927. Explaining his decision in a March press release, Bolden noted that Hilldale was "through losing money in an impossible league" and would return to independent baseball where the team had once made "plenty of money." In addition, Bolden cited the league's rejection of his plan for rotating umpires and the profound lack of cooperation among league owners. In less than subtle references to James Keenan and Nat Strong, Bolden remarked in disgust that "when one man quits this week and then comes back a few weeks later and when one team plays forty home games and another four, then it is time for a halt." Bolden issued another thinly veiled swipe at Strong, complaining that "some clubs come to a park and during the season, take away thousands of dollars, yet they never have a park to give anything in return."

Local reaction to Hilldale's withdrawal was mostly favorable as many fans had tired of the league's incessant problems and controversies. As Joe Rainey, a local African American athlete and sportswriter would note, "Many a fan will welcome, instead of mourn, over the latest step." The *Baltimore Afro-American*, often a harsh critic of Bolden's leadership as league chairman, applauded Bolden's decision, noting that "justice to players and managers as well, seems to be the guiding force in all of Bolden's dealings with his fellow moguls in the national pastime." Yet William "Doc" Lambert, a trainer connected with several NNL and ECL teams, suggested that Bolden's timing had been poor, observing that some viewed the move as a further example of compliance with Nat Strong. In addition, Lambert argued that Bolden, as "one of the smartest men in the business," should have remained in the league to enact necessary reforms from within and warned that the "league will prevail in the end."[20]

To the surprise of many, the ECL's anticipated collapse failed to materialize. Shortly after Bolden's announcement, the league reorganized in a meeting in Trenton presided over by reelected president Isaac Nutter. The Black Sox, Lincoln Giants, and Bacharachs agreed to remain in the league, and Nutter managed to lure the wavering Cuban Stars with a promise to receive 40 percent of the gross for league games instead of the usual 35 percent. Meanwhile, the league began negotiations with the Eastern League All-Stars, a recently organized Philadelphia area team owned by gambler Smitty Lucas primarily comprised of former league players. Nutter hoped that Hilldale would be unable to compete with the revitalized league, particularly with a competing Philadelphia franchise, and would be forced to seek readmission. In addition, Nutter predicted the ECL, "which is synonymous to organized baseball, . . . will go on and become stronger and more effective despite the efforts of Bolden and Strong to wreck the league."

As expected, the Eastern League All-Stars, renamed the Philadelphia Tigers, joined the ECL by April and attempted to obtain home grounds at the strategically located Elks Park at 48th and Spruce Streets in West Philadelphia. Bolden, however, still well connected to local white park owners, quickly blocked the move by securing the park for Hilldale. With the Tigers unable to obtain grounds in Philadelphia, the league's most profitable city, the ECL seemed all but finished. A last-minute desperate attempt to lure Bolden back failed, and on April 13, 1928, the league was apparently dissolved in a meeting attended by Bolden, Pompez, Rossiter, and Ike Washington, the new owner of the Bacharachs. Once again the league refused to die as the Philadelphia Tigers managed to rent Penncoyd Park, a less accessible semipro ballfield at Ridge Avenue and Lincoln Drive. While the ECL bravely began the season on April 29, the Cuban Stars dropped out within three weeks and were soon followed by the Lincoln Giants. Although Nutter insisted the league would continue and attempted to find replacement franchises, the Eastern Colored League had finally breathed its last by June 1928, a mere five and a half years after its formation.[21]

Economics had played a significant role in the ECL's final disintegration with a steady attendance decline in the league's four major cities of Baltimore, New York, Atlantic City, and Darby since 1923 as well as franchise failures in Washington, Wilmington, and Newark. Yet as Bolden noted, the lackadaisical and selfish attitudes of the league's owners had also contributed to the league's downfall. As the West had predicted, Nat Strong proved to be a liability, although he could not be blamed entirely for the league's failures. Strong, with his still considerable booking power and control of Dexter Park, might have been equally destructive had he been excluded from the circuit. Nevertheless, his refusal to secure grounds for the league's two traveling teams, the Cuban Stars and the Royal Giants, ensured the league's scheduling problems and attendant difficulties.

Several black sportswriters, citing the multitude of difficulties, viewed the league's collapse as inevitable. Randy Dixon of the *Philadelphia Tribune* noted, "Little regard was given to the fact that the schedules were lopsided, the teams varying in the number of games played. They opined that the next year such trifles would be adjusted. But that next year never came." Bill Gibson of the *Baltimore Afro-American* felt the ECL had "always remained rather a puny thing, never developing the robustness and virility of its relative, the National League." Other observers optimistically hoped that a new league would arise from the ashes of the ECL, and Black Sox owner George Rossiter stated, "I have always had faith in organized baseball and it is still my contention that a league is the best thing for all concerned."

Any future league, however, still required the participation of Hilldale, which remained the backbone of professional black and independent white baseball in the Midatlantic region, despite its recent decline. Yet after suffering a nervous breakdown probably related to his five years of ECL frustrations, Bolden refused to commit to league participation. Bolden's cryptic statement that he was "in favor of league ball, but only when it is run on a business-like basis" gave little hint of the future course of Hilldale or eastern black baseball.[22]

8

"A General Understanding": Organized Baseball and Black Professional Baseball, 1900–1930

> We do not believe that there exists any rule or bylaw excluding the colored man from organized baseball, but there appears to be a general understanding all along the line that Cubans, (provided they do not come too black), Chinese, Indians and every one else under the sun, be allowed his chance to measure, except the black man.... Perhaps, some day, a Regular American baseball man will establish a precedent — maybe.
> — *Black sportswriter Ira Lewis, 1920.*

While the outlook for professional black baseball appeared increasingly negative in the spring of 1928, African Americans were momentarily encouraged by renewed discussion in several daily newspapers of the long dormant issue of organized baseball's color barrier, triggered by the appearance of Andy Cohen, a Jew, in the New York Giants starting lineup. In the nearly 30 years since the last appearance of a black player in the minor leagues, black baseball had developed dramatically, yet its sportswriters, fans, and players continued to hope for the integration of the white professional game. Even Rube Foster's formation of the NNL in 1920 had been partially motivated by a desire to prepare black players for their eventual entrance into major league baseball. Although the pre-Depression era is usually considered insignificant in the fight for integration, several noteworthy developments influenced the subsequent course of the assault on baseball's color line in the 1930s and early 1940s.

Organized baseball, despite its unwritten yet unyielding ban of African Americans after 1899, hardly remained isolated from black professional baseball. Eager to supplement their modest salaries, major and minor league players arranged exhibition games against black professional clubs and strong white semipro teams during spring training, on off days, and at the end of the season. As early as 1885, the Cuban Giants booked games against the New York Metropolitans and Philadelphia Athletics of the American Association and later faced other league clubs, including the St. Louis Browns and Cincinnati Red Stockings as well as the National League's Kansas City Cowboys, Indianapolis Hoosiers, Boston Beaneaters, and Detroit Wolverines. Bud Fowler's Page Fence Giants also competed against major leaguers, losing twice to the Cincinnati Reds in 1895.

Some major league players, however, objected to all forms of interracial competition and refused to play black teams. Cap Anson, the star first baseman and manager of the Chicago White Stockings of the National League and perhaps the most vocal advocate of the color line in baseball, threatened to cancel several games in the 1880s rather than take the field against white professional teams with black players in their lineups. In September 1887 the St. Louis Browns, with the exception of Charles Comiskey and Ed Knauff, petitioned the team's owner, Chris Von der Ahe, to protest a scheduled exhibition game in West Farms, New York, against the Cuban Giants, noting they would "cheerfully play against white people at any time." To the disappointment of a large crowd, the game was canceled, Von der Ahe offering the alibi that injuries had prevented his team's appearance.[1]

With the accelerated development and increased strength of black teams after 1900, interracial professional competition became more common as white players began to realize its lucrative possibilities. Simultaneously, African American teams began to defeat organized baseball clubs with regularity, largely due to the ascendancy of Rube Foster, who provided black baseball with a pitcher capable of stopping any major league lineup. During his four years in the East with the Philadelphia Giants and Cuban X-Giants from 1903 through 1906, Foster reportedly defeated the New York Giants, Philadelphia A's, Philadelphia Phillies, Brooklyn Dodgers, and clubs from the New England, Tri-State, and Eastern leagues. Foster continued to baffle major league opponents after jumping to the West, winning all four of the Leland Giants' victories over an outlaw team featuring major leaguers Mike Donlin and Jake Stahl in 1907.

Often heavily attended, postseason barnstorming games were invaluable in showcasing the outstanding talents of African American players to unsuspecting white players, fans, sportswriters, and owners. After attending the Leland Giants' series against Mike Donlin's All-Stars in 1907, Chicago White Sox owner Charles Comiskey noted that he would have signed at least three Giants had they been white, a refrain often repeated by major league officials during the next 40 years. The complimentary treatment and continued strong showing of black clubs against major and minor league teams during the early 1900s raised hopes that African American players or teams might be allowed in some of the lower-ranked leagues in organized baseball. In 1907, the Boston Braves' signing of pitcher Bill Joy, supposedly a Malay from Honolulu, was enthusiastically applauded by the *Indianapolis Freeman* and viewed as a potential step toward integration. Sol White claimed that one of the "leading players and a manager in the National League" was advocating the entry of Billy Matthews, an African American who had starred on Harvard's baseball team and was currently playing in white semipro leagues in New England.

While organized baseball remained closed to blacks, the formation of the United States League in 1910 temporarily attracted national attention to the issue. Organized by G.H. Lawson, a former minor league pitcher and brother of former major leaguer Alfred Lawson, the new league hoped to equal the major leagues in scope and prestige and took the unusually progressive step of allowing unrestricted access to African American players. Not surprisingly, the league received only lukewarm response from black players, who doubted the wisdom of joining an outlaw circuit outside organized baseball run by a promoter whose similar projects had ended in failure. The Brooklyn Royal Giants and Cuban X-Giants rejected offers from Lawson, and the "Black and Tan League," as it was labeled by some cynics, never got off the ground.[2]

Despite the failure of the United States League, the question of black participation in organized baseball was continually discussed during 1910, particularly after African American boxer Jack Johnson's dramatic triumph over James Jeffries for the heavyweight championship on July 4 drew increased attention to the concept of interracial competition. In August, a Milwaukee newspaper endorsed the entrance of blacks to organized baseball, citing the hypocrisy of white players who "never hesitate about playing games against the Negro clubs in the off season" yet refused to play alongside them in the major leagues. The sentiment was echoed by the prominent sportswriter Bill Phelon, who noted, "Nowhere is the color line drawn so strictly as among the big and minor leaguers, and yet the color line fades away when there is a chance to make any money by playing black teams on the outside." In addition, Phelon observed that even flagrant racists such as Georgia-born Ty Cobb had recently participated in a postseason series against a Cuban team that featured several African Americans.

Since the 1890s, organized baseball teams had traveled to Cuba in the winter to face increasingly stiff local competition. In 1908, the Cincinnati Reds, led by former manager Frank Bancroft, lost seven of 11 games to Cuban teams, incurring the wrath of team president Garry Herrmann. The Reds, however, were impressed by the brilliant pitching of Jose Mendez, the future manager of the Kansas City Monarchs, who won two games in the series without allowing a run in 25 innings. Like Foster, Mendez would prove to be a nemesis for major league teams and was the subject of generous praise from white players and journalists, who constantly bemoaned the black skin that kept him out of organized baseball.

Despite the Reds' defeat in 1908, major league teams continued to compete against Cuban clubs with only modest success. Hampered by the absence of stars Ty Cobb and Sam Crawford, the American League champion Detroit Tigers were also dealt a series loss during their trip to Cuba in 1909. A year later, the Tigers returned for a 12-game set against the Almendares and Havana clubs, the latter supplemented by African Americans Home Run Johnson, Bruce Petway, Pete Hill, and John Henry Lloyd. While the Tigers took seven of the 12 games with one tie, the four black players were particularly impressive in defeat, as John Henry Lloyd (.412) and Pete Hill (.389) encountered little trouble with major league pitching. Meanwhile, catcher Bruce Petway along with future major leaguer Mike Gonzalez achieved the remarkable feat of throwing out the great Ty Cobb (second in stolen bases in 1910 with 65) in each of his three stolen base attempts during the five games in which he appeared during the series. After one unsuccessful attempt, the frustrated Cobb insisted that the bases had been placed too far apart and was proven correct after measurement. While contemporary press accounts also blamed sandy basepaths for Cobb's poor base-running performance, the Tigers' George Moriarty, who stole only 33 bases in 1910, managed to swipe seven during the series. Unhappy with his showing, Cobb reportedly vowed never to play against blacks again.[3]

To the chagrin of American League president Ban Johnson, the world champion Philadelphia Athletics also journeyed to Cuba in 1910. Fearful of humiliating defeats at the hands of clubs outside organized baseball, Johnson particularly objected to exhibition games by World Series participants, especially since few barnstorming teams were representative of the champions at full strength. Despite Johnson's opposition, the Athletics proceeded with their tour as planned, barely managing to split the eight-game series after losing three of the first four games. Alarmed by the mediocre showing of the Athletics, the National Commission promptly enacted a new law that forbade barnstorming by league champions and required other teams to obtain both league and owner permission. As the *Sporting News* approvingly stated, "The world's championship title therefore will not be besmirched by post-season tragedies such as the series between the Athletics and the Cuban teams." While Cuban barnstorming would be largely halted after 1911, controversy over postseason tours by "unrepresentative" major league teams would continue to rage in the future.

The postseason barnstorming, however, forced organized baseball to acknowledge the high caliber of baseball played by Cuban players and paved the way for their admission to organized baseball. In 1910, four light-skinned Cuban players were signed by New Britain of the Connecticut League, and a year later, Armando Marsans and Rafael Almeida appeared in the major leagues with the Cincinnati Reds. While others such as Mike Gonzalez and Adolfo Luque would follow, organized baseball remained closed to darker Cubans like Jose Mendez despite several wins over major league opponents between 1908 and 1911 and praise from Larry Doyle, Christy Mathewson, and manager John McGraw of the New York Giants. Yet Lester Walton of the *New York Age* hoped the appearance of lighter Cuban players would prepare fans and players for the future signing of "coal black" Cubans like Mendez and perhaps lead to the participation of African Americans. In the meantime, Walton suggested that some black players might "keep their mouths shut and pass for Cubans."[4]

Among major league officials, New York Giants manager John McGraw seemed the most likely candidate to acquire a black player. While managing the American League's Baltimore Orioles in 1901, McGraw signed Charlie Grant, a well-known black professional player he had discovered working during the winter as a bellhop at the Eastland Hotel in Hot Springs, Arkansas, and subsequently attempted to pass him off as a Native American named Charlie Tokohama. McGraw's plan failed, however, as Grant's identity was inadvertently revealed by black fans who publicly congratulated him. In addition, Chicago White Sox president Charles Comiskey recognized Grant from his previous appearances in Chicago as a member of the Columbia Giants. McGraw, according to Dave Wyatt of the *Freeman*, wept after being forced to release Grant, and the incident established McGraw's reputation as a friend of black players.

Numerous black sportswriters praised McGraw for his seemingly sympathetic attitude toward African Americans. In 1909, McGraw's donation of the receipts from a benefit game in Waco, Texas, to a local black college was noted in the African American press, as was his later signing of Native American catcher Chief Meyers. An admirer of the skills of black players, McGraw reportedly claimed that he would pay $30,000 for Mendez if he were white, leading observers such as the *Chicago Defender*'s William White to predict that McGraw would sign African Americans if allowed. A list of noted black baseball players that included Spottswood Poles, Dick Redding, Joe Williams, and John Henry Lloyd, discovered by McGraw's widow after his death, apparently confirmed his intentions.

While McGraw was not as "chuck full of color prejudice" as other major league officials, his reputation for racial tolerance was somewhat overrated. McGraw's autobiography contains numerous references to "darkies," and as his biographer Charles Alexander has suggested, he was no "crusader for racial justice." Except for the Charlie Grant incident, McGraw made no real attempt to challenge the color line in baseball despite his reported interest in black players. Ironically, of the six leading major league officials polled by Jimmy Powers of the *New York Daily News* at the 1933 Baseball Writers Dinner, only McGraw openly objected to the presence of blacks in organized baseball.[5]

McGraw's American League contemporary Connie Mack was also viewed as favorably inclined toward black players. Like McGraw, Mack's use of Native Americans such as Chief Bender seemed to suggest an inherent racial tolerance that might lead to a signing of an African American. Sol White, meanwhile, cited Mack's rental of Columbia Park to the Philadelphia Giants and Cuban X-Giants, his willingness to allow his Athletics to barnstorm against black professional teams, and his supposed signing of a black player while manager of Milwaukee in 1900. In 1918 the *Chicago Defender* praised Mack as a "white man with a white heart" after learning that Mack had enrolled four black children from the South in northern private schools and paid their tuition. Judy Johnson also praised Mack as a "wonderful man" and claimed that Mack once told him that the integration of major league baseball was blocked only by the vast number of blacks who would have to be allowed in. Despite his respect for black players, Mack was opposed to integration, and the Athletics showed little interest in signing black players after the color line was broken in 1946.

While hardly in favor of integration, White Sox owner Charles Comiskey had been viewed positively by African Americans since his refusal to sign a petition protesting a game against the Cuban Giants in 1887. Anxious to attract the numerous black fans who resided near his park, Comiskey hired African American trainers and groundskeepers, donated money to charitable black causes, and leased his park on numerous occasions to black teams. Comiskey also remained friendly with Rube Foster despite his competition for patronage with the nearby American Giants. Comiskey's true racial views, however, were more accurately suggested by his comments on the supposed stinginess of black fans, particularly in Baltimore.[6]

Although harsh by modern standards, the racial views of Comiskey, McGraw, and Mack were still more enlightened than those of most white players, who, like the majority of Americans during the Progressive era, continued to believe in the inferiority of African Americans. In 1911 the *St. Louis Post-Dispatch* offered a typically racist explanation for the skills of black players:

> Less removed from the anthropoid ape, he gets down on ground balls better, springs higher for liners, has a much stronger and surer grip, and can get in and out of a base on all fours in a way that makes the higher product of evolution look like a bush leaguer.[7]

Some players' racist views translated into violence toward blacks. In 1909 George McConnell of the New York Highlanders attempted to hang a black bellboy accused of stealing from him while at spring training in Macon, Georgia. The *Indianapolis Freeman* reported that McConnell, a Tennessee native, was stopped only by the intervention of his teammates.

Another southerner, Ty Cobb, made no attempt to hide his abhorrence of African Americans. One teammate recalled, "Cobb hated a colored person worse than anything." Cobb was involved in numerous racial incidents early in his career, including an altercation with a groundskeeper in Augusta, Georgia, in 1907; a fight with a laborer who objected to Cobb's stepping in freshly laid concrete in Detroit in 1908; and assaults of a black watchman at a Cleveland hotel in 1909, a fan in 1910, and a butcher in 1914. Not surprisingly, Cobb's attack of an abusive white fan in 1912 that led to his famous suspension was reportedly precipitated by taunts of "coon" or "half-nigger."

Cobb, who particularly objected to blacks he perceived as "uppity," was accused of kicking Ada Morris, a black chambermaid, down a flight of stairs in a Detroit hotel in 1919 after she protested a racial insult. While the incident was suppressed by the daily papers and the Tigers, black sportswriters such as Sol White denounced Cobb, noting that his name "should never pass the lips of colored baseball fans." Yet Cobb's brilliant baseball skills continued to intrigue African Americans, and even Rollo Wilson admitted that despite a "'low down' opinion of the Georgia Screech as an individual . . . his ability as an athlete makes us forget that when he is in action." In 1927 John Howe of the *Philadelphia Tribune* disgustedly noted the excitement shown by some local black fans at Cobb's presence with the Philadelphia Athletics. The usually unfriendly Cobb, however, surprised black Philadelphians in August 1928 by tossing two baseballs to a group of young African American fans after pregame practice at Shibe Park.[8]

Cobb's overt bigotry and refusal to play against blacks after 1910 perhaps represented the extreme of racial intolerance in organized baseball. Yet the financial lure of postseason barnstorming led many players to set aside their prejudices, at least temporarily, and as Frank Forbes, a veteran of several professional clubs, recalled, "They didn't allow Negroes in the Majors, but hell, we were very attractive to them in October." Despite the restrictions placed on barnstorming by the National Commission in 1911, major league teams continued to schedule postseason games with black professional teams, several in the East involving the recently organized Lincoln Giants. In 1911, Lincoln was defeated by an all-star team led by Walter Johnson but bounced back a year later to beat Rube Chalmers of the Philadelphia Phillies and Louis Drucke of the New York Giants. In 1913 Lincoln took four of five postseason games against teams partially or entirely composed of white major leaguers as Joe Williams won four games, including an impressive 9–2 victory over Grover Cleveland Alexander of the Phillies (22-8, 2.79) and a 2–1 outdueling of the Athletics' Chief Bender (21-10, 2.21). A year later, Williams won another game for Lincoln, defeating the Philadelphia Phillies 10–4 at Olympic Field.

The defeats of major league barnstorming teams by black clubs elicited a variety of reactions from white fans and players. The excuse of an unrepresentative lineup was frequently employed, occasionally with some justification. In 1911 the Pittsburgh Pirates featured only one regular player in the starting lineup and were beaten by Dizzy Dismukes and the West Baden Sprudels, while other "all-star" teams featured only a few legitimate major league players. Other clubs, after initially underestimating an African American team, subsequently rationalized their defeat by citing their opponent's atypically high caliber of play. After crushing several white minor league teams during their winter tour of California in 1913, the Chicago American Giants earned the respect of their rivals and lavish praise from the local press such as the *San Francisco Chronicle*, which gushed, "We hate to say how good this ball club really is."[9]

Realizing the strength of black professional teams and fearful of potential "disgrace" from defeat, some major league players continued to be leery of interracial competition. In 1912, the New York Giants nearly canceled a scheduled exhibition game at Paterson, New Jersey, after learning that the opponent would not be the semipro team they had expected but the Smart Sets, a black professional club. The Giants finally agreed to play, although pitcher Louis Drucke, fearful of gaining a reputation of being easily beaten by blacks, refused to participate unless announced under an assumed name. With the score tied 3–3 in the tenth inning, the Giants left the field, protesting the supposed use of an old baseball by Smart Sets pitcher Danny McClellan. While a few angry fans reportedly pelted the departing Giants with sticks and stones, the headline in the following day's *New York Times* (*GIANTS PLAY NEGRO TEAM, ENDS IN RIOT*) typically distorted the incident, providing a tacit condemnation of interracial competition.

With white players pressured by fans who expected easy victories and questioned defeats, a number of officials in organized baseball continued to voice increasing objections to all forms of barnstorming, particularly against black teams. In 1914, a planned series between the Lincoln Stars and an all-star team featuring five players from the world champion Boston Braves was canceled because of the opposition of Braves manager George Stallings. Meanwhile, manager Walter McCredie of the Portland Beavers of the Pacific Coast League was harshly criticized for booking his team to play Rube Foster's American Giants despite being "badly beaten" by them during the previous year. Dan Long, a former league manager, felt that no PCL team should play African American clubs, stating that "colored players are barred in organized baseball, and I can see no reason why white players should even meet them in exhibition games, if they are barred by the baseball powers." League president Baum voiced his disapproval, and one owner proudly revealed that there were "two classes I bar from playing on my ball park — colored tossers and bloomer girls." In response, the *New York Age* asserted with some logic that opposition to interracial games stemmed more from a fear of humiliation rather than actual color prejudice.[10]

In 1915 two controversial postseason games held in New York and Indianapolis compelled organized baseball once again to take decisive action against barnstorming. With both leagues already irate over a planned postseason western tour by two decidedly inferior "all-star teams," the Lincoln Giants' 1–0 defeat of the National League champion Philadelphia Phillies (with six regulars in the lineup) on October 17 confirmed the need to enforce stricter restrictions. Questioned by National League president John Tener, who was prepared to halt all barnstorming, Phillies owner William Baker insisted that his team had been given permission to play locally. While most observers expected the following week's scheduled game between Lincoln and Philadelphia to be canceled, the Phillies were allowed to play and won 4–2. The National Commission, however, vowed to address the barnstorming issue during the winter months.

A second disturbing incident occurred simultaneously in Indianapolis as violence erupted at an October 24 game at Washington Park between the Indianapolis ABCs and a barnstorming team led by Donie Bush of the Detroit Tigers. The arrest of Bingo DeMoss and Oscar Charleston of the ABCs for attacking an umpire prompted hundreds of fans to swarm onto the field, the disturbance eventually handled by club-brandishing police. Typically, the local white newspaper, the *Indianapolis Star,* exploited the racial angle, stating that a race riot had been "narrowly averted." Although manager C.I. Taylor and Charleston apologized for the incident, the National Association of Professional Baseball Leagues announced plans to limit future competition in Indianapolis between black professional and white all-star teams.

Hoping to halt the embarrassing defeats and avoid the controversies of the prior season, the American and National leagues restricted barnstorming privileges prior to the 1916 season. Players now required written consent from their team to participate in barnstorming or other sports such as football or basketball in the off-season. While exhibition games were played as usual during 1916, league barnstorming rules were enforced more strictly than in the past. The National Commission blocked the participation of Bill Rariden of the Giants, Edd Roush of the Reds, and Doc Crandall of the Browns, and the Indianapolis club of the American Association prevented several of its players from playing in a postseason game with the ABCs. Meanwhile, a total of 51 players from 13 of the 16 clubs were fined by the National Commission for illegal barnstorming activities during 1916.[11]

To the chagrin of organized baseball, professional black teams continued to register victories over major and minor league clubs despite the new league policy. During October 1917, organized baseball officials were forced to contend with not only Hilldale's landmark victory over the All-Americans but the Lincoln Giants' defeat of Rube Marquard (19-12, 2.55 with Brooklyn), with both games won by Joe Williams. In response, Brooklyn Dodgers owner Charles Ebbets fined Marquard $100, the action rationalized in a subsequent press release:

> The Brooklyn team is averse to permitting its team, or any of its players, participating in games with Negroes. There are only semi-professional

Negro teams, and when there is an outcome like yesterday's game, when Rube was beaten, President Ebbets believes it tends to lower the calibre of ball played by the big leagues in the eyes of the public, and at the same time make the major league team the subject of ridicule at the hands of the more caustic fans.[12]

The National Commission, meanwhile, took dramatic steps to block barnstorming by the 1917 league champions New York Giants and Chicago White Sox, holding $1,000 of each player's World Series share as bond to be disbursed only after both teams had signed an agreement not to barnstorm. During the following season, the National Commission again attempted to suppress postseason activity, disciplining several players from the world champion Boston Red Sox for barnstorming against Hilldale and white semipro clubs.

Facing diminished opportunities to compete in lucrative games against organized baseball teams, most black players reacted negatively to the new policy. Some observers, including the *Indianapolis Freeman*, felt that the recent barnstorming restriction had been enforced solely because of embarrassing defeats to black teams: "They have a very good reason for not letting their men play, and it isn't the fear of them getting hurt either." Yet veteran columnist Dave Wyatt argued that black baseball benefited little from postseason exhibitions, noting that victories by black teams could often be blamed on weak competition while white victories exposed the weaknesses in black professional baseball. As Wyatt observed, postseason games were not particularly meaningful unless a white team's lineup was intact and had been playing together over a period of time rather than assembled haphazardly, as was increasingly the case.

The regulation of postseason barnstorming reduced the already limited interaction between white major leaguers and black professional players and helped suppress discussion of the color line in baseball for several years. The successful formation of a third major league, the outlaw Federal League in 1914, led some African Americans to hope the expected depletion of major league talent would pave the way for the entrance of blacks to organized baseball. In 1914 Rube Foster told the *Seattle Post Intelligencer* that he expected blacks to be allowed in the minor leagues by 1915. While the Federal League's eventual collapse dashed hopes of integration, the league provided several parks that would later be used by black teams in Indianapolis, St. Louis, and Newark.[13]

With the color line still firmly intact, major league scouts turned their attention to several talented black players perceived as suitable candidates to pass as white, Cuban, or Native American in organized baseball.

The great Cuban shortstop Pelayo Chacon was followed by scouts throughout his career but was eventually judged too dark, while fellow islander Christobel Torriente was rejected because of kinky hair. In the Pacific Coast League, Walter McCredie's attempt to sign a half-Hawaiian–half-Chinese player was blocked by league officials, although Jimmy Claxton of the Oakland Oaks managed to pass as white long enough to appear on a baseball card in 1916. Various schemes to sign black players would continue, and by 1929 the *Chicago Whip* claimed that 20 black players were passing for white in the major leagues.[14]

The devastating effect of World War I on organized baseball provoked renewed discussion of the issue. With numerous leagues shut down during 1918, several observers suggested that the admission of blacks might stimulate interest, and even the usually conservative *Sporting News* asked whether the "new era of World Democracy [would] change their status." An article by the nationally syndicated sportswriter Hugh Fullerton in early 1919 provided additional favorable publicity to black players. Fullerton, however, was opposed to integration of organized baseball because of potential racial conflict and suggested a black professional league with the franchises to lease major league parks when idle.

Unbeknownst to Fullerton, several black teams had already established a working relationship with organized baseball by leasing parks for important games. Prior to 1910, the Cuban X-Giants and Philadelphia Giants had leased Columbia Park in Philadelphia, and New York teams had rented the Polo Grounds, Hilltop Park, and Washington Park. By the end of World War I, Rube Foster's Chicago American Giants had played at Comiskey Park in Chicago, Navin Field in Detroit, Redland Field in Cincinnati, Forbes Field in Pittsburgh, and American League Park in Washington, D.C. In 1919 Hilldale and the Bacharach Giants became the first two black teams to play at Shibe Park in Philadelphia, and a black team made its initial appearance at Ebbets Field in Brooklyn, with the first all-black game scheduled a year later. During the week of October 4–10, 1920, Hilldale made its first appearance at Phillies Park, and the New York Bacharachs and Chicago American Giants were simultaneously scheduled at Shibe Park.[15]

The continued development of black professional baseball in the postwar era resulted in expanded use of major league parks. Some teams secured grounds for an entire season. In 1921 the Cuban Stars of the NNL leased Redland Field as their home grounds, and the Washington Potomacs of the ECL used Griffith Stadium for local games in 1923 and 1924. In Pittsburgh the Homestead Grays began to lease Forbes Field on a regular basis during the 1920s as Cum Posey formed a profitable working relationship with Pirates owner Barney Dreyfuss. Yet the recently built Yankee Stadium, despite its proximity to New York's African American community, remained off-limits to black teams until July 5, 1930, when the park was leased for a benefit game for the Brotherhood of Sleeping Car Porters, featuring the Lincoln Giants and Baltimore Black Sox. The game reportedly drew 14,000 fans leading to expanded access to Yankee Stadium, as the Lincoln Giants rented the park in September 1930 and the newly formed Harlem Stars in 1931. In 1931 Hilldale made its first and only appearance at Yankee Stadium and played at Griffith Stadium, Forbes Field, and Phillies Park during the same season.

Despite the superior caliber of organized baseball's parks, black teams faced considerable disadvantages as tenants. Heavy attendance was necessary to offset rental fees ranging from 25 to 33 ⅓ percent on occasion, yet the more expensive major league ticket prices sometimes limited the patronage of black fans. In 1931 a second benefit game played at Yankee Stadium for the Brotherhood of Sleeping Car Porters lost money after the Yankee management received its share of the gross receipts. In addition, black teams received no profits from concessions, were forced to contend with white park personnel, and were usually forbidden to use dressing rooms and showers. By the 1940s, most grounds in organized baseball had been occupied by black teams, the New York Yankees and the Washington Senators maintaining especially profitable rental agreements.[16]

While park rentals helped establish relationships between white and black baseball officials, organized baseball's attitude toward integration changed little in the postwar era. In addition, the formation of the NNL in 1920 contributed to ambivalence among some fans. Already increasingly committed to building separate communities, race-conscious African American fans feared that black players would be overshadowed in the white major leagues and felt that black professional baseball should be established on a profitable basis without the intrusion of whites.

Not surprisingly, the December 1920 founding of the ambitious fully integrated Continental League by the redoubtable G.H. Lawson was perceived as a predictable white reaction to the NNL's successful debut season. Ten years after his United States League failure, Lawson once again seemed determined to capitalize on the appeal of black players and announced that four of the new circuit's 10 eastern-based franchises would be black. While Lawson's statement that at least 100 black players were of major league caliber suggested an admiration of their skills, the new league seemingly planned to utilize African Americans as one of a number of publicity gimmicks. Unlike organized baseball, the Continental

Hilldale, 1923. Left to right: John Henry Lloyd, Red Ryan, Pud Flournoy, Clint Thomas, Biz Mackey, Jake Stephens, Nip Winters, Ed Bolden, Judy Johnson, Otto Briggs, George Johnson, George Carr, Frank Warfield, Toussaint Allen, Holsey Lee, Louis Santop. Perhaps the greatest Hilldale team, the 1923 club finished its remarkable season by taking five of six games against two barnstorming major league teams (Cash-Thompson Collection, courtesy Afro-American Historical and Cultural Museum, Philadelphia, Pennsylvania).

League planned no reserve clause, each team instead to be affiliated with the American Federation of Labor. In addition, hitters would be allowed two bases on a walk and were not required to circle the bases on home runs. The publicity-conscious Lawson also announced the hiring of boxer Jack Johnson as a league umpire at $1,500 per week and reportedly planned to use other black umpires.

As in 1910, Lawson secured national coverage for his project, including several articles in the *New York Times*. Despite heavy press coverage, most organized baseball officials regarded the Continental League as little more than a curiosity, and Charles Ebbets, Jr., of the Brooklyn Dodgers particularly noted the league's lack of substantial financial backing. Other observers objected to Lawson's integration policy. While offering tentative support, *Baseball Magazine* was quick to note that "through all the ages the effort to mix oil and water has failed.

BASE BALL! Shibe Park
21st St. and Lehigh Avenue
HILLDALE vs. BACHARACHS

Playing off tie, each team has won Four (4) Games

Monday, Sept. 8th 3:30 p.m.

SEATS, 30c, 55c, and 85c.

Cars marked "21" on Market Street and "33" on Arch Street direct to park.

A 1919 advertisement for the deciding game of a series between Hilldale and the Bacharach Giants. The game marked the first appearance of two black teams at Shibe Park (*Philadelphia Tribune*, September 6, 1919).

In this country at least all efforts to mix black and white on an [equal basis] have also failed." Meanwhile, the *Sporting News* refused to grant coverage to Lawson except to criticize the new league for reportedly planning to play games against the recently expelled members of the 1919 Chicago White Sox.

Although suspicious of Lawson's intentions, the black press was generally supportive of the Continental League, at least initially. The league's extensive involvement of African American players, umpires, and league officials was commended as was Lawson's promise not to encroach upon NNL territory. In March 1921 the *Chicago Defender* endorsed the league, noting that "any institution that has the tendency to try and break down the color prejudice and treat all as Americans should have the patronage of all citizens." Lawson, however, alienated blacks by attempting to lure the American Giants into the league and later made an effort to seize Washington Park from the Indianapolis ABCs. Meanwhile, one press release even claimed that "Darby, Pennsylvania resident Eddie Bohon was attempting to secure the Camden franchise."

With Lawson appearing an increasing threat to the NNL, opposition to the Continental League mounted, led by veteran sportswriter Ira Lewis. To Lewis, the Continental League represented another example of white baseball men "casting an eye to the possibilities of colored baseball," coincidentally after the NNL had enjoyed a successful season and had recently expanded by luring eastern teams into the fold. In addition, Lewis questioned the advisability of black players joining an outlaw league seemingly destined to fail. As Lewis noted, "After struggling along this far, under conditions that have been worse than bitter to the pioneers, it would be the height of folly to form any kind of a deal with white baseball men that would not assure to the colored player all the advantages given any other baseball player; and particularly the chance to ride into major league baseball." Lewis's misgivings proved correct. Despite continued announcements from Lawson, the league apparently never began its season, although the existence of a black Continental League franchise in Philadelphia was noted locally.[17]

The collapse of the Continental League, however, was largely overshadowed by the recent appointment of Judge Kenesaw Mountain Landis as commissioner of baseball in the aftermath of the 1919 Black Sox scandal. Black baseball fans hoped that Landis, viewed as friendly toward African Americans, might take steps to begin the integration of organized baseball. As the *Baltimore Afro-American* enthused, Landis was "eminently fair and if it was left to him, there would be colored major league baseball clubs tomorrow." Shortly after Landis took office, former Harvard black baseball star and attorney Billy Matthews wrote to the new commissioner soliciting his support for the fight against the color barrier:

> You will note that every other class of people are counted eligible to play in the big leagues. Why keep the Negro out if he can play the same grade of baseball demanded of the other groups? Are the big leagues more exclusive than the best colleges and athletic clubs in the land? Does an attitude on the part of the National Commission square with your plea of injustice to Afro-Americans? If baseball leaders would adopt the open door policy toward the Negro player, don't you think it would be another guarantee on their part that baseball in the future is to be on the level?

Despite his reputation for racial tolerance and supposed interest in black professional baseball, Landis was hardly an advocate for integration. During his lengthy tenure as commissioner, Landis avoided public discussion of the issue until the late 1930s, and then only to state that the time was still not right for black players in organized baseball. While pressure for integration would mount in the early 1940s, Landis continued to remain firmly opposed, even blocking an attempt by Bill Veeck to purchase the moribund Philadelphia Phillies and restock the team with black players. Shortly before his death in 1944, Landis finally addressed the issue of blacks in baseball: "There is no rule in organized baseball prohibiting their participation and never has been to my knowledge."[18]

Although Landis did nothing to advance the cause of integration during the 1920s, his famous 1922 suspension of Babe Ruth for violating rules prohibiting barnstorming by World Series participants would drastically affect the postseason interaction of white and black players. In response to the Ruth case, the National League and American League subsequently allowed barnstorming by World Series participants but limited barnstorming squads to no more than three players from a single team with league and commissioner permission required. Black teams, who had continued to fare well in exhibition games with major leaguers, viewed the ruling as yet another attempt to suppress interracial professional competition, which in recent years had faced increasing opposition from white officials. In 1921 several St. Louis sportswriters had severely criticized the St. Louis Cardinals for barnstorming against the NNL's St. Louis Giants. According to Robert Crepeau, the *Sporting News* "commented that it might be all right for the players to pick up a few extra dollars. On the other hand, in the eyes of the Cardinal fans it was 'bad stuff' to see their heroes participate in 'the grand African show.'"

Initially the new barnstorming rules had a limited effect on postseason exhibition games. In 1922 black professional teams had little difficulty securing organized baseball opponents in the off-season and achieved unparalleled success. The New York Bacharachs twice beat the world champion New York Giants, defeating Rosie Ryan (17-12, 3.01 ERA, ranked first in the National League) and Jack Scott, who had recently shut out the Yankees in the third game of the World Series. In the Midwest, the St. Louis Stars took two of three games against the Detroit Tigers (minus Ty Cobb and Harry Heilmann), and the Monarchs won five of six from the Kansas City Blues of the American Association. Other professional teams, including the Brooklyn Royal Giants, Cuban Stars, Indianapolis ABCs, and Cleveland Tate Stars, won several games against opponents from organized baseball. In 1923 black teams once again made a strong showing as Hilldale took five of six games against two barnstorming teams of Philadelphia Athletics, the Detroit Stars won two of three from the fifth-place St. Louis Browns, and the American Giants divided two games and tied a third with the Detroit Tigers.

The numerous defeats of organized baseball teams offered proof of the major league caliber of black professional teams. Noting Hilldale's victories over the barnstorming Athletics in 1923, A. Philip Randolph's *The Messenger* asked: "And now, who are really the World's Champions? Who are America's best players? Is there any reason why these Negroes should not play in the big leagues?" The *Baltimore Afro-American* hailed the postseason competition as the "real world's series" but bemoaned the limited coverage of the games in the white press. Several white sportswriters, however, did acknowledge the miserable showing of white teams in 1922 and 1923, although most chose to castigate major leaguers for their participation and gave little credit to their black opposition. In October 1922 the *North American* observed that "several teams with prominent major leaguers have been beaten in the last week by colored semipro teams and the showing made by the big league stars was said not to be first class." Commenting on the 1923 series between the St. Louis Browns and "a bunch of Negroes," a writer for the St. Louis based *Sporting News* voiced his dismay at the "spectacle of white major league players taking the abuse of mobs of our colored brethren and liking it or seeming to because of the few dollars netted."[19]

Despite restrictions, postseason barnstorming continued throughout the decade with Hilldale, Homestead, and the Baltimore Black Sox regular participants in the East, and the American Giants in the West. After mid-decade, however, black teams competed rarely against intact major league lineups and increasingly faced "all-star" teams of varying degrees of skill. After barnstorming against a powerful team of major leaguers featuring Lefty Grove, Heinie Manush, and Jimmy Dykes in 1926, Hilldale competed against two nondescript teams with barely a recognizable name in their lineups in 1928 and 1931, winning six of eight games. With permission required, many star players were prevented from participation, such as Jack Quinn and Mickey Cochrane of the Athletics, who were forced to sit out a game with the Lincoln Giants in 1925 for failing to secure prior authorization. Black professional teams, however, continued to face strong opposition yet continued to dominate postseason competition, to the chagrin of organized baseball. In reality, the superior showing of black professional teams was hardly surprising, as Bill Foster, Rube Foster's half brother and a successful pitcher in the Negro Leagues during the 1920s and 1930s, explained:

> The major league all-stars just didn't beat those teams, those Negro teams. See, we were organized as a unit, but they just came down there with one from here, one from there. They didn't have a whole lot of signals or anything like that. . . . An all-star, picked ball club is at a disadvantage in the technical part of baseball.[20]

Gene Benson observed that black players "played harder when we played the major leaguers because we were trying to prove something to them that we could play." Yet a number of major leaguers during the 1920s continued to show little respect for black players despite their skills and remained outwardly hostile toward all African Americans. In 1923 the Philadelphia Athletics were rocked by a controversy involving the Ku Klux Klan membership of several team members and the ineligibility of certain players because of religion or ethnicity. The later indictment (and subsequent acquittal) of Athletics pitcher Robert Hasty in the whipping of an African American woman in Marietta, Georgia, forced the usually conservative *Sporting News* to address the subject of racism in baseball, noting that the exclusion of the "Ethiopian" had deprived baseball of some of the "greatest players the game ever has known."

Although several prominent major league players were reportedly members of the Klan, racial attitudes differed widely in organized baseball, as in American society. Baltimore-born Babe Ruth, for example, considered being called "nigger" by bench jockeys "the worst insult of all," although his biographer Robert Creamer has observed that "his personal relationship with blacks over the years was amiable." Ruth regularly barnstormed against black teams, praised the ball-playing skills of John Henry Lloyd and Dick Redding, and even met publicly with black boxer Harry Wills in 1924. Nip Winters of Hilldale noted that the Babe was "a fine man to get along with, very friendly," and Bill Drake assessed him as "a regular fellow. . . . He used to chew tobacco. I'd say, 'Ruth, give me a chew.' He'd pull out a plug, give me a bite, he'd take a bite, put it back in his pocket." Ruth, however, was less than friendly in his comments about Cuban players after his tour of the island with the New York Giants in 1920: "Them greasers are punk players. Only a few of them are any good. This guy they calls after me [Christobel Torriente of the Chicago American Giants] because he made a few homers is as black as at a ton-and-a-half of coal in a dark cellar."[21]

While hardly outspoken advocates of integration, several noted players such as Casey Stengel, Lou Gehrig, Frankie Frisch, Walter Johnson, and Honus Wagner had no qualms about barnstorming against black players and appreciated their abilities. Cool Papa Bell, meanwhile, recalled Dizzy Dean as a "good guy" and praised the racial attitudes of Paul and Lloyd Waner as well as Jimmie Foxx, who was friendly with several black players, including Gene Benson, Oscar Charleston, and Webster McDonald.

Yet like Ty Cobb, the great Rogers Hornsby, a Texas native, openly expressed his contempt for African Americans. Hornsby occasionally boycotted games against black teams and as manager of the New York Giants in 1927, reportedly orchestrated the firing of the team's black trainer. Nearly 20 years later, Hornsby would react to the signing of Jackie Robinson: "They've been getting along all right playing together and should stay where they belong in their league."[22]

In Philadelphia, Lefty Grove and Al Simmons of the Athletics were known for their less than enlightened views of African Americans. Judy Johnson recalled his first appearance against Grove in 1926:

The best was beating Lefty Grove. He just hated us. It was nigger this and nigger that. I never wanted a hit so bad in my life as the first time I came up against him. I hit the first pitch he threw me right back at him. It took the cap right off his head and went right into center field for a single. Grove was pretty rattled. . . . I remember that hit more than any I ever got.

In later years, Grove denied ever playing against blacks, although there is ample evidence of postseason defeats to Hilldale in 1926 and the Baltimore Black Sox in 1928.[23]

The racial views of major and minor league officials also varied considerably during the 1920s. According to William Gibson of the *Baltimore Afro-American*, owner Jack Dunn of the Baltimore Orioles of the International League was "so full of race hate" that he would not allow his club to play the Black Sox and refused to lease his park to the team. In Chicago, the Cubs, owned by rumored Klan member William Wrigley, were hardly receptive to blacks. As Willie Powell of the American Giants noted, the Cubs were "very uppity. The White Sox didn't mind us playing in their park. But the Cubs didn't want us." In Washington, Senators owner Clark Griffith was a complex figure whose reputation for racial tolerance was primarily based on his liberal use of Cuban players during his managerial career, including Armando Marsans and Rafael Almeida in 1911 with the Cincinnati Reds, as well as Merito Acosta and Jacinto Calvo with the Washington Senators in 1913. Yet Griffith later refused to allow interracial games at Griffith Stadium during the 1920s and incurred the wrath of the local NAACP in 1925 by failing to include African American youths in a promotion at the park.

Despite occasionally shoddy treatment from Griffith and other major league owners, many African Americans remained dedicated fans of organized baseball, a dilemma never entirely resolved by black baseball officials. With Griffith Stadium located within easy access to black Washingtonians, African Americans eagerly patronized the Senators, to the chagrin of one *Washington Tribune* columnist: "All of us are quite interested in major league baseball and rightly so, but why not develop an interest in the semi-pros and sand-lotters?" After watching the Senators receive greater African American support than the newly organized Potomacs in 1923, local sportswriter H. Scott asked, "Why then, should we continue to support, foster and fill the coffers of a national enterprise that has no place or future for men of color, although they have the ability to make the grade." Comiskey Park, also located in a black residential area, attracted numerous African American fans, and in Philadelphia, John Howe of the *Philadelphia Tribune* criticized "colored adorers of the Athletics" who had no interest in black professional baseball. In St. Louis, blacks continued to patronize the St. Louis Cardinals and St. Louis Browns despite being forced to sit in a separate screened-in section at Sportsman's Park. In 1929, a St. Louis black newspaper chided fans who would rather "fork over six bits to see a game at Sportsman's Park . . . and get jim-crowed in the bargain" than attend games of the NNL's St. Louis Stars.[24]

As with white fans, World Series games were particularly popular with African Americans. Rube Foster regularly attended the fall classic each season, and C.I. Taylor kept a promise to take his entire team to a series game in 1917. With the Polo Grounds easily accessible to black fans, the 1921 series between the New York Giants and New York Yankees reportedly attracted over 25,000 blacks, causing the *Chicago Whip* to scold, "It is bad enough to ride on Jim Crow cars, but to go into ecstacies over a Jim Crow sport is unforgivable." In 1932 one commentator estimated that 20 percent of the 30,000 fans at Yankee Stadium for game 2 of the World Series were black. Even the black World Series was occasionally overshadowed by its white counterpart. During game 2 of the 1924 black World Series at Phillies Park, results of the white World Series game between the Senators and Giants were periodically announced, and many fans remained in the park to learn the final score.[25]

Some observers attributed the popularity of major league baseball to superior publicity available in the daily press. In Philadelphia, Otto Briggs noted that some blacks read only white newspapers and "very seldom go to see colored teams play." The *New York Amsterdam News* claimed in 1929 that there were "scores of people in Harlem that do not know there is a colored baseball club in the city." Another sportswriter agreed that the black press did not reach enough fans, remarking, "It is not uncommon to hear even youngsters calling the names of white players with ease — while it would give them a headache to name a Negro star." The *Philadelphia Tribune* noted that a group of young black children attending their first Hilldale game as guests of Bolden "had heard of the Cobb, Speaker, Hornsby, and Babe Ruth and other pale-faced stars but knew not that they had players of their own group who could hold their own with any stars of any league."[26]

Although white players attended black professional games on occasion, most had only limited contact with African Americans. In addition, the subservient position occupied by African Americans in organized baseball, as in American society, helped reinforce racial prejudices and stereotypes. As early as the 1900s, several major league teams hired African Americans as trainers, including Bill Buckner of the White Sox, Ed Mackal of the New York Giants, and Ed LaForce of the Pittsburgh

Pirates — all enjoying lengthy careers. (Trainers at this time performed no medical function but mostly handled equipment, like the clubhouse attendant of the modern game.) By the 1920s, several African Americans were employed as trainers in the American Association, Pacific Coast League, and other minor leagues. Yet black trainers, like all African American laborers, were susceptible to dismissal at the behest of whites. After the 1917 season Bill Buckner was terminated as trainer of the White Sox, reportedly because of Eddie Collins's dislike of African Americans. While Buckner was eventually rehired, trainer Doc Jamieson of the New York Giants would be fired because of manager Rogers Hornsby's prejudices.

The continued use of blacks as mascots or good-luck charms also undermined white racial respect. As early as the 1900s, several major league teams featured African American mascots, including the Pittsburgh Pirates, who hired Lovell Miller for $35 a month in 1902. By the 1920s, black mascots were still a common sight. The Nashville team of the Southern Association employed a "comical" mascot named "Rubber," and some semipro teams used mascots in games against black professional clubs. In Philadelphia, Mickey Cochrane of the Athletics had an "anonymous bat boy" named "Black Cat," and Connie Mack added two black mascots as good luck for the team's pennant run in 1925. Desperate for any progress in the fight for integration, the *New York Amsterdam News* applauded Mack's decision to hire mascots as "the most radical move any major league manager has made in the annals of baseball" and hoped that the presence of blacks in the Philadelphia clubhouse might change racial attitudes.[27]

The enthusiastic reaction to a black mascot underscored the lack of progress toward integration by the end of the decade. Yet the 1920s had been noteworthy for the continued strong showing by African American teams against opponents from organized baseball, offering convincing proof that their skills were equal if not superior to those of white players. As sportswriter and NNL official A.D. Williams noted, black players had not only defeated major league barnstorming teams but outperformed white players in the Cuban winter leagues. In addition, Williams cited Cuban players like Ramon Herrera, a veteran of both the Eastern Colored League's Cuban Stars and the Boston Red Sox, as proof of the caliber of black baseball. Several white journalists and officials had also attested to the high quality of professional black teams. In 1924, Mike Doolan, a former major league player and one of the umpires during the eastern games of the 1924 Hilldale–Kansas City series, classified both teams as "far better" than the International League, and Rodger Pippen, a sportswriter with the *Baltimore News*, lavished praise upon several Black

Sox in 1925: "Their ability astounded me. If colored players were permitted in the National, American and International Leagues, three or four of the Sox would have their names in big type in every sports page in the country."

Few white journalists, however, outwardly advocated integration during the late 1920s and would remain mostly silent on the issue until the early 1930s. One national publication, *The Nation*, briefly raised the issue in 1926, noting that while blacks participated alongside whites in college athletics, "the major leagues never admit even the most brilliant colored baseball player." Meanwhile, the short-lived journalistic discussion during the spring of 1928 typically accomplished little to change the status of black players, to their increasing frustration. As Jake Stephens noted, "You just knew you were better than the major leaguers. . . . Why, Chick Galloway of the Athletics didn't have anywhere near the range I had at shortstop. He couldn't carry my glove."

The early belief that the color line would fall if black baseball continued to develop proved a fallacy. The ECL and NNL, despite their numerous financial and administrative problems, had offered an exciting brand of baseball featuring some of the finest players in the country, yet the color line remained firmly intact. With race relations continuing to deteriorate nationally in the late 1920s, there seemed little immediate hope for relief, leaving African American players and their fans to contend as usual with the precarious fortunes of professional black baseball.[28]

9

A New Bolden and a
New League, 1928–1929

I still am ready to join a real league, which I
hope will be in existence some day.
— *Ed Bolden, April 1928*

Hilldale's return to independent ball was the first of several steps taken by Bolden in 1928 to ensure the club's survival in the increasingly bleak economic environment of black Philadelphia. Determined to restore team discipline and remain budget conscious, Bolden warned that "every player will earn his money or get out" and promised to "get rid of dissatisfied players and men who won't stay in condition." Bolden refused to sign Scrip Lee, a five-year veteran of the club, because of supposedly excessive salary demands and traded disciplinary problems George Carr and Nip Winters to Lincoln for first baseman Walter "Rev" Cannady and former Hilldale pitcher Red Ryan. In addition, Bolden overturned Charles Freeman's uneconomical decision to hire Bill Francis as a non-playing field manager and brought back outfielder Otto Briggs as captain. Hilldale's most important preseason move, however, was the acquisition of two of the disbanded Harrisburg Giants' best players, center fielder Oscar Charleston and pitcher Dalty Cooper.

The success of Bolden's revamped club during 1928 helped local fans forget the numerous disappointments and controversies of the prior two seasons. Featuring a powerful hitting attack led by sluggers Charleston, Mackey, and Thomas and a strong pitching staff spearheaded by Cooper and Cockrell, Hilldale won 52 of its first 68 games as an independent club, including nine consecutive victories in a preseason training tour through Virginia and the Carolinas. With the continued decline of the local semi-professional scene, few white teams were able to compete with Hilldale's

187

fearsome lineup, and the *Philadelphia Tribune* reported in June that "white clubs are refusing to meet the stronger race clubs." Hilldale, however, continued to obtain bookings throughout the season, especially in Northeast Philadelphia where the team was scheduled nearly every Friday against Wentz-Olney, Harrowgate, Frankford Caseys, Frankford Arsenal, and other white teams. Still, the disparity in strength was often apparent, and Briggs occasionally ordered Hilldale pitchers to let up or switched players from their usual positions to avoid embarrassing white clubs and losing subsequent bookings.[1]

In addition, Hilldale continued to book games against black teams, despite the collapse of the ECL, and had no trouble securing former league clubs as attractions for Hilldale Park. Commenting on Hilldale's full schedule, Bill Gibson of the *Afro-American* wrote, "There's any number of baseball men who would be willing to swap their right leg for Bolden's rabbit foot. No wonder he smiles despite his reported losses of yesteryear." Other eastern clubs fared less well in their return to independent baseball. The Baltimore Black Sox and Lincoln Giants were increasingly forced by late season to import white teams or weaker black professional clubs as opponents for Sunday games, and the Atlantic City Bacharachs, now under Ike Washington, owner of the Blue Kitten cafe in Atlantic City, also did poorly. The Cuban Stars spent much of the summer barnstorming through New England, and the Brooklyn Royal Giants toured upstate New York.

Not surprisingly, Nat Strong, still the major eastern park owner and booking agent, was least affected by the demise of the ECL. Along with his partner, Max Rosner, Strong continued to book black teams to face the Brooklyn Bushwicks nearly every Sunday at Dexter Park as well as scheduling two black teams on holidays. Interviewed in June 1928 by Romeo Dougherty of the *New York Amsterdam News*, Strong claimed that "Dexter Park is going just as big as it ever did . . . and you can tell the world that the colored teams get more money here than at any other place." Strong's $600 flat guarantee for a Sunday doubleheader at Dexter Park, though representing far less than what a team would earn on a percentage basis at the park, continued to remain alluring to black professional teams in the East. Meanwhile, Strong invested little money or interest in his Brooklyn Royal Giants, a club characterized by Rollo Wilson as "an old soldiers' home, a port for foundering hulks which have walloped through the seven seas of baseball."[2]

The collapse of the ECL also facilitated the ascension of Cum Posey's Homestead Grays, who added a number of former ECL stars to their already formidable lineup, including John Beckwith of the Harrisburg Giants and Martin Dihigo of the Cuban Stars. While the Grays had

Signed by Bolden after the collapse of the Harrisburg Giants, the temperamental superstar Oscar Charleston spent the 1928 and 1929 seasons with Hilldale. Charleston replaced Otto Briggs as team captain after a brilliant performance against the Homestead Grays at the close of the 1928 season (National Baseball Library and Archive, Cooperstown, N.Y.).

become an exceptionally popular drawing card in recent years and had successfully debuted against the Lincoln Giants in New York and Philadelphia in 1927, the team had yet to face Hilldale. With both clubs enjoying remarkable seasons in 1928, a meeting seemed inevitable, and Bolden made plans for Hilldale to travel to Pittsburgh for a series at Forbes Field in early September. To the disappointment of fans, Bolden was forced to cancel the series after he was unable to arrange the additional bookings necessary between Philadelphia and Pittsburgh to defray the substantial travel costs.

Finally Posey agreed to take his team to Philadelphia for a four-game series with Hilldale September 13–15. Heavy attendance was expected, and as *Tribune* sportswriter Randy Dixon noted, "No series that has been played in this town in recent years is creating as much interest as the Hilldale-Homestead engagement." The opening game at Elks Park at 48th and Spruce Streets drew 824 fans, the largest Thursday crowd of the year as Hilldale breezed to an easy 10–2 victory behind Dalty Cooper's eight-hit pitching. On Friday, Homestead, led by three home runs by Grover Lewis, evened the series with a 10–6 victory over Phil Cockrell before a crowd of 1,219 at Elks Park. Hilldale took the final two games, played at Hilldale Park on Saturday, September 15, sparked by brilliant performances by Oscar Charleston (two triples, a single, and a homer in game 1) and Rev Cannady (single and home run in game 2). The crowd of 2,948 on Saturday represented the team's highest paid attendance since May and would be surpassed at Hilldale Park only three times in the next three years. In a rematch two weeks later, Homestead won three of four games played at Pittsburgh and Columbus, although Hilldale was weakened by the absence of Mackey, Warfield, and Cannady, who had left to freelance with other clubs after the regular season's end on September 15.

The financial success of the Homestead series culminated Hilldale's successful return to independent baseball, and the team was reportedly the only eastern club to remain profitable in 1928, with the possible exception of the Grays. Yet attendance at Hilldale Park had continued to drop as a crippling recession had devastated the African American community in Philadelphia, resulting in vacated black stores and food lines for the unemployed. In the eight Saturday games at Hilldale Park prior to the Grays' appearance on September 15, the team drew only 7,019 fans, less than 900 per game. Meanwhile, Bolden had been forced to transfer Thursday games at Hilldale Park to Elks Park at 48th and Spruce in Philadelphia in June after attendance had averaged barely 300 fans per game.[3]

Ignoring economic realities, the *Tribune* blamed the attendance decline on the disbanding of the Eastern Colored League, claiming black fans had "acquired a taste for League baseball" and would "no longer support the other kind wholeheartedly." A number of sportswriters voiced similar sentiments, suggesting that a new league would revitalize sagging regional interest in black baseball and curb the sudden return of contract jumping among players. In August 1928 the Eastern Sportswriters Association (formed in 1927) proposed the formation of a new league and appealed to Bolden as "the man of the hour . . . the one individual . . . who can work order out of the present chaos." Despite Bolden's disagreements with newspapermen in the past, most respected his 18 years of baseball experience with Hilldale and his involvement with the NNL, ECL, and PBA. Bolden was cautiously optimistic in his response, noting that while he was "most heartily in favor of organized baseball," he was "not sure the time is opportune" because of financial difficulties. Still, Bolden suggested that "if parks can be procured, if the promoters will be unselfish and cooperate much good can be accomplished."

Cum Posey also seemed receptive to the idea of a league, especially after the Grays' successful swing through the East during 1928 with victories against Hilldale, Lincoln, and Baltimore. During the off-season, the possibility of a new eastern league featuring Hilldale and Homestead, the two most popular drawing cards in the region, was enthusiastically discussed in the black press. Yet Otto Briggs, a veteran of the strife-ridden ECL, remained pessimistic, noting that there were "too many little petty grievances among the owners . . . and rather than let bygones be bygones . . . they would rather run their teams independently and at the same time losing money." In December, however, Bolden announced that "after a careful survey of conditions existing last season," the Hilldale corporation had recommended the "reorganization of the Eastern Colored League" with an organizational meeting to be held in January 1929 in Philadelphia.

While supportive of a new league, players, fans, and sportswriters were anxious that the past mistakes of the ECL not be repeated. As Sol White, now a columnist with the *New York Amsterdam News,* wryly observed, "Several clubs can organize a league any time, but the thing of it is, what they will do with it after they get it." Briggs, for example, argued that a fair schedule, rotating umpires, nonpartisan president, and agreement with the NNL were necessary for success, and others called for stronger finances and greater cooperation among league owners. Not surprisingly, a general consensus developed against the involvement of Nat Strong's Brooklyn Royal Giants or any other traveling team. Although White claimed that Strong had been invited to the January meeting, Strong did not attend, secure in his profits at Dexter Park and indifferent to the progress of his Brooklyn Royal Giants.[4]

On January 15, 1929, the much anticipated organizational meeting was held at the Citizens Republican Club in Philadelphia with most of the former ECL owners in attendance as well as Posey and a representative of the Washington Black Sox. With Bolden as the driving force, the American Negro Baseball League (ANL) was launched with Hilldale, the Baltimore Black Sox, Lincoln Giants, Cuban Stars, Homestead Grays, and the Atlantic City Bacharach Giants as members. To no one's surprise, Bolden was unanimously elected the league's first president, demonstrating to doubters that his power was still considerable despite Nat Strong's absence and his recent disability. Posey, however, remained out of the league government as Lincoln Giants owner James Keenan was chosen as vice president and George Rossiter of the Black Sox was named treasurer. To handle league statistics, publicity, and various administrative functions, the league took the unprecedented step of appointing Rollo Wilson, a well-respected eastern sportswriter, as league secretary.

With five of the six original ECL franchises as members, the American Negro Baseball League initially appeared little more than a refurbished version of the earlier circuit. An 80-game split season similar to the ECL's was adopted, along with reserve clause, a system of fines and suspensions, and a plan for rotating umpires. As usual, scheduling was hampered by the presence of two traveling teams, the Homestead Grays and Cuban Stars, who lacked regular home grounds. The Grays, however, arranged to continue their occasional use of Forbes Field in Pittsburgh and leased Hooper Field in Cleveland; the Cuban Stars were to use league parks in Baltimore, Darby, and New York when available or neutral grounds like Dexter Park in Brooklyn and Island Park in Harrisburg.

Yet the ANL offered several promising contrasts to the Eastern Colored League. Its racial composition differed substantially from its predecessor with the involvement of only two white owners, James Keenan and George Rossiter, compared to four at the inception of the ECL. The new league was also less "top-heavy" than the ECL or NNL, with four of the six teams (Hilldale, Lincoln, Baltimore, and Homestead) closely matched in strength. In addition, Bolden's powers as league president exceeded his severely limited authority as chairman of the ECL and allowed him to implement several progressive policies. The ECL's seemingly unenforceable system of fines (from $25 to $100) was modified, and attacks on umpires or players were now punishable by a $50 fine or a 30-day suspension. In response to numerous complaints from fans of overlong games, the league imposed a new $5 fine for players whose arguments with umpires caused delays. Finally, the ANL attempted to hold down salary expenditures by setting roster limits at 14 players per team until June 15, with expansion to 16 by July.[5]

The appointment of Rollo Wilson as league secretary and the subsequent invitation of sportswriters to several league meetings conveyed the ANL's desire for a more positive relationship with the press. As chairman of the ECL, Bolden had not actively solicited press support and had alienated black sportswriters by limiting access to meetings and choosing white journalist Bill Dallas as the league's ill-fated umpire supervisor in 1924. After the ECL's collapse, however, Bolden had admitted that league publicity had been insubstantial and now realized the necessity of greater press involvement, especially with attendance and interest in decline. With Wilson as secretary, access to league information expanded substantially, although by July Sol White would request the ANL to "let us in on some things. . . . We might help you." League publicity, thanks to Wilson's outstanding efforts, would vastly improve, with statistics and standings published more regularly than in the past.[6]

Bolden's most significant accomplishment as president was the near completion of the league schedule. Following the NNL's precedent, a $500 deposit was required of all teams, contributing to greater adherence to the published schedule. In addition, the absence of Nat Strong, the ECL's largest stumbling block, facilitated cooperation by league owners. The Black Sox, for instance, vacated their park on Sunday, July 7, to play the Lincoln Giants in New York, yet their grounds in Baltimore remained occupied with a scheduled game between Hilldale and the Cuban Stars. While rain resulted in several cancellations, the ANL, in contrast to its predecessor, made a genuine attempt to replay postponed games. By the season's conclusion, five of the six league teams had played at least 60 of the 80 games scheduled, only the Cuban Stars falling short with 54.

Praised by Sol White as the "best we have had in the East," the more efficiently operated ANL represented a significant step above the ECL but still fell victim to the problems that had dogged the earlier circuit. The ANL was equally ineffective in its enforcement of league rules, as players who tested the new league's authority soon realized. For the second time in three years, Biz Mackey, accompanied by George Carr, Ping Gardner, and Connie Day of the Bacharach Giants, failed to report to Hilldale on time, choosing to barnstorm in Honolulu. While ANL rules specified that players who reported late would be suspended for each day missed, the four players were back in action within weeks upon their return in mid–June, setting a precedent for further evasions of league policy.

The league also proved unable to handle the argumentative and overly confrontational tactics of Homestead manager Cum Posey. As his critics anticipated, Posey was involved in a series of disputes with umpires and rival players, particularly in Philadelphia. On May 17 at Passon Field (formerly Elks Park) at 48th and Spruce, Posey refused to leave the game after being ejected by the umpire, and the game continued. In the ninth inning, an attack on an umpire by several Grays precipitated a near riot involving fans and several Hilldale players. Only two players were eventually suspended, and Posey received no disciplinary action. Two months later, on July 26, Posey once again refused to abide by an umpire's decision, resulting in a forfeit to Hilldale. Eager to placate the quick-tempered Posey, Bolden hired an additional umpire for the following day's game at Hilldale Park, causing one fan to remark that "Bolden seems to be afraid of Posey" as he "accedes to his every demand." Bolden, however, was apparently unwilling to risk alienating Posey, who was a valuable league ally.[7]

Despite the presence of Posey, the ANL was less marred by violence than the ECL had been in its last two seasons. Nevertheless, several players, particularly Jud Wilson of the Black Sox, continued to terrorize umpires without repercussion. In June the Bacharachs played the second game of a doubleheader in Baltimore under protest after Wilson was allowed to appear despite striking an umpire in the first game. Later in the season Wilson was involved in two more confrontations during a single week in August, throwing a bat at one umpire's feet in Baltimore and shoving another at Hilldale Park. Yet Wilson's status as a major star for the Black Sox protected him and other notorious umpire baiters like Oscar Charleston from serious penalty and symbolized a chronic difficulty faced by organized black baseball — the reluctance of most owners and officials to discipline players who were valuable drawing cards.

As president, Bolden once again received most of the blame for the league's failings. In August, Syd Pollock, the white owner of the independent Havana Red Sox, claimed in a widely published press release that Bolden had not "upheld the league rules, nor enforced 50 percent of them this season." Labeling the league a "joke," Pollock noted that several players who had jumped contracts with Alex Pompez's Cuban Stars to join the newly organized Stars of Cuba (reportedly backed by Nat Strong) had been allowed later to return to the ANL without penalty. While Bolden failed to respond, Posey denied the charges and defended Bolden's leadership. Attacking Pollock's credibility, Posey depicted him as an exploitive owner who underpaid his players at $90–$100 a month, accepted any guarantee offered, and deceived fans by prominently advertising a player named Smokey Joe Williams who was not the legendary pitcher.

League secretary and sportswriter Rollo Wilson also rushed to Bolden's defense with a surprisingly sympathetic column in the *Pittsburgh Courier* that simultaneously revealed the personal pressures faced by Bolden in his everyday life:

> The recent attacks on President Ed Bolden, of the new league . . . have been unfounded, unjust, and unethical. . . . This writer has occasion to know just how hard a job it is trying to run a baseball league where money is scarce, economic conditions are bad and a critical public expects perfection in everything. . . . Running the Hilldale club and directing the affairs of the American Negro League are together a job which few men would attempt and fewer still would succeed at. In addition to that, Ed Bolden is a man who works every day to make a living for his family. From 11 at night until 8 in the morning, six times a week, he can be found at the Central Post Office, Philadelphia, sorting mail. That's how much of a sinecure he has.
>
> Hilldale is handicapped by Bolden being the head of the league, if the truth must be known. It takes time which should be devoted to the affairs of his corporation. And being president of the league is a job which is open to anyone who is willing, and able, to take it under the same terms Mr. Bolden has it. There is no salary attached, you know.[8]

Despite external attacks, Bolden received his most hostile criticism during the season from local Hilldale fans, whom he had alienated with a series of mostly unpopular management decisions. In January, Bolden had continued his dismantling of his pennant-winning clubs of 1923–1925 by trading Frank Warfield and Red Ryan to the Black Sox for second baseman Dick Jackson and outfielder Crush Holloway. A month later Bolden pulled off another surprising deal, sending Jake Stephens and Rev Cannady to Homestead for Cuban superstar Martin Dihigo and George Britt. Yet Bolden's most startling move was the release of 37-year-old Otto Briggs, who had been replaced by Oscar Charleston as team captain after the Homestead series at the end of the 1928 season. With Clint Thomas already gone, Hilldale entered the season with only Phil Cockrell, Joe Lewis, Judy Johnson, and the still absent Biz Mackey remaining from the world championship team of 1925.

Local fans reacted negatively to Bolden's preseason moves, particularly the loss of Stephens and Briggs, two of the team's most popular players. The release of the highly respected Briggs, an 11-year veteran of the club, prompted a written protest from Hilldale fans, but to no avail. In a letter to the *Philadelphia Tribune*, one fan claimed that he was "surrounded by Hilldale fans who claim they have lost interest . . . and will follow the progress of the Athletics this summer." Bolden, however, gambled that fans would eventually accept his new club, especially with

Future Hall-of-Famer Martin Dihigo was acquired from the Homestead Grays prior to the 1929 season in an unpopular trade involving Jake Stephens. Despite earning the team's highest salary ($400), Dihigo proved to be a disappointment and reportedly sought his release by August (National Baseball Library and Archive, Cooperstown, N.Y.).

the presence of Oscar Charleston and Martin Dihigo, two of the best players in black baseball. Blessed with a powerful throwing arm, the 24-year-old Dihigo could play several positions and was also a fine hitter. On May 9, 1927, while a member of the Cuban Stars, Dihigo had belted two grand-slam home runs and a solo shot against Hilldale, and Bolden hoped for similar production.[9]

Despite the much anticipated pairing of Charleston and Dihigo, the team got off to a slow start and quickly fell behind in the ANL standings. Bolden's new club, assembled mostly through trades, lacked the cohesion and harmony of earlier Hilldale teams, a problem exacerbated by the temperamental Oscar Charleston's leadership. While Phil Cockrell replaced Charleston as team captain in mid–May, a tragedy at Hilldale Park disrupted the team soon after. On May 18, 1929, Lena Mitchell Strickland was shot and killed by Clifton Voinges, her estranged common-law husband, during the third inning of a game between Homestead and Hilldale with 1,909 fans in attendance. Strickland, involved in the local numbers scene, had recently separated from Voinges after a stormy four-year relationship. Voinges had searched for Strickland in vain until finding her at Hilldale Park where she was a regular spectator each Saturday.

Although a stunned Hilldale managed to win the game, the team would drop three of its next four league games, and eventually staggered to a 15-20 fourth-place finish in the first half of the ANL race, nine games behind Frank Warfield's Baltimore Black Sox. The Black Sox, rejuvenated by the acquisition of Dick Lundy and Oliver Marcelle in a pair of preseason trades with the Bacharachs, now featured one of the greatest infields of the 1920s with Jud Wilson at first base, Warfield at second, Lundy at shortstop, and Marcelle at third. A strong pitching staff also contributed to the team's success, anchored by Laymon Yokely with key contributions from former Hilldale pitchers Red Ryan, Scrip Lee, and Nip Winters.

Thanks to Phil Cockrell's steadying field leadership and the return of Biz Mackey and Jake Stephens, Hilldale substantially improved in the second half and led the league as late as mid–August. The team eventually finished second with a 24-15 record after being overtaken by the Black Sox, who won 12 of their final 13 league games. Hilldale's improved performance, however, would be overshadowed by a series of controversies during July and August that would nearly destroy the once solid franchise.[10]

Initially hailed by fans, Bolden's reacquisition of the popular Jake Stephens soon became a public relations nightmare for the club. Stephens, unhappy with the Grays, had jumped the team in early May to join Danny McClellan's New England–based Philadelphia Giants, earning him a suspension from the ANL. In late June, Bolden worked out a deal with Posey that sent Britt back to the Grays in exchange for Stephens, effectively negating half of the earlier trade. Stephens's return to Hilldale was short-lived as a dispute over his $206 debt to Homestead provoked a serious altercation with Bolden. On August 1, Stephens refused to appear in a game, claiming that the Hilldale corporation had agreed to pay his debt but had instead docked part of his salary. Yet Bolden insisted that Stephens's return to Hilldale had been contingent upon his payment of all prior obligations. After reportedly using "abusive and insulting language" during a subsequent meeting with Bolden, Stephens was suspended for "insubordination and slander," then left the club to rejoin the Philadelphia Giants.

Stephens, denounced by Bolden as an ungrateful "troublemaker," later denied that he had used bad language and claimed that Bolden had "informed me if I didn't give in, I was through playing ball." In addition, he maintained that his team loyalty was still intact and attributed the entire incident to Bolden's misguided acquisition of Martin Dihigo, a "high priced star who didn't fill my place because he couldn't." In response, Bolden noted that the corporation had once been "willing to make concessions" to Stephens but had "now decided that ball players must deliver the goods, pay their debts and be gentlemen or seek elsewhere for employment." Bolden's somewhat abrupt suspension of Stephens, however, exemplified his increasing impatience and frustration with professional ballplayers who unlike his amateur teams of 20 years earlier, would not respond to his "fatherly" leadership.

Bolden would exhibit a similar intolerance after another disquieting incident only four weeks later on August 29, 1929. After attending a party at a "questionable house" at 15th and Naudain, three Hilldale players, Joe Strong, Sam Warmack, and Dick Jackson, became involved in a violent brawl over 40 cents owed to Warmack by Strong. When Strong supposedly reached for a weapon, Jackson struck him with a brick, fracturing his skull. Bolden blamed Strong for the episode and showed surprisingly little sympathy to the injured player: "It's [Strong's] fault. He shouldn't be found in those kind of places. He was not in condition to play anyway, so if he has been fired it is no more than could be expected. We can't afford to be paying him while he is laying up in a hospital." In addition, Bolden, acutely aware of the team's diminishing public image, noted that "the club will suffer more than the one or two men directly concerned in the matter." Afterward, Randy Dixon, sports editor of the *Tribune*, would aptly remark, "All is not well in Hilldale camp. The fans sense it. The players admit it. And, the results prove it."[11]

Bolden's failure to secure an all-black umpiring staff at Hilldale Park provided a final devastating blow to the team's flagging image. Since the formation of the NNL in 1920, African American fans had increasingly demanded "race" umpires. Yet with the predominance of white umpires in the past, only a handful of blacks possessed the experience and training necessary to umpire, forcing team owners to make a difficult choice between race consciousness or business sense. The NNL, after considerable pressure from league fans, had launched a comprehensive attempt to hire black umpires in 1923, only to dismiss most of them within two years. The league continued to employ black umpires after 1925 but failed to commit to an exclusively black umpiring crew. Meanwhile, the ECL had used several black umpires during its existence, although most were paired with a white umpire, as at Hilldale Park. No black umpires had been used in the World Series, except for 1927 when the NNL's Billy Donaldson officiated in the western games.

While some players argued that white umpires were no more competent than black umpires, many owners still believed that whites were more capable of enforcing discipline on the playing field. The presence of white umpires was seen as a greater deterrent to violence. Players were perceived as less willing to rebel against white authority and could expect harsher punishments for attacks on white umpires. In addition, white umpires, as nonresidents of the local African American community, were less susceptible to the taunts and threats of players and fans, especially after the game's end. S.B. Wilkins, a former western sportswriter, noted that fans often refused to accept the "word of the arbiter of color" and "are of the belief that a white man cannot be mistaken." Even Rube Foster reportedly stated that he "never saw a 'nigger' yet that could umpire."

Others, like A.D. Williams of the *Kansas City Call*, argued that white umpires were no more successful in suppressing violence in the NNL and "had suffered more harm at the hands of the players than have Negro umpires," particularly in Chicago. Williams maintained that the NNL's black umpires, when supported by league officials, "rendered about as good service as could be expected from any umpires anywhere and of any color." Yet black umpires, like their white counterparts, were constantly undermined by weak and inconsistent enforcement of league policies and the interference of owners. In the early 1920s, the owner of the NNL's short-lived Pittsburgh Keystones, fearful of the possible effect on attendance, prevented Franklin Miller, an Afro-American umpire, from ejecting Rube Foster from a game in Pittsburgh. Meanwhile, manager C.I. Taylor of the ABCs reportedly attempted to use his league authority to prevent his ejection from games.[12]

By the late 1920s, local African Americans were less tolerant of white umpires, especially with the continued deterioration of race relations in Philadelphia during the decade. The increase in residential segregation had resulted in a corresponding decline in contact between blacks and whites, undermining any attempts at improving interracial understanding. Even sporting events, one of the few opportunities for positive interracial interaction, had become characterized by mounting segregation. In 1927 fans attending a basketball game at the Arena at 46th and Market between the black Renaissance team of New York and the white Phillies of the National Court League were segregated into black and white seating sections, and a year later, black golfers found themselves barred from the Cobbs Creek golf course.[13]

The *Tribune*, recognizing the growing prejudice toward African Americans, forcefully addressed the subject of black umpires in an editorial in 1927 but avoided directly criticizing Bolden and Hilldale:

> Regardless of the reason for colored ball games having white umpires it is a disgusting and indefensible practice. . . . It will require much thought and perhaps time and money . . . but the owners of ball clubs owe [it] to their patrons to discontinue a practice that is a reflection upon themselves, the ballplayers and the Negro race.[14]

While racially mixed umpiring crews continued to be employed at Hilldale Park through the 1928 season, the formation of the ANL in 1929 resulted in a greater commitment to hire African Americans. The ANL, eager to avoid the criticisms faced by the ECL over the use of whites, selected several blacks for its umpiring staff, including veteran arbiter Caesar Jamison and former players Bill Gatewood at Atlantic City, Frank Forbes at Lincoln, and Judy Gans at Hilldale. White umpires, however, continued to be used, and with the release of Gans in early July, local fans began to note the conspicuous absence of a black umpire at Hilldale Park.

In August, "Dubria Ardee" (probably a pseudonym for *Tribune* sports editor Randy Dixon) noted that other league cities, including Pittsburgh, Atlantic City, and New York, had retained black umpires and warned of a "genuine revolt among local fans" if Hilldale didn't "adjust the umpire situation." Yet Bolden, always the racial pragmatist, was seemingly no longer willing to take chances with inexperienced black umpires, especially with the presence of the argumentative Cum Posey. Nevertheless, white umpires proved no better, including one umpire, MacDonald, whose obvious bias toward Hilldale ("Come on, fellows, let's get some runs") angered rival league teams and earned him a quick dismissal.[15]

With economic conditions worsening for many black Philadelphians, the employment of whites by an African American corporation was viewed as particularly objectionable and seemed to provide a convenient rationale for the continued exclusion of blacks from local industries like Bell Telephone and American Stores on the basis of racial inferiority. Echoing this sentiment, the *Philadelphia Tribune* took the unusual step of criticizing Bolden and the Hilldale corporation in two strongly worded editorials appearing on August 1 and August 8, 1929:

NEGRO UMPIRES AT HILLDALE

> In order to maintain order and discipline it is necessary according to the reasoning of Hilldale's management — to have a white man oversee the

game. It is a reflection on the ability and intelligence of colored people. *Are we still slaves?* Is it possible that colored baseball players are so dumb that they will resent one of their own race umpiring their game? Or is it that the management of Hilldale is so *steeped in racial inferiority that it has no faith in Negroes?* Aside from the economic unfairness of such a position the employment of white umpires at Negro ball games brands Negroes as inferior. It tells white people in a forceful manner that colored people are unable to even play a ball game without white leadership. It is a detestable mean attitude. There is no excuse for it. Hilldale depends on colored people for its existence. If the management lacks sufficient racial respect to employ Negro umpires the public should make it listen to reason.

HILLDALE AGAIN

The *Tribune* believes that the only reason the Hilldale management has white umpires is because it has an inferiority complex. The officials believe that everything white is better than everything colored. Their attitude proves it. As a matter of fact Hilldale can secure the services of better colored umpires than it can white. Then, too, colored ball players may have sense enough to rebel against an unfair white umpire. They might resent the thought which seems to obsess *certain owners* that colored ball players will accept any decision so long as it comes from a white man. Thank God ball players are no longer slaves. They do not think that everything white is perfect and everything black is evil.[16]

The controversy at Hilldale provoked a similar incident in Baltimore, where no black umpires had been used at Maryland Park during the season. In contrast to Bolden, Black Sox owner George Rossiter responded to the public outcry and attributed the absence of "race umpires" at Maryland Park to the usual claims of black incompetence and inexperience. Observing that his attempted use of black umpires in preseason games had been greeted with "numerous squawks from players and fans," Rossiter predicted the continued presence of white umpires until better black umpires had developed. Nevertheless, Rossiter recognized the dilemma facing black umpires: "The colored umpire does not have the advantage that the white umpire has, in passing from sandlot ball to the minor leagues and then to the majors. He must come just as the average player does, from the sandlot right to the 'big show' and as a result of his inexperience is not able to deliver the goods." Despite Rossiter's promise to use black umpires "if any first-class arbiters apply," the *Baltimore Afro-American* insisted that "if the Sox management were colored, we'd have colored umpires tomorrow. . . . White umps at Black Sox park must go, and the sooner the better." White umpires, however, remained in place in Hilldale and Baltimore through the end of the season, although changes were expected for 1930.

The future of the ANL seemed very much in doubt at the season's close. The league's significant advances in schedule completion and owner cooperation had been largely overshadowed by the unfavorable publicity generated by the umpiring controversy. In addition, the ANL's efficient operation could not compensate for the declining economic prospects of urban blacks, who increasingly found baseball more a luxury than a necessity. In Atlantic City, the Bacharachs reportedly averaged only 300–400 fans per game, prompting manager Ben Taylor to quit the team in disgust after remarking that "no man can make any money out of baseball there." At Hilldale Park, average attendance fell for the third consecutive year, dropping from 1,600 per game in 1928 to less than 1,400 in 1929. The team was also burdened by a heavy payroll of nearly $4,000 per month, led by Martin Dihigo at $400 and Oscar Charleston at $375.[17]

The Homestead Grays, despite high preseason expectations, were also a disappointment, financially and on the playing field. Weakened by a midseason car crash, the Grays managed only a 35-28 overall record in the ANL and were involved in a number of violent disputes with umpires. Meanwhile, Cum Posey's interest in league baseball had gradually waned, and his attempt to seize several western players, including a young pitcher by the name of Satchel Paige of the Birmingham Black Barons, had prevented a new agreement with the NNL. By August, Posey was ready to return to independent baseball and began planning a series of raids on eastern clubs. Posey's addition of Judy Johnson and Oscar Charleston of Hilldale, Clint Thomas of the Bacharach Giants, and Jake Stephens of the Philadelphia Giants for Homestead's postseason barnstorming tour suggested his intentions for 1930.

Meanwhile, the NNL, still headed by Hueston, had continued to flounder financially. The league operated with only six teams in 1929 after the 1928 collapse of yet another ill-fated Cleveland franchise and the demotion of the Cuban Stars to associate status. Like the ANL, the league was plagued by bad publicity, with several incidents involving the Detroit Stars. The team was threatened with expulsion after several players were accused of throwing a game to the Chicago American Giants in 1927 and the arrest of two team officials for robbery in 1928. The Stars were revived under new ownership but were devastated by a fire at Mack Park in July 1929 that injured over 100 fans and the subsequent disclosure that the team's black "owner," Mose Walker, was actually a front for white park owner John Roesink. The ascension of Roesink, who reportedly refused to compensate fans injured in the fire, and the increasing presence of white backing in Chicago, Kansas City, and other league cities was an unhappy reminder to midwestern fans of the NNL's failure to achieve Rube Foster's dream of an entirely African American–financed league.

After reaching its financial peak in the early 1920s, organized black baseball appeared to be at a crossroads entering 1930, a mere decade after the ground-breaking formation of the Negro National League. Despite Foster's optimistic predictions, league baseball had failed to eradicate the involvement of white owners, umpires, park owners, and booking agents and had been unable to prevent the resumption of player raids between East and West. In addition, the expected growth of salaries and profits did not materialize, as a result of the deteriorating conditions of African Americans after mid-decade. While Foster's American Giants had been paid salaries totaling nearly $4,000 a month in 1920, NNL teams were limited to a monthly salary cap of $2,750 in 1929. With seemingly little progress in recent years, several sports commentators, including Al Monroe of the *Chicago Whip* and Bill Gibson of the *Baltimore Afro-American*, expressed disgust at the stagnation of the two leagues and claimed to be "fed up on colored baseball."[18]

With the stock market crash in October 1929 dealing another crushing blow to the nation's African Americans, the future of Hilldale and other black professional teams seemed more shaky than ever. As expected, the American Negro League collapsed in February 1930, and Bolden, confident that Hilldale could no longer exist in its present form in the current economic climate, quietly began to dissolve the club. Bolden did not renew the lease at Hilldale Park and began to ship the team's property to Passon Field at 48th and Spruce in Philadelphia where he expected to launch a new team, "Ed Bolden's *Hillsdale* Club," financed by local white promoter Harry Passon. Commenting on the presumed end of the original Hilldale corporation, Rollo Wilson expressed dismay that "the members of the corporation could not adjust the personal differences which have shattered the morale of the outfit for the past three years! The labors and renown of almost twenty years, have been dissolved in a menstruum of bitterness. The grown men responsible should be treated as boys and thoroughly spanked."

With the 1930 season ready to begin, the fate of Hilldale was still undecided with rumors circulating that Lloyd Thompson's Darby Phantoms of the racially mixed Inter-Urban League would replace Hilldale. Finally, three members of the corporation, James Byrd, Lloyd Thompson, and former president Charles Freeman, joined to block the dissolution of the club and succeeded in obtaining a new lease at Hilldale Park. Hilldale's last-minute revival, compounded by the Lincoln Giants' move to Philadelphia for weekday games, forced Bolden to abandon his plan for a new team.[19]

To most observers, Bolden seemed all but finished. Despite his eagerness to please the fans, build a winning team, and organize a successful league, Bolden's willingness to make concessions to white promoters, backers, and umpires had made him an increasingly unpopular figure, as had his decisions to trade or release favorite Hilldale players in recent years. Randy Dixon of the *Tribune* provided a devastating critique of the Hilldale president's 20-year career:

> The history of the success of the erstwhile postal clerk reads like a dime best seller. He led a group of mediocre performers through the pitfalls of public opinion, built up a real following and guided the Hilldale Corporation to the heights of Negro baseball. . . .
>
>   . . . Bolden proved himself a traditional if not typical cullud man by playing "Uncle Tom" and taking his advantages to the Nordic faction. He cut the Negro Press off his list. He favored the white brethren on all sides. . . .
>
>   . . . When the American League folded up, Bolden came through with a subsequent statement that Hilldale had dissolved. The Daisy dynasty had ended. He got Nordic backing. Made arrangements to take something that had been nurtured by colored people and was a colored institution and bend it in such a manner as to fill the coffers of the Nordic. Not maliciously or intentionally perhaps, but such was the case or almost the case.
>
>   Lloyd Thompson had stepped in and thwarted Bolden at every turn and now the man who was once a king is now a piker and Ed Bolden is through. We mean THROUGH![20]

10

End of a Team,
End of an Era, 1930–1932

Don't forget Hillsdale [*sic*]. That organization has helped the game wonderfully in days
past.
— *Sol White, 1930*

Twenty years after joining the Hilldale Field Club as a 14-year-old
boy in 1910, Lloyd Thompson now found himself in the unlikely position
of corporation president. Employed as a carpenter, Thompson had been
heavily involved in black baseball as secretary of the Hilldale corporation,
press agent for the ECL, freelance sportswriter and cartoonist for the
Philadelphia Tribune, and most recently manager of the amateur Darby
Phantoms. Thompson, however, was faced with the unenviable task of
replacing Ed Bolden and rebuilding a team nearly destroyed by recent
front office conflict. With the team's existence in doubt until late spring,
several of the club's best players, including Judy Johnson, Jake Stephens,
and Oscar Charleston, had defected to Cum Posey's Homestead Grays,
leaving Thompson and manager Phil Cockrell with a severely weakened
lineup of inexperienced youngsters and fading veterans.

Operating once again as an independent team, Hilldale continued
to defeat most white semipro opponents during 1930 but could no longer
compete against black professional clubs. Hampered by weak pitching,
the team lost 11 of its first 12 games against former league rivals Baltimore
and Lincoln, including a May 11 doubleheader sweep by Lincoln by the
humiliating scores of 22–4 and 14–3. In a desperate attempt to secure
talent, Thompson gave tryouts to dozens of local players, including several from his Darby Phantoms club, and signed several castoffs from other
eastern teams. In May, Thompson lured Oliver Marcelle, Dick Seay, and

Otis Starks from the Brooklyn Royal Giants but was forced to withdraw his offer after threats of retaliation from Nat Strong. Although Thompson managed to sign two former Hilldale players, Chaney White and Martin Dihigo, neither remained with the club for the entire season, White joining the Homestead Grays in July and Dihigo returning to the Stars of Cuba. Noted pitcher Webster McDonald left Hilldale after only a month, returning for his annual summer engagement with Little Falls, Minnesota, of the white Northern League.

The reliable play of Hilldale veterans Biz Mackey and Phil Cockrell provided the season's rare highlights, as Cockrell hurled his sixth no-hitter, a 5–0 decision over Cape May on August 14. Otto Briggs, resigned after a one year absence, helped stabilize the outfield defense, and newcomers Oscar Levis and Jess Hubbard also made solid contributions. Nevertheless, the team's general mediocrity and the onset of the Depression severely limited interest among local fans, who disgustedly denounced the Darby Daisies (as they were increasingly referred to) as "an apology for a real ball club." The team's 16 Saturday games at Hilldale Park drew a total of only 7,319 fans, and attendance failed to exceed 1,000 except for Memorial Day, July 4, and Labor Day. By August, the team was taken off salary and was placed on the co-op basis for the first time since 1916. Overshadowed by Lincoln, Homestead, and Baltimore, Hilldale's future appeared in jeopardy, and as Randy Dixon warned, "Unless the Daisies want to pass out, they must produce a winner."[1]

The 1930 season, however, proved a financial nightmare for much of black baseball. In the East, the Atlantic City Bacharachs finally disbanded after a series of disastrous seasons. Alex Pompez's Cuban Stars failed to reorganize and were replaced by Pelayo Chacon's Stars of Cuba. Homestead, Baltimore, and Lincoln also struggled financially despite dominating the opposition. In September, a much anticipated 10-game series between Homestead and Lincoln (won by Homestead, six games to four) played at Yankee Stadium, Forbes Field, and Bigler Field in Philadelphia was a financial failure for Lincoln owner James Keenan. Within six months, the Lincoln Giants would disband after losing their grounds at the Catholic Protectory Oval.

The NNL also fared poorly despite president Hueston's preseason assertion that there was "nothing the matter with the league." By July, Hueston was forced to admit that "something must be done for Negro baseball" and advocated the formation of a new eight-team league consisting of four eastern and four western teams. Hueston's circuit, hardly feasible in the current economic climate, failed to materialize, and similar proposals for eastern-based leagues attracted little support. In the Phila-

Lloyd Thompson (Cash-Thompson Collection, courtesy Afro-American Historical and Cultural Museum, Philadelphia, Pennsylvania).

delphia area, a six-team mixed league with Hilldale, Baltimore Black Sox, and four white semipro clubs (Trenton, Camden, Wilmington, and Chester) was briefly considered but eventually rejected. Despite gaining considerable support from local promoters, a later proposal for the similarly organized InterState League would also be rejected in 1931.

With no league baseball, eastern teams returned to the barnstorming practices of a decade earlier but found opponents fewer and less lucrative. Paying games became rare as guarantees were cut to $50 to $75 per game or eliminated altogether. The heavy competition for bookings led several teams to avoid the congested Midatlantic black baseball scene, including Danny McClellan's Philadelphia Giants (based in Providence, Rhode

Dignitaries at Opening Day at Hilldale Park, May 3, 1930. First row, left to right: Royal Weaver (mortician), E. Washington Rhodes (editor of *Philadelphia Tribune*), Magistrate Ed Henry (politician). Second row: John Drew (politician), William Allmond (mortician), John Long. Third row: George Godfrey (boxer), Lloyd Thompson. Within a year, Drew would assume ownership of Hilldale (Cash-Thompson Collection, courtesy Afro-American Historical and Cultural Museum, Philadelphia, Pennsylvania).

Island, in 1930), Frank Wickware's Burlington Giants (Burlington, Vermont, and Bridgeport, Connecticut), and Chappie Johnson's Colored Stars (Canada). Other clubs returned to the gimmicks of the past such as the clowning Harlem Black Sox and Syd Pollock's Havana Red Sox, who donned beards and became the Cuban House of David in 1931. Like Hilldale, most clubs abandoned salaries and returned to the cooperative plan with profits shared between club and players.[2]

Despite numerous setbacks, the season was salvaged by the advent of night games, a development that would profoundly transform and revitalize baseball. Experimentation with various lighting arrangements had continued during the 1920s, and in 1930 the Kansas City Monarchs became the first club successfully to employ a portable lighting system. The Monarchs' portable lights initiated night baseball in numerous parks, including Forbes Field in Pittsburgh and Hamtramck Stadium in Detroit, and allowed games to be scheduled at more convenient hours for fans unable to attend afternoon or twilight games. Realizing the lucrative financial possibilities of night games, several teams began to obtain lighting arrangements. Despite Nat Strong's initial opposition, a permanent lighting system was installed at Dexter Park, with night baseball debuting on July 23, 1930, and achieving instant popularity among fans.

In Philadelphia, Hilldale scheduled its first night game on July 1, 1930, at the recently built Sesqui Stadium against a team from the South Philadelphia League. The game was postponed because of rain, and other night games scheduled at the stadium were marred by poor lighting. In 1931, several night games were played locally through the use of portable lighting systems provided by visiting barnstorming clubs such as Grover Cleveland Alexander's bearded House of David team. On August 26, 1931, the first night game at Hilldale Park was played, Hilldale defeating the House of David 8–1. An amazing 2,166 fans attended the Wednesday night game, surpassing the season's largest Saturday crowd of 1,915 on opening day. Within a year, permanent lighting arrangements would be installed in Philadelphia at PRR Field at 44th and Parkside and Frankford Legion Field at Pratt and Large Streets.[3]

The season was also noteworthy for a new wave of players, teams, and owners who would play a significant role in the future history of black baseball. The Pittsburgh Crawfords, formed as a local sandlot team in the 1920s, became a professional club in 1930 under the control of numbers boss Gus Greenlee and began to challenge the Homestead Grays for superiority in western Pennsylvania. While operating less prominent teams, owners Abe Manley of the Camden Leafs and Syd Pollock of the Cuban House of David continued to gain valuable experience and would soon be major powers in organized black baseball. Meanwhile, the Homestead Grays featured a young slugging catcher named Josh Gibson, who was picked off the sandlots and soon dazzled fans with his home-run prowess. Another future great, Satchel Paige, began to attract nationwide attention in 1930. Paige, pitching for the Baltimore Black Sox, beat Hilldale twice in 1930, including a five-hit shutout on June 8, 1930. A year later, Phil Cockrell would outduel the young Paige on a four-hitter, beating him 3–1 on August 15, 1931.

In contrast, Bolden and Foster, the two dominant leaders of black baseball during the 1920s, remained inactive during 1930. Despite early optimism, Foster never fully recovered from his mental collapse in 1926 and died on December 9, 1930, at 51. Foster's death, mourned by thousands of African Americans nationwide, foreshadowed the imminent final collapse of the Negro National League and underscored the leadership void in black baseball since his collapse in 1926. Foster, while brusque and heavy-handed at times, had managed to provide a vision and sense of purpose that no eastern or western owner had been able to duplicate. While even a healthy Foster may have been unable to offset the effects of the Depression on black baseball, the aimlessness that had characterized the game in recent years might have been avoided.

Bolden, meanwhile, already reeling from his thwarted attempt to dissolve Hilldale, received another blow in August with the news of a possible demotion. Perhaps due to league, team, and personal pressures, Bolden's annual efficiency rating at the post office had slipped from 100 percent in 1926 to 91.7 percent in 1930, below the 95 percent necessary to retain his status as special clerk. In a letter to the Philadelphia postmaster, Bolden cited his prior excellent record and asked for a chance "to show my efficiency by checking up on my conduct and amount of work accomplished." In addition, Congressman James Wolfenden of Bolden's voting district in Delaware County wrote a letter on his behalf, noting that "he is one of the outstanding men in the community in which he lives and, in fact, a leader in civic affairs among his people." Although Bolden was placed on probationary status at the post office for six months, he was eventually allowed to retain his position with no loss of pay.

With his employment situation resolved, Bolden began to orchestrate a comeback. In early 1931 the *Philadelphia Tribune* reported that Bolden, "much the better after a year's rest and in improved health," planned to organize a new team backed by white booking agent and park owner Harry Passon, with John Henry Lloyd, who had recently resigned from the Lincoln Giants, to manage. Bolden's proposed club appeared especially threatening to Hilldale, which despite the efforts of Lloyd Thompson and his associates, had ended the 1930 season on the verge of bankruptcy.[4]

Yet for the second consecutive season Bolden would find his ambitions blocked by unexpected developments involving Hilldale. Lacking the finances to attract superior talent, Lloyd Thompson turned to John Drew, a wealthy black Delaware County politician and businessman who had made his fortune by starting a bus line in Darby, later selling to Philadelphia Rapid Transit at a substantial profit. Drew, realizing that investment in Hilldale would be not only a popular public-relations move but a chance to restore the team to its past glory and profitability, agreed to provide the backing for a new Hilldale team in 1931. The original Hilldale corporation was dissolved, and on March 11, 1931, the team was reincorporated as the Hilldale Club, Inc., with Drew as principal owner

Action at Hilldale Park c. 1930 (Cash-Thompson Collection, courtesy Afro-American Historical and Cultural Museum, Philadelphia, Pennsylvania).

with 197 shares and Byrd, Freeman, and Thompson holding one share each. With Hilldale preserved for another season, John Henry Lloyd announced that he would not join any team threatening the existence of an established club, and Bolden's plans quickly dissolved.

With his most formidable competition removed, the diminutive Drew began his comprehensive rebuilding project. While admittedly a "rank novice" as a baseball magnate, Drew's ownership philosophy soon attracted the notice of players:

> The initial plank in my base ball platform is that the Negro player has never received his worth in monetary consideration. . . . I will never be satisfied to operate baseball along lines that have produced nothing but failure. The player is the source of the game. The Negro player has never received enough salary for his contribution to the game.[5]

Reinstituting salaries, Drew succeeded in coaxing back Judy Johnson (as manager), Nip Winters, Jake Stephens, Martin Dihigo, and other former Hilldale players. After purchasing Hilldale Park, Drew invested over $14,000 in improvements, adding a clubhouse with plumbing facilities, administrative offices, a ladies' rest room, and a new grandstand featuring box seats with individual chairs. Two large cars were obtained for team travel, and arrangements were made for local radio station WELK to broadcast Hilldale news. Drew even enlisted Oscar DePriest, the country's only black congressman, to throw out the first ball on opening day on May 2 and secured the presence of NNL president Hueston. In response to past complaints, a greater effort to hire black umpires was promised by the new Hilldale leader.

A 4–0 victory over the Baltimore Black Sox on opening day at Hilldale Park quickly revealed the team's new direction to local fans, leading Randy Dixon to note, "It is a foregone fact that the Daisies are going to emerge from their cellar hideout of last season." Under Drew's ownership, Hilldale had its last great season in 1931, compiling a 120-31-4 record, and regained much of the good will lost after the disastrous 1929 and 1930 seasons. The team featured a hard-hitting yet strong defensive outfield of Martin Dihigo, Chaney White, and former Harrisburg Giant Rap Dixon, reliable play from still-productive veterans Mackey and Judy Johnson, and a pitching staff spearheaded by Phil Cockrell (23-3 overall record) and Webster McDonald. McDonald sandwiched a 9-1-1 record with Hilldale around his summer stint in Little Falls and helped offset the disappointing return of Nip Winters, who was released in June for various rules infractions. After returning to Hilldale in August, McDonald threw three consecutive shutouts and later defeated a mediocre team of major league players in October.

Despite a successful season on the playing field, Hilldale's financial difficulties continued during 1931. While average Saturday attendance at Hilldale Park jumped from 652.7 in 1930 to 1,108.4 in 1931, crowds still failed to approach their pre–1930 standards. In addition, the return of Thursday games at Hilldale Park after a three-year absence attracted only marginal interest, as attendance averaged less than 200 fans per game. Meanwhile, twilight games with local white semipros became increasingly unprofitable, forcing Hilldale to schedule an unprecedented three games per day on September 13 and September 19, a practice soon to be common in black baseball during the 1930s. As the *Philadelphia Tribune* observed, Hilldale and other professional teams had fallen victim to the "depression wave. The clubs have played top notch ball but the old gold is not there as in the past."[6]

In New York interest in black baseball continued to decline during 1931 despite the formation of a successor to the disbanded Lincoln Giants that featured several former Lincoln players, including manager John Henry Lloyd. Organized with the assistance of African American dancer-entertainer Bill "Bojangles" Robinson, the new team, known as the Black Yankees, was rumored to be partially financed by major league owners Jake Ruppert of the New York Yankees and Charles Stoneham of the New York Giants, who agreed to lease the Polo Grounds and Yankee Stadium to the club. Both owners recognized the potential income from park rentals to African American teams, especially after the successful debut of black baseball at Yankee Stadium for a benefit game for the Brotherhood of Sleeping Car Porters on July 5, 1930. Ruppert, however, apparently objected to the use of the name Black Yankees, and the team underwent several name changes during the season, including Bill Robinson's Brown Buddies, Bill Robinson's New York Stars, and Harlem Stars. Black Yankees would eventually prevail, despite the complaints of its "'Uncle Tom' ring" by some sportswriters, and the team was even outfitted with uniforms previously worn by the New York Yankees.

To the disappointment of local fans, the Black Yankees would play only a handful of games at Yankee Stadium and the Polo Grounds during 1931 due to low patronage and exorbitant rental fees totaling 33 percent of the gross receipts on occasion. Hoping to spark local interest, the Black Yankees attempted a return to "theatrical ball" without success, and by August the team's major financial backers — Bill Robinson's manager, Marty Forkins, and John Powers — withdrew their support. At the end of the season, the team was even forced to return its uniforms to the Yankees, culminating, as Romeo Dougherty of the *Amsterdam News* would lament, New York's "worst season in Negro baseball." While a rumored return by James Keenan never materialized, the Black Yankees were rescued by the subsequent involvement of African American nightclub owner M.E. Goodson, his associate James Semler, and the omnipresent Nat Strong, the team's New York booking agent.[7]

Despite unfavorable economic conditions during 1931, the eastern black professional baseball scene remained saturated, as numerous teams attempted to obtain bookings. Several professional clubs were formed in the Midatlantic region during 1930 and 1931, including the Newark Browns, Washington Pilots, and a new Philadelphia-based version of the Bacharach Giants under the ownership of Harry Passon, whose earlier attempts to organize teams with Bolden had failed. Initially consisting of players from former Hilldale pitcher Charles Henry's ill-fated Detroit Giants team, the Bacharachs eventually attracted a number of former Hilldale stars, including Otto Briggs and Nip Winters, and obtained home grounds at Passon Field at 48th and Spruce.

In New England, the Providence Giants were launched in 1931 with backing provided by Jude James Dooley, a local white football and hockey franchise owner, and "Daddy" Black, underworld leader of Providence's African American community. Featuring a number of former ECL stars, including Oliver Marcelle, Jess Hubbard, Luther Farrell, and Cliff Carter, the Giants became a member of the mostly white Boston Twilight League. Other eastern teams such as the Brooklyn Royal Giants, Pennsylvania Red Caps, Stars of Cuba, Baltimore Black Sox, Danny McClellan's Philadelphia Giants, Syd Pollock's Cuban House of David, and the Homestead Grays continued to operate, as well as the fast-rising Pittsburgh Crawfords, who now featured Satchel Paige, Jimmy Crutchfield, and other established players. With most clubs forced to cut expenses to survive, rosters and salaries continued to shrink, and luxuries such as train travel became increasingly a thing of the past.[8]

As in 1929, a number of observers advocated a league to cure black baseball's ills. Randy Dixon felt that a league would provide "an interest and a purpose" currently lacking in eastern black baseball and represented "the only solution . . . enabling the owners to pay their minions salaries commensurate with their talents." As in 1930, several league rumors surfaced during the season, including Black Yankees promoter Marty Forkins's suggested 12-team American Negro Baseball League, to be headed by local African American politician Ed Henry and proposals from Dixon and Washington Pilots secretary S.B. Wilkins. A planned 26-game round-robin series to be held in Philadelphia in September received strong support from eastern clubs but was rejected because of scheduling difficulties.

Once again, Cum Posey of the Homestead Grays provided the driving force necessary to launch a new organization and quickly gained support after announcing his intention to form a league in October. While the Grays had enjoyed another successful season in 1931, fashioning a 143-22-2 record and a 4-3 mark against Hilldale, Posey had become increasingly alarmed by competition and player raids from Gus Greenlee's Pittsburgh Crawfords and hoped to destroy or weaken the Crawfords by excluding them from his proposed circuit. Although Posey did not formally bar the Crawfords, his insistence that Greenlee sign a five-year league contract and allow Posey or his brother to run the team ensured the team's nonparticipation. Rejected by Posey, Greenlee focused his efforts on the construction of Greenlee Field, the Crawfords' new stadium, which would be completed in time for the 1932 season and would provide more access to local black fans than Forbes Field.[9]

In January 1932 Posey presided over an initial two day organizational meeting held at the Majestic Hotel in Cleveland with most of the leading figures in black baseball in attendance, including John Drew and Lloyd Thompson of Hilldale. The new East-West League was formed, consisting of the Homestead Grays, Hilldale, Baltimore Black Sox, Cleveland Stars, Newark Browns, Washington Pilots, Detroit Wolves, and Syd Pollock's Cuban House of David (who would be known as the Cuban Stars after agreeing to shave their beards in time for the start of league play). The presence of Pollock, an enemy of Posey's only three years earlier, was a surprise, as was the inclusion of the barely established Newark Browns. Yet Posey was determined to shun all contact with Nat Strong and had chosen the Browns instead of the Strong-booked Black Yankees as his New York–area representative.

The inclusion of Cleveland and Detroit was questionable as well, particularly in view of the expensive travel involved. Yet Posey hoped to exploit the considerable void in the Midwest left by the virtual collapse of the NNL during 1931. Despite the apparent consensus for league baseball, the NNL had proved equally susceptible to the devastating effects of the Depression. Unable to remain profitable in the current economic climate, the Kansas City Monarchs had withdrawn from the NNL in April 1931 and did not reorganize until July. The loss of the Monarchs, the league's most stable franchise, and the simultaneous defection of the Birmingham Black Barons and Memphis Red Sox to the reorganized Negro Southern League severely crippled the already fragile NNL, causing Frank Young of the *Chicago Defender* to remark: "Has the death of Rube Foster ended all possibilities of a successful western league? Our answer is that it looks very much that way." While the league survived a miserable 1931 season, the NNL would finally collapse in March 1932, leaving the Midwest open to Posey's newly formed East-West circuit.

While the East-West League adopted the commission form of government employed during the first four years of the ECL, Posey as chairman clearly dominated league proceedings. Determined to avoid the mistakes of prior leagues and provide "competition to big time white baseball," Posey mapped out an ambitious program with several features unique to black baseball. To cut down on the reliance on white independent teams and their booking agents, daily league games were planned for the first time, and a 112-game split season was adopted. The league took the unprecedented step of hiring the renowned Al Munro Elias Baseball Bureau to compile and distribute regular batting and pitching statistics to 50 newspapers, secured a $3,000 radio contract to broadcast game results, and planned to use major league parks at Pittsburgh, Washington, and Cleveland when available. In addition, an exclusively black umpiring staff was recruited, placed on monthly salary, and freed from the control of individual owners. A reserve clause was to be enforced, each team allowed until June 1 to reach a roster limit of 15 players.[10]

With the wealthy Drew as league treasurer and $1,000 deposits received from each team, the EWL seemed assured of success, leading the usually critical Romeo Dougherty to characterize Posey as the "smartest man in baseball." Posey and other black baseball owners, however, did not suspect that the crippling effects of the Great Depression had only begun to be felt by African Americans. As the nation's economic woes worsened during 1932, black workers, typically the last hired and first fired, would suffer more acutely than whites. Unemployment rose dramatically as increasing numbers of black workers found their positions eliminated or held by whites. In Philadelphia, black unemployment during the Depression would peak at 56 percent in 1932 as thousands of blacks lost jobs due to severe cutbacks in the building and construction trades. Victimized by low-paying jobs and high rents, few African Americans had adequate savings to survive a prolonged period of unemployment, forcing many to turn to public assistance for survival. In 1931 blacks had comprised over 35 percent of the families receiving aid in Philadelphia despite constituting only 11 percent (220,000) of the city's population.[11]

John Drew, while supportive of Posey's project, realized the need to address the current economic crisis. At a March 31, 1932, Hilldale corporation meeting, the monthly salary limit was slashed to $2,200 with "all other expenses . . . curtailed as much as possible." Angered by expected salary cuts, several players did not return to the club as Rap Dixon and Rev Cannady signed with the Pittsburgh Crawfords, Bill Yancey with the New York Black Yankees, and Webster McDonald with the Washington Pilots. Martin Dihigo and Biz Mackey rejected contract offers as well, and as one local columnist noted, "There is much dissatisfaction brewing out Hilldale way." The corporation's decision to discontinue the use of a team chauffeur also irritated Hilldale players, particularly Bud Mitchell, who was increasingly forced to handle driving duties. Mitchell, the lowest-paid Hilldale player in 1931 at $100 a month, would later be released in May after refusing to drive without a raise in pay.

Meanwhile, the EWL became embroiled in a controversy prior to the season's outset with the disclosure of league chairman Cum Posey's involvement with three league teams. Posey had assumed control of the newly formed Detroit Wolves (mostly composed of the recently disbanded St. Louis Stars) yet continued to maintain his management of the Homestead Grays by placing his brother Seward at the helm and had also obtained a financial interest in the Cleveland Stars. The news confirmed the suspicions of John Clark, the Crawfords' publicity man, who since the league's inception had relentlessly attacked the organization as a "Posey League" designed to benefit only the Homestead owner. Posey downplayed the charges, but not even Rube Foster, who had lent financial assistance to weaker teams and had helped establish others, had ever attempted to operate more than a single NNL franchise. Randy Dixon, citing the league's "weak supports," predicted that "despite denials to the contrary, the early death of the East West League is almost a sure thing."

As anticipated, the EWL was a disaster from the onset, crippled by poor attendance in league cities, high travel expenses, and several rainouts. By June, Posey was forced to suspend his feud with Gus Greenlee, accepting the Crawfords and the New York Black Yankees into the league as associate members, and agreeing to schedule 11 league games at Greenlee Field. As the EWL continued to flounder in June, Posey in desperation discontinued daily league games and the use of salaried umpires and canceled the league's arrangement with the Elias Bureau for weekly statistics. In addition, to reduce traveling expenses, the Homestead Grays absorbed the Detroit Wolves, a move perceived by some as a further example of Posey's opportunism. The league, however, was virtually near collapse with the last-place Newark Browns on the verge of bankruptcy and Syd Pollock's Cuban Stars preparing to withdraw to participate in tournaments in Denver and Iowa.[12]

For Hilldale, the season was a failure on and off the playing field. Decimated by the loss of Mackey, Dihigo, and Rap Dixon, the team found itself in sixth place in mid–June with a 9-16 record, playing before record low crowds at Hilldale Park. Only 910 fans had attended Hilldale's May 7 opener against the Newark Browns, and attendance during June averaged less than 200 fans per Saturday and under 50 for weekday games. With local fans incapable of financially supporting the team, Drew lowered grandstand ticket prices at Hilldale Park from 75 cents to 50 cents and bleacher seats from 50 cents to 35 cents in hopes of stimulating attendance. In addition, Hilldale, like several other EWL teams, abandoned monthly salaries and returned to the cooperative plan, management to receive 25 percent of each game's net profits, the remainder to be divided among the players. As a result of the EWL's decision to halt daily baseball, the team also began booking games with local independent teams.

The corporation's maneuvers proved futile as attendance remained modest at Hilldale Park and net profits from semipro bookings failed to exceed $40-$50 per game. Sensing the team's ultimate fate, manager

Judy Johnson jumped to the Pittsburgh Crawfords in late June and was replaced by Phil Cockrell. A general exodus of Hilldale players followed with the defection of Chaney White, Frank Dallard, and Porter Charleston on July 17 providing the final blow. After playing a previously arranged game in Newark that day, the club disbanded on Monday, July 18, 1932. The team's future had been sealed by the sparse crowds at Hilldale Park on the prior two Saturdays with only 99 fans in attendance on July 2 and 196 for the team's final game in Darby on July 9. After the team's collapse, the remaining Hilldale players jumped to other professional clubs, and others joined a new "Hillsdale" club under Charles Freeman, which briefly secured local bookings.

In a terse statement to the press explaining his decision, Drew perceptively noted that "present conditions are such that the fans do not have money to spend on baseball." Nevertheless, local African Americans mourned the loss of the team that had provided exciting entertainment for over 20 years and whose victories had been a rare source of community and racial pride. While the collapse of Hilldale was only one of numerous black business failures during the Depression, the *Philadelphia Tribune* took the unusual step of eulogizing Hilldale in its July 28, 1932, edition:

HILLDALE'S PASSING

John Drew put money and time into Hilldale Baseball Club last year with the hope that this club, which had grown from an amateur sand-lot aggregation to a world championship, might continue to set records and give recreation to thousands of those who love the national sport.

Box office receipts continued to fall off in spite of greatly improved park facilities and good games. This year Hilldale failed to attract the fans in large numbers.

The folding up of Hilldale is most unfortunate, regardless of the cause. The general business depression may be responsible for the passing of one of America's greatest baseball organizations.

Hilldale paid many thousands of dollars to its players. Many of these men were valuable citizens with buying power.

The *Tribune* hopes that when next season comes around Hilldale will be carrying on again with flying colors. Philadelphia needs Hilldale. It is a business institution which has contributed much to the financial advancement of Colored citizens.[13]

Drew's substantial income from his numerous investments would have allowed him to continue to operate Hilldale at a loss during 1932, and the growth of night baseball in 1933 and the legalization of Sunday baseball in 1934 might have reversed the team's financial misfortunes. Yet

With Hilldale near collapse during the 1932 season, Judy Johnson jumped to the Pittsburgh Crawfords where he spent the remainder of his career (National Baseball Library and Archive, Cooperstown, N.Y.).

Drew, disheartened by reported losses of $8,000 in 1931 and $10,000 in 1932, refused to revive the club. In later years he was surprisingly bitter about his short-lived involvement with Hilldale and would claim that he had been "brainwashed" into believing the team would earn money. Drew was particularly disappointed by a perceived lack of cooperation by local fans:

> Negro fans do not have the proper sense of values. . . . Last year [1931] I was criticized for having dollar box seats and they told me that was too much to charge for a colored team. When we played the white All Stars up at the Phillies' park I saw at least eight hundred Negro fans sitting in the grandstand seats which cost them a dollar. Among them were many who had refused to pay a dollar at Hilldale.[14]

Former Hilldale pitcher Webster McDonald, however, would later blame the team's demise on Drew's failure to cultivate profitable relationships with white promoters and his unwillingness to conform to standard practices in black baseball:

> Johnny Drew . . . didn't last long. He didn't believe in some of the systems we had in our league. See, back then most of the teams would come here to Philadelphia to play us because we had a park exclusively to ourselves in Darby, south of town. We could play three games a week at night. And we'd also play a six o'clock twilight game somewhere against one of these industrial teams. But on a Sunday when some of our teams weren't booked up against each other, we used to have some good spots in New York against the Bushwicks. Anyway, a booking agent booked you to play where you couldn't book yourself, to keep your team from being idle, and you had to pay him 10 percent. And that, Johnny Drew refused to do. He said he would sit down and pay his ball club for the season even if he didn't play a ball game, rather than play an exhibition game. So he finally dropped out.[15]

The deteriorating economic situation undoubtedly exerted the most profound influence on Drew's decision to suspend operation. Syd Pollock, whose Cuban Stars also lost heavily in 1932, noted that with the "existing Depression . . . no one can blame promoters who have sunk hundreds of dollars into the game when they decide to call in their uniforms until such a time as conditions pick up and the baseball fans go back to work at regular wages." By August, Cum Posey was forced to shut down the East-West League, admitting that he had "picked the wrong time." Most teams would finish the season in debt, including Posey's Homestead Grays, who would suffer their most unprofitable year to date. Posey's rival, Gus

Greenlee, did poorly as well; his seemingly stable Pittsburgh Crawfords reportedly lost $16,000 in 1932.

White organized baseball, after surviving the 1930 and 1931 seasons reasonably intact, would also feel the full effects of the Depression in 1932. Minor league baseball was hit especially hard, and by August several leagues had collapsed, including the Southeastern League, Cotton States League, Inter-State League, Three-I League, Eastern League, Arizona-Texas League, and Western Association. Higher minor league classifications like the Pacific Coast League and American Association reduced ticket prices, and the International League cut team rosters from 20 to 18 players. Major league and minor league salaries were slashed, and by 1933 a Class D player was lucky to make $50 a month. As in black baseball, the advent of night games and improving economic conditions would revitalize the minor leagues by the close of the decade.

Major league owners reportedly lost $1.2 million in 1932 as total attendance fell to 3.5 million, a nearly 70 percent drop since 1930. In Philadelphia, the Phillies and Athletics combined to draw only 674,414 fans at Shibe Park and the Baker Bowl in 1932, a far cry from the previous decade's peak attendance of 1.1 million in 1925 and 1929. The Phillies, despite finishing in fourth place with their best record since 1917, drew only 268,914 fans, and the second place A's fell to 405,500 after reaching 839,176 only three years earlier. Both teams would continue their attendance slide in 1933, perhaps somewhat exacerbated by Connie Mack's breakup of his pennant-winning 1929–31 clubs, and would combine to draw 453,559 fans, less than Mack's sixth-place A's had drawn at Shibe Park in 1923. By 1936, major league baseball would finally stabilize, although a series of poor Philadelphia teams would limit attendance growth locally until after World War II.[16]

Black baseball would also survive the Depression, and its local revival would be spearheaded by the familiar figure of Ed Bolden. After two years of inactivity, Bolden launched a comeback beginning in February 1932 with a speech, "Progressive Ideas in Modern Baseball," delivered before the Darby Phantoms athletic club. Bolden, a compelling and eloquent speaker, so impressed the organization that he was named an honorary member and then asked to assume control of the Phantoms' football, basketball, and baseball teams. After being assured of absolute authority, Bolden accepted the offer and quickly focused his attention on the promising Darby Phantoms baseball team, which had won three consecutive championships in the mixed Inter-Urban League from 1929 through 1931 and sent several players to professional teams. Bolden began aggressively promoting the team and his return and launched ambitious plans to elevate the Phantoms to professional status, as he had done with Hilldale two decades earlier.

Despite regular bookings and the addition of several professional players, the young Phantoms attained only modest success as a traveling team and were consistently overmatched by more experienced opponents. By 1933, Bolden had abandoned the club to return to professional black baseball with white booking agent Eddie Gottlieb as co-owner of the recently organized Philadelphia Stars. Disillusioned by Bolden's abrupt withdrawal, Ray Macey of the Phantoms questioned how "a mind completely encompassed with the thought of enacting another Horatio Alger, has suddenly lost interest." In addition, Macey suggested the team of young amateurs had been manipulated by Bolden's "flowery scented words" into a premature and near fatal leap into professionalism. While Bolden's desire to return to professional baseball was understandable, his apparent exploitation of the Phantoms once again revealed a callousness and cynicism that had become increasingly apparent after his 1927 breakdown, particularly in his tactless handling of veteran players in 1929 and calculated attempt to dissolve the club in 1930.[17]

Not surprisingly, Bolden's new club featured the involvement of several former Hilldale players with Biz Mackey named as team captain, Dick Lundy as manager, and Webster McDonald as secretary. Frank Dallard, Rap Dixon, Jake Stephens, Chaney White, Cliff Carter, and Porter Charleston were added and Bolden confidently expected the team would "make this city forget its baseball headaches of recent seasons." As Bolden continued preparations for the Stars' inaugural season, Gus Greenlee finalized plans for a new Negro National League that would include the Chicago American Giants, the Homestead Grays, Detroit Stars, Indianapolis ABCs, and the Columbus Blue Birds in addition to his Pittsburgh Crawfords. In contrast to Posey's ill-fated EWL, the new NNL planned no "extravagant policy of every-day league baseball" and promised to cut admission prices in "keeping with the times." The Kansas City Monarchs and New York Black Yankees, however, declined to join the circuit, which would be victimized by contract jumping and unstable franchises during its first season of play.

While Bolden and Gottlieb had attended a March meeting of the new league held in Philadelphia, the Stars also remained outside of the circuit during 1933 and operated as an independent. Like nearly all Depression black professional teams, the Stars were unsalaried with receipts divided among Bolden, Gottlieb, and the players. Securing regular local bookings during its first season, the team was positively received by fans, who viewed the club as the logical successor to Hilldale. Bolden, careful to emphasize

Ed Bolden. After yielding control of Hilldale in 1930, Bolden later revived his career as part owner of the Philadelphia Stars (Cash-Thompson Collection, courtesy Afro-American Historical and Cultural Museum, Philadelphia, Pennsylvania).

the connection between his past and present clubs, reportedly promoted the Stars as "Hilldale" for a Sunday doubleheader in Brooklyn and leased Hilldale Park briefly in August.

Harry Passon's Bacharach Giants, still featuring Nip Winters, Phil Cockrell, Otto Briggs and other former Hilldale players, also attracted a strong local following and provided the Stars with their most serious competition during 1933. Ironically, the Bacharachs and Stars, the two most logical successors to Hilldale's local throne, had both been organized with the financial assistance of white promoters. Bolden's initial alliance with Passon and subsequent affiliation with Gottlieb suggested his realization that an African American corporation like Hilldale could no longer function in the current Depression environment. The influence of individual African American entrepreneurs like Bolden and Posey would be considerably lessened in the future as professional teams would be increasingly financed by black vice leaders like Abe Manley in Newark or with the assistance of Abe Saperstein and other white promoters.[18]

Although the Stars and Bacharachs joined Greenlee's league in 1934, the Bacharachs found themselves overmatched and would remain for only a single half season. Meanwhile, the Stars, led by young pitching sensation Stewart "Slim" Jones, captured the second half flag and then defeated Robert Cole's Chicago American Giants for the league championship in a series marred by disputes over ineligible players. While the Stars would never win another league championship, the club would survive the Depression and eventually stabilize, thanks to the increasing popularity of night baseball, the legalization of Sunday ball in 1934, and the return of economic prosperity during World War II. The success of the Stars would help to rekindle local interest in black amateur and semi-pro baseball, exemplified by the development of the Suburban Colored League in 1934 and the Eastern Seaboard League in 1937 as well as the ascendancy of Black's Meteors in the early 1930s. Formed by South Philadelphia mortician George Black in 1932, the team began to build a strong local following at their home grounds, the Sons of Italy Field at 26th and Snyder, and continued their success into the 1940s under Ben Cain.

Surpassed by Bolden's Philadelphia Stars, the Bacharach Giants continued to operate locally into the 1940s, functioning as a lower level club where local sandlot products like future stars Gene Benson and Roy Campanella could receive needed experience and fading veterans could prolong their careers. Other once formidable eastern teams followed similarly undistinguished paths, such as the Brooklyn Royal Giants, who managed to survive into the late 1930s despite the death of Nat Strong in 1935 at the age of 61. In Baltimore, the Black Sox were sold by George Rossiter by 1934 and were eventually supplanted by the NNL's Baltimore Elite Giants as the leading local club. In New York, the Black Yankees paled as successors to the Lincoln Giants and would gain notoriety as the weakest team in the Negro National League. An attempted revival of the Harrisburg Giants was aborted by the death of Colonel Strothers in 1933.[19]

Yet several leading eastern clubs of the 1920s would outlast the Depression and continue to prosper into the following decade. The Homestead Grays recovered from the 1932 East-West League debacle as Posey secured the financial assistance of black racketeer Rufus Jackson, joined the NNL permanently, and began operating out of Washington at Griffith Stadium and the Pittsburgh area by the late 1930s. While the rival Pittsburgh Crawfords were forced to disband after 1938, the Grays successfully operated through the 1950 season, four years after Posey's death in 1946. Former Cuban Stars owner and numbers banker Alex Pompez also remained actively involved, resurfacing as the owner of the New York Cubans of the NNL in the late 1930s after fleeing the country, receiving immunity for testifying against several gamblers. After the integration of organized baseball, Pompez helped sign several Latin American players to major league contracts and later served on a committee to select Negro League players for the Baseball Hall of Fame before his death in 1974 at the age of 84. Syd Pollock, owner of the Cuban Stars in Posey's ill-fated EWL, later became owner of the Cincinnati-Indianapolis Clowns. In 1952, the Clowns' traveling secretary, former Hilldale infielder Bunny Downs, signed Hank Aaron to his first professional contract.

Bolden remained active with the Stars and held several offices with the Negro National League yet would never achieve the influence that he had enjoyed during the 1920s with Hilldale. The NNL was dominated by Cum Posey's Homestead Grays, who won 10 pennants during the league's existence from 1933 to 1948. In the West, the Kansas City Monarchs achieved remarkable success as a member of the Negro American League, a second professional circuit formed in 1937 with several of the original NNL cities included. With two leagues once again in existence, the black World Series of the 1920s was revived in 1942, as the Monarchs defeated the Grays. The Grays, however, would eventually recover to win three World Series, including the final one played in 1948.

While eagerly anticipated by fans, the postseason contests were overshadowed by the annual East-West game at Comiskey Park. The East-West game and its white major league counterpart, the All-Star game, made their initial appearance in 1933 and featured the game's best players, usually chosen by fans. Attracting huge crowds that reportedly topped 50,000 on two occasions, the East-West game consistently generated considerable publicity in white and black newspapers and accomplished in a single game what longer championship series had failed to do in several.

Ironically, the unparalleled success of the East-West game would contribute to the ultimate collapse of organized black baseball. Recognizing the exceptional skills of black professional players and the existence of their numerous fans for the first time, several white sportswriters began to advocate the integration of organized baseball in the 1930s. Discussion of the issue would escalate by the end of the decade and continue into the 1940s with the African American press assuming an increasingly active role. The signing of Jackie Robinson, a 26-year-old shortstop with the Kansas City Monarchs, in October 1945 by general manager Branch Rickey of the Brooklyn Dodgers climaxed the long assault on major league baseball's color line. Yet Dave Malarcher, a veteran observer of black baseball and former Chicago American Giant, argued that the path to integration had actually been paved "when the major leagues saw those 50,000 Negroes in the ball park [at the East-West game]."

Bolden, unlike several of his contemporaries, was heartily in favor of the integration of organized baseball, and was hopeful that it would accelerate the development of black professional baseball, as he related to Rollo Wilson in May 1945:

> If any player of mine is considered good enough for any manager of the majors to want to sign, I am willing for him to have his opportunity to advance and I would be willing to talk terms for his contract. . . .
>
> Contrary to what Cum Posey and some of the others think, I believe that so-called colored baseball would be improved. The players would give you their best efforts for they would know that they were in a position to make the big leagues and to get in they would have to be on their toes at all times. Our leagues, therefore, would have a better brand of baseball and there would be more youngsters coming into the game because it would have a real future.
>
> The majors could then use our leagues as developing posts for the colored boys not quite able to stand the pace. They would get more experience and our clubs would be strengthened.

Robinson's successful debut with the Brooklyn Dodgers in 1947 and subsequent signings of other black players effectively destroyed professional black baseball. Attendance dropped substantially as African American fans shifted their attentions to the performance of Robinson and other black big leaguers. Simultaneously, the growth of television caused interest in white semipro baseball to wane by the early 1950s, exemplified by the disbanding of the Brooklyn Bushwicks and Doherty Silk Sox in 1951. With few profitable bookings available and patronage and interest in decline, the Negro National League collapsed in 1948. Absorbing several NNL franchises, including Bolden's Philadelphia Stars, the Negro American League managed to survive until 1963.

Biz Mackey with Joe DiMaggio c. 1938 (courtesy John Holway).

Ed Bolden lived to see his dream of an effectively operating African American professional baseball league shattered. After retiring from the post office in 1946 after 42 years, Bolden was finally able to devote his attention fully to his "hobby" and spent the final years of his life operating the Philadelphia Stars with Eddie Gottlieb. With the loss of the team's home grounds at 44th and Parkside after the 1947 season, the Stars' final years were spent mostly on the road except for occasional games scheduled at Shibe Park. Bolden remained with the club until his death at 69 on September 27, 1950, fittingly occurring as professional black baseball neared its demise, a victim of the recent integration of the major leagues.[20]

Hilldale remained a part of the collective memory of the local African American community for years after the team's collapse in 1932. The half-white-owned Philadelphia Stars never evoked the emotional response that Hilldale had elicited, and many fans looked nostalgically back to the 1920s when Hilldale had stood atop the black baseball world. In addition, Hilldale Park continued to be used by black semipro clubs like the Darby

Cubs in the 1930s and would later be equipped with lights and serve as the home grounds for a new Hilldale Daisies team in the 1940s. Organized in 1942 by former league players Webster McDonald and Fats Jenkins, the club eventually joined Branch Rickey's ill-fated United States Baseball League in 1945 but passed out of existence soon after.

The team's legacy was also preserved by a number of former players who remained in the Philadelphia area after their playing days were over, like Louis Santop, who became a bartender and was involved with local Republican politics. Meanwhile, former Hilldale stars Biz Mackey, Martin Dihigo, and Oscar Charleston enjoyed lengthy careers in professional black baseball as managers or players. Mackey, nearly 50, managed the NNL's Newark Eagles to the world championship in 1946 and continued to make occasional pinch hitting appearances. Others, like Crush Holloway and Phil Cockrell, desperate to stay in baseball, became Negro League umpires after their careers had ended. Sadly, several notable Hilldale players did not reach their sixtieth birthdays. Frank Warfield, still active as a second baseman and captain of the EWL's Washington Pilots, died in 1932, closely followed by former teammates George Johnson in 1940, Louis Santop in 1942, and Otto Briggs in 1943. Phil Cockrell was tragically murdered in 1951 in a case of mistaken identity, and Oscar Charleston dropped dead of a heart attack in 1954 after managing the Philadelphia Stars for several years.

With the death of Bolden in 1950, the aging of local fans familiar with the team, and the subsequent collapse of professional black baseball, memories of Hilldale faded by the 1960s. The park was demolished, the property converted into a farm and eventually sold to Acme Markets by John Drew. A supermarket occupies the spot today. Meanwhile, most players, unlike their white contemporaries, were doomed to live out their lives in relative obscurity and poverty. Webster McDonald waited on tables and distributed linen in the dining rooms of two Philadelphia banks after his retirement from baseball. Clint Thomas and John Henry Lloyd both became janitors. Biz Mackey became a forklift operator in Los Angles but lived to see his protégé Roy Campanella become a successful major league catcher. As manager of the Baltimore Elite Giants in the late 1930s, Mackey helped shape the development of Campanella, a 16-year-old South Philadelphia native who had joined the Elites in 1937 after stints with the Bacharach Giants and other local semipros. Mackey's influence would also benefit Earl Battey, a young Los Angeles catcher who later spent 13 years in the major leagues from 1955 to 1967.[21]

In the last 25 years, renewed interest in the history of professional black baseball sparked by the publication of Robert Peterson's *Only the*

10. End of a Team, End of an Era

Ball Was White in 1970 and the election of Satchel Paige to the Baseball Hall of Fame in 1971, has allowed Hilldale players to escape years of anonymity. Four of the 10 former Negro Leaguers subsequently enshrined in the Hall of Fame appeared with Hilldale during their careers, including Judy Johnson (1918, 1921–1929, 1931–1932), Oscar Charleston (1928–1929), Martin Dihigo (1929–1931), and John Henry Lloyd (1923). Judy Johnson, who granted numerous interviews before his death in 1989, contributed invaluable recollections of Hilldale and black baseball during the 1920s and 1930s. In addition, Negro League historian John Holway was able to interview several former Hilldale players, including Jake Stephens, Clint Thomas, Doc Sykes, Webster McDonald, Scrip Lee, Nip Winters, and Crush Holloway before their deaths.

Lloyd Thompson, the only individual involved in both the formation and the disbanding of Hilldale, continued to chronicle the team's exploits in various local articles until his death in 1987 at 91. Thompson's extensive collection of Hilldale financial documents, correspondence, scorebooks, and photographs is now housed in the Afro-American Historical and Cultural Museum in Philadelphia. Like Thompson, other members of the Hilldale corporation would enjoy remarkable longevity. George Mayo, who spent 18 years with Hilldale as a player and corporation member and later operated a successful house-painting business, died at 93 in 1987, and former owner John Drew died at 93 in 1976. In 1988 the *Philadelphia Inquirer* ran a brief feature on 94-year-old Charles Freeman, former corporation member and reportedly the last survivor of the 1915 Hilldale Club, who recalled, "The thing I miss the most is seeing all my teammates. I'll tell you something, playing baseball with them is something I'll never forget."[22]

The achievements of the Hilldale baseball club between 1910 and 1932 instilled a new sense of racial pride in the black population of Philadelphia. The corporation, "working for a combination solely controlled by colored men and maintained by our race," had offered tangible proof that black enterprises could succeed, make a profit, and benefit the community.[23]

The *Tribune* best expressed the significance of Hilldale:

> [Hilldale's] accomplishments have made glad the heart of every school boy of our race, and we believe impregnated many with the determination to duplicate their stand, and soar to the heights they have reached in their chosen profession. . . . The ability of Negroes to do things on a par with the best of any group has again been clearly demonstrated.[24]

Hilldale's remarkable success, occurring at a time when the majority of Philadelphia's black businesses failed, was largely due to the efforts of its

ident, Ed Bolden, from 1910 through 1929. His canny
l reputation for "fair dealing and clean playing" had
he very top of black professional baseball in the 1920s,
tion of the Eastern Colored League in 1922. Worsen-
.....ic conditions and the fragility of all black enterprises, however, proved more potent than Bolden's considerable entrepreneurial
skills. The post–World War I boom that carried Hilldale and other black
businesses in Philadelphia to prosperity in the early 1920s would eventually
fade, and the mid-decade industrial recession initiated a steady decline in
attendance at Hilldale Park that Bolden was powerless to stop. The onset
of the Depression virtually destroyed professional black baseball in Philadelphia and other cities, only to be revived with a fresh infusion of capital
from black vice leaders and white booking agents.

Bolden's nearly unparalleled 40-year career from 1910 to 1950 encompassed the beginning and virtual end of professional black baseball, and
as Roscoe Coleman, sports editor of the *Philadelphia Independent,* noted, his
death "ended an era in race baseball and the attempt on the part of its
pioneers and successors to elevate it to a big time level."[25]

Appendix A: Attendance

The Hilldale ledgers contain detailed financial information for the 1926–1932 seasons, including ticket sales for games at Hilldale Park. These figures are based on my calculations from these records:

	Total Attendance for Saturday/Holiday Games	Dates	Average
1926	46,123	26	1,844.9
1927	41,366	26	1,591.0
1928	39,572	25	1,582.9
1929[a]	38,411	28	1,371.9
1930	14,361	22	652.8
1931[a]	27,711	25	1,108.4
1932	3,735	11	339.5

[a]Some games estimated.
Excludes Thursday games at Hilldale Park as well as preseason games.

Appendix B:
Yearly Records

Hilldale

1910	0-2	1922	94-57-2
1911	23-6	1923	137-43-6
1912	19-6-1	1924	112-51-9
1913	16-7	1925	121-48-5
1914	18-7	1926	117-57-2
1915	20-8-2	1927	84-61-5
1916	19-9-2	1928	119-40-3
1917	23-15-1	1929	67-50-8
1918	41-7	1930	77-58-5
1919	40-23-2	1931	120-31-4
1920	102-34-6	1932	29-30-1
1921	105-41-3		

(Based on final published records or author's calculations from newspaper game accounts.)

Eastern Colored League
(Based on final published standings.)

1923	HILLDALE	32-17
	Cuban Stars	23-17
	Brooklyn Royal Giants	18-18
	Atlantic City Bacharach Giants	19-23
	Lincoln Giants	16-22
	Baltimore Black Sox	19-30
1924	HILLDALE	47-22
	Baltimore Black Sox	32-19
	Lincoln Giants	32-25
	Atlantic City Bacharach Giants	30-29

Harrisburg Giants	26–28
Brooklyn Royal Giants	16–26
Washington Potomacs	21–37
Cuban Stars	17–31

1925
HILLDALE	45–13
Harrisburg Giants	37–18
Baltimore Black Sox	31–19
Atlantic City Bacharach Giants	26–26
Brooklyn Royal Giants	13–20
Cuban Stars	15–26
Lincoln Giants	7–39
Wilmington Potomacs	8–20 (disbanded in July)

1926
Atlantic City Bacharach Giants	34–20
Harrisburg Giants	25–17
HILLDALE	34–24
Cuban Stars	28–21
Lincoln Giants	19–22
Baltimore Black Sox	18–29
Brooklyn Royal Giants	7–20
Newark Stars	1–10 (disbanded in July)

1927 *First half:*
Atlantic City Bacharach Giants	29–17
Baltimore Black Sox	23–17
Cuban Stars	24–19
Harrisburg Giants	25–20
HILLDALE	17–28
Brooklyn Royal Giants	10–21
Lincoln Giants	12–18 (left league in June)

Second half:
Atlantic City Bacharachs	25–18
Harrisburg Giants	16–12
HILLDALE	19–17
Baltimore Black Sox	12–18
Cuban Stars	9–13
Brooklyn Royal Giants	5–10

American Negro League

1929 *First half:*
Baltimore Black Sox	24–11
Lincoln Giants	22–11
Homestead Grays	15–13
HILLDALE	15–20
Atlantic City Bacharach Giants	11–20
Cuban Stars	6–16

Second half:

Baltimore Black Sox	25–10
HILLDALE	24–15
Lincoln Giants	18–15
Homestead Grays	19–16
Cuban Stars	9–23
Atlantic City Bacharach Giants	8–25

East-West League

1932 *(based on last standings published; league disbanded in July)*

Baltimore Black Sox	20–9
Homestead Grays	16–8
Cuban Stars	12–15
Washington Pilots	13–18
HILLDALE	10–17
Cleveland Stars	8–16
Newark Browns	3–14
Detroit Wolves	13–5 (at time of merger with Grays in June)

Appendix C:
Rosters, 1910–1932

(Compiled from available box scores.)

Albritton, Alex p, 1921
Allen, Clyde p, 1932
Allen, Toussaint 1b, 1919–1924
Anderson, Sam rf, 1910–1911
Arnold, Paul "Sam" lf, 1926
Ash, Rudolph lf, 1926
Awkward, Bob p, 1925
Balw'n 3b, 1910
Banks 2b, 1930
Barber (Barbour), Jess of, 1920
Barnard cf, 1917
Baxter 1b, 1930
Beckwith, John ss (1926, 1929, 1931
  postseason only)
Berkely, Randolph c, 1919
Bombay 1930
Bram p, 1930
Brice, Leon rf, 1911
Briggs, Otto of, 1917, 1919–1928, 1930
  (captain, 1917, 1927–1928)
  (postseason 1914, 1929)
Britt, George 3b-p-1b, 1929
Brockman 2b, 1927
Brooks, O. 3b (1929 postseason)
Brown p, 1930
Brown, Arnold "Scrappy" ss, 1920–1921
Brown, Elias "Country" lf, 1918
Buchanan, Floyd "Buck" p, 1914–1916
Burbage, Buddy cf, 1930
Burgee, Louis 2b, 1915–1917
Burgin, Ralph 3b, 1930–1931
Burke rf, 1919

Campbell, Bill "Bullet" p, 1924–1928
Cannady, Rev 1b-2b-p, 1928, 1931
Capers, Lefty p, 1932
Carr, George 1b-lf-c-rf, 1923–1927
  (preseason only 1928/postseason only
  1929)
Carter, Cliff p, 1924 (postseason only
  1928), 1929–1930, 1932
Carter, Paul p, 1930–1932
Casey p, 1931
Casey, Mickey c (split squad with
  Baltimore only 1930)
Cason, John c, 1920
Chacon, Pelayo ss (1920 postseason
  only)
Charleston, Oscar cf-1b (1926 post-
  season) 1928–1929 (captain, 1928–
  1929)
Charleston, Porter p, 1927–1929, 1931–
  1932
Clark, Harry "Lefty" p, 1915–1917
Clarkson, Leroy "Cannonball" 1b-3b-
  p-of, 1911–1915
Clift ss, 1921
Cockrell, Phil p-rf-lf, 1918–1932 (cap-
  tain, 1929–1930, 1932)
Cooper, Dalty p, 1928–1929, 1932
Corbett, Charles p, 1927
Cottrell c, 1923
Crump 2b-3b, 1921–1922
Crump 2b, 1932
Cummings, Nap 1b-lf, 1918–1919,

1921–1922; 1925 (one game only)
Currie, Rube p, 1924–1925
Curry rf (split squad with Baltimore only 1930)
Dallard, William "Eggie" c-lf-1b, 1921, 1928–1932
Davis, Earl ss, 1930
Day, Connie (split squad with Baltimore only 1930)
Deas, Yank c, 1918–1919
Denby 1913
DeWitt, Eddie 3b, 1930
Dials, Lou of, 1932
Dickerson, Lou p, 1921
Dick'n cf, 1911
Dihigo, Martin ss-2b-p-3b-rf, 1929–1931
Dilworth, Arthur p, 1918
Dixon 2b, 1930
Dixon, Rap lf, 1931
Dixon, Tom c-3b-2b, 1932
Dobbins, Nat ss, 1921
Downs, McKinley "Bunny" ss-3b,rf 1917–1922 (captain, 1918–1919) (1929 postseason)
Durant lf, 1932
Easte p, 1923
Ellis, Glen "Rocky" of-ph-team mascot, 1924–1928
Farrell, Luther p, 1925
Fiall, Tom cf-3b, 1918
Flournoy, Pud p, 1919–1923
Ford, Frank p-c, 1915–1917
Foreman, Buddy ss, 1921
Francis, Bill 3b-ss, 1920–1922 (captain, 1920–1922)
Freeman, Charles 3b-cf, 1913–1917
Fuller, William 2b, 1917–1918
Gadsden, Gus of-2b, 1932
Gardner, Kenneth "Ping" 1922–1923; 1930
Garner, Raymond of, 1912–1914
Gar'v 1b, 1910
Gaskins, Charles of, 1911
Gaston 1921
Gillespie, Henry p-rf, 1916–1917, 1920–1922, 1930
Goldman c, 1915
Graham of, 1923
Hackey p (postseason 1930 only)
Hamilton p, 1927

Hampton p, 1923
Hargett, L. p, 1918
Harper ss, 1920
Harris 1b-2b-cf, 1910–1912
Harris, A. 3b, 1917
Harris, A. p, 1922
Haynes, Bill p, 1922
Henry, Charles p, 1922, 1926
Hill, Billy "Stump" lf, 1912–1913 (captain, 1913)
Hocker, Bruce 1b, 1918
Holloway, Crush rf, 1929, 1932
Holmes cf, 1910
Holmes 3b-rf, 1914
Hubbard, Jess lf-1b-p, 1919, 1930
Hudspeth, Bob "Highpockets" 1b, 1929
Huhns c, 1910
Jackson p, 1910
Jackson 2b-3b, 1912
Jackson, Dick 2b-3b, 1929–1930
Jackson, Hubert "Lefty" of, 1911–1914
Jeffries, Harry 3b, 1932
Jenkins, Fats of (postseason only 1928, 1931)
Jenkins, Thomas c-rf, 1913–1917
Johnson c-2b, 1912
Johnson, Cecil "Ces" 3b-p-ss, 1918, 1920
Johnson, Dan p, 1917–1918
Johnson, George of, 1918–1925, 1927
Johnson, Jimmy ss, 1932
Johnson, Judy 3b-ss, 1918, 1921–1929, 1931–1932 (captain, 1931–1932)
Johnson, W. c-1b-lf, 1927
Jones cf, 1910
Jones, Willie c-1b, 1930
Keifer p, 1932
Kelly, Roy 3b, 1914
Kemp, George p-c-rf, 1910–1917
Kenner ss, 1921
Kenyon, Harry 1922
Kimbro, Jess 3b (postseason 1917), 1918
Lackey, Obie ss-2b, 1929–1932
Layton, Obie p, 1931
Lee, Holsey "Scrip" p-3b-lf, 1923–1927, 1930
Levis, Oscar p-1b, 1930–1931
Lewis, Joe c, 1924–1925, 1927–1932
Lindsay 2b, 1932
Lloyd, John Henry ss, 1923 (captain, 1923)

Lundy, Dick ss (postseason 1917, 1923), 1918–1920
McDonald, Webster p, 1930–1931
Mackey, Raleigh "Biz" c-ss-3b-1b-p-lf-rf, 1923–1931
Marcelle, Oliver 3b (Bacharachs series only 1919)
Mason, Hugh "Scrappy" p, 1912–1913
Maul c-2b, 1912
Mayo, George 1b, 1912–1918
Meade, Arthur "Chick" 3b, 1919
Mitchell, Bud p-c-lf-1b, 1929–1932
Mungin p, 1927
Muse, H. p, 1922
Naughton lf, 1914
Perry, Hank p, 1926
Pettus, Bill c-1b-3b, 1917–1918
Phillips, Harry 2b, 1916
Pinder, Earnest "Monk" cf, 1916
Pinder, Fred ss, 1914–1917 (captain, 1916)
Poles, Spottswood cf, 1917, 1919
Porter, Clarence of, 1911–1912
Pritchett, Wilbur p, 1921, 1924, 1929–1930
Purgen, John ss-2b, 1921
Raylon (Baylon?) p, 1931
Rector, Connie p, 1920–1922
Reed p, 1929
Reese, John cf-lf, 1918–1919
Reid, Ambrose 2b-3b, 1930
Rhoades, Neal c-lf, 1917–1918
Richardson, Dewey c, 1922
Rivers, Dewey "Deep" lf, 1926
Roberts, Elihu 2b-of, 1919–1920
Roberts, Roy p, 1930
Robinson, Bill "Newt" ss, 1925–1926 (preseason 1927)
Ross, Bill p, 1923
Ryan, Merven "Red" p-rf, 1922–1929, 1931
Santop, Louis c (postseason 1917; Bacharachs series only 1919), 1918, 1920–1926
Scott cf, 1910
Scott, Robert lf, 1927
Sheffey, Douglas p, 1915–1916
Shell p, 1923
Sherkliff, Ed p, 1931
Simmons, Paul cf, 1915
Smith ss, 1910

Smith 3b-of, 1919
Smith p, 1927
Smith p, 1930
Smith, Jacob p, 1913–1914
Smith, W. p-ss, 1921
Stanley, Neck p, 1928–1929
Starks, Otis "Lefty" p, 1919–1920
Stephens, Paul "Jake" ss-2b, 1921–1929, 1931 (postseason 1930)
Stone 2b, 1929
Stratton c, 1930
Strong, Joe p, 1928–1929
Strothers, Hulett ss-rf-3b-lf, 1911–1914
Studevan, Mark 3b-2b-of, 1910–1916
Sykes, Frank "Doc" p, 1917–1918 (captain, 1918), 1922–1923
Sykes, Melvin lf, 1926
Taylor, Ben 1b (postseason only 1919)
Taylor, John p, 1917
Thomas, Clint lf-cf-2b, 1923–1928
Thomas, Jules of (postseason 1917)
Thomas, Lefty p, 1930
Thompson, Lloyd 2b-ss-of-3b, 1910–16
Thorpe, Jim p, 1928
Triplett cf, 1917
Tucker, Orval 2b, 1930
Tyler, Ed p, 1926
Underhill, Bob p, 1924
Valentine rf, 1917
Wagner, Bert "Bill" 1b, 1927
Wallace 1919
Warfield, Frank 2b, 1923–1928 (captain, 1923–1927)
Warmack, Sam of-3b, 1929, 1932
Washington, Namon ss-2b-lf-c, 1925–1927
Waters, Ted of, 1927 (postseason 1930 only)
Webster, Pearl "Speck" lf (postseason 1917), 1918
West 2b, 1914
Weston p, 1930
White, Burlin c, 1919
White, Chaney lf, 1920–1922, 1930–1932 (postseason 1929)
White, Moak (postseason 1929)
Whitworth, Dick p, 1920–1921
Wicks, E. ss, 1921
Willetts 2b, 1914
Williams, Smokey Joe (7/26 game and postseason only, 1917; postseason only 1919)

Williams, Tom p-of, 1918–1919
Wilson, Frank "Chink" p-ss-lf-c, 1910–
   1915
Wilson, J. rf, 1910

Winters, Nip p-1b, 1923–1927, 1931
Yancey, Billy ss, 1927, 1931
York, Jim c, 1919–1921

Notes

Chapter 1

1. Proceedings from *Philadelphia's Baseball History*, symposium held on February 24, 1990, sponsored by the Historical Society of Pennsylvania, 3-15, 27-32; David Voight, "America's Game: A Brief History of Baseball," in *Baseball Encyclopedia*, 8th ed. (New York, 1990), 3-13; Bill James, *Bill James Historical Baseball Abstract* (New York, 1988), 11.

2. Harold Seymour, *Baseball: The People's Game* (New York, 1990), 161, 213-218, 258-269; Edward "Dutch" Doyle, "Philadelphia's Ball Parks," unpublished paper, SABR Research Exchange, 1-7; Edward "Dutch" Doyle, "Sandlot Baseball in the Philadelphia Area," unpublished paper, SABR Research Exchange, 8-17; Riess, *City Games*, 67. Harold Seymour noted that white independent teams were often called semipros "to differentiate them from teams in Organized Baseball" while independent black teams were given this label "in order to denigrate them." On the distinction between amateurs and semipros, see Seymour, *People's Game*, 258-260.

3. *North American*, May 15, 1910 ("50,000"); May 21, 1911 ("baseball virus"); August 25, 1912; May 31, 1914; May 6, 1915. *Philadelphia Press*, April 3, May 8, 15, July 31, 1910. *Philadelphia Inquirer*, August 14, 1910. Seymour, *People's Game*, 261; Harold Seymour, *Baseball: The Golden Age* (New York, 1971), 42. Although commercialized Sunday baseball was allowed in Chicago, St. Louis, and Cincinnati as early as 1902, it remained illegal in New York until 1919 and in Pennsylvania until 1934. See John Lucas, "The Unholy Experiment—Professional Baseball's Struggle Against Pennsylvania Sunday Blue Laws 1926-1934," *Pennsylvania History* 38 (1971), 170.

4. *North American*, May 15, 1910; May 21, 1916. Seymour, *People's Game*, 261-262, 220-232.

5. *North American*, April 14, 1912; May 11, 1913; May 16, 1915; May 7, 21, June 11, 1916; September 14, 1919; July 17, 1921. Seymour, *People's Game*, 215, 221, 227, 228. Philip Scranton and Walter Licht, *Work Sights: Industrial Philadelphia, 1890-1950* (Philadelphia, 1986), 165-166, 246. *Philadelphia Public Ledger*, July 5, 1914; September 3, 1916. *Philadelphia Inquirer*, May 29, 1910; August 25, 1923. *Philadelphia Press*, July 21, 1912; July 23, 1913; May 3, 1914.

6. John Betts, *America's Sporting Heritage: 1850-1950* (Reading, 1974), 179-184; *Philadelphia Inquirer*, May 21, 1911; *North American*, May 16, 1915; *Indianapolis Freeman*, May 5, 1917; Seymour, *People's Game*, 53-85.

7. *North American*, July 7, 1912; July 19, August 13, 27, 1922. Seymour, *People's Game*, 261.

239

8. *Philadelphia's Baseball History*, 7–17; Charles Alexander, *Our Game* (New York, 1991), 100–102, 106; Doyle, "Philadelphia's Ball Parks," 1–7; Doyle, "Sandlot Baseball in the Philadelphia Area," 8–17; Voight, "America's Game: A Brief History of Baseball," 3–13. On Ban Johnson and the formation of the American League, see Eugene Murdock, *Ban Johnson, Czar of Baseball* (Westport, CT, 1982), 43–68.

9. *North American*, May 10, 1914; Riess, *City Games*, 69; Robert Obojski, *Bush League: A History of Minor League Baseball* (New York, 1975), 390. With the formation of the National Association of Professional Baseball Leagues in 1901, minor leagues were given rankings of A to D, with a higher AA classification adopted in 1908. The AAA minor league ranking familiar to baseball fans today was not in use until 1946; the B, C, and D rankings were eliminated in 1963. On the evolution of the minor league classification system, see Obojski, 14–30.

10. *Sporting Life*, April 15, 1922; *North American*, July 2, 1911; May 9, 16, June 1, August 8, 1915; June 18, 1916; May 6, 1917; July 4, 1918. *Philadelphia Public Ledger*, June 10, 1917. *New York Times*, October 14, 1917; February 1, 1919. Seymour, *People's Game*, 264–268.

11. Harry Silcox, "Efforts to Desegregate Baseball in Philadelphia: The Pythian Baseball Club, 1866–1872," unpublished manuscript, National Baseball Library, 1–8. Seymour, *People's Game*, 533–543; *Philadelphia's Baseball History*, 8; *Philadelphia Tribune*, July 17, 1920; Jerry Malloy, "Out at Home," in *The National Pastime* (1982), 14, 25 (quote). On the Pythians, see the papers of the Pythian Baseball Club located in the Historical Society of Pennsylvania, Philadelphia.

12. On the Cuban Giants, see Jerry Malloy, "The Birth of the Cuban Giants: The Origins of Black Professional Baseball" (courtesy of Jerry Malloy), 1–15; Sol White, *Sol White's Official Base Ball Guide* (1907; repr. ed., Columbia, SC, 1984), 11–13; Seymour, *People's Game*, 539; *New York Amsterdam News*, January 30, 1929. While Sol White claimed that Frank Thompson formed the team from his black waiters at the Argyle Hotel, Malloy's article strongly suggests that the team was composed of ballplayers who were later given hotel positions to supplement their incomes. Harold Seymour asserted that the Orions of Philadelphia and Black Stockings of St. Louis may have predated the Cuban Giants as professionals, although neither team traveled as extensively or was as well known as the Giants.

13. Seymour, *People's Game*, 545–548, 556–557; Leslie Heaphy, "The Growth and Decline of the Negro Leagues," unpublished M.A. thesis, University of Toledo, 1989, 13; Kenneth Kusmer, *A Ghetto Takes Shape: Black Cleveland, 1870–1930* (Chicago, 1976), 53; Malloy, "Birth of the Cuban Giants," 8. Of the approximately 70 black players in organized baseball between 1878 and 1899, only Moses Fleetwood Walker and his brother Welday played in the major leagues, appearing with Toledo in the American Association in 1884.

14. *Philadelphia Evening Item*, April 15, April 23 (quote), April 26, October 3, October 7, 1902. Sol White, *Sol White's Official Baseball Guide*, 1–8, 33. On White, see also John Holway, *Blackball Stars: Negro League Pioneers* (Westport, CT, 1988), 1–7; James Bankes, *Pittsburgh Crawfords: The Lives and Times of Black Baseball's Most Exciting Team* (Dubuque, IA, 1991), 7; Alexander, *Our Game*, 50–51; *Chicago Defender*, February 2, 1918. While occasionally inaccurate, White's 1907 *Official Base Ball Guide* is considered to be one of the primary sources for the study of early black baseball.

15. White, *Official Base Ball Guide*, 35, 37, 49, 84; *Philadelphia Sunday Item*, May 8, 1910; *New York Age*, August 3, 1911; *Philadelphia Inquirer*, August 28, 1922; *Baltimore Afro-American*, October 10, 1924; *New York Amsterdam News*, March 27, 1929. Later versions of the Philadelphia Giants included a traveling team under Charles Bradford in New York and a New England–based club managed by Danny McClellan.

16. Ruck, *Sandlot Seasons*, 45 (quote); *Indianapolis Freeman*, September 14, 28, 1907; March 13, 1909; April 9, 1910. *Philadelphia Press*, May 29, 1910; July 28, 1912. *Philadelphia Sunday Item*, June 12, 1910; *Philadelphia Inquirer*, May 31, 1911. *North American*, April 14, May 19, 31, 1912; June 15, 29, August 10, 1913; August 2, 16, 1914. *Philadelphia Tribune*, March 8, 22, 1912; July 15, 1913. Seymour, *People's Game*, 569–585. Beginning with the Cuban Giants in 1885 and continuing into the 1920s, Giants remained a popular name in black baseball as well as a means to distinguish black teams from similarly named white clubs. One Afro-American newspaper, the *Indianapolis Freeman*, observed in 1907, "If your team is not called 'Giants' you can believe that no one thinks that they can play ball" (*Indianapolis Freeman*, April 27, 1907).

17. Charles Hardy, "Race and Opportunity: Black Philadelphia During the Era of the Great Migration, 1916-1930," Ph.D. diss., Temple University, 1989, 169. *Chicago Defender*, October 21, 1916; August 9, 1919. *Philadelphia Tribune*, March 30, 1912. *Administrative Survey of Darby Township — Delaware County, Pennsylvania: A Report for the Board of Township Commissioners Bureau of Municipal Research and Pennsylvania Economy League* (1957); Armstrong Association of Philadelphia, *A Study of Living Conditions Among Colored People in Towns in the Outer Part of Philadelphia and in Other Suburbs Both in Pennsylvania and New Jersey* (Philadelphia, 1915), 21–22. *Philadelphia Inquirer*, March 19, 1989. In 1910 the population of Darby Borough was 6,305, with 676 blacks composing 10.7 percent of the population (*Thirteenth Census of the United States*).

18. *Philadelphia Sunday Item*, May 29, 1910. A second notice appeared in the *Item* two weeks later, soliciting opponents for upcoming open dates; see June 12, 1910, *Sunday Item*.

19. *Philadelphia Tribune*, February 23, 1928. U.S. Bureau of the Census, Manuscript Schedules of Population, 1910. Lloyd Thompson, Mark Studevan, and Thomas Jenkins became members of the Hilldale Corporation and would remain involved with the club for the next 20 years.

20. *Philadelphia Inquirer*, June 12, 1910, July 31, 1910. *North American*, June 12, 1910. The box score of Hilldale's first known game appeared in the June 12, 1910, *Philadelphia Inquirer* and *North American*. The only other documented game was played on July 30, 1910. More detailed coverage of Hilldale's first season probably appeared in the *Philadelphia Tribune*; unfortunately, no issues are extant before 1912.

21. *New York Amsterdam News*, March 7, 1923 (quote); *Philadelphia Tribune*, April 23, 1920; *Philadelphia Independent*, October 7, 1950. U.S. Bureau of the Census, Manuscript Schedules of Population, 1910. Official Personnel Folder, Edward W. Bolden, United States Office of Personnel Management. Phil Dixon and Patrick Hannigan, *Negro Baseball Leagues: A Photographic History* (Mattituck, NY, 1992), 60. Bolden continued to work at the post office until his retirement in 1946.

22. Unidentified newspaper clipping, September 22, 1953, courtesy of John Holway (quote); *Darby, PA. 1682-1982 Tricentennial* (commemorative booklet) in Lloyd Thompson-Bill Cash Collection, Archives of Afro-American Historical and Cultural Museum, Philadelphia, PA; *Philadelphia Tribune*, August 29, 1914. While the details of Bolden's early life are obscure, his background is suggested by his employment as a government postal worker, a civil service position that typically attracted well-educated blacks stifled elsewhere. See Hardy, "Race and Opportunity," 20–21; Allen Spear, *Black Chicago: The Making of a Negro Ghetto, 1890-1920* (Chicago, 1967), 36.

23. *North American*, May 15, 1910; May 21, 1911 ("gossip"); May 19, 1912. *Philadelphia Inquirer*, July 10, 1910; *Philadelphia Record*, July 10, 1910. The *North American*'s annual "Rosters of Local Amateurs" listed a total of approximately 800 teams in 1910, 1911, and 1912; less than 10 were known to be black. Scanning the Philadelphia daily papers from 1910 to 1912, I found approximately 20 black teams mentioned. Most

faced white opponents regularly and represented the upper echelon of the local black baseball scene.

24. *Philadelphia Tribune*, March 23 ("good grounds"), March 30, June 1, June 22, 1912 ("fast, colored").

25. Seymour, *Golden Age*, 91; David Q. Voight, *American Baseball: Vol. 2, From the Commissioners to Continental Expansion* (University Park, PA, 1966–1970, repr. 1983), 68–72; Betts, *America's Sporting Heritage*, 121–122; *Philadelphia Inquirer*, August 28, 1922. Increased ballpark security, improved umpiring, and a rise in college players all contributed to the decline in rowdyism.

26. *Philadelphia Tribune*, March 30, September 7, 1912; September 6, 1913; October 17, 1914.

27. *Philadelphia Tribune*, September 28, 1912; June 7, July 15, August 30, 1913; April 25, 1914, June 6, 1914 (quote). *North American*, August 4, 1912. Newspaper estimates of crowd sizes were often exaggerated as well as inaccurate. Rollo Wilson of the *Pittsburgh Courier* commented on this tendency in 1923. Assessing a crowd at Hilldale Park, he noted that the attendance was estimated at "7,000 to 50,000, dependent upon one's ignorance of how many people make 1,000" (*Pittsburgh Courier*, July 14, 1923). In comparing Hilldale's actual attendance from 1926 to 1932 to published estimates, I have noted a general tendency toward overestimation. According to the Hilldale ledgers, the largest crowd at Hilldale Park during this period was on May 31, 1926, with a paid attendance of 5,565. Newspaper accounts in the June 1, 1926, *Philadelphia Inquirer* and June 5, 1926, *Baltimore Afro-American*, however, incorrectly estimated the crowd at 10,000–12,000 fans.

28. The 1914 and 1915 Hilldale ledgers, Lloyd Thompson–Bill Cash Collection; *Philadelphia Tribune*, April 4, 1914. In 1910, ticket prices at Phillies Park and Shibe Park ranged from 25 cents to $1, while black professional teams charged about 25 cents for admission. See *Philadelphia Press*, April 15, 1910; *Philadelphia Bulletin*, May 23, 1910; *New York Age*, August 8, 1912.

29. *Philadelphia Tribune*, March 22, 1913; February 3, 1917; August 3, 1912.

30. *Philadelphia Tribune*, September 26, October 17, 1914; August 28, 1915 (quote). 1915 Hilldale ledger.

31. *Philadelphia Tribune*, August 17, 1912.

32. *Baltimore Afro-American*, May 13, 1921; *Chicago Defender*, April 23, 1921. *North American*, May 22, 1919; April 4, 1920; March 25, March 27, March 28, 1921. University of Pennsylvania Archives.

33. Lloyd Thompson, "Darby Hilldale Baseball Team," in *Darby, PA. 1682–1982 Tricentennial* (commemorative booklet), Lloyd Thompson–Bill Cash Collection; *Philadelphia Tribune*, September 25, 1915; February 19, March 11, April 8, 1916. 1916 Hilldale ledger book.

34. The 1916 Hilldale ledger book.

35. *Philadelphia Tribune*, April 15, 1916 (quote), May 20, 1916, October 13, 1917.

36. *Chicago Defender*, May 13, 1922. Until the 1920s, white organized baseball was similarly plagued by unruly fan behavior; see Seymour, *Golden Age*, 90–115.

37. *Chicago Defender*, October 21, 1915; August 24, 1918; June 21, 1919, September 6, 1919; May 22, 1920; June 4, 1921, August 13, 1921; June 4, 1923. *Baltimore Afro-American*, January 10, 1925; Janet Bruce, *The Kansas City Monarchs: Champions of Black Baseball* (Lawrence, KS, 1985), 51; Donn Rogosin, *Invisible Men: Life in Baseball's Negro Leagues* (New York, 1985), 89.

38. *Chicago Defender*, July 15, 1916 ("Giants Park"); *New York Amsterdam News*, May 16, 1923 ("Protectory Oval").

39. *Philadelphia Tribune*, January 13, February 17, March 24, 1917. *Baltimore Afro-*

American, July 27, 1923; *Pittsburgh Courier*, August 4, 1923. The 1929 murder at Hilldale Park of a woman involved in the local numbers scene suggests that Bolden was never entirely able to eradicate the presence of gamblers; see *Philadelphia Tribune*, May 23, 1929.

40. *Philadelphia Tribune*, August 21, 1915.

41. The 1916 Hilldale ledger book. *Philadelphia Tribune*, February 3, 17, 1917. Tentative plans for Hilldale sponsored football and basketball teams were soon abandoned. The "old fellows" were Charles Freeman, George Mayo, Thomas Jenkins, Edward Bolden, Mark Studevan, Lloyd Thompson, George Kemp, and William Anderson. James Byrd became part of the corporation on October 22, 1916. Most of the "old fellows" would remain with the original corporation until its demise in 1930.

Chapter 2

1. *Indianapolis Freeman*, May 26, 1917 (Wyatt quote); White, *Base Ball Guide*, 25, 27, 35, 83; Seymour, *People's Game*, 535, 545; Dixon and Hannigan, *Negro Baseball Leagues* (appendix); Kusmer, *Ghetto Takes Shape*, 35–40, 50, 113–115, 148–153, 154 (quote). Spear, *Black Chicago*, 53–54; Malloy, "Birth of the Cuban Giants," 11–12. *New York Age*, April 8, 1909 (Walton quote); April 8, 1915. Ocania Chalk, *Pioneers in Black Sport* (New York, 1975), 44. *Brooklyn Daily Eagle*, August 15, 1904. Black teams, even when white owned, did control their own destinies on the playing field. The team's playing manager (usually called the captain) typically handled field decisions and strategy while white or black business managers (the "manager") oversaw finances.

2. Malloy, "Birth of the Cuban Giants," 11–12; *Baltimore Afro-American*, February 8, 1924 (Foster quote).

3. *New York Amsterdam News*, December 18, 1929 (White quote); *New York Times*, January 11, 1935; *Chicago Defender*, April 19, 1919; January 13, 1923; *Philadelphia Tribune*, January 2, 1926; April 12, 1928; Robert Peterson, *Only the Ball Was White* (Englewood Cliffs, NJ, 1970), 60; Ruck, *Sandlot Seasons*, 115–122; "King Nat of the Bushers" (undated photocopy, 1914?), National Baseball Library.

4. *Indianapolis Freeman*, September 28, December 7, 1907; March 21, 1908; February 27, December 4, 11, 18, 1909; December 23, 1911. *New York Age*, April 14, May 5, 1910; July 20, August 3, 10, 1911; May 2, 1912; March 13, 1913. *Chicago Defender*, December 13, 1919. Champions of the association included the Philadelphia Giants from 1905 to 1907 and the Brooklyn Royal Giants from 1908 to 1909.

5. "King Nat of the Bushers," *New York Age*, February 15, 1909; *Indianapolis Freeman*, May 26, 1917; *New York Amsterdam News*, December 18, 1929; White, *Base Ball Guide*, 25–33, 79 (quote); Dixon and Hannigan, *Negro Baseball Leagues*, 69–78; Caroline Golab, "The Immigrant and the City: Poles, Italians, and Jews in Philadelphia, 1870–1920," in *Peoples of Philadelphia: A History of Ethnic Groups and Lower-Class Life, 1790–1840*, ed. Allen F. Davis and Mark Haller (Philadelphia, 1973), 209. Fowler's All-American Black Tourists, formed after the collapse of the Page Fence Giants, outdid the Giants in showmanship, parading into towns clad in dress suits with silk umbrellas. Among early black players, Rube Foster, Danny McClellan, and Kid Carter were known for their more serious approach to the game in contrast to the antics of foghorn-voiced baseball comedians Bill Monroe and Clarence Williams. See *Norfolk Journal and Guide*, April 21, 1923.

6. Seymour, *People's Game*, 262, 573; White, *Base Ball Guide*, 29–31, 45–46; Peterson, *Only the Ball*, 63–64; *Indianapolis Freeman*, August 31, September 7, 1907; October 2, 1909; Betts, *America's Sporting Heritage*, 181; Spear, *Black Chicago*, 78–79, 117;

Dixon and Hannigan, *Negro Baseball Leagues*, 96, 144. While several sources list the Unions as being formed in the mid-1880s, a press release in the March 13, 1909, *Indianapolis Freeman* notes the team's thirtieth year of operation. The Union Giants would continue as a traveling barnstorming club into the 1930s under Peters and later Robert Gilkerson.

7. *Indianapolis Freeman*, September 21, 1907; February 15, March 21, August 1, 1908; February 13, May 15, September 4, October 2, December 4, 1909; April 2, April 30, May 14, 21, August 27, October 8, December 24, 1910; December 23, 1911; March 6, 1915; May 19, 1917. *New York Age*, April 14, May 5, 1910. *Chicago Defender*, June 25, October 8, 1910; November 2, 1918. *Pittsburgh Courier*, January 16, 1926. White, *Base Ball Guide*, 47–51; Dixon and Hannigan, *Negro Baseball Leagues*, 90–101; *Half Century Magazine*, March 1919, 8; Holway, *Blackball Stars*, 8–35; Holway, *Voices*, 76; Bankes, *Pittsburgh Crawfords*, 16–17; Chicago Commission on Race Relations, *Negro in Chicago* (Chicago, 1922), 178. In 1926 Rube Foster claimed the Lelands posted a 123-6 record in 1910, but this has not been verified. Frank Leland and R.R. Jackson continued to own the Chicago Giants, with Joe Green as manager, until Leland's death in 1914 at the age of 45. As late as 1916, the Chicago Giants were still being referred to as the Leland Giants. The team operated as a traveling club under Joe Green into the 1920s. See *Indianapolis Freeman*, May 10, June 21, July 12, 1913; August 19, 1916; *Chicago Defender*, May 9, November 21, 1914.

8. *Indianapolis Freeman*, June 20, 1908; June 12, 1909; April 16, August 27, 1910, January 21, September 9, 1911; April 24, 1915. Holway, *Voices*, 28–29. Conrad Kuebler, the white owner of Kuebler's Park, also provided financial backing to the Giants.

9. *Indianapolis Freeman*, July 27, 1907; October 3, 1908; April 24, May 29, June 12, October 30, 1909; March 5, 1910; February 26, May 27, 1916. Dixon and Hannigan, *Negro Baseball Leagues*, 33, 36, 51, 101.

10. *Indianapolis Freeman*, August 1, 1908; March 12, 1910; May 26, 1917. White, *Base Ball Guide*, 90; *New York Age*, July 17, 1913; Rogosin, *Invisible Men*, 152–177; Peterson, *Only the Ball*, 60–62; Bruce, *Kansas City Monarchs*, 14. Operating in New Jersey from 1912 through 1917, the Long Branch Cubans, a mixed Cuban team, featured several future and former major league players, including pitcher Dolf Luque. The Cuban team was a regular Sunday opponent for New York's major league teams affected by the city's Sunday baseball ban.

11. *Indianapolis Freeman*, October 19, 1907; August 1, 1908; March 20, April 24, May 9, June 12, 1909; June 18, 25, 1910; April 24, 1915. Dixon and Hannigan, *Negro Baseball Leagues*, 85; White, *Base Ball Guide*, 53, 84. In 1906, 108 of the Philadelphia Giants' 145 games were against white teams.

12. *Indianapolis Freeman*, June 20, July 18, 1908; June 17, 1909; April 30, 1910; February 28, April 11, 1914. *Chicago Whip*, March 4, 1922; *Baltimore Afro-American*, July 23, 1927; Seymour, *People's Game*, 561–563; Dixon and Hannigan, *Negro Baseball Leagues*, 111. The original Kansas City Monarchs of the early 1900s had no connection to the later professional team formed in 1920 by J.L. Wilkinson.

13. *Indianapolis Freeman*, December 12, 1908; March 20, April 24, May 29, 1909; January 22, June 25, 1910; June 1, 1912; August 23, 1913. *Half-Century Magazine* (June 1919), 8; *Chicago Broad Ax*, May 18, 1912, cited in Spear, *Black Chicago*, 118; Holway, *Voices*, 193; *Cleveland Advocate*, April 12, 1919. White semipro and black professional teams often leased major league parks for important games. Prior to 1911, several parks, including Columbia Park (Philadelphia A's), the Polo Grounds (New York Giants), Hilltop Park (New York Highlanders), Washington Park (Brooklyn Dodgers), and Comiskey Park (Chicago White Sox) were used in games featuring two black clubs. See *Indianapolis Freeman*, June 29, September 14, 1907; September 17, 1910.

New York Age, September 3, 1908; June 9, 1910; October 31, 1912. Seymour, *Golden Age*, 70.

14. *New York Age*, March 30, 1911, February 2, 1918. *Indianapolis Freeman*, December 11, 1909 ("belittle"); August 1, 1914; May 12, 1917; September 7, 1918. *Chicago Defender*, May 25, August 31, 1918. *Cleveland Advocate*, April 12, 1919 (White quote).

15. *Indianapolis Freeman*, February 28, April 11, 1914; August 7, 14, 1915 (Taylor quote); April 29, 1916. *Chicago Defender*, November 4, 11, 18, 25, 1916. Peterson, *Only the Ball*, 226, 251; Dixon and Hannigan, *Negro Baseball Leagues*, 111–114; Holway, *Voices*, 50 (Malarcher quote). In 1916, the ABCs took five of nine games against the American Giants in a championship series. Rube Foster disputed the results, claiming that both teams agreed to a 12-game series, with seven wins necessary to claim the championship.

16. *Indianapolis Freeman*, January 7, July 24, 1911; December 20, 1913. *New York Age*, February 16, April 20, June 29, August 10, 1911; August 21, September 4, 1913. *Pittsburgh Courier*, November 21, 1925; July 3, 1926. *New York Amsterdam News*, June 23, 1926; August 25, 1927. *Chicago Defender*, April 26, 1919; *New York Times*, November 22, 1954. Peterson, *Only the Ball*, 70; Dixon and Hannigan, *Negro Baseball Leagues*, 107–109. While the McMahons were viewed as the sole owners of the Lincoln Giants through 1913, there is evidence to suggest that Keenan and Harvey provided backing as well and later bought out the club from the McMahons. See *Baltimore Afro-American*, November 27, 1928; *New York Amsterdam News*, April 27, 1932; *Pittsburgh Courier*, May 8, 1926. During the 1920s, the McMahons owned the Commonwealth basketball team. Roderick McMahon, meanwhile, became well known as Tex Rickard's matchmaker at the newly built Madison Square Garden in New York. He died in 1954 at the age of 72.

17. *Indianapolis Freeman*, March 8, 1913; March 4, May 27, 1916. *North American*, May 21, October 8, 1916. *New York Age*, May 2, 1912; July 20, 1916. *Chicago Defender*, March 18, 1922. *Philadelphia Tribune*, January 2, 1926; May 10, 1928; May 28, 1931. James DiClerico and Barry Pavelec, *Jersey Game* (New Brunswick, 1991), 140; Peterson, *Only the Ball*, 67. An alternate version of the Bacharachs' formation suggests that Mayor Bacharach discovered the team in Jacksonville, Florida, and brought the team north in 1916. See Holway, *Blackball Stars*, 32, 136; Rogosin, *Invisible Men*, 28.

18. *Indianapolis Freeman*, June 25, 1910; December 23, 1911 (Wyatt quote); May 3, December 20, 1913; July 4, 1914. *Chicago Defender*, September 9, 1916; September 7, 1918, June 28, November 29, 1919. Dixon and Hannigan, *Negro Baseball Leagues*, 62. Before World War I, teams typically received guarantees for weekday games ranging from $50 to $60, with an option of receiving 40–50 percent of the gross receipts.

19. *Indianapolis Freeman*, April 18, 1914; August 28, 1915. *New York Age*, August 17, 1911; August 15, 1912 (Walton quotes); July 24, 1913 (Walton quote). *Chicago Defender*, September 5, 1914; August 28, 1915; January 1, 1916. African American umpires were not exclusively used in any Chicago-area black league until 1915.

20. *Indianapolis Freeman*, March 10 (Foster quote), May 12, 1917; *New York Age*, August 4, 1910; *Chicago Defender*, April 15, 1914.

21. White, *Base Ball Guide*, 79 (quote); *Indianapolis Freeman*, July 11, 1908 (quote); January 15, April 16, 1910; *Norfolk Journal and Guide*, April 21, 1923; *New York Amsterdam News*, February 20, 1929; Jules Tygiel, *Baseball's Great Experiment: Jackie Robinson and His Legacy* (New York, 1983), 18–19; Rogosin, *Invisible Men*, 145; Peterson, *Only the Ball*, 145–151; Bruce, *Kansas City Monarchs*, 80. Black teams advertising in the white press often emphasized both their ballplaying skills and entertainment value. Philadelphia's Anchor Giants were touted as a "star attraction of ball players and fun makers" in 1911, while other teams were promoted for their "witty sayings and repartee" with fans. In 1919 a press release for the first game at Shibe Park featuring two

black teams (Hilldale and the Bacharach Giants) noted the clubs kept "spectators in constant laughter by their droll coaching and witty sayings." Clowning would fade in the 1920s, although Elias "Country" Brown, an outfielder for several clubs, kept the practice alive. As late as 1924, Ira Lewis of the *Pittsburgh Courier* scorned a touring "monkey team" attempting to pass as Cubans as a "collection of chattering jackasses" without talent. See *North American*, June 25, 1911; September 8, 1919. *Indianapolis Freeman*, March 3, 1917; *New York Amsterdam News*, September 29, 1926; *Pittsburgh Courier*, April 25, 1925.

22. *Indianapolis Freeman*, August 7, 1915; *Chicago Defender*, July 24, 31, 1915. Kusmer, *Ghetto Takes Shape*, 189; Seymour, *People's Game*, 575–576; *Baltimore Afro-American*, June 30, 1917.

23. Hardy, "Race and Opportunity," 322–323; Kusmer, *Ghetto Takes Shape*, 157–159; Sadie Tanner Mossell, "Standard of Living Among One Hundred Negro Migrant Families in Philadelphia," *Annals of the American Academy of Political and Social Science*, 98 (November 1921), 174–175; *Philadelphia Tribune*, February 3; 10, May 26, July 28, 1917. *Chicago Defender*, March 31, 1917.

24. *Philadelphia Tribune*, February 10, 1917 (Bolden quote); March 21, 1929. *Indianapolis Freeman*, April 24, June 26, 1915; Otto Briggs File, National Baseball Library; Peterson, *Only the Ball*, 319; *Chicago Defender*, September 16, 1916; September 27, 1924. Bolden had apparently made earlier attempts to sign Briggs. Briggs appeared in Hilldale's final game of 1914 and was listed as a prospective team member for 1915 but remained in the Midwest during the season. *Philadelphia Tribune*, February 13, 1915.

25. *North American*, April 22, 1917; *Philadelphia Tribune*, May 12 (Bolden quote), June 9, 16, 30, July 28, 1917; *Baltimore Afro-American*, March 27, 1926; telephone conversation with Jim Riley, November 22, 1992. Sykes later became a dentist in Alabama and was a witness in the famous 1931 Scottsboro case. He died in 1986 at age 94.

26. *Indianapolis Freeman*, September 8, October 20, 1917; *Chicago Defender*, February 3, 1917.

27. *Chicago Defender*, September 1, 8, 1917; July 6, August 10 (Wyatt quote), 1918. *Philadelphia Tribune*, August 25, 1917; Rube Foster letter to W.T. Smith, July 2, 1919, National Baseball Library.

28. *North American*, July 27, 1917; *Philadelphia Tribune*, July 15, 1916 (quote). Bolden still insisted upon gentlemanly behavior from his players, even in the later years of the club. Jake Stephens, Hilldale's shortstop for much of the 1920s, remembered, "If you weren't a gentleman, you didn't play on his ball club. When he called you in his office, you didn't do it again or you didn't play again [until] next year. Your baseball ability didn't mean a thing, you had to be a gentleman" (John Holway notes, courtesy John Holway). Proper dress was important as well. Bolden bought the young Stephens two suits and two Stetson hats when he first made the team in 1921. Rogosin, *Invisible Man*, 69.

29. *Chicago Defender*, October 11, 1913; October 23, 1915. Holway, *Blackball Stars*, 61–78; Bankes, *Pittsburgh Crawfords*, 63; Rogosin, *Invisible Men*, 183–184. According to author John Holway, Joe Williams won 22 games against teams of white organized baseball players between 1912 and 1932.

30. *Philadelphia Record*, October 7, 1917; *Philadelphia Tribune*, October 13, 1917; *Chicago Defender*, October 13, 1917; February 22, 1919. Hilldale Ledger, 1917. Other sources assessed the crowd at 12,000 fans. The team earned $1,966.39 for the October 6 game, $1,560.69 for October 13, and $1,397.17 for the October 20 game, for a total of $4,924.25.

31. *Philadelphia Tribune*, October 13, 1917.

32. On the Chester race riots of 1917, see Hardy, "Race and Opportunity," 390.

Chapter 3

1. Robert Creamer, *Babe: The Legend Comes to Life* (New York, 1974), 158–164, 159 ("mills and shipyards"); Murdock, *Ban Johnson, Czar of Baseball*, 119–131; Seymour, *People's Game*, 233–235; *Chicago Defender*, August 31, 1918 (quote); *North American*, July 19, 26, 28, September 2, 7, 15, 1918; *Sporting News*, October 3, 1918; *Philadelphia Public Ledger*, October 19, 1918. On the impact of World War I on semiprofessional baseball, see also Rob Ruck, *Sandlot Seasons: Sport in Black Pittsburgh* (Cocoa, FL, 1983), 39–46; Seymour, *Golden Age*, 245–255; David Voight, *American Baseball*, 121–122; Seymour, *People's Game*. In 1918, major league baseball was forced to suspend operations a month early in September, and only one of nine minor league organizations managed to complete its season. Obojski, *Bush Leagues*, 18.

2. *Chicago Defender*, August 31, 1918 (quote); Hardy, "Race and Opportunity," 135, 314–378; Fourteenth Census 1920 (Washington, 1921); Allen Ballard, *One More Day's Journey: The Story of a Family and a People* (New York, 1984), 171.

3. *Chicago Defender*, December 29, 1917; January 5, October 19, November 9, 1918; March 1, April 5, September 6, 1919; January 3, April 10, 1920; March 19, 1921. *Baltimore Afro-American*, September 10, 1920; July 29, 1921. *Philadelphia Tribune*, January 18, 1919; April 17, 1920. *New York Times*, February 21, 1920. Murdock, *Ban Johnson*, 121–122; *New York Age*, August 17, 1918; Seymour, *People's Game*, 592–593; *The Competitor*, May 1921; Holway notes; L. Robert Davids, ed., *Insider's Baseball* (New York, 1983), 268–270. While Harold Seymour has noted that many blacks who served were "arbitrarily assigned to labor battalions," several black ballplayers saw action overseas. Spottswood Poles received five battle stars and a Purple Heart while serving with the 369th Infantry, and future Hilldale pitcher Scrip Lee also was wounded. Speck Webster died of pneumonia in France in 1919. Like their white counterparts, several black professional ballplayers who served in the military also managed to play baseball overseas, like Dizzy Dismukes, who led the only black team in the AEF League to a third-place finish. Black soldiers, however, usually had separate recreation programs and were often segregated while attending interracial games.

4. *Chicago Defender*, June 15, 22, 1918; December 13, 1919; December 24, 1921. List of Hilldale's Expenses for 1918 in Lloyd Thompson–Bill Cash Collection; *Philadelphia Tribune*, September 28, 1918; *Baltimore Afro-American*, March 7, 1925. In 1920, according to Rube Foster, there were only five salaried clubs in existence: the Lincoln Giants, Hilldale, Brooklyn Royal Giants, New York Bacharach Giants, and the Chicago American Giants. By 1921, twelve teams paid a total of $166,000 in salaries. In the late 1920s, Hilldale's salaries ranged from $125 to $400. Since players were docked for various expenses, including equipment, salary advances, and transportation, they seldom received the full amount each month. On salaries in the major and minor leagues, see Steven A. Riess, *Touching Base: Professional Baseball and American Culture in the Progressive Era* (Westport, CT, 1980), 156–165.

5. Holway, *Blackball Stars*, 88–95, 91 (quote); Peterson, *Only the Ball*, 224; *Chicago Defender*, September 27, 1924; Louis Santop File, National Baseball Library.

6. *Philadelphia Tribune*, April 6, July 13, 1918; April 3, 7, 1951. *Chicago Defender*, May 18, 1918; September 27, 1924. *Baseball Encyclopedia*, 8th ed. (New York, 1990), 2613–2614; Holway, *Blackball Stars*, 150–166; Peterson, *Only the Ball*, 237; James A. Riley, *All-Time All-Stars of Black Baseball* (Cocoa, FL, 1983), 252; Bankes, *Pittsburgh Crawfords*, 152; Judy Johnson File, National Baseball Library. Cockrell's no-hitters were against the All-Nationals of New York in 1919, the Detroit Stars in 1921, Chicago American Giants and Paterson Silk Sox in 1922, South Phillies in 1923 (six innings), and Cape May in 1930.

7. *Chicago Defender*, June 28, 1918; October 16, 1920. *Philadelphia Tribune*, June 1, July 6, September 21, 1918 (quote); October 16, 1920. *Philadelphia Record*, September 15, 1918; October 5, 12, 1919; October 9, 1920. Ruth was hitless in the first game, while Santop had two singles and a double. During the week of October 4–10, 1920, both of Philadelphia's major league parks were occupied by black teams, Hilldale at Phillies Park and the New York Bacharachs and Chicago American Giants at Shibe Park.

8. Douglas Novell and Lawrence Ziewacz, *Games They Played: Sports in American History, 1865–1980* (Chicago, 1983), 67–96; Betts, *America's Sporting Heritage*, 67, 136–139, 181 (quote); *New York Times*, June 28, 1919 (quote), cited in Betts, 139; Joel Zoss and John Bowman, *Diamonds in the Rough: The Untold Story of Baseball* (New York, 1989), 93; Seymour, *People's Game*, 236–249. Between 1909 and 1923, the percentage of industrial employees working less than 54 hours per week jumped from 15.2 percent to 68 percent.

9. Seymour, *People's Game*, 236–270; *Philadelphia Inquirer*, April 25, 27, June 4, 9, 18, July 13, August 2, 5, 1922; June 4, 9, 1923. *North American*, June 9, 1919; April 11, 18, 19, May 16, 26, 30, June 21, August 22, 29, September 25, 1920; April 24, June 17, July 17, 1921; Edward "Dutch" Doyle, "Sandlot Babe," in *Ol' Ball Game: A Collection of Baseball Characters and Moments Worth Remembering* (Harrisburg, 1990), 31–33; *Philadelphia Tribune*, July 26, 1924. Other notable women's teams were the Philadelphia Bobbies, the Quaker City Bloomer Girls, and the Seger Flashes, an African American team.

10 Ruck, *Sandlot Seasons*, 43; *Chicago Defender*, March 30, July 13, 1918; July 17, 1920. *North American*, July 24, 1921 (Isaminger quote); February 11, 19, May 14, 1922. *Philadelphia Inquirer*, April 24, 1922 ("Old Sport" quote). While twilight baseball had been tried in the western states before World War I, its appearance in New York, Chicago, Philadelphia, and other cities was triggered by a need to accommodate the later hours of war workers unable to attend afternoon games. Daylight savings time returned to local option in 1920 but continued to be retained in Philadelphia. By September, darkness limited most twilight games to seven innings. Semiprofessional teams attempted various lighting arrangements, but night baseball did not become a significant factor until 1930. *Philadelphia Public Ledger,* March 29, 1919; March 24, 31, April 6, 1920; May 21, 1921; March 3, 1922.

11. *Baseball Encyclopedia*; Frank Bilovsky and Rich Westcott, *Phillies Encyclopedia* (New York, 1984), 476; photocopy from *Baseball Dope Book* (1985), 42–43, Baseball Hall of Fame Library; *Philadelphia Tribune*, March 20, 1920 (Steele quote); *North American*, July 24, 1921; *Indianapolis Freeman*, January 5, 1918.

12. *North American*, April 19, May 2, 16, 30, 1920; February 17, 19, March 5, April 19, 23, May 14, June 11, August 6, 1922; May 5, 1923. *Philadelphia Inquirer*, June 29, 1922; April 29, 1923. *Philadelphia Public Ledger*, September 2, 1921.

13. *Chicago Defender*, August 7, 1920; *Philadelphia Tribune*, July 5, 12, August 23, September 20, 1919; October 16, 1920; April 30, 1921; April 19, 1924. *North American*, June 29, 1919; April 11, May 18, 24, July 18, 21, September 5, 1920; April 17, 1921, August 20, 1922; July 6, 1924. *Philadelphia Inquirer*, May 10, July 6, 1922; May 29, 1929. *Sporting Life*, March 18, 1922; *Philadelphia Record*, September 9, 1930; Bruce Kuklick, *To Every Thing a Season* (Princeton, NJ, 1991), 50–51; Doyle, "Sandlot Baseball," 13–14. Other former major league players playing locally in the 1920s and early 1930s included Socks Seibold, Lefty York, Claude Hendrix, Marty Kavanaugh, Ed Lennox, Ralph Young, Dick Spalding, Denny Sothern, and Ed Roetz. See *Philadelphia Inquirer*, June 27, July 9, 1922; June 24, 1925; June 6, 1926. *North American*, April 1, May 20, 1923. *Philadelphia Tribune*, August 6, 1931.

14. Holway, *Black Diamonds*, 84 (Benson quote); *Sporting Life*, March 18, 1922; *North American*, July 31, August 1, 21, 1921. Other future major leaguers who played

against Hilldale included Bucky Walters of the Trenton team in 1930 and Hank Greenberg with Bay Parkway of New York in 1929; see *Philadelphia Tribune*, July 3, 1930; *New York Amsterdam News*, April 24, 1929.

15. *Philadelphia Tribune*, February 8, August 2, 23, September 20, 1919; March 20 (quote), May 8, 29, June 19, 1920; September 10, 1921. *Philadelphia Inquirer*, September 2, 1989; *Pittsburgh Courier*, August 4, 1923 (Wilson quote); *North American*, July 6, 25, 1919. Financial figures are based on my reading of the Hilldale ledger books from 1921 to 1924, which list the amount and percentage paid for each game (Lloyd Thompson–Bill Cash Collection).

16. 1916 Hilldale Ledger (November 1916 entry); *Philadelphia Tribune*, April 13, 1918; January 24, February 14, March 6 (Madison Stars quote), April 17, June 26, July 17, August 28, 1920. Holway, *Voices*, 74 (McDonald quote); *Washington Bee*, June 8, 1918; *Philadelphia Daily News*, August 23, 1982.

17. *North American*, August 28, 1920; June 15, 1921. Peterson, *Only the Ball*, 10–11 (Johnson quote); *Philadelphia Tribune*, September 8, 1932. While Hilldale successfully drew on Saturdays, the failure of another Pennsylvania club, the Pittsburgh Keystones. was blamed on the absence of Sunday baseball; see *Chicago Defender*, December 16, 1922.

18. *Philadelphia Tribune*, February 28, 1920; April 4, 1925; February 14, 1928 (quote); May 28, 1931 (DePriest quote). *Pittsburgh Courier*, June 2, 1923; May 2, 1925; *Baltimore Afro-American*, October 15, 1920. Peterson, *Only the Ball*, 123 (Johnson quote). In the early 1920s, the field was occasionally used for football games during the off-season. Actual seating capacity and dimensions of Hilldale Park are not known. Unreliable estimates have appeared in Michael Benson's *Ballparks of North America* (Jefferson, NC, 1989), 419. Hilldale pitcher Scrip Lee told John Holway that "left field was about 350, it might have been a little bit longer. Center field had a big tree, there was plenty of room back there for the outfielders to run" (courtesy of John Holway). The *Tribune* estimated the distance to center field at 320 feet in 1925.

19. *Philadelphia Tribune*, April 29, August 3, 1918; May 17, 1919; April 24, 1920; April 30, 1921. For major league ticket prices, see Riess, *Touching Base*, 32–34; Seymour, *Golden Age*, 68. At black baseball parks in Atlantic City, Chicago, New York, Baltimore, Brooklyn, and Newark during the early 1920s, ticket prices ranged from 25 cents for bleacher seats to 85 cents for box seats. See *Chicago Defender*, April 30, 1910; August 9, 1913; May 31, June 7, August 30, 1919; April 10, June 5, July 3, 1920; August 13, 1921. *Philadelphia Tribune*, May 17, 1919; May 8, 1920. *Baltimore Afro-American*, June 23, 1922.

20. *Philadelphia Tribune*, April 15, May 13, 1916; April 28, 1917; June 5, July 3, July 17, 1920; April 23, 1921; September 5, 1929. *Baltimore Afro-American*, September 10, 17, 1920; Seymour, *Golden Age*, 363–366. On Rhodes, Williams, and Stevens, see Hardy, "Race and Opportunity," 314–370. African American female fans were common at Hilldale Park and other black baseball parks. As early as 1911, the *Indianapolis Freeman* noted that black female fans "know what they are talking about." See *Indianapolis Freeman*, August 5, 1911, *Chicago Defender*, May 13, 27, 1911; May 2, 1914; April 17, 1920. *Baltimore Afro-American*, June 20, 1919; August 18, 1922. *Philadelphia Tribune*, May 25, 1912; May 9, 1925. Seymour, *People's Game*, 565–566, 577, 600.

21. *Philadelphia Tribune*, August 31, 1918 (Bolden quote); September 6, 1924; December 13, 1928 ("losing their" quote). *Pittsburgh Courier*, June 6, 1925 (Wilson quote); *Chicago Defender*, September 19, 1924; *North American*, July 18, 1920; *Baltimore Afro-American*, July 3, 1926 (Black Sox quote). Even the *Chicago Defender*, never an ardent supporter of Bolden or his team, acknowledged that Hilldale had "the most loyal bunch of fans in the country."

22. John Holway notes (Johnson and Lee quotes). *Philadelphia Tribune*, November 12, 1921. Eddie Gottlieb, a white promoter who later co-owned the Philadelphia Stars with Ed Bolden, also attested to the significant presence of whites at Hilldale games in the early 1920s (cited in Rust, *"Get That Nigger off the Field!"* 16). An item for "white tickets" in the Hilldale ledger book of 1926 indicates that segregated seating may have existed occasionally at Hilldale Park. During the early 1920s, grandstand seating was segregated at the Kansas City Monarchs' park at Twentieth and Olive, which they shared with the American Association's Kansas City Blues; see Holway, *Blackball Stars*, 330.

23. Bankes, *The Pittsburgh Crawfords*, 85 (Johnson quote); *Philadelphia Tribune*, May 31, 1924; July 26, August 30, 1928. *Chicago Defender*, September 20, 1919; *Pittsburgh Courier*, October 3, 1925; Holway, *Black Diamonds*, 15; Bill Klink, "Our Friend Willie," in *Ol' Ball Game*, 127–128. From 1919 to 1931, Hilldale made only rare appearances at Shibe Park, although the New York Bacharachs leased the park on several occasions between 1919 and 1921. Several historians of black baseball have confused Shibe Park, the home of the A's from 1909 to 1954 (and the Phillies from 1938 to 1970), with Phillies Park (Baker Bowl), the Phillies' grounds from 1887 to 1938.

24. Robert Eisen, "Dexter Park and the Bushwicks," *Times Newsweekly of Ridgewood, Long Island*, September 19, 26, 1991; telephone conversation with Bob Potts, November 29, 1992; Seymour, *People's Game*, 264. Hilldale debuted against the Bushwicks on June 20, 1920, and against Paterson on August 17, 1918.

25. *Philadelphia Tribune*, November 12, 1921 (information abstracted from a list of Hilldale's games for 1921); June 7, 1928. *North American*, July 16, August 13, 1922. Frederic Kelly, "Judy Johnson: From Snow Hill to the Hall of Fame," *Sun Magazine*, February 1, 1976, 18 (Johnson quote). *Baltimore Afro-American*, March 20, 1926 (Taylor quote). Twenty-three teams defeated Hilldale in 1921, 16 white and seven black.

26. *Philadelphia Tribune*, May 31 (Hilldale fan quote), December 20, 1928 (Briggs quote). *Chicago Defender*, July 31, 1920 ("white lads"), October 21, 1922; October 13, 1923. *Philadelphia Inquirer*, August 28, 1923. Racially motivated "sandlot riots" occurred in Philadelphia in June 1918 and July 1920. See *Chicago Defender*, June 15, 1918; *Philadelphia Tribune*, July 31, August 14, 1920.

27. *Pittsburgh Courier*, August 30, 1924; *Philadelphia Tribune*, July 31, August 14, 1920; Rogosin, *Invisible Men*, 134 (Johnson quote). Strawbridge and Clothier began playing black teams in 1924.

28. Rogosin, *Invisible Men*, 128 (Hubbard quote); Kelly, "Judy Johnson," 16 (Johnson quote). In border cities like Baltimore and Washington, interracial baseball remained less common than in Philadelphia, New York, or Chicago. See *Baltimore Afro-American*, July 27, 1929.

29. Kusmer, *Black Cleveland*, 214; *Baltimore Afro-American*, April 11, 1925 (Bolden quote); May 12, September 22, 1928 (quotes); *Chicago Defender*, December 31, 1921 (Foster quote); Ruck, *Sandlot Seasons*. Interracial teams were comparatively rare. On July 3, 1920, however, Bolden lent the white St. Agatha team a Hilldale player after two of its catchers had been injured. In 1926, Mike Yaffe, a white political leader of Philadelphia's black Thirtieth Ward, operated a multiracial All-Nations team; see *Philadelphia Tribune*, July 10, 1920; August 28, September 4, 1926.

30. *Philadelphia Tribune*, February 10, 1917; April 19, June 7, June 14, 1924; June 27, 1925; June 23, 1927; August 16, 1928; September 30, 1950. Hilldale ledger, 1920; Hardy, "Race and Opportunity," 233 ("Jim Crow" quote); *Pittsburgh Courier Magazine*, April 14, 1951 ("dour" quote); inventory of property, Edward Bolden (courtesy Delaware County Courthouse, Media, Pennsylvania). Hilda Bolden was the only African American woman to graduate from the premed program at the University of

Pennsylvania in 1928 and later received her medical degree from Meharry Medical College; see *Philadelphia Tribune*, June 21, 1928.

31. Steven Riess, "Professional Sunday Baseball: A Study in Social Reform, 1892–1934," *Maryland Historian*, Fall 1973, 95–108; John A. Lucas, "The Unholy Experiment: Professional Baseball's Struggle Against Pennsylvania Sunday Blue Laws, 1926–34." *Pennsylvania History* (38), April 1971, 163–175; *North American*, May 19, 1919; July 18, August 8, 1920; June 6, 1921; July 30, 1922. *New York Times*, November 2, 1919; March 9, 1920; May 9, 1921. *Philadelphia Public Ledger*, July 15, 1920; May 9, 1921. *Philadelphia Tribune*, July 17, 1920; *Baltimore Afro-American*, September 10, 1920; Alexander, *Our Game*, 149; Kuklick, *To Every Thing*, 70–72. On similar crackdowns on commercialized Sunday baseball in Darby, see *North American*, August 30, 1920; *Public Ledger*, August 30, 1920. Like other local teams, Hilldale participated in several illegal Sunday games during 1920 and sporadically through 1922.

32. *North American*, July 12, 25, August 9, 29, September 1, 1921. *Philadelphia Public Ledger*, June 21, July 25, August 29, September 2, 1921 (Moore quote). Sunday baseball continued to be a controversial topic in several Philadelphia area communities, including National Park and Audubon in southern New Jersey and Upper Darby in Delaware County. In 1926 the Philadelphia Athletics played a test game at Shibe Park to challenge the constitutionality of the state's Sunday baseball ban but eventually were defeated in the Pennsylvania Supreme Court and gave up. As late as 1930, Philadelphia police were still breaking up Sunday games. On Sunday, September 28, 1930, 23,000 fans attended a game at Phillies Park (Baker Bowl) to benefit the family of a man killed while trying to prevent his son from being arrested for a Sunday baseball violation. See *North American*, August 7, 27, 1922; *Philadelphia Inquirer*, February 4, 1923; John Lucas, "Unholy Experiment," 167–169; *Philadelphia Record*, September 29, 1930; Doyle, "Philadelphia Sandlot Baseball," 13.

33. *Philadelphia Inquirer*, April 5, May 9, 14, 24, June 2, 12, 25, 27, July 10, August 18, October 20, 1922. *North American*, February 8, 10, 13, 18, 25, May 9, 12, 23, June 18, June 27, July 2, 9, 16, August 6, September 3, 1922 (quote). *Sporting Life*, March 18, April 8, June 10, 1922. *Chicago Defender*, April 22, 1922; January 13, 1923. *Baltimore Afro-American*, October 6, 1922; *Pittsburgh Courier*, October 13, 1923 ("Jim Crow sections"), August 30, 1924; *New York Amsterdam News*, January 17, 1923; Seymour, *People's Game*, 249. In 1922 the proposed elimination tournament was canceled because of various delays. Winners of the three divisions in 1922 were Fleisher (local), American Chain (regional), and Richmond Giants ("colored"). The American Chain team of York, Pennsylvania, later joined organized baseball as part of the newly formed Class B New York–Pennsylvania League. In 1923, Hilldale defeated Chester to win the PBA championship.

34. *Pittsburgh Courier*, July 14, 1923; July 24, 1926. *Philadelphia Inquirer*, May 7, July 22, 29, 1928; June 8, 1930. *Philadelphia Record*, August 12, 1930; *Philadelphia Tribune*, February 20, 1930; *North American*, July 31, 1921; Betts, *America's Sporting Heritage*, 253, 271–272, 314–315; Robert Crepeau, *Baseball: America's Diamond Mind, 1919–1941* (Orlando, 1980), 184; *New York Times*, February 22, 1925; December 31, 1931. "To Rescue Baseball in the Small Towns," *Literary Digest*, April 18, 1925; Seymour, *People's Game*, 71, 84–85, 250, 257; Hugh Fullerton, "Earnings in Baseball," *North American Review*, June 1930, 743–744; Vincent Franklin, *Education of Black Philadelphia* (Philadelphia, 1979), 105; Scranton and Licht, *Work Sights*, 266.

35. Bilovsky and Westcott, *Phillies Encyclopedia* (New York, 1984), 476; photocopy from *Baseball Dope Book* (1985), 42–43, Baseball Hall of Fame Library; Riess, *City Games*, 223; *Baseball Encyclopedia*. *Philadelphia Tribune*, July 15, 1925; May 29, 1926; June 7, July 12, 1928; June 27, 1929; April 17, 1930. *Baltimore Afro-American*, August

28, 1926; *Philadelphia Inquirer*, June 15, 24, 1926; Bruce, *Kansas City Monarchs*, 45; Seymour, *Golden Age*, 443; Voight, *American Baseball*, 43–44, 89–90, 247–248. There is evidence to suggest that the local absence of a strong professional team attracted whites to black ballparks or to white semiprofessional games. In Kansas City, white attendance at Monarch games began to diminish as the fortunes of the local minor league club, the Kansas City Blues, steadily improved. Similarly, the popularity of semipro ball in Cleveland during 1924 increased as the Indians struggled to a sixth-place finish in the American League. In 1934, with the Athletics and Phillies both fighting to stay out of last place, Rollo Wilson claimed that "hundreds of white fans" in Philadelphia preferred to watch black professional baseball instead of local major league baseball. See Seymour, *People's Game*, 244; *Crisis*, October 1934, 305.

36. *Philadelphia Tribune*, March 19, 1921; *North American*, May 28, 1922 ("colored championship"); *Pittsburgh Courier*, June 2, 30, July 14, October 13, 1923; John Saunders, *100 Years After Emancipation*, 191 ("short, chunky").

Chapter 4

1. Rogosin, *Invisible Men*, 12 ("absolute zenith"); Ruck, *Sandlot Seasons*, 43–44; Kusmer, *Ghetto Takes Shape*, 283. *Chicago Defender*, September 23, 1916; February 22, March 1, 1919. *Indianapolis Freeman*, September 7, 1918; July 5, 1919. Bruce, *Kansas City Monarchs*, 36–45, 67–77. Despite Taylor's absence, the ABCs continued to operate in 1919, functioning as a semiprofessional club under George Abram at Northwestern Park. There is evidence to suggest that Foster planned to place a club in Indianapolis at Washington Park in 1920 under John Henry Lloyd; see Foster letter to W.T. Smith, July 2, 1919.

2. *Chicago Defender*, December 13, 1919 (Foster quote); Bankes, *Pittsburgh Crawfords*, 23–28, 91–96; Ruck, *Sandlot Seasons*, 136–169. Involvement of black underworld figures was less pronounced during the 1920s, although Baron Wilkins of the Bacharach Giants, Alex Pompez of the Cuban Stars, and Dick Kent of the St. Louis Stars all operated franchises. As economic conditions for blacks worsened during the Depression and available finances became scarce, black vice leaders, especially involved in the illegal numbers lottery, invested in baseball as a money-laundering scheme and to avoid paying income tax. These men, including Gus Greenlee (Pittsburgh Crawfords), Rufus Jackson (Homestead Grays), Abe Manley (Newark Eagles), and Jim Semler (New York Black Yankees), virtually dominated the ownership of Negro league teams in the mid-1930s. Notably, neither Foster nor Bolden, the acknowledged powers of black baseball in the 1920s, had ties to illegal activities, although Bolden has been erroneously depicted as a vice leader in several histories, perhaps due to his later involvement with gambler-promoter Eddie Gottlieb (see especially Bankes, *Pittsburgh Crawfords*, 28; Rogosin, *Invisible Men*, 17, 107). In Philadelphia, Smitty Lucas, a local "hotel man and cabaret owner" heavily involved in the Philadelphia numbers scene, organized the Eastern League All-Stars in 1927. Later known as the Philadelphia Tigers, the team was a member of the Eastern Colored League in the last year of its existence in 1928 and disappeared soon after. See *Philadelphia Tribune*, June 30, August 11, 1927; May 3, 1928; Hardy, "Race and Opportunity," 457–471.

3. *Cleveland Advocate*, April 12, 1919 (White quote); Rich Bak, *Cobb Would Have Caught It: The Golden Age of Baseball in Detroit* (Detroit, 1991), 92–107. *Baltimore Afro-American*, December 27, 1924; January 3, 10, 1925. *Chicago Defender*, March 13, 1920; February 12, 1921. *Pittsburgh Courier*, December 27, 1924. In 1919 Hilldale made its first trip west, traveling to Detroit for a series against the newly formed Stars.

4. *Philadelphia Tribune*, April 13, 1918.

5. *Philadelphia Tribune*, April 13, 20 (Miller quote), June 15, 1918. *New York Age*, June 8, 1918 (Walton quote); *Chicago Defender*, November 9, 1918. While several railroad stations in the East featured strong red cap teams, including Union Station in Washington and Broad Street Station in Philadelphia, the Pennsylvania Red Caps of Pennsylvania Station, New York, were the best known and often attracted professional players to their ranks. See Seymour, *People's Game*, 585; *Philadelphia Tribune*, May 14, 1931.

6. *Chicago Defender*, April 19, 26, May 10, 17, 31, June 7, 14, 21, 28, July 5, 12, 1919; January 1, 1921. *Cleveland Advocate*, April 26, 1919; *Philadelphia Tribune*, May 28, 1931; March 10, 1932. *New York Amsterdam News*, July 14, 1926; *Baltimore Afro-American*, May 19, December 22, 1922; March 16, 1923; June 6, 1924. *Pittsburgh Courier*, May 31, 1924. In 1921 Chase was permanently banned from organized baseball for his involvement in throwing games. On Chase, see Bill James, *Bill James Historical Baseball Abstract*, 337–342.

7. Kusmer, *Ghetto Takes Shape*, 174–189. *Baltimore Afro-American*, July 25, August 1, November 28, 1919. *Chicago Defender*, April 26 (White quote), August 9, 30, September 6, 1919; *Cleveland Advocate*, April 26, 1919 ("leashed"). Race riots also occurred in Wilmington, Delaware, and Washington, D.C., during 1919.

8. C.I. Taylor, "Future of Colored Baseball," *The Competitor*, February 1920, 76; Holway, *Voices*, 28–29; *Chicago Defender*, November 2, 1918; August 30, September 20, 1919. *North American*, September 9, 1919; Foster letter to W.T. Smith, July 2, 1919; *Negro in Chicago*, 178.

9. Rogosin, *Invisible Men*, 26 ("structural problem"), 44, 93; Ruck, *Sandlot Seasons*, 116–122; *Philadelphia Tribune*, September 19, 1925; January 28, 1932. *Chicago Defender*, August 10, 1918; April 19, 1919. Bruce, *Kansas City Monarchs*, 30, 74; Wyatt, "'Stove League': Smoking 'Em Across with the Winning Run on the Sacks," *The Competitor*, January 1920, 65. *Indianapolis Freeman*, August 17, 1918; December 27, 1919. *Washington Tribune*, September 23, 1922. The St. Louis Giants, Winston-Salem Giants, Pittsburgh Giants, Baltimore Black Sox, and Madison Stars of Philadelphia all incorporated between 1917 and 1921, selling shares at prices ranging from $1 to $100. See *Chicago Defender*, December 29, 1917, April 10, 1920; March 19, 1921. *Philadelphia Tribune*, April 17, 1920; *Baltimore Afro-American*, September 10, 1920; July 29, 1921.

10. Bill Plott, "Southern League of Colored Base Ballists," in *Baseball Historical Review*, ed. L. Robert Davids, SABR, 1981, 75–78; *New York Amsterdam News*, February 6, 1929; White, *Base Ball Guide*, 15–19, 41–51; Malloy, "Out at Home," 19–20; *New York Age*, April 14, 1910; *Cincinnati Enquirer*, November 10, 1904, cited in Robert L. Davids, "John (Bud) Fowler: Nineteenth Century Black Baseball Pioneer," unpublished paper, SABR Research Exchange, 8; *Indianapolis Freeman*, November 9, 23, 30, December 7, 21, 28, 1907; February 15, March 7, October 31, 1908; April 16, December 24, 1910; January 14, 1911. *Chicago Defender*, December 31, 1910; May 27, 1911 (quote).

11. *Indianapolis Freeman*, May 2, June 20, October 31, 1908; March 13, 1909; January 22, 29, July 2, 23, August 20, 1910; July 8, 1911; April 20, 1912; February 1, 1913; September 26, 1914. *New York Age*, July 9, 1908; June 3, 1909; May 19, 1910. *Chicago Defender*, May 7, 1910; *North American*, May 21, 1916; Seymour, *People's Game*, 576; Dixon and Hannigan, *Negro Baseball Leagues*, 104.

12. *Indianapolis Freeman*, November 29, December 20, 1913; April 18, 1914; August 14, 1915; May 19, October 20, 1917. *New York Age*, June 29, 1911; *Cleveland Advocate*, February 15, 1919; *Chicago Defender*, March 1, October 4, 1919; Taylor, "Future of Colored Baseball," 76–79; *New York Times*, November 18, 1913. In November 1913

the *New York Times* reported that a "Colored National Baseball League" had been capitalized in Pierre, SD, with backing from a group of Chicago men.

13. For Foster's articles, see *Chicago Defender*, November 29, December 13, 20, 27, 1919; January 3, 10, 17, 1920. Several historians of black baseball have erroneously suggested that financial losses suffered in 1919 because of a supposed decline in the popularity of semipro baseball motivated Foster to form a league. For examples of this view, see Bankes, *Pittsburgh Crawfords*, 17; Holway, *Blackball Stars*, 21. Ira Lewis observed that Foster, operating an already enormously successful club, had the least to gain from a risky league venture and could have easily "defied organization for many years"; see Lewis, "National Baseball League Formed," 66-67.

14. Dave Wyatt, "'Stove League,'" 65-66; C.I. Taylor, "Future of Colored Baseball," *The Competitor*, February 1920, 76-79.

15. *Indianapolis Freeman*, January 17, February 28, 1920; *Baltimore Afro-American*, September 4, 1926; *Pittsburgh Courier*, January 10, 1925; Bruce, *Kansas City Monarchs*, 36-45, 67-77; *Chicago Defender*, September 23, 1916; Holway, *Blackball Stars*, 327-343.

16. *Chicago Defender*, January 31, February 14, 21, March 20, 1920; *Baltimore Afro-American*, February 27, 1920; Ira F. Lewis, "National Baseball League Formed," 66-67; Dixon and Hannigan, *Negro Baseball Leagues*, 123-124; Bruce, *Kansas City Monarchs*, 13-14; Peterson, *Only the Ball*, 113-114; Ruck, *Sandlot Seasons*, 124. The Negro Southern League, a regional semiprofessional organization, was formed in March 1920 with franchises in Knoxville, Montgomery, Atlanta, Birmingham, New Orleans, Nashville, and Jacksonville. The league was later reorganized under Bert Roddy in 1926; see *Chicago Defender*, March 6, April 17, September 11, 1920; Rogosin, *Invisible Men*, 7-10; Peterson, *Only the Ball*, 101.

17. *Chicago Defender*, April 24, May 15, July 24 (Wyatt quote), July 31, August 28, 1920. In 1921 the NNL would rent American Association parks in Kansas City, Indianapolis, and Columbus as well as Redland Field, home of the Cincinnati Reds.

18. "Big League Making Progress," *The Competitor*, July 1920, 69; *Chicago Defender*, August 7, 1920; January 5, 1924. *Chicago Whip*, July 8, July 29, August 12, November 4, 1922; January 5, 1924. *Baltimore Afro-American*, February 2, 1923; *Pittsburgh Courier*, December 27, 1924; Murdock, *Ban Johnson*, 80.

19. *Chicago Defender*, January 17, February 21, March 13, May 1, 8, 1920 (Strong quote); *Philadelphia Tribune*, January 31, June 12, 1920; March 1, 1924. *Indianapolis Freeman*, April 24, 1920; *North American*, May 2, 1920. In 1920 Hilldale initiated separate legal proceedings against Deas and Lundy for contract violation. Citing the Pennsylvania Supreme Court's ruling in the 1902 Nap Lajoie case in support of organized baseball's reserve clause, Judge Stern of the Philadelphia Court of Common Pleas granted a temporary injunction that prevented Deas from playing for the Bacharachs until a final hearing on the case. Unwilling to pay the $2,000 bond required to protect Deas against any loss of income during the injunction, Hilldale eventually abandoned the case. On the Lajoie case, see Murdock, *Ban Johnson*, 54-55.

20. *Philadelphia Tribune*, August 21, 1920.

21. *Chicago Defender*, December 11, 1920; *Philadelphia Tribune*, November 20, 1920; *Baltimore Afro-American*, February 11, March 4, 1921; February 2, 1923. *Indianapolis Freeman*, November 27, December 11, 1920; Ira F. Lewis, "Baseball Men Hold Successful Meeting," *The Competitor*, January–February 1921, 51-54; Ira F. Lewis, "Big Clubs Ready for Season," *The Competitor*, April 1921, 37-39; Ira F. Lewis, "'New' League Not Needed," *The Competitor*, May 1921, 39-41; Peterson, *Only the Ball*, 86; *Pittsburgh Courier*, January 23, 1923. Other associate members in 1921 included the Cleveland Tate Stars, Pittsburgh Keystones, Pittsburgh Giants, Homestead Grays, Calgary Black Sox, and Dayton Marcos; see *Chicago Whip*, April 9, 1921.

22. *Philadelphia Tribune*, July 24, 1920; February 26, August 6, November 5, 1921; January 12, 1924; December 8, 1927. Holway, *Black Diamonds*, 2; *Chicago Defender*, August 9, 1919.

23. *Philadelphia Tribune*, July 9, September 10, October 15, 22, November 5, 12 (Thompson quote), 1921; *Chicago Defender*, June 11, October 8, 15, 22, December 31, 1921 (Foster quote); *Philadelphia Record*, October 13, 1921. According to Lloyd Thompson, Foster's demand for ground rules at Hilldale Park stemmed from a 1919 incident in which Hilldale outfielder Johnny Reese had secretly hidden a ball in one of the concealed tree stumps and used it to retire an American Giant player; see *Philadelphia Tribune*, February 14, 1929.

24. *Baltimore Afro-American*, November 11, December 2, 1921; February 10, December 15, 1922; April 6, 1923. *Chicago Defender*, November 26, December 10, 24, 1921; February 4, 1922. *Chicago Whip*, January 21, February 11, April 21, 1922. Foster claimed that at least half of the 12 major black baseball teams lost money in 1921; see *Chicago Defender*, December 24, 1921.

25. *Baltimore Afro-American*, January 13, December 15 ("slack"), 1922; February 16, April 6, 1923. *Pittsburgh Courier*, December 27, 1924 (Blount quote); January 24, 1925. *Chicago Defender*, November 26, 1921; December 22, 1923; January 5, 1924. *Chicago Whip*, October 28, 1922; *Philadelphia Tribune*, January 3, September 13, 1925 (Womack quote). Foster reportedly paid $945 to $1,346 a month for renting Schorling Park, supposedly equal to or greater than the cost of operating a "first class" minor league park; see *Chicago Defender*, November 29, 1919; April 3, 1920.

26. *New York Amsterdam News*, January 17, 1923; *Chicago Defender*, March 4, 11 (quotes), August 26, September 2, 1922; *Philadelphia Inquirer*, June 19, 26, July 31, December 23, 1922. On July 30, 1922, Cockrell pitched and won both games of a doubleheader against the East New York team, allowing a total of 14 hits in two games.

27. *New York Amsterdam News*, January 17, 1923 ("we have"); November 15, 1922, Rube Foster letter to W.T. Smith, National Baseball Library; *Chicago Whip*, December 16, 1922 ("legal shakedown"); *Baltimore Afro-American*, December 8, 22, 1922 ("disadvantage"); *Chicago Defender*, December 16, 1922; January 13, February 24, 1923.

28. *Chicago Defender*, January 13, 1923 (quote); *Baltimore Afro-American*, February 8, 1924 (Foster quote); *Philadelphia Tribune*, December 1, 1923; *Baltimore Afro-American*, December 1, 22, 1922; January 25, 1924. *Chicago Defender*, January 12, 1924. While the ECL had only two teams financed entirely by blacks (Hilldale and the Cuban Stars), whites had exerted considerable influence in the background of Foster's NNL. In addition to J.L. Wilkinson's ownership of the Kansas City Monarchs, the St. Louis Giants received considerable financial backing from whites despite the presence of a black "owner," and John Schorling continued to hold the lease to the American Giants' home at Schorling Park. In 1933, Rollo Wilson noted that "mighty few teams have been entirely financed by Negro capital, if you want to know the truth. There have been many instances of so-called Negro 'owners' being nothing but a 'front' for the white interest behind them" (*Pittsburgh Courier*, September 24, 1933, cited in Ruck, *Sandlot Seasons*, 116).

Chapter 5

1. Eisen, "Dexter Park and the Bushwicks," *Norfolk Journal and Guide*, February 26, 1921 ("Hebrew"); July 22, 1922. *New York Amsterdam News*, January 17, 1923 ("fallen in line"); July 14, 1926. *Chicago Defender*, March 10, 1923; *Chicago Whip*, December 23, 1922; *Baltimore Afro-American*, May 30, June 6, 1924; *New York Times*, May 25, 29, 1924;

Pittsburgh Courier, July 17, 1926. Baron Wilkins, Connors's former partner, was murdered in front of his New York city cabaret on May 24, 1924. Connors remained unaffiliated with black baseball until his death in 1926.

2. *New York Amsterdam News*, January 17 (Foster, Bolden quotes), March 7, 1923; *Chicago Defender*, February 24, 1923. *Baltimore Afro-American*, February 16, 1923 ("merits and demerits"); February 29, 1924; September 5, 1925. Bruce, *Kansas City Monarchs*, 32; *Chicago Whip*, October 28, December 16, 1922; *Philadelphia Tribune*, February 16, 1924. During the mid-1920s, Hilldale was able to travel by train to Baltimore, its most distant league rival, at a Sunday excusion fare of only $3.00 per player. In contrast, railroad fare between NNL cities ranged from $6.72 to $23.72 per player in 1925.

3. *Chicago Whip*, March 4, 1922; *Washington Tribune*, February 24, March 24, 1923; *Baltimore Afro-American*, March 2, 1923.

4. *Chicago Defender*, November 13, 1920; January 13, March 17, March 24, 1923 ("older heads"). *Baltimore Afro-American*, October 29, 1920; August 18, 1921; January 12 ("don't care to have me"), March 2, March 23 ("haphazard"), April 6, 1923. *Washington Tribune*, January 20, 1923.

5. *New York Amsterdam News*, April 18, 1923; November 4, 1925; June 23, 1926; August 25, 1927 ("To see"). *Chicago Defender*, March 13, 1920; *Philadelphia Tribune*, January 2, 1926; Holway, *Black Diamonds*, 158–160. There is little evidence to support Bruce Chadwick's claim that New York was a "hotbed of black baseball." During the 1920s, the absence of an easily accessible black baseball park and the close proximity of the Polo Grounds and Yankee Stadium led many of Harlem's fans to shift their support to major league baseball. In addition, the popularity of cricket among the city's substantial population of Caribbean-born blacks also undermined the growth of baseball locally. By 1932 Romeo Dougherty of the *New York Amsterdam News* would characterize the city as the "biggest hick town" in black baseball. See *New York Amsterdam News* March 5, December 31, 1930; March 9, 30, June 15, 1932; March 29, 1933. Art Rust, Jr., *"Get That Nigger,"* 55–56; Bruce Chadwick, *When the Game Was Black and White* (New York, 1992), 30.

6. *Baltimore Afro-American*, April 22, June 17, July 29, August 5, 1921; February 10, March 10, June 9, August 4, November 3, 1922; May 18, 1923; January 11, April 18, September 5, October 3, 1925; February 12, 1927; March 31, 1928. *Chicago Defender*, October 11, 1924; *Philadelphia Tribune*, January 2, 1926; April 25, 1929; February 12, 1931. *Washington Tribune*, June 9, 1923; Holway, *Voices*, 67–68; John Holway notes. Hilldale's much anticipated debut at Maryland Park on May 7, 1922, was cut short by the team's uncharacteristic decision to walk off the field in the second inning after a heated dispute over ground rules. The *Baltimore Afro-American* condemned Hilldale's "poor sportsmanship," and the team was fined $50 by the PBA for disappointing the large crowd. See *Baltimore Afro-American*, May 12, 1922; *Philadelphia Inquirer*, May 8, 1922; *North American*, May 23, 1922.

7. *Washington Tribune*, April 21, 1923 ("race affair"); March 1, 1924. *Chicago Defender*, January 13, 1923; *Baltimore Afro-American*, December 22, 1922; January 26, February 16, July 13, 1923. *Pittsburgh Courier*, December 27, 1924; 1923 Hilldale ledger; *New York Amsterdam News*, September 12, 1923 ("petty differences"). Ongoing research by members of the Negro League Committee of the Society of American Baseball Research has revealed the inaccuracy and incompleteness of most published NNL and ECL statistics and standings.

8. *Baltimore Afro-American*, December 8, 1922; April 6, June 1, July 13, 20, August 31, September 21, 1923. *Pittsburgh Courier*, September 29, October 27, 1923 (Wilson quote); *Chicago Defender*, January 27, September 29, 1923; Holway notes; *Philadelphia*

Tribune, January 5, March 15, 1924; Holway, *Blackball Stars,* 9 (Stephens quote), 45; *New York Amsterdam News,* September 26, 1923 (Bolden quote). On Lloyd, see Holway, *Blackball Stars,* 36–49.

9. *Philadelphia Public Ledger,* October 10–14, 1923; *North American,* October 10, 1923; *Pittsburgh Courier,* October 20, 27, 1923; *Philadelphia Inquirer,* June 23 ("million dollar"), October 10–14, 20–21, 1923; *Philadelphia Record,* October 11–14, 1923; *Washington Tribune,* July 21, 1923 (quote); *Chicago Whip,* December 23, 1922 ("wealth"); *Baltimore Afro-American,* October 19, 1923; *New York Amsterdam News,* June 20, 1923. Sixteen Philadelphia Athletics appeared in the six games with Hilldale in 1923.

10. *Baltimore Afro-American,* March 30 ("ping pong"), July 20, August 10, 1923; *Washington Tribune,* August 4, 1923; *Norfolk Journal and Guide,* September 15, 1923; *Chicago Defender,* February 16, 1924; *Philadelphia Tribune,* December 15, 1923; March 15, April 26, 1924; July 20, 1933. The Harrisburg Giants were probably formed about 1903; an item submitted by Strothers appearing in the February 28, 1909, *Philadelphia Sunday Item* notes the team's seventh season of operation.

11. *Chicago Defender,* February 2, 1924; *Washington Tribune,* August 2, 1924; *Baltimore Afro-American,* February 22, 29, 1924; Holway, *Voices,* 67. Salaries in the professional black baseball leagues ranged from about $100 to $500 a month during the 1920s, comparable to pay in the A or B minor leagues. In contrast, the average major league salary reached $7,500 by 1929. See *Chicago Defender,* January 26, 1924, *Baltimore Afro-American,* August 28, 1926; Alexander, *Our Game,* 158; *New York Times,* December 9, 1919; January 12, 1921.

12. *Baltimore Afro-American,* January 11 (Spedden quote), February 8 (Foster quote), February 29, May 30, August 1, 1924; *Philadelphia Tribune,* April 19, 1924; *Pittsburgh Courier,* August 1, 1924. Organized baseball utilized a comparable system of fines to punish umpire assaults in the early 1920s. In 1922 players were fined $50 in the AA American Association and $25 in the class A Eastern League. Under Commissioner Kenesaw Mountain Landis, a 90 day unpaid suspension later became the standard penalty for attacks on umpires. See *North American,* August 8, 25, 1922; Obojski, *Minor Leagues,* 22.

13. *Philadelphia Tribune,* May 31, June 7, 1924; January 31, 1925. *Baltimore Afro-American,* April 22, 1921; January 18, June 6, 27, August 1, September 12, 19 ("league bosses"), October 3, December 20, 1924; February 14, 1925 (Taylor quote). *Pittsburgh Courier,* June 7, 1924; *Washington Tribune,* August 27, 1921; September 23, 1922; June 7, 14, 28, August 16, 1924. Despite a substantial African American population, Washington-based professional clubs were hindered by local restrictions on interracial competition, a shortage of available grounds that necessitated the expensive rental of Griffith Stadium, and the popularity of the Washington Senators among black fans. The Washington Braves, an earlier attempt at a local professional team, presented President Warren Harding with a gold pass for admission to their home games in 1921 but still failed to last beyond a single season. Not until the Homestead Grays began playing at Griffith Stadium in the late 1930s did black baseball become consistently profitable in Washington.

14. *Baltimore Afro-American,* December 27, 1924 (Taylor quote); *Philadelphia Tribune,* March 22, April 5, July 12, 26, September 13, 1924; January 17, February 7, 1925. Holway notes (Stephens-Winters quotes); *Pittsburgh Courier,* September 13, 1924. An alternate account in the *Pittsburgh Courier* credits Winters with a one-hitter. With the common absence of an official scorer in the Negro Leagues as well as independent baseball, published box scores of the same game sometimes differed from newspaper to newspaper, dependent on the original source of the account.

15. *Philadelphia Tribune,* July 12, August 16, September 6 (Bolden quote), September

13, 1924 ("sanctity"); January 3, 10, 1925. *Washington Tribune*, September 6, 1924; *Pittsburgh Courier*, September 13 (Wilson quote), November 15, December 27, 1924; *Baltimore Afro-American*, August 29, September 12, 1924; *The Competitor*, January–February 1921.

16. *Baltimore Afro-American*, September 26, October 3 ("disinterested"), 10, 1924; *Philadelphia Inquirer*, September 13, 1925. Ticket prices for major league World Series games ranged from $1.10 to $6.60.

17. *Baltimore Afro-American*, September 19, 26, October 3 ("on paper"), October 10, 1924; March 28, 1925. While John Holway and others have attributed the absence of Stephens to a "case of jitters," at least two contemporary accounts refer to Stephens's ankle injury; see Holway, *Blackball Stars*, 158; *Philadelphia Tribune*, February 7, September 26, 1925.

18. *Philadelphia Tribune*, November 1, 1924; January 17, 1925. *Pittsburgh Courier*, October 11, 1924 (Dismukes quote); *Chicago Defender*, October 4, 11, 1924; *Philadelphia Record*, October 4–5, 1924.

19. *Baltimore Afro-American*, October 10, 1924. Several historians of black baseball have mistakenly credited Shibe Park as the location of games 1 and 2 of the 1924 World Series.

20. *Philadelphia Tribune*, October 18, 1924 (Thompson quote); February 7, 1925. *Pittsburgh Courier*, October 18, 1924; August 8, 1925. *Baltimore Afro-American*, October 17, 1924.

21. *Philadelphia Tribune*, June 28, July 12, September 13 (Womack quote), October 18, 25, November 1, 1924; *Pittsburgh Courier*, October 18, 25, November 1, 1924 ("impromptu parade" and Briggs quotes); August 8, 1925. Holway, *Blackball Stars*, 94 (Thomas quote). World Series averages are based on the author's compilations. Jack Dunn, owner of the Baltimore Orioles of the International League, and manager Jack Hendricks of the Cincinnati Reds attended the final game of the series.

22. *Philadelphia Tribune*, October 25, November 1, 22, 1924 (Foster quote); January 10, 1925 (Johnson quote). *Pittsburgh Courier*, October 25 (Wilson quote), November 8, 1924; January 10, 1925 (Wilkinson quote). Financial returns from the 1924 World Series compare favorably to the Junior World Series, an annual event since 1920 featuring the pennant winners of the International League and the American Association. Receipts totaled $68,010.50 for a six-game series between Baltimore and St. Paul in 1920 and $54,757.35 for an eight-game Louisville-Baltimore series in 1921. In general, minor league baseball, with its smaller rosters, lower pay, and often arduous traveling conditions, offers a better comparison with black baseball than the major league teams, who as Rube Foster noted, were operated by "rich men." See *Baseball Magazine*, February 1922, 686; *Chicago Defender*, January 5, 1924.

23. *Philadelphia Tribune*, October 25 (*Kansas City Call* quote), November 22, 1924; *Chicago Defender*, October 4 (quote), 25, 1924. Local coverage of the World Series was sporadic at best, as most newspapers provided only brief summaries and box scores. The *North American*, for example, published accounts of only six of the 10 series games.

Chapter 6

1. *Philadelphia Tribune*, April 26, 1924; January 17, 1925; January 30, February 6, 1926. W.E.B. Du Bois, *Philadelphia Negro: A Social Study* (New York, 1967 [1899], 322–367; Armstrong Association of Philadelphia, *Study of Living Conditions*, 7; Theodore Hershberg, et al., "Tale of Three Cities: Blacks, Immigrants, and Opportunity

in Philadelphia, 1850-1880, 1930, 1970," 461-491; Golab, "Immigrant and the City," 209-213; H. Viscount Nelson, Jr., "Race and Class Consciousness of Philadelphia Negroes with Special Emphasis on the Years between 1927 and 1940," Ph.D. diss., University of Pennsylvania, 1969, 61; Kusmer, *Ghetto Takes Shape*, 52-55; *Philadelphia Inquirer*, April 25, 1993. Blacks continued to remain excluded from Philadelphia's thriving textile industry. As late as 1930, less than 2 percent of the city's 45,000 textile workers were African Americans, employed mostly in janitorial positions.

    2. Kusmer, *Ghetto Takes Shape*, 63-109; *Baltimore Afro-American*, July 21, 1928. Charles Fred White, *Who's Who in Philadelphia* (Philadelphia, 1912), 193-242; Records of Edward Bolden; United States Office of Personnel Management; Spear, *Black Chicago*, 36; *Negro Survey of Pennsylvania* (Harrisburg, 1927), 58; *Philadelphia Tribune*, July 3, 1926. In its employment of black postal workers, Philadelphia lagged behind Chicago, which had 500 in 1910 despite a population half as large. Despite a considerable growth in the local African American population, Philadelphia still had only 300 black postal workers by 1926.

    3. Talcott Parsons and Kenneth Clark, eds., *Negro American* (Boston, 1966), 568; Kusmer, *Ghetto Takes Shape*, 115; Armstrong Association of Philadelphia, *Negro in Business in Philadelphia: An Investigation by the Armstrong Association of Philadelphia* (Philadelphia, n.d.), 4-5; *Negro Survey of Pennsylvania*, 29-37; Hardy, "Race and Opportunity," 339, 359, 368, 438, 545; R.R. Wright, Jr., *Negro in Pennsylvania: Study in Economic History* (Philadelphia, 1912), 173 (quote); Armstrong Association, *A Study of Living Conditions*, 3-6; William Ziglar, "'Community on Trial': The Coatesville Lynching of 1911," *Pennsylvania Magazine of History and Biography* 106 (1982), 245-270 (*Philadelphia Tribune* quote cited on 269-270).

    4. *Philadelphia Public Ledger*, November 5, 6, 1914; September 10, October 3, December 21, 1915 (Colwyn quote); January 20, 1917. Vincent Franklin, "Philadelphia Race Riot of 1918," *Pennsylvania Magazine of History and Biography* 99 (1975), 336-338; White, *Who's Who in Philadelphia*, 148 ("benevolent feudalism"); Kusmer, *Ghetto Takes Shape*, 35-36.

    5. Sadie Tanner Mossell, "Standard of Living Among One Hundred Negro Migrant Families in Philadelphia," *Annals of the American Academy of Political and Social Science* 98 (1921), 171-222; Ballard, *One More Day's Journey*, 173, 185; *Philadelphia Public Ledger*, February 24, March 4, 1917; Armstrong Association, *Study of Living Conditions*, 3-7; Kusmer, *Ghetto Takes Shape*, 157-173.

    6. Hardy, "Race and Opportunity," 390-392; Franklin, "Philadelphia Race Riot of 1918," 314-378; Works Progress Administration, *Ethnic Survey: The Negro in Philadelphia*, 1938-1939, 1941; Kusmer, *Ghetto Takes Shape*, 190-196.

    7. *Philadelphia Tribune*, February 26, March 12, 1921; Parsons and Clark, *Negro American*, 567; Vincent Franklin, *Education of Black Philadelphia* (Philadelphia, 1979), 71; Hardy, "Race and Opportunity," 513; Vincent Franklin, "'Voice of the Black Community': The Philadelphia Tribune, 1912-41," *Pennsylvania History* 51 (1984), 270-271; Kusmer, *Ghetto Takes Shape*, 174-189; *Philadelphia Inquirer*, April 9, 1993. Future opera great Marian Anderson, a native of South Philadelphia, was refused admission to a prestigious Philadelphia music school in the early 1920s simply on the basis of skin color.

    8. *Philadelphia Tribune*, May 31, 1924; October 30, December 25, 1926; July 11, 1929; June 11, 1931; February 25, March 3, 1932. *Baltimore Afro-American*, December 27, 1924; Hardy, "Race and Opportunity," 407-411; Charles Haley, "To Do Well and to Do Good: Philadelphia's Black Middle Class During the Depression, 1929-1940," Ph.D. diss., SUNY Binghamton, 1980, 81; *Philadelphia Public Ledger*, November 11, 1922 (quote).

9. Spear, *Black Chicago*, 158, 316; Fredric Miller, "Black Migration to Phila-delphia: A 1924 Profile," *Pennsylvania Magazine of History and Biography* 108 (1984), 315–350; *Pittsburgh Courier*, July 14, 1923; *Philadelphia Public Ledger*, July 9, July 17, 1923 ("mills and factories"); *Philadelphia Tribune*, January 30, February 6, July 3, 1926; Sam Bass Warner, *Private City: Philadelphia in Three Periods of Its Growth* (Philadelphia, 1968), 179–182; Haley, "To Do Well," 37–38; Gilbert Osofsky, "Harlem Tragedy: An Emerg-ing Slum," in *American Urban History: An Interpretive Reader with Commentaries*, ed. Alex-ander Callow, Jr. (New York, 1982), 318. By 1926 the average weekly wage in Phila-delphia was about $25 for black male workers and $16 for women.

10. Works Progress Administration, *Ethnic Survey*; Philip Foner and Ronald Lewis, eds., *Black Worker: A Documentary History from Colonial Times to the Present*, Vol. 6, *The Era of Post-War Prosperity and the Great Depression, 1920–1936* (Philadelphia, 1981), 143–150; Miller, "Black Migration to Philadelphia," 344–345; Franklin, *Education of Black Philadelphia*, 105; Hardy, "Race and Opportunity," xiv, 71, 100, 135, 322, 349, 366; Nelson, "Race and Class Consciousness," 31; Haley, "To Do Well," 54; *Baltimore Afro-American*, February 14, 1925.

11. Forrester Washington, "Recreational Facilities for the Negro," *Annals of the American Academy of Political and Social Science* 130 (1928), 272–282; Spear, *Black Chicago*, 107–116; *Negro Survey of Pennsylvania*, 53–55; Works Progress Administration, *Ethnic Survey*; *Philadelphia Tribune*, June 12, 1920; May 7, 1921; May 10, 1924; April 3, October 23, November 13, 1930; March 31, 1932. Hardy, "Race and Opportunity," 347, 441–446; Mossell, "Standard of Living Among One Hundred Negro Migrant Families in Philadelphia," 198–199; *Baltimore Afro-American*, September 9, 1921. While baseball remained the most popular sport among blacks in Philadelphia during the 1920s, other commercialized sports began to attract attention. Boxing, legalized in Philadelphia early in the decade, became especially popular after mixed bouts were finally per-mitted in the city in 1924. Black college football also maintained supporters, and the annual Thanksgiving game between Howard University and Lincoln University, played alternate years in Philadelphia, became a major national sports event for Afri-can Americans. Basketball also advanced in popularity by the late 1920s as numerous black semipro teams were formed, some competing against white teams as well.

12. Hardy, "Race and Opportunity," 438–459; *Philadelphia Tribune*, January 30, February 6, 1926; March 19, 1927. Works Progress Administration, *Ethnic Survey*; Mossell, "Standard of Living," 210; Ballard, *One More Day's Journey*, 174; Kusmer, *Ghetto Takes Shape*, 92; Seymour, *People's Game*, 569, 595; Franklin, *Education of Black Phila-delphia*, 93. Few suitable public recreational facilities were accessible to African Amer-icans in Philadelphia and other cities. While the Progressive era playground move-ment had stimulated the building of numerous public parks supposedly open to all, most were located in white neighborhoods where black patronage was strongly dis-couraged. With local YMCAs also discriminating against blacks, a separate branch was built in 1914 at 1724 Christian Street in South Philadelphia and became an impor-tant social, recreation, and educational center as well as the site of the founding of the Eastern Colored League in 1922. By the mid-1920s, two YMCAs and two YWCAs served the city's black population of 165,000, although none were located in North Philadelphia, the home of over 35,000 blacks.

13. *Philadelphia Tribune*, November 29, December 13, 1924; January 3, February 14, 1925. *Pittsburgh Courier*, November 15, December 20, 27 (Blount quote), 1924; Jan-uary 10, 24, 1925 (Lewis quote). *Baltimore Afro-American*, September 26, 1924; January 3 (Foster quote), 10, February 14, 1925. *Indianapolis Freeman*, April 21, 1917. The NNL-ECL agreement paralleled the settlement reached in 1903 between the American League and National League, which established the territorial rights of each league

and uniform contracts with a reserve clause in place. See Murdock, *Ban Johnson*, 43–68.

14. *Philadelphia Tribune*, January 31, March 28, April 4, 18, May 2, June 27, 1925; July 17, 1926 (Howe quote). *Baltimore Afro-American*, March 14, 28, April 4, 1925; *New York Amsterdam News*, March 11, 1925. League scheduling was also disrupted by the limited availability of the Harrisburg Giants' Island Park, which functioned primarily as the home of the Harrisburg Senators of the New York–Pennsylvania League.

15. *Philadelphia Tribune*, March 28 (Howe quote), April 4 (Bolden quote), 11, 1925; September 18, 1926. *Pittsburgh Courier*, March 28, 1925 (Wilson quote), August 8, September 12, 1925. *Baltimore Afro-American*, August 8, 1925.

16. *Pittsburgh Courier*, August 1 (Wilson quote), September 12, 1925; *Baltimore Afro-American*, July 25, August 1, 8, 1925; *New York Amsterdam News*, July 29, 1925 (Bolden quote).

17. *New York Amsterdam News*, July 22, 29, 1925; *Baltimore Afro-American*, June 20, July 4 (Mackey quote), 25, August 15, 1925; *Washington Tribune*, June 24, August 8, 1925; *Philadelphia Tribune*, June 27, August 1, September 19, 1925; *Pittsburgh Courier*, August 1, 8 (Thompson, Nunn quotes), September 12, 1925.

18. *Baltimore Afro-American*, February 7, June 20 ("farce"), July 4, 1925 (Lloyd quote); June 26, July 3, August 7, 1926. *Pittsburgh Courier*, December 20, 1924; January 30, April 4, August 1 ("taciturn"), August 8, 1925 (Robinson quote). *Philadelphia Tribune*, September 19, 1925 (Howe); January 30, 1926. *Washington Tribune*, August 29, 1925 ("pigmy"); *New York Amsterdam News*, July 29, 1925 (Bolden quote).

19. *Philadelphia Tribune*, February 21, March 14, April 4, 11, June 20, 27 ("attacks"), November 14, 1925; *Baltimore Afro-American*, May 16, 1925 (Mackey quote). Louis Santop and Red Ryan were released in February 1925, reportedly because of poor performances in the 1924 series but were re-signed prior to the beginning of the season.

20. *Philadelphia Tribune*, September 26, October 3, 10, 17, 24, 1925; *Chicago Defender*, October 3, 10, 1925; *Baltimore Afro-American*, October 17, 24, November 7, 1925. Attendance at Phillies Park during the 1924 and 1925 World Series totaled 19,197 fans for four games (4,799.25 average), while 27,987 fans attended the seven games played at Muehlebach (3,998.1 average).

21. *Philadelphia Tribune*, November 1, 1924; October 24, 1925; September 18, October 2, 1926; January 22, November 3, 1927. *Baltimore Afro-American*, November 6, 1926; *Pittsburgh Courier*, June 27, 1925; April 17, November 20, 1926 (Wilson quote). Financial statements of the 1924, 1925, and 1926 World Series (1927 not available):

	1924	1925	1926
Attendance	45,857	20,067[a]	21,369
Gross receipts	$52,113.90	$21,044.60	$23,343.50
Average	5,211.39	3,006.37	2,122.14
Expenses	28,650.46	15,172.65	15,724.17
Available	23,463.44	5,871.95	7,733.48
Eastern Commission	1,173.17	293.59	386.68
Western Commission	1,173.17	293.60	386.68
Winning team	4,927.32	1,233.11	1,624.04
Losing team	3,284.88	822.08	1082.68
Winning players	4,927.32	1,233.11	1,624.04
Losing players	3,284.88	822.08	1,082.68

	1924	1925	1926
Second place in East	$1,407.80	$352.31	$464.01
Second place in West	1,407.80	352.32	464.01
Third place in East	938.53	234.88	309.33
Third place in West	938.53	234.87	309.33

[a]includes exhibition game

22. *Philadelphia Tribune*, December 6, 1924; January 10, October 17, October 24 ("Hilldale won the pennant!"), November 14, 1925 ("seem to like it"); March 15, 1928. *Washington Tribune*, October 17, 1925; *Baltimore Afro-American*, August 15, 1925; *New York Amsterdam News*, December 22, 1926; Hardy, "Race and Opportunity," 325.

Chapter 7

1. Foner and Lewis, *Black Worker*, 2 ("Great Depression"); *Pittsburgh Courier*, October 17, 1925; April 17, 1926 (Wilson quote). *Baltimore Afro-American*, January 16, March 20, 1926 (Taylor); *Philadelphia Tribune*, November 29, 1924; January 16, 1926; February 26, 1927; June 7, 1928 ("overhead"). *New York Amsterdam News*, January 13, 1926; 1926 Hilldale ledger.

2. *Baltimore Afro-American*, October 17, 1925; *New York Amsterdam News*, January 17, 1926 (Dougherty quote); August 17, 1927. Holway, *Blackball Stars*, 299–326; Ruck, *Sandlot Seasons*, 124–136; Ocania Chalk, *Black College Sport*, 23–25. For similar criticisms of Posey, see *Chicago Defender*, February 26, 1921, and *New York Amsterdam News*, January 19, 1927. Clint Thomas also recalled Posey as a "greedy guy."

3. *Philadelphia Tribune*, January 16, 1926; October 6, 13, 1927. *Pittsburgh Courier*, April 18, June 28, October 4, 1924; August 22, September 5, November 14, December 19, 1925; May 15, June 19, August 28, September 4, November 27, 1926. *Baltimore Afro-American*, January 4, June 27, July 11, September 5, 1924; April 18, October 17, 1925. Holway, *Blackball Stars*, 305.

4. *Philadelphia Tribune*, January 16, April 17, July 10, 17, 31, August 7, 21, October 2, 1926; *New York Amsterdam News*, July 7, December 22, 1926; *Philadelphia Inquirer*, April 17, 1928; *Baltimore Afro-American*, March 27, July 31, October 9, 1926; *Pittsburgh Courier*, April 17, August 14, 1926 (Wilson quote).

5. *Baltimore Afro-American*, July 3, 31, August 14 ("same level"), 21, 28 (Pompez quote), 1926; *Pittsburgh Courier*, August 14, 21, 1926; *Philadelphia Tribune*, July 17, August 7, 14, 1926; *New York Amsterdam News*, August 11, 1926 (Bolden quotes).

6. *Philadelphia Tribune*, June 6, 1925; January 16, March 27, May 1, June 19, 26 ("spiritual slump"), July 10, 31, October 2, 9, 1926; January 1, 1927. *Pittsburgh Courier*, January 16, June 26, July 24, 31, September 4, October 16, 1926 ("You'd never"). *Baltimore Afro-American*, April 6, 1925; June 19, July 31, August 7, September 11, October 16, 1926. *Philadelphia Inquirer*, July 4, 1926 ("hitless wonders"); *New York Amsterdam News*, September 22, 1926; Bankes, *Pittsburgh Crawfords*, 87; 1926 Hilldale ledger and scorebook; *Philadelphia Record*, October 2, 3, 7, 8, 9, 1926; *Philadelphia Public Ledger*, October 3, 10, 1926. Phil Cockrell shut out major league teams in 1919, 1923, and 1926.

7. *Philadelphia Tribune*, April 5, 26, June 14, 1924; March 5, April 9, August 4, 1927; February 2 ("in sight of the major leagues"), April 19, May 3 ("minor league"), 24, June 14, 1928; January 10, 1929. *Baltimore Afro-American*, August 11, 1922; March

17, 1928. *New York Amsterdam News*, July 15, 1925 (Keenan quote); Seymour, *People's Game*, 601; Heaphy, "Growth and Decline of the Negro Leagues," 72–75; *Pittsburgh Courier*, May 29, 1926. Darby native Rocky Ellis, the team's mascot, was allowed to play in occasional one-sided games and later pitched in the Negro Leagues during the 1930s.

8. *Philadelphia Tribune*, May 10, July 12, December 13, 1924; May 14, 1927; July 19, 1928. *New York Amsterdam News*, January 30, 1926; *Pittsburgh Courier*, January 30, 1926; *Chicago Defender*, April 6, 1918 (Foster quote); *Baltimore Afro-American*, April 18, 1924; February 20, June 12, October 2, 1926.

9. Holway, *Black Diamonds*, 58–59; Holway, *Voices*, 95 (Allen quote), 115 (Bell quote); Holway, *Blackball Stars*, 91 (Stephens quote); *Baltimore Afro-American*, January 17, 1925; August 14, 1926. Kelly, "Judy Johnson," 15; *Philadelphia Tribune*, July 17, 1926; July 30, 1931 ("almost"). Kevin Kerrane and Rob Beaton, "Judy Johnson: Reminiscences by the Great Baseball Player," *Delaware Today*, May 1977, 16 ("cut up"). The spitball and emery ball, both illegal in organized baseball, were permitted in the ECL.

10. *Baltimore Afro-American*, September 21, November 2, 1923; February 8, 29, 1924; January 3, 10, 1925; August 14, September 4, 11, 1926; April 16, 1927; July 7, 1928. *Pittsburgh Courier*, November 28, 1925; Holway, *Blackball Stars*, 221, 333; Kelly, "Judy Johnson," 16; *Philadelphia Tribune*, September 12, 1928; August 6, 1931. John Holway, "Before You Could Say Jackie Robinson," *Look*, July 13, 1971, 50 (Stephens quote). Though not known to be a heavy drinker, Bolden's personnel folder notes a 1905 suspension for arriving at work intoxicated.

11. *New York Amsterdam News*, May 16, 1923; June 10, 1925. *Baltimore Afro-American*, September 21, November 2, 1923; June 28, 1925; May 14, 1926; July 30, December 31, 1927; June 15, July 20, 1929. *Pittsburgh Courier*, May 29, September 25, 1926; *Philadelphia Tribune*, May 10, June 7 ("cleanest"), July 7, August 23, 1928; February 27, 1930; May 14, 1931. *Washington Tribune*, May 16, 1925; *Indianapolis Freeman*, December 16, 1916; February 24, 1917; Holway, *Blackball Stars*, 254. Farrell also played on the mostly white Atlantic City police baseball team. In 1929 Farrell was prevented from participating in a game against the Baltimore police team, who refused to allow him to wear his uniform and forced him to sit in the stands away from his teammates.

12. *Pittsburgh Courier*, January 17, November 28, 1925; *Baltimore Afro-American*, April 17 ("Buick Roadster"); August 28, 1926; March 12 ("pretty"), October 15, 1927. Hardy, "Race and Opportunity," 556; *Washington Tribune*, August 2, 1924; *Philadelphia Tribune*, April 19, 1924 (Howe quote); June 20, 1929. Seymour, *Golden Age*, 346–347. Nearly 60 percent of American families earned less than $2,000 annually in 1929.

13. *Pittsburgh Courier*, November 20, December 25, 1926 (Posey quotes); *New York Amsterdam News*, December 22, 1926; *Philadelphia Tribune*, January 8, 1927.

14. *Philadelphia Tribune*, January 15, 22, March 19, 1927; March 29, 1928. *Baltimore Afro-American*, February 5, 12, 19, April 23, 1927; *Pittsburgh Courier*, November 20, December 25, 1926. Six franchises were placed in Cleveland during the NNL's existence: Tate Stars (1922), Browns (1924), Elites (1926), Hornets (1927), Tigers (1928), and Cubs (1931).

15. *Philadelphia Tribune*, March 26, June 23, 30, July 14, 21, 28, August 11 (Howe quote), 1927; *Baltimore Afro-American*, April 30, May 14, 21, 28, June 4, July 9, 30, 1927; *New York Amsterdam News*, June 29, 1927; *Chicago Defender*, July 2, 1927; Dixon and Hannigan, *The Negro Baseball Leagues*, 147.

16. *Philadelphia Tribune*, January 15, 22, February 26, April 2, June 23, August 18, 1927; *Baltimore Afro-American*, February 12, April 23, June 25, July 9, 23 ("What's"), August 13, 20, 1927; *Pittsburgh Courier*, September 10, 1927 ("internal"); *New York Amsterdam News*, June 29, July 6, September 14, 1927. As early as 1924, Hilldale

had been referred to as the Darby Daisies; in 1927 the team featured embroidered daisies on their caps.

17. *Philadelphia Tribune*, April 30, May 7, June 9 ("lack of discipline"), 23, 30, July 14, 21, 28, August 4, 11, September 29, 1927; *Pittsburgh Courier*, July 16, 1927 ("Hilldale Ball Fan"); *Baltimore Afro-American*, March 5, 1927. In March 1927, a similar trade of Charleston for Jud Wilson of the Black Sox was announced but subsequently called off because of Charleston's dislike of the racial atmosphere in Baltimore.

18. *Philadelphia Tribune*, September 1, 29, October 13 (Howe quote), December 15, 22, 1927; *Baltimore Afro-American*, October 1, 1927; *New York Amsterdam News*, September 28, November 30, December 14, 1927; official personnel and employee medical folder of Ed Bolden.

19. *New York Amsterdam News*, February 15, 29, April 11, 1928; *Philadelphia Tribune*, February 2, 16, 1928; *Baltimore Afro-American*, February 25 ("highly successful"), March 10, 17, 24, 1928; *Chicago Defender*, October 22, 1927.

20. *Philadelphia Tribune*, February 2 ("narrow minds," "curb underhand work"), 16, March 15 (Rainey quote), 22, 29, 1928; *New York Amsterdam News*, March 28, April 11 (Lambert quote), 25 ("plenty of money," "when one man"), 1928; *Pittsburgh Courier*, March 17, 1928 ("through losing money"); *Baltimore Afro-American*, March 17 ("justice"), 31, 1928 ("some clubs").

21. *Philadelphia Tribune*, March 15, 22 (Nutter quote), April 12, 19, 26, May 3, 31, 1928; *Baltimore Afro-American*, March 24, 31, April 7, 21, 1928; *New York Amsterdam News*, May 2, 30, June 6, 1928.

22. *Philadelphia Tribune*, April 19, 1928 (Dixon, Bolden quotes); *Baltimore Afro-American*, April 21 (Rossiter quote), 28 (Gibson quote), 1928.

Chapter 8

1. *Philadelphia Tribune*, May 24, 1928; Malloy, "The Birth of the Cuban Giants"; Malloy, "Out at Home," 26 ("cheerfully") ; White, *Base Ball Guide*, 17–19; Dixon and Hannigan, *Negro Baseball Leagues*, 72–81. Gerald Scully, for example, has noted that "with few exceptions, little of importance concerning the Negro in organized baseball seems to have occurred from 1898 to the 1930s," and Robert Crepeau has similarly asserted that the "issue was only rarely mentioned" during the 1920s; see Scully, "Discrimination: The Case of Baseball," 226; Crepeau, *Baseball: America's Diamond Mind*, 168.

2. White, *Base Ball Guide*, 85 ("leading players"), 127–128; *Half-Century Magazine*, March 1919, 8; *Indianapolis Freeman*, September 14, 21, 1907; March 19, April 16, 1910. *New York Age*, March 10, 1910; *New York Times*, March 4, 1910; *Chicago Whip*, January 22, 1920. Foster reportedly earned the nickname "Rube" after his defeat of Rube Waddell of the Athletics in the early 1900s. A newspaper account of the game has yet to be found.

3. *Indianapolis Freeman*, February 13, 1909; September 3, 1910 ("never hesitate"); February 4, 1911; February 24, 1912. *New York Age*, December 8, 1910; January 21, 1911 ("Nowhere is the"). Charles Alexander, *John McGraw* (New York, 1988), 17–20; Holway, *Blackball Stars*, 50; Michael Oleksak and Mary Adams Oleksak, *Béisbol: Latin Americans and the Grand Old Game* (Grand Rapids, 1991), 20–21; Charles Alexander, *Ty Cobb* (New York, 1984), 98–99; Dixon and Hannigan, *Negro Baseball Leagues*, 102–103; Okeksak and Oleksak, "Cuba No Vacation for U.S. Teams in 1900s," *USA Today Baseball Weekly*, May 24–30, 1991, 18.

4. *Sporting News*, November 24, December 1, 15, 29, 1910; January 12, 1911 ("will

not be"). Oleksak and Oleksak, "Cuba No Vacation," 18; Murdock, *Ban Johnson*, 66–69; Lee Allen, *Cooperstown Corner* (Cleveland, 1990), 7–9; *Indianapolis Freeman*, December 23, 1911; *New York Age*, September 28, 1911 (Walton quote).

5. *Indianapolis Freeman*, February 19, 1910; September 29, 1917. *Baltimore Afro-American*, October 27, 1928; Alexander, *John McGraw*, 75 ("crusader"); White, *Base Ball Guide*, 85; *New York Amsterdam News*, February 27, 1929; Chalk, *Pioneers of Black Sport*, 20; *New York Age*, April 1, 1909; August 24, September 28, 1911 ("chuck full"). *Chicago Defender*, May 10, 1919; Zoss and Bowman, *Diamonds in the Rough*, 143; Dixon and Hannigan, *Negro Baseball Leagues*, 92; Davids, *Insider's Baseball*, 270.

6. *Indianapolis Freeman*, May 10, 1913; September 29, 1917. *Chicago Defender*, August 13, 1910; September 21, 1918 ("white man with a white heart"); May 10, 1919. *New York Amsterdam News*, February 27, 1929; Judy Johnson file, National Baseball Library ("wonderful man"); *Philadelphia Tribune*, November 5, 1931; Seymour, *Golden Age*, 243; Kuklick, *To Every Thing*, 145–146; Holway, *Voices*, 87. In 1928, Rollo Wilson noted that Mack was the "only owner or promoter" who refused to recognize his press standing. *Pittsburgh Courier*, May 19, 1928.

7. *New York Age*, September 28, 1911 ("less removed"); Kusmer, *Ghetto Takes Shape*, 174–175.

8. *Indianapolis Freeman*, June 20, 1908; March 20, 1909. Alexander, *Ty Cobb*, 50, 67–68, 94, 98–99, 119; *New York Age*, September 16, 1909; *North American*, May 19, 1912; Zoss and Bowman, *Diamonds in the Rough*, 144–145; *Chicago Defender*, May 3, 1919; *Cleveland Advocate*, May 10, 1919 (White quote); *Pittsburgh Courier*, August 2, 1924 (Wilson quote); *Philadelphia Tribune*, February 12, 1927; August 30, 1928. Bak, *Cobb*, 178. Several other players were involved in racial violence. In 1917, Danny Shay, a former major leaguer and manager of Milwaukee of the American Association, was indicted in the murder of a black waiter but acquitted after claiming self-defense. In May 1928 in the Texas League, future major leaguer Art Shires reacted to the booing of black fans by firing a baseball into the segregated black section of the park in Waco, striking a fan who later died of his injuries; Shires was also acquitted. In 1930, Shanty Hogan of the New York Giants was stabbed by a black elevator operator after Hogan, objecting to his presence, attempted to evict him from a party. See *Baltimore Afro-American*, April 6, 1928; December 29, 1928. *New York Amsterdam News*, January 2, 1929; *Chicago Defender*, December 1, 1917; *Philadelphia Tribune*, October 16, 1930; *Philadelphia Public Ledger*, October 9, 1930.

9. Holway, *Blackball Stars*, 67 (Forbes quote), 68; *New York Age*, October 5, 19, 1911; October 31, November 7, 1912; October 2, 9, 16, 23, November 6, 1913. *Indianapolis Freeman*, September 16, 1911; April 12, December 20, 1913 ("hate to say").

10. *New York Age*, May 30, 1912; February 5 (Long, Baum quotes), October 8, 15, 22, 29, 1914; *Chicago Defender*, June 1, 1912; *New York Times*, May 27, 1912. In 1913 the *New York Times* would similarly distort an incident occurring at a game in Schenectady, New York, between the Mohawk Giants and a barnstorming team led by Walter Johnson of the Washington Senators. After the Mohawk Giants announced their refusal to participate until receiving back pay owed by the club's owner, the crowd surged onto the playing field, creating a "near riot" according to the *Times*. Order was eventually restored, and a five-inning game was played with Johnson, despite allowing only two hits and fanning 11 batters, being defeated by Frank Wickware 1–0. See *North American*, October 6, 1913; *New York Times*, October 6, 1913.

11. *New York Age*, October 7, 14, 21, 28, 1915; *New York Times*, October 14, 18, 21, 22, 23, 26, 1915; March 10, October 24, 27, December 9, 1916. *Indianapolis Freeman*, October 30 ("narrowly averted"), November 13, December 11, 1915; October 14, 1916. *Chicago Defender*, October 30, November 6, 1915; October 14, 1916.

12. *New York Age*, October 18, 1917; *Baltimore Afro-American*, October 27, 1917 ("The Brooklyn team"); *Chicago Defender*, October 27, 1917; *Philadelphia Tribune*, October 13, 1917.

13. *New York Times*, October 14, 16, 17, 1917; October 6, 1918. *Indianapolis Freeman*, May 2, 1914; October 14, 1916 ("They have"); March 24, 1917.

14. *Indianapolis Freeman*, July 10, 1915; *Chicago Defender*, January 16, 1915; July 5, 1919. *Baltimore Afro-American*, February 28, 1925; October 26, 1929. *Philadelphia Tribune*, March 21, 28, 1929; Holway, *Blackball Stars*, 126. Davids, *Insider's Baseball*, 58–62. In a strange reversal of typical practice, Chick Meade, who appeared with Hilldale in 1919 and with several other clubs during the early 1920s, reportedly passed as an African American to appear in black professional baseball after his failure to make the major leagues. See *Philadelphia Tribune*, June 25, 1931; September 22, 1932.

15. *Sporting News*, December 5, 1918 ("new era"); *Cleveland Advocate*, February 15, 1919; *Half Century Magazine*, April 1919, 8; *Indianapolis Freeman*, September 14, 1907; *New York Age*, June 9, 1910; October 31, 1912; August 8, 1917. *Chicago Defender*, August 25, September 1, 1917; August 3, 31, 1918; September 20, 1919.

16. *Chicago Whip*, October 15, 1921; *Baltimore Afro-American*, March 24, 1924; *Philadelphia Tribune*, July 10, 1930; May 14, December 31, 1931. *New York Amsterdam News*, July 9, 1930; August 19, 26, 1931. *Washington Tribune*, July 28, 1923; Tygiel, *Baseball's Great Experiment*, 22; *Pittsburgh Courier*, December 27, 1924.

17. *Indianapolis Freeman*, May 2, 1914; David Pietrusza, *Major Leagues: The Formation, Sometimes Absorption and Mostly Inevitable Demise of 18 Professional Baseball Organizations, 1871 to Present* (Jefferson, NC, 1991), 253–256 ("Eddie Bohon"); *Chicago Defender*, March 12 ("any institution"), April 9, May 28, 1921; *Philadelphia Tribune*, April 9, 1921; Crepeau, *America's Diamond Mind*, 168 ("Through all the ages"); *Chicago Whip*, January 22, February 5, March 5, 1921; *Norfolk Journal and Guide*, February 19, April 16, 1921; *North American*, June 5, 1921; *Baltimore Afro-American*, April 29, 1921; Ira Lewis, "'New' League Not Needed," *The Competitor*, May 1921, 39, 41 (Lewis quotes). The Philadelphia representative of the Continental League was organized by George Victory, manager of the Pennsylvania Giants, and Monroe Young, a former Negro Southern League official.

18. Murdock, *Ban Johnson*, 183; *Baltimore Afro-American*, May 14, 1927 ("eminently fair"); *New York Amsterdam News*, May 11, 1927; Rogosin, *Invisible Men*, 184, 198; Tygiel, *Baseball's Great Experiment*, 31; David Wiggins, "Wendell Smith, The Pittsburgh Courier-Journal and the Campaign to Include Blacks in Organized Baseball, 1933–1945," *Journal of Sports History* 10(2), Summer 1983, 5–29; Dixon and Hannigan, *Negro Baseball Leagues*, 242–243 (Landis quote). With interracial teams rare during the 1920s, most observers predicted that the integration of organized baseball would involve the admission of entire black teams rather than individual players.

19. *New York Times*, June 10, July 29, 1922; *Philadelphia Inquirer*, July 28, August 15, October 4–13, 1922; Tygiel, *Baseball's Great Experiment*, 26; *Chicago Whip*, October 15, 22, 1921; Crepeau, *America's Diamond Mind*, 168 ("commented that," "bunch of Negroes"); *Chicago Defender*, October 14, 21, 1922; October 20, 27, 1923. Bak, *Cobb*, 99; *Baltimore Afro-American*, November 3, 1922 ("real world series"); *North American*, October 3, 21 ("Several league teams"), 1922; *The Messenger*, December 1923, 939 (quote).

20. *New York Amsterdam News*, October 14, 1925; *Baltimore Afro-American*, October 9, 1926; Holway, *Voices*, 191 (Foster quote). While John Holway has estimated that blacks won over 60 percent of nearly 450 games against barnstorming major leaguers between 1887 and 1950, no attempt was made to differentiate the levels of competition faced.

21. *Philadelphia's Baseball History*, 83 (Benson quote); *Chicago Defender*, December

29, 1923; Crepeau, *America's Diamond Mind*, 90 ("Them greasers"), 163 ("Ethiopian"); *Philadelphia Record*, November 22, 29, 1923; *Baltimore Afro-American*, February 28, 1924; *New York Amsterdam News*, October 19, 1927; Creamer, *Babe*, 185 ("the worst insult," "his personal"); John Holway notes (Winters quote); Holway, *Voices*, 25 (Drake quote).

22. *New York Amsterdam News*, October 28, 1925; November 10, 1926. Zoss and Bowman, *Diamonds in the Rough*, 338; Holway, *Blackball Stars*, 65–66; Bankes, "Magnificent Pittsburgh Crawfords," 51, 56 ("good guy"); Bankes, "Pittsburgh Crawfords," 63–81; *Philadelphia Tribune*, January 26, 1928; Chalk, *Pioneers of Black Sport*, 78 (Hornsby quote); Holway, *Voices*, 30.

23. Bankes, "Pittsburgh Crawfords," 63, 87 (Johnson quote); Holway, *Black Diamonds*, xiii; Holway, *Voices*, 67.

24. *Baltimore Afro-American*, November 3, 1922; January 5, 1923; October 3, 1925; July 27 ("so full of race hate"), September 28, 1929. Holway, *Black Diamonds*, 41 (Powell quote); Allen, *Cooperstown Corner*, 7–9; *Chicago Defender*, May 10, 1919; June 18, 1921. *Washington Tribune*, June 10, 1922 ("All of us"); July 21, 1923; January 12, April 12, 1924 ("Why then,"); September 5, 12, 1925. *Philadelphia Tribune*, September 9, 1925; February 12, 1927 ("colored adorers"); July 25, 1929 ("fork over"). Tygiel, *Baseball's Great Experiment*, 25; *Chicago Whip*, June 23, 1928; Seymour, *People's Game*, 600.

25. *Indianapolis Freeman*, September 29, 1917; *Chicago Whip*, October 11, 1919; October 22, 1921 ("It is bad enough"). *Philadelphia Tribune*, November 22, 1924; October 6, 1932. *Philadelphia Record*, October 5, 1924. Black professional players often watched major league games to assess their own abilities. Rube Foster gave his players passes to Comiskey Park with the order "See what you can learn." While with Hilldale, Judy Johnson often attended games at Shibe Park during off days at the invitation of Connie Mack. By the 1930s, according to Johnson, black professional players were allowed free in most major league parks with the exception of St. Louis. See Holway, *Blackball Stars*, 29 (Foster quote); Bankes, "Pittsburgh Crawfords," 88; Kerrane and Beaton, "Judy Johnson," 32.

26. *Philadelphia Tribune*, August 30 ("had heard"), December 27, 1928 (Briggs quote); June 30, 1932 ("It is not uncommon"). Rust, *"Get That Nigger*, 5; Zoss and Bowman, *Diamonds in the Rough*, 158; *New York Amsterdam News,* May 15, 1929 ("scores").

27. *Chicago Defender*, August 5, October 7, 1916; March 23, 1918. Ritter, *Glory of Their Times*, 191; *Indianapolis Freeman*, March 8, 1913; *Philadelphia Tribune*, January 26, 1928; June 20, 1929. *Baltimore Afro-American*, July 23, 1920; April 29, 1921; August 25, 1922; February 5, 19, 1927. *New York Amsterdam News*, September 16, 1925 ("The most radical move"); June 8, 1927. *Sporting Life*, September 1922; *Chicago Whip*, February 4, June 17, 1922; *Half-Century Magazine*, April 1919, 8; *Philadelphia Public Ledger*, October 16, 1930; Zoss and Bowman, *Diamonds in the Rough*, 144–145; Dixon and Hannigan, *Negro Baseball Leagues*, 101.

28. *Philadelphia Tribune*, June 19, 1926; July 12, 1928. *Baltimore Afro-American*, October 10, 1924 ("far better"); May 23, 1925 (Pippen quote). *The Nation*, August 25, 1926, 161 (quote); Holway, *Voices*, xviii (Stephens quote); Kusmer, *Ghetto Takes Shape*, 187–189; *Indianapolis Freeman*, December 23, 1911. Many white sportswriters continued to regard Hilldale and other black professional teams as only semiprofessional. In response, the *Philadelphia Tribune* of October 1, 1931, noted that this identification was "really a misnomer because the Hilldale Club is not a semi-pro but a professional team and those who are in the know class realize that it is merely that of cuticle pigments that keep players like Biz Mackey, Judy Johnson, Webster McDonald, Walt Cannady and a host of others from being playmates of Babe Ruth, Chuck Klein, Goose Goslin and others who have made the grade in the majors."

Chapter 9

1. *Pittsburgh Courier*, March 17, 1928 ("earn his money"); *Baltimore Afro-American*, April 28, 1928 ("get rid of"); Holway notes; *Philadelphia Tribune*, March 29, April 5, 12, 26, May 31, June 7 ("white clubs"), 28, 1928; *Philadelphia Inquirer*, May 24, June 19, 1928. Hilldale's lineup against Kensington on June 1, 1928, featured Oscar Charleston as starting pitcher and two pitchers, Dalty Cooper and Bill Campbell, in the outfield.

2. *Baltimore Afro-American*, May 12 (Gibson quote), June 16, September 22 (Wilson quote), 1928; *New York Amsterdam News*, January 17, 1923; June 23, 1926; June 27 (Strong quote), September 8, 1928; March 2, 1932. *Philadelphia Tribune*, April 12, September 12, October 4, 1928; Ruck, *Sandlot Seasons*, 118. Strong reportedly continued to charge a high booking fee (10 percent), although Bolden claimed that he "never paid Mr. Strong one cent for booking the Hilldale Club."

3. *Philadelphia Tribune*, October 6, 1927; February 16, 23, April 26, June 28, July 5, 19, 26, August 23, September 13 (Dixon quote), 20, 27, October 4, December 27, 1928; January 10, 1929. *New York Amsterdam News*, August 5, 1927; 1928 Hilldale ledger; *Baltimore Afro-American*, July 28, 1928; Hardy, "Race and Opportunity," 361. Unofficial figures credit John Beckwith with 59 home runs in 1928 against black and white competition.

4. *Philadelphia Tribune*, June 7, July 5, 1928 (quote), August 16, December 13 (Briggs quote), 1928; *New York Amsterdam News*, June 6, August 15, 1928 ("man of the hour"), August 22, 1928 ("most heartily in favor"); January 16 (White quote), 23, 1929. *Baltimore Afro-American*, July 21, August 18, September 29, December 15, 1928 ("recommended the reorganization"). There is evidence to suggest that Strong sold most or all of his interest in the Brooklyn Royal Giants prior to the beginning of the 1929 season, although several contemporary accounts continued to list him as the team's owner, perhaps because of his control over their bookings. See *Philadelphia Tribune*, June 27, July 25, 1929; April 17, May 22, 1930. *New York Amsterdam News*, March 20, July 31, 1929, June 4, 1930. *Baltimore Afro-American*, March 2, 1929.

5. *Philadelphia Tribune*, January 3, 10, February 28, March 7, 21, April 25, May 9, June 6, June 27, July 4, 25, 1929; *Baltimore Afro-American*, January 5, 19, April 13, June 29, August 10, 1929; *New York Amsterdam News*, July 26, 1933; *Pittsburgh Courier*, January 19, 1929.

6. *Philadelphia Tribune*, February 2, April 19, 1928; May 30, 1929. *New York Amsterdam News*, July 17, 1929 (White quote); *Baltimore Afro-American*, April 13, July 6, 1929.

7. *Baltimore Afro-American*, May 25, July 13, September 21, 1929; *Philadelphia Tribune*, April 29, May 23, 30, June 6, 13, 20, 27, July 11, August 1 ("seems to be afraid"), September 19, 1929; February 13, 1930; *New York Amsterdam News*, July 17, 1929 (White quote); *Pittsburgh Courier*, June 8, 1929.

8. *Philadelphia Tribune*, June 20, July 4, August 8, 15 (Pollock quote), 22, September 5, 1929; *Baltimore Afro-American*, June 22, July 13, 27, August 17, 1929; *New York Amsterdam News*, August 14, 1929; *Pittsburgh Courier*, August 31, 1929 (Wilson quote).

9. *Philadelphia Tribune*, May 19, 1927; January 31, March 7, 21, April 4 ("surrounded by Hilldale fans"), 18, May 2, August 1, 1929. Holway, *Black Diamonds*, 11; *Baltimore Afro-American*, April 20, 1929. Dihigo was reportedly Hilldale's first Cuban-born player since Pelayo Chacon, who appeared briefly with the team during a 1920 postseason series. On Dihigo, see Holway, *Blackball Stars*, 236–247.

10. *Philadelphia Tribune*, May 23, July 4, 11, August 22, 1929; April 24, 1930; May

28, 1931. *Baltimore Afro-American*, January 26, August 17, 1929; *New York Amsterdam News*, March 27, 1929. In 1931, a similar shooting incident during an Indianapolis ABCs game left one fan dead and two wounded.

11. *Philadelphia Tribune*, May 9, August 8 (Stephens, Bolden quotes), September 5 (Bolden, Dixon quotes, "questionable house"), 12, 1929; *Baltimore Afro-American*, May 18, 1929; *New York Amsterdam News*, September 25, 1929. On September 22, 1929, less than a month after the incident, Strong and Warmack appeared in Hilldale's lineup against the Farmers in Brooklyn.

12. *Indianapolis Freeman*, March 27, 1920; *Philadelphia Tribune*, August 22, 1925; November 10, 1927, January 24, June 27, 1929 (Foster quote); June 19, 1930. *Chicago Defender*, December 31, 1921; March 24, 1923. *Baltimore Afro-American*, January 13, 1922; February 9, March 23, April 13, 27, December 14, 1923; February 22, October 3, 1924; August 22, 1925; August 17 (S.B. Wilkins quote), 31 (Williams quote), September 21, 1929. *Pittsburgh Courier*, November 1, 1924; July 25, 1925. *Washington Tribune*, August 25, 1924; Peterson, *Only the Ball*, 90; Bruce, *Kansas City Monarchs*, 28–30; Hardy, "Race and Opportunity," 180. As early as 1921, Hilldale fans had questioned the use of white umpires. See *Chicago Defender*, June 18, 1921.

13. *New York Amsterdam News*, August 8, 1928; Hardy, "Race and Opportunity," 180, 361, 540; Kusmer, *Ghetto Takes Shape*, 174–189; *Philadelphia Tribune*, March 5, 1927.

14. *Philadelphia Tribune*, September 8, 1927.

15. *Philadelphia Tribune*, April 18, May 23, 30, June 20, July 11, August 1 ("genuine revolt"), 8 ("Come on fellows"), 1929; *Baltimore Afro-American*, July 20, 1929; *New York Amsterdam News*, May 1, July 31, 1929.

16. *Philadelphia Tribune*, August 1 ("Negro Umpires at Hilldale"), 8 ("Hilldale Again"), 1929. Boots Evans, Spike Halliday, James Locke, and former Philadelphia Giants pitcher William Bell were among the black umpires employed by Hilldale in the 1920s. By 1929, umpires were paid $7-$8 per game at Hilldale Park.

17. *Baltimore Afro-American*, July 20, August 10 (Rossiter quote), 17 (quote), October 19 (Taylor quote); *Philadelphia Tribune*, September 19, 1929; 1929 Hilldale ledger. Hilldale's 1929 financial records indicate that the team grossed $28,865.99.

18. *Philadelphia Tribune*, June 27, July 11, 18, August 1, September 19, 1929; August 7, 28, 1930. *Baltimore Afro-American*, March 3, April 7, May 19, 1928; April 13, October 5, 1929. Oliver Arata, "Colored Athlete in Professional Baseball," *Baseball Magazine*, May 1929, 555–556; *Chicago Whip*, June 23, 1928 ("fed up on colored baseball"); *Chicago Defender*, February 5, 1927. Roesink's racist attitudes and comments about "shine newspapers" caused many black fans to boycott the Detroit Stars' home games at Hamtramck Stadium in Detroit in 1930.

19. *Philadelphia Tribune*, February 20, March 27, April 3, 10, 17, 24, 1930; *Public Ledger*, February 18, 1930; *Pittsburgh Courier*, March 1 (Wilson quote), April 19, 1930.

20. *Philadelphia Tribune*, April 24, 1930 (Dixon quote). Dixon was apparently a strong fan of neither Hilldale nor Bolden. In 1930, Rollo Wilson observed that Dixon's "pet hobby" was seemingly to "hate Hilldale"; see *Pittsburgh Courier*, February 15, 1930.

Chapter 10

1. *Philadelphia Tribune*, April 24, May 1, 22, July 24, 31, August 7 ("apology," Dixon quote), 21, 1930; 1930 Hilldale ledger; *New York Amsterdam News*, May 14, June

4, 1930; *Philadelphia Record*, July 22, 1930. On July 21, 1930, the Darby Phantoms, supplemented by a few Hilldale players, were booked as Hilldale in a game against Manoa. The team's assistant manager, Bob Clark, was Hilldale's mascot in the early 1920s.

2. *Philadelphia Tribune*, April 3 ("nothing the matter"), March 6, May 22, July 3, 24 ("something must be done"), August 28, September 11, 18, 25, October 2, 1930; March 12, 26, 1931. *New York Amsterdam News*, June 4, 11, August 13, December 31, 1930; August 12, 1931. 1930 Hilldale ledger; Peterson, *Only the Ball*, 83–84.

3. Eisen, "Dexter Park and the Bushwicks"; *Philadelphia Tribune*, January 16, July 10, 1930; July 14, 28, August 4, 1932. *Philadelphia Record*, July 1, 1930; *Philadelphia Inquirer*, July 10, 14, 1932; Crepeau, *Diamond Mind*, 188–193; 1931 Hilldale ledger; *New York Amsterdam News*, July 16, 1930; *Philadelphia Record*, September 4, 1930. According to Sol White, the Cuban X-Giants played a night game in 1901 in Philadelphia using an extra large and soft baseball. While major league teams did not begin night baseball until 1935, the Phillies played an exhibition game in September 1930 in Allentown under lights.

4. Ruck, *Sandlot Seasons*, 46–62, 137–169; Bankes, *Pittsburgh Crawfords*; *Philadelphia Tribune*, September 12, 1929; May 8, June 12, July 3, August 28, September 18, October 2, December 11, 1930; January 29 ("much the better"), February 26, August 20, 1931. Office of Personnel Management, official personnel folder and employee medical folder of Edward Bolden (Wolfenden quote).

5. *Philadelphia Tribune*, February 26, March 5 ("rank novice," "initial plank"), May 7, 1931; Lloyd Thompson, "Darby's John M. Drew: Business Man, Pioneer Bus Line Owner," in *Darby, PA, 1682–1982 Tricentennial*, Lloyd Thompson–Bill Cash Collection; March 11, 1931, certificate of incorporation, Lloyd Thompson–Bill Cash Collection.

6. *Philadelphia Tribune*, March 5, 26, April 2, 23, May 7 ("cellar hideout"), 21, August 6, 13, 27, September 10 ("depression wave"), 17, 24, November 5, 1931; 1931 Hilldale ledger.

7. *Philadelphia Tribune*, April 16, 30, May 7, 14, 28, June 11 ("Uncle Tom ring"), July 9, August 6, 1931; *New York Amsterdam News*, August 5, 26, September 16 ("worst season"), 1931; January 27, June 15 ("theatrical"), 1932.

8. *New York Amsterdam News*, April 9, 1930; *Philadelphia Tribune*, April 16, May 14, June 18, 25, July 20, August 27, 1931; April 21, 1932.

9. *Philadelphia Tribune*, March 12, 19, July 16, 23, August 6 (Dixon quote), September 3, 10, 17, October 15, 22, 29, 1931; February 25, 1932; Dixon and Hannigan, *Negro Baseball Leagues*, 155–159.

10. *Philadelphia Tribune*, December 18, 1930; March 12, April 23, July 9, 1931; January 21, 28, February 4, 11, 18, March 17, 24, 31, April 21, 28, May 5, 1932. *New York Amsterdam News*, January 27, February 17, March 9, April 20 ("competition"), May 4, 1932; *Chicago Defender*, April 11, 1931 (Young quote); Dixon and Hannigan, *Negro Baseball Leagues*, 149–152; Heaphy, "Growth and Decline of the Negro Leagues" 74. The Cuban Winter League and Palm Beach Hotel League were forced to shut down early during the winter of 1930–31, and the Texas Oklahoma Louisiana League (TOL), a lesser organization formed in 1929 by Kansas City Monarchs publicity man Quincy Gilmore, collapsed in 1931.

11. *New York Amsterdam News*, February 17, 1932 ("smartest man"); Franklin, "'Voice of the Black Community': The Philadelphia Tribune, 1912–41," 273; Haley, "To Do Well," 55–57; Joseph Willits, "Some Impacts of the Depression Upon the Negro in Philadelphia," *Opportunity* (July 1933), 200–204. Between 1929 and 1935, black unemployment averaged 45 percent annually in Philadelphia.

12. Minutes of March 31, 1932, Hilldale Corporation meeting ("all other expenses"), Bill Cash–Lloyd Thompson Collection; *Philadelphia Tribune,* February 18 ("Posey League"), March 10, 31, April 21 ("much dissatisfaction"), 28, May 5 (Dixon quote), 19, 26, June 2, 9, 23, 1932; 1931 Hilldale ledger; *New York Amsterdam News,* April 20, June 15, 1932.

13. *Philadelphia Tribune,* June 16, 23, 30, July 21, July 28 ("do not have money to spend on baseball," "HILLDALE'S PASSING"), 1932; 1932 Hilldale ledger.

14. Saunders, *100 Years After Emancipation,* 193 ("brainwashed"); William Brashler, *Josh Gibson: A Life in the Negro Leagues* (New York, 1978), 99 ("do not have the proper sense of values"). Although Bolden had severed all ties to Hilldale by early 1930, John Saunders unfairly and incorrectly blamed him for the team's financial woes in 1931 and 1932, claiming he knew "little or nothing about the financial end of an operation of Hilldale's magnitude."

15. Holway, *Voices,* 81-82. During 1931 and 1932, Hilldale took only five Sunday trips to New York and made no appearances at Dexter Park. Drew, however, routinely paid 5 percent to Eddie Gottlieb, a Philadelphia area promoter and associate of Strong's, for booking a number of Hilldale games in 1931 and 1932; see July 25, 1932, letter to Ed Gottlieb, Bill Cash–Lloyd Thompson Collection; *New York Amsterdam News,* April 20, 1932.

16. *Philadelphia Tribune,* June 30, 1932 (Pollock quote); *Pittsburgh Courier,* July 16, 1932; undated photocopy, Baseball Hall of Fame Library; Dixon and Hannigan, *Negro Baseball Leagues,* 168; Alexander, *Our Game,* 155-162; Bill Rabinowitz, "Baseball and the Depression," in *Baseball History: An Annual of Original Baseball Research — Premier Edition,* ed. Peter Levine (Westport, CT, 1989), 49-59; Obojski, *Minor Leagues,* 153, 326, 343, 351, 354, 384, 394; *New York Times,* May 13, October 9, 29, December 6, 1932; Crepeau, *Diamond Mind,* 173-195; Bilovsky and Westcott, *Phillies Encyclopedia,* 476; photocopy from *Baseball Dope Book* (1985), 42-43, Baseball Hall of Fame Library. Between 1934 and 1947, neither the Phillies nor the Athletics finished higher than fifth place in their leagues.

17. *Philadelphia Tribune,* August 13, September 24, 1931; February 18, March 31, April 28, May 19, June 9, 1932; March 23, 1933 (Macey quotes).

18. Holway, *Voices,* 82-84; *Philadelphia Tribune,* February 9, 23, March 9, 16 ("make this city forget"), April 27, June 29, 1933; *New York Amsterdam News,* February 5 ("extravagant," "keeping"), June 7, 14, 1933; Dixon and Hannigan, *Negro Baseball Leagues,* 159-161; John Holway notes.

19. *Philadelphia Tribune,* May 18, July 20, 1933; July 5, October 11, 1934; August 7, 1943. Saunders, *100 Years After Emancipation,* 144, 196; Holway, *Black Diamonds,* 75; *New York Times,* January 11, 1935.

20. Heaphy, "Growth and Decline," 186; Alexandro Pompez file, courtesy National Baseball Hall of Fame Library; Bankes, *Pittsburgh Crawfords,* 91-93; Hank Aaron with Lonnie Wheeler, *I Had a Hammer: The Hank Aaron Story* (New York, 1991), 32; Dixon and Hannigan, *Negro Baseball Leagues,* 19, 160-329, 299 (Malarcher quote); Eisen, "Dexter Park and the Bushwicks"; telephone conversation with Bob Potts; *Philadelphia Tribune,* May 5, 1945 (Bolden on integration); October 3, 1950. Bolden's wife Nellie died on October 12, 1949, at the age of 68. On Gottlieb, see Ruck, *Sandlot Seasons,* 115-122, and Ed Gottlieb file, National Baseball Hall of Fame Library. Gottlieb was a highly successful coach and owner of several basketball teams, including the South Philadelphia Hebrew Association and the Philadelphia Warriors, and was later elected to the Basketball Hall of Fame. He died in 1979 at the age of 81.

21. *Philadelphia Tribune,* July 28, 1932; May 4, 1933; May 27, 1937; August 15, 1940; April 25, 1942; November 6, 1943; April 3, 7, 1951. Heaphy, "Growth and

Decline," 154–155; Holway, *Blackball Stars*, 47–124, 217–247; Holway, *Voices*, 68; Saunders, *100 Years After Emancipation*, 193–195; *Philadelphia Daily News*, August 23, 1982; John Holway, "Clash of the Black League Titans," in *Ol' Ball Game* (Harrisburg, 1990), 65–66; Phillip Hoose, *Necessities: Racial Barriers in American Sports* (New York, 1989), 124–127.

22. *Philadelphia Tribune*, May 1, 1987; March 2, 1976; *Philadelphia Inquirer*, August 25, 1987; August 21, 1988 (Freeman quote). The probable last surviving member of the 1925 Hilldale championship team was Clint Thomas, who died in 1990 at the age of 94.

23. *Philadelphia Tribune*, February 23, 1918.

24. *Philadelphia Tribune*, December 1, 1923.

25. *Philadelphia Tribune*, May 10, 1919; *Philadelphia Independent*, October 7, 1950 (Coleman quote).

Bibliography

Books

Aaron, Hank, with Lonnie Wheeler. *I Had a Hammer: The Hank Aaron Story.* New York: Harper Paperbacks, 1991.

Administrative Survey of Darby Township, Delaware County, Pennsylvania: A Report for: The Board of Township Commissioners Bureau of Municipal Research and Pennsylvania Economy League. November 1957.

_____. *The Negro in Business in Philadelphia: An Investigation by the Armstrong Association of Philadelphia.* Philadelphia: Armstrong Association of Philadelphia, n.d.

Alexander, Charles. *John McGraw.* New York: Viking Press, 1988.

_____. *Our Game.* New York: Henry Holt, 1991.

_____. *Ty Cobb.* New York: Oxford University Press, 1984.

Allen, Lee. *Cooperstown Corner: Columns from the Sporting News, 1962-1969.* Cleveland: Society of American Baseball Research, 1990.

Aptheker, Herbert, ed. *A Documentary History of the Negro People in the United States, 1910-1932.* Secaucus, NJ: Citadel Press, 1973.

Armstrong Association of Philadelphia. *A Study of Living Conditions Among Colored People in Towns in the Outer Part of Philadelphia and in Other Suburbs Both in Pennsylvania and New Jersey.* Philadelphia: Armstrong Association of Philadelphia, 1915.

Ashe, Arthur, Jr. *A Hard Road to Glory: A History of the African-American Athlete, 1619-1918.* New York: Warner, 1988.

Bak, Rich. *Cobb Would Have Caught It: The Golden Age of Baseball in Detroit.* Detroit: Wayne State University Press, 1991.

Ballard, Allen. *One More Day's Journey: The Story of a Family and a People.* New York: McGraw-Hill, 1984.

Bankes, James. *The Pittsburgh Crawfords: The Lives and Times of Black Baseball's Most Exciting Team.* Dubuque, IA: William C. Brown, 1991.

The Baseball Encyclopedia. 8th ed. New York: Macmillan, 1990.

Benson, Michael. *Ballparks of North America.* Jefferson, NC: McFarland, 1989.

Betts, John. *America's Sporting Heritage: 1850-1950.* Reading, MA: Addison-Wesley, 1974.

Bilovsky, Frank, and Rich Westcott. *The Phillies Encyclopedia.* New York: Leisure Press, 1984.

Brashler, William. *Josh Gibson: A Life in the Negro Leagues.* New York, Harper and Row, 1978.

Bruce, Janet. *The Kansas City Monarchs: Champions of Black Baseball.* Lawrence, KS: University Press of Kansas, 1985.

273

Burkett, Randolph K., Nancy Hall Burkett, and Henry Louis Gates, Jr., eds. *Black Biography 1790–1850: A Cumulative Index.* Alexandria, VA: Chadwyck-Healy, 1991.

Callow, Alexander B., Jr., ed. *American Urban History: An Interpretive Reader with Commentaries.* New York: Oxford University Press, 1982.

Chalk, Ocania. *Black College Sport.* New York: Dodd, Mead, 1976.

―――――. *Pioneers of Black Sport.* New York: Dodd, Mead, 1975.

Chicago Commission on Race Relations. *The Negro in Chicago: A Study of Race Relations and a Race Riot.* Chicago: University of Chicago Press, 1922.

Creamer, Robert. *Babe: The Legend Comes to Life.* New York: Penguin, 1974.

Crepeau, Richard. *Baseball: America's Diamond Mind, 1919–1941.* Orlando, FL: University Presses of Florida, 1980.

Daniels, Walter. *Black Journals of the United States.* Westport, CT: Greenwood Press, 1982.

Darby, PA. 1682–1982 Tricentennial (commemorative booklet).

Davids, L. Robert, ed. *Insider's Baseball.* New York: Scribner, 1983.

DiClerico, James, and Barry Pavelec. *Jersey Game.* New Brunswick, NJ: Rutgers University Press, 1991.

Dixon, Phil, and Patrick Hannigan. *The Negro Baseball Leagues: A Photographic History.* Mattituck, NY: Amereon House, 1992.

Du Bois, W.E.B. *The Philadelphia Negro: A Social Study.* New York: Schocken, 1967 (first published 1899).

Fleming, G. James, and Christian E. Burckel, eds. *Who's Who in Colored America.* 7th ed. Yonkers-on-Hudson, NY: Christian E. Burckel, 1950.

Foner, Philip, and Ronald Lewis, eds. *The Black Worker: A Documentary History from Colonial Times to the Present.* Vol. 6, *The Era of Post-War Prosperity and the Great Depression, 1920–1936.* Philadelphia: Temple University Press, 1981.

Franklin, Vincent. *The Education of Black Philadelphia.* Philadelphia: University of Pennsylvania Press, 1979.

Gilmore, Al-Tony. *Bad Nigger! The National Impact of Jack Johnson.* Port Washington, NY: Kennikat Press, 1975.

Grobani, Anton. *Guide to Baseball Research.* Detroit: Gale Research, 1975.

Hall, Charles. *Negroes in the United States, 1920–32.* Washington, DC: U.S. Government Printing Office, 1935 (Kraus reprint, 1969, New York).

Holway, John. *Black Diamonds: Life in the Negro Leagues from the Men Who Lived It.* Westport, CT: Meckler, 1989.

―――――. *Blackball Stars: Negro League Pioneers.* Westport, CT: Meckler, 1988.

―――――. *Voices from the Great Black Baseball Leagues.* New York: Dodd, Mead, 1975.

Hoose, Phillip. *Necessities: Racial Barriers in American Sports.* New York: Random House, 1989.

James, Bill. *The Bill James Historical Baseball Abstract.* New York: Villard Books, 1988.

Kennedy, Louise. *The Negro Peasant Turns Cityward.* New York: AMS Press, 1930.

Kerlin, Robert T. *Voice of the Negro — 1919.* New York: Arno Press, *New York Times,* 1968, reprint (first published 1920).

Kuklick, Bruce. *To Every Thing a Season.* Princeton, NJ: Princeton University Press, 1991.

Kusmer, Kenneth. *A Ghetto Takes Shape: Black Cleveland, 1870–1930.* Urbana: University of Illinois Press, 1976.

Levine, David Allan. *Internal Combustion: The Races in Detroit, 1915–1926.* Westport, CT: Greenwood Press, 1976.

Lynch, Hollis, comp. *The Black Urban Condition: A Documentary History, 1866–1971.* New York: Thomas Crowell, 1973.

McBride, David. *The Afro-American in Pennsylvania: A Critical Guide to Sources in the Pennsylvania State Archives.* Harrisburg: Pennsylvania Historical and Museum Commission, 1979.

Murdock, Eugene. *Ban Johnson, Czar of Baseball.* Westport, CT: Greenwood Press, 1982.

_____. *Baseball Players and Their Times: Oral Histories of the Game, 1920–1940.* Westport, CT: Meckler, 1991.

Nearing, Scott. *Black America.* New York: Vanguard Press, 1929 (reprint 1970, Johnson Reprint, NY).

Negro Survey of Pennsylvania. Harrisburg: Commonwealth of Pennsylvania, Department of Welfare, 1927.

Nielson, David Gordon. *Black Ethos: Northern Urban Negro Life and Thought, 1890–1930.* Westport, CT: Greenwood Press, 1977.

Novell, Douglas, and Lawrence Ziewacz. *The Games They Played: Sports in American History, 1865–1980.* Chicago: Nelson-Hall, 1983.

N. W. Ayer & Son's American Newspaper Annual and Directory. Philadelphia: N.W. Ayer, 1914.

Obojski, Robert. *Bush League: A History of Minor League Baseball.* New York: Macmillan, 1975.

The Ol' Ball Game: A Collection of Baseball Characters and Moments Worth Remembering. Harrisburg: Stackpole, 1990.

Oleksak, Michael, and Mary Adams Oleksak. *Béisbol: Latin Americans and the Grand Old Game.* Grand Rapids, MI: Masters Press, 1991.

Osofsky, Gilbert. *Harlem: The Making of a Ghetto.* New York: Harper and Row, 1971.

Parsons, Talcott, and Kenneth Clark, eds. *The Negro American.* Boston: Houghton Mifflin, 1966.

Peterson, Robert. *Cages to Jump Shots.* New York: Oxford University Press, 1990.

_____. *Only the Ball Was White.* Englewood Cliffs, NJ: Prentice-Hall, 1970.

Pietrusza, David. *Major Leagues: The Formation, Sometimes Absorption and Mostly Inevitable Demise of 18 Professional Baseball Organizations, 1871 to Present.* Jefferson, NC: McFarland, 1991.

Proceedings from *Philadelphia's Baseball History.* Symposium, February 24, 1990, sponsored by the Historical Society of Pennsylvania.

Riess, Steven A. *City Games: The Evolution of American Urban Society and the Rise of Sports.* Urbana: University of Illinois Press, 1989.

_____. *Touching Base: Professional Baseball and American Culture in the Progressive Era.* Westport, CT: Greenwood Press, 1983.

Riley, James A. *The All-Time All-Stars of Black Baseball.* Cocoa, FL: TK, 1983.

_____. *The Biographical Encyclopedia of the Negro Baseball Leagues.* New York: Carroll and Graf, 1994.

Ritter, Lawrence. *The Glory of Their Times.* New York: Vintage Books, 1984.

Robinson, Jackie (as told to Alfred Duckett). *I Never Had It Made.* New York: Putnam, 1972.

Rogosin, Donn. *Invisible Men: Life in Baseball's Negro Leagues.* New York: Atheneum, 1985.

Ruck, Rob. *Sandlot Seasons: Sport in Black Pittsburgh.* Urbana: University of Illinois Press, 1987.

Rust, Art, Jr. *"Get That Nigger Off the Field!"* New York: Delacorte Press, 1976.

_____, with Edna Rust. *Confessions of a Baseball Junkie.* New York: William Morrow, 1985.

Saunders, John. *100 Years After Emancipation: History of the Philadelphia Negro, 1787–1963.* Philadelphia: FRS, 1964.

Scranton, Philip, and Walter Licht. *Work Sights: Industrial Philadelphia, 1890–1950.*
      Philadelphia: Temple University Press, 1986.
Seymour, Harold. *Baseball: The Golden Age.* New York: Oxford University Press, 1971.
_____. *Baseball: The People's Game.* New York: Oxford University Press, 1990.
Smith, Myron. *Baseball: A Comprehensive Bibliography.* Jefferson, NC: McFarland,
      1986.
Spear, Allan. *Black Chicago: The Making of a Negro Ghetto, 1890–1920.* Chicago: Univer-
      sity of Chicago Press, 1967.
Spink, J.G. Taylor. *Judge Landis and Twenty-Five Years of Baseball.* New York: Thomas
      Crowell, 1947.
Sullivan, Neil. *The Minors: The Struggles and the Triumph of Baseball's Poor Relation from
      1876 to the Present.* New York: St. Martin's Press, 1990.
Tebbel, John. *The Compact History of the American Newspaper.* New York: Hawthorn,
      1969.
Tygiel, Jules. *Baseball's Great Experiment: Jackie Robinson and His Legacy.* New York: Ox-
      ford University Press, 1983.
Voight, David Q. *American Baseball.* Vol.2, *From the Commissioners to Continental Expan-
      sion.* University Park: Pennsylvania State University Press, 1966–1970 (reprint
      1983).
Warner, Sam Bass. *The Private City: Philadelphia in Three Periods of Its Growth.* Phila-
      delphia: University of Pennsylvania Press, 1968.
White, Charles Fred. *Who's Who in Philadelphia.* Philadelphia: AME, 1912.
White, Sol. *Sol White's Official Base Ball Guide.* Columbia, SC: Camden House, 1984,
      reprint (originally published 1907).
Woodward, C. Vann. *The Strange Career of Jim Crow.* New York: Oxford University
      Press, 1974.
Woofter, T.J., Jr. *Negro Problems in Cities.* Garden City, NY: Doubleday, Doran, 1928.
Works Progress Administration. *Ethnic Survey: The Negro in Philadelphia,* 1938–1939,
      1941.
Wright, Giles. *Afro-Americans in New Jersey: A Short History.* Trenton: New Jersey
      Historical Commission, Department of State, 1988.
Wright, R. R., Jr. *The Negro in Pennsylvania: A Study in Economic History.* Philadelphia:
      AME, Philadelphia, 1912.
Zoss, Joel, and John Bowman. *Diamonds in the Rough: The Untold Story of Baseball.* New
      York: Macmillan, 1989.

Articles, Unpublished Documents

Antonucci, Mike. "Negro League Cards Are Legacy to History." *Sporting News,* De-
      cember 30, 1991, p. 47.
Arata, Oliver S. "The Colored Athlete in Professional Baseball." *Baseball Magazine,*
      May 1929, pp. 555–556.
Bankes, James. "The Magnificent Pittsburgh Crawfords." In *The Ol' Ball Game: A Col-
      lection of Baseball Characters and Moments Worth Remembering.* Harrisburg: Stackpole,
      1990, pp. 44–57.
Bjarkman, Peter. "First Hispanic Star? Dolf Luque, of Course." *Baseball Research Jour-
      nal* 19, 1990, pp. 28–32.
"Big League Making Progress." *The Competitor,* July 1920, p. 69.
Blockson, Charles L. "A History of the Blackman in Montgomery Co." *Bulletin of the
      Historical Society of Montgomery County* 18 (4), Spring 1973, pp. 337–362.

Campbell, Roy H. "The Times of Yeadon's Black Enclave." *Philadelphia Inquirer*, February 26, 1987.

Casway, Jerrold. "Hits and Errors in Catalogue of Ballparks." *Philadelphia Inquirer*, April 5, 1992, p. N2.

Cattau, Daniel. "Forgotten Champions." *Washington Post Magazine*, June 3, 1990, pp. 22–29.

Clark, Dick, and John B. Holway. "Charleston No. 1 Star of 1921 Negro League." *Baseball Research Journal* 14, 1985, pp. 63–70.

————. "1930 Negro National League." *Baseball Research Journal* 18, 1989, pp. 81–86.

Clark, Mark, and Phil Mullen. "Black Involvement in the Early Years of Professional Baseball." In *Cooperstown Symposium on Baseball and the American Culture*, ed. Alvin Hall. Westport, CT: Meckler, 1989, pp. 375–385.

Colimore, Edward. "Telling the Story of Black Migration in the 20th Century." *Philadelphia Inquirer*, January 16, 1990.

Conk, Margo. "Essay Review: Industrial Philadelphia." *Pennsylvania Magazine of History and Biography* 106(3), 1982, pp. 423–432.

Davids, Robert L. "John (Bud) Fowler: Nineteenth Century Black Baseball Pioneer." Unpublished paper, SABR Research Exchange, 17 pp.

Doyle, Edward "Dutch." "Baker Bowl Comments." Unpublished paper, SABR Research Exchange.

————. "Philadelphia's Ball Parks." Unpublished paper, SABR Research Exchange, 7 pp.

————. "Sandlot Babe." In *The Ol' Ball Game: A Collection of Baseball Characters and Moments Worth Remembering*. Harrisburg: Stackpole, 1990, pp. 31–33.

————. "Sandlot Baseball in the Philadelphia Area." Unpublished paper, SABR Research Exchange, 10 pp.

Eisen, Robert. "Dexter Park and the Bushwicks." *Times Newsweekly of Ridgewood, Long Island*, September 19, 1991, pp. 64–68; September 26, 1991, pp. 65–68.

Elfers, James. "Pro Diamonds in the Diamond State." Unpublished paper, SABR Research Exchange, 1986, 23 pp.

Emlen, John. "The Movement for the Betterment of the Negro in Philadelphia." *Annals of the American Academy of Political and Social Science*, September 1913; reprinted in *Black Politics in Philadelphia*, ed. Miriam Ershkowitz, Joseph Zikmund II. New York: Basic Books, 1973, pp. 40–52.

Fish, Larry. "From Dusty Records, Tales of Philadelphia Labor." *Philadelphia Inquirer*, March 1, 1993.

Franklin, Vincent. "The Philadelphia Race Riot of 1918." *Pennsylvania Magazine of History and Biography* 99, 1975, pp. 336–350.

————. "'Voice of the Black Community': The Philadelphia Tribune, 1912–41." *Pennsylvania History* 51 (4), October 1984, pp. 261–284.

Fullerton, Hugh. "Earnings in Baseball." *North American Review*, June 1930, pp. 743–748.

Gelber, Steven. "'Their Hands Are All Out Playing' Business and Amateur Baseball, 1845–1917." *Journal of Sports History* 11(1), Spring 1984, pp. 5–27.

Golab, Caroline. "The Immigrant and the City: Poles, Italians, and Jews in Philadelphia, 1870–1920." In *The Peoples of Philadelphia: A History of Ethnic Groups and Lower-Class Life, 1790–1840*, ed. Allen F. Davis and Mark Haller. Philadelphia: Temple University Press, 1973, pp. 201–230.

Gordon, Eugene. "The Negro Press." *American Mercury*, June 1926, pp. 207–215.

Green, James "Joe," with John Holway. "I Was Satchel's Catcher." *Journal of Popular Culture* 6(1), Summer 1972, pp. 157–170.

Hallgren, Mauritz. "Mass Misery in Philadelphia." *The Nation*, March 9, 1932, pp. 275–277.

Harlow, Alvin. "Unrecognized Stars." *Esquire*, August 1938.

Hershberg, Theodore, Alan Burnstein, Eugene Ericksen, Stephanie Greenberg, and William Yancey. "A Tale of Three Cities: Blacks, Immigrants, and Opportunity in Philadelphia, 1850–1880, 1930, 1970." In *Philadelphia: Work, Space, Family, and Group Experience in the Nineteenth Century*. New York: Oxford University Press, 1981, pp. 461–491.

Hicks, John. "St. Louis: Is It the Toughest Town for Negro Baseball Players?" *Crisis*, October 1950; in Lynch, Hollis, comp., *The Black Urban Condition: A Documentary History, 1866–1971*. New York: Thomas Crowell, 1973, pp. 573–576.

Holway, John B. "Before You Could Say Jackie Robinson." *Look*, July 13, 1971, pp. 46–50.

————. "Clash of the Black-League Titans." In *The Ol' Ball Game: A Collection of Baseball Characters and Moments Worth Remembering*. Harrisburg: Stackpole, 1990, pp. 58–66.

————. "The One Man Team: Cristobel Torriente." In *Baseball Historical Review*, ed. L. Robert Davids. Society of American Baseball Research, 1981.

————. "Rube Foster: Father of Black Game." *Sporting News*, August 8, 1981, pp. 19–20.

————. "Where Have All the Black Fans Gone?" National Baseball Library, n.d., pp. 70–71.

Kelly, Frederic. "Judy Johnson: From Snow Hill to the Hall of Fame." *Sun Magazine*, February 1, 1976, pp. 15–20, National Baseball Library.

Kerrane, Kevin, and Rob Beaton. "Judy Johnson: Reminiscences by the Great Baseball Player." *Delaware Today*, May 1977, pp. 15–16, 33–34, 44–46.

Kieran, John. "Big League Business." *Literary Digest*, May 31, 1930, pp. 16–17, 149–150, 154.

"King Nat of the Bushers." Undated photocopy (1914?), National Baseball Library.

Kleinknecht, Merl. "The Cleveland Buckeyes." Paper presented on behalf of the Negro Leagues Committee, SABR XX, Cleveland, Ohio, 1990.

Klink, Bill. "Our Friend Willie." In *The Ol' Ball Game: A Collection of Baseball Characters and Moments Worth Remembering*. Harrisburg: Stackpole, 1990, pp. 126–133.

Lanctot, Neil. "Fair Dealing and Clean Playing: Ed Bolden and the Hilldale Club, 1910–1932." *Pennsylvania Magazine of History and Biography*, January–April 1993, pp. 3–49.

Lenthall, Bruce. "Covering More Than the Game: Baseball and Racial Issues in an African-American Newspaper, 1919–1920." In *Cooperstown Symposium on Baseball and the American Culture*, ed. Alvin Hall. Westport, CT: Meckler, 1990, pp. 57–65.

Leonard, Buck, with John Holway. "Grays Brought Night Baseball to Washington." *Sporting News*, March 11, 1972, pp. 27–28.

Lewis, Gregory. "Black Ball." *Image*, April 8, 1990, pp. 22–28.

Lewis, Ira F. "Baseball Men Hold Successful Meeting." *The Competitor*, January–February 1921, pp. 51, 54.

————. "National Baseball League Formed." *The Competitor*, March 1920, pp. 66–67.

————. "'New' League Not Needed." *The Competitor*, May 1921, pp. 39, 41.

————. "Who'll Be the Next?" *The Competitor*, October–November 1920, pp. 221–223.

Lucas, John A. "The Unholy Experiment: Professional Baseball's Struggle Against Pennsylvania Sunday Blue Laws, 1926–34." *Pennsylvania History* 38, April 1971, pp. 163–175.

Malloy, Jerry. "The Birth of the Cuban Giants: The Origins of Black Professional Baseball." Unpublished manuscript, courtesy of Jerry Malloy.

_____. "Out at Home." *The National Pastime: A Review of Baseball History*, Fall 1982, pp. 14–28.

Manly, A.L. "Where Negroes Live in Philadelphia." *Opportunity*, May 1923, pp. 10–15.

Miller, Fredric. "The Black Migration to Philadelphia: A 1924 Profile." *Pennsylvania Magazine of History and Biography*, July 1984, pp. 315–350.

Mossell, Sadie Tanner. "The Standard of Living Among One Hundred Negro Migrant Families in Philadelphia." *Annals of the American Academy of Political and Social Science* 98, November 1921, pp. 171–222.

Mullen, Phil, and Mark Clark. "Blacks in Baseball: An Historical Perspective, 1867–1988." In *Cooperstown Symposium on Baseball and the American Culture,* ed. Alvin Hall. Westport: Meckler, 1989, pp. 123–137.

Nardinelli, Clark. "Judge Kenesaw Mountain Landis and the Art of Cartel Enforcement." In *Baseball History: An Annual of Original Baseball Research,* ed. Peter Levine. Westport, CT: Meckler, 1989, pp. 103–114.

Newman, Bernard. "The Housing of Negro Immigrants in Pennsylvania." *Opportunity*, February 1924, pp. 46–48.

O'Leary, John. "The Memphis Red Sox." *Memphis Magazine*, reprint of June 1979 article, pp. 42–52.

Oleksak, Michael, and Mary Adams Oleksak. "Cuba No Vacation for U.S. Teams in 1900s." *USA Today Baseball Weekly*, May 24–30, 1991, p. 18.

Ordine, Bill. "A Better Team Than Money Could Buy." *Today Magazine, Philadelphia Inquirer*, April 17, 1977, pp. 33–40.

Osofsky, Gilbert. "Harlem Tragedy: An Emerging Slum." In *American Urban History*, ed. Alexander B. Callow, Jr. New York: Oxford University Press, 1982, pp. 309–327.

Phelps, Howard. "Inter-Racial Baseball Should Come to Fruition." *Half-Century Magazine*, April 1919, p. 8.

Plott, Bill. "The Southern League of Colored Base Ballists." In *Baseball Historical Review*, ed. L. Robert Davids. Society of American Baseball Research, 1981, pp. 75–78.

Rabinowitz, Bill. "Baseball and the Great Depression." In *Baseball History: An Annual of Original Baseball Research,* ed. Peter Levine. Westport, CT: Meckler, 1989, pp. 49–59.

Riess, Steven. "Professional Sunday Baseball: A Study in Social Reform, 1892–1934." *Maryland Historian*, Fall 1973, pp. 95–108.

Samuel, Terence. "Central Morton Confronts Change." *Philadelphia Inquirer*, November 19, 1989.

_____. "The Heritage That Divides Darby." *Philadelphia Inquirer*, March 19, 1989.

Scully, Gerald W. "Discrimination: The Case of Baseball." In *Government and the Sports Business*, ed. Roger Noll. Washington, DC: Brookings Institution, 1974, pp. 221–273.

Silcox, Harry. "Efforts to Desegregate Baseball in Philadelphia: The Pythian Baseball Club, 1866–1872." National Baseball Library, 1973.

Smith, Shelley. "Remembering Their Game." *Sports Illustrated*, July 6, 1992, pp. 81–92.

Strauss, Robert. "Oy, How They Played the Game." *PhillySport*, February 1989, pp. 40–47.

Taylor, C.I. "The Future of Colored Baseball." *The Competitor*, February 1920, pp. 76–79.

Thorn, John, and Jules Tygiel. "Jackie Robinson's Signing: The Real, Untold Story."

The National Pastime: A Review of Baseball History. Vol. 10. Cleveland: Society of American Baseball Research, 1990, pp. 7–12.

"To Rescue Baseball in the Small Towns." *Literary Digest,* April 18, 1925, pp. 68–72.

Voight, David Q. "America's Game: A Brief History of Baseball." In *The Baseball Encyclopedia,* 8th ed. New York: Macmillan, 1990, pp. 3–13.

Washington, Forrester. "Recreational Facilities for the Negro." *Annals of the American Academy of Political and Social Science* 130, November 1928, pp. 272–282.

Weaver, Bill. "The Black Press and the Assault on Professional Baseball's 'Color Line,'" October, 1945–April, 1947." *Phylon* 40(4), Winter 1979, pp. 303–317.

Wiggins, David. "Wendell Smith, the Pittsburgh Courier-Journal and the Campaign to Include Blacks in Organized Baseball, 1933–1945." *Journal of Sports History* 10(2), Summer 1983, pp. 5–29.

Williams, Nudie. "Footnote to Trivia: Moses Fleetwood Walker and the All-American Dream." *Journal of American Culture* 11(2), Summer 1988, pp. 65–72.

Willits, Joseph. "Some Impacts of the Depression Upon the Negro in Philadelphia." *Opportunity,* July 1933, pp. 200–204.

Wilson, W. Rollo. "Ed Bolden's Hilldale Club Was Tops." *Pittsburgh Courier Magazine,* April 14, 1951, p. 11.

———. "They Could Make the Big Leagues." *Crisis,* October 1934, pp. 305–306.

Wyatt, Dave. "The 'Stove League': Smoking 'Em Across with the Winning Run on the Sacks." *The Competitor,* January 1920, pp. 65–66.

Ziglar, William. "'Community On Trial': The Coatesville Lynching of 1911." *Pennsylvania Magazine of History and Biography* 106(2), April 1982, pp. 245–270.

Dissertations/Theses

Farmer, Greene, Jr. "Social Implication of Black Professional Baseball in the United States." Ph.D. diss., United States International University, 1975.

Haley, Charles. "To Do Well and To Do Good: Philadelphia's Black Middle Class During the Depression, 1929–1940." Ph.D. diss., SUNY Binghamton, 1980 (alternate title: "To Do Good and Do Well: Middle Class Blacks and the Depression Philadelphia, 1929–1941").

Hardy, Charles. "Race and Opportunity: Black Philadelphia During the Era of the Great Migration, 1916–1930." Ph.D. diss., Temple University, Philadelphia, 1989.

Heaphy, Leslie. "The Growth and Decline of the Negro Leagues." M.A. thesis, University of Toledo, 1989.

Nelson, H. Viscount, Jr. "Race and Class Consciousness of Philadelphia Negroes with Special Emphasis on the Years between 1927 and 1940." Ph.D. diss., University of Pennsylvania, 1969.

Periodicals/Newspapers

Newspapers

Baltimore Afro-American	Cleveland Advocate
Chicago Defender	Indianapolis Freeman
Chicago Whip	New York Age

New York Amsterdam News
Norfolk Journal and Guide
Philadelphia Bulletin
Philadelphia Independent
Philadelphia Inquirer
Philadelphia Item
Philadelphia North American

Philadelphia Press
Philadelphia Public Ledger
Philadelphia Record
Philadelphia Tribune
Pittsburgh Courier
Washington Bee
Washington Tribune

Periodicals

Baseball Magazine
The Competitor
The Crisis
Half-Century Magazine (1919)
Journal of Negro History

The Messenger
Opportunity
The Sporting Life (1922, edited
    by Edgar Wolfe)
Sporting News

Archives, Documents, Manuscript Collections

Bill Cash–Lloyd Thompson Collection, Afro-American Historical and Cultural Museum, Philadelphia, PA.

Delaware County Courthouse, Media, PA.

Eddie Gottlieb file, National Baseball Library.

John Holway notes, courtesy of John Holway.

Judy Johnson file, National Baseball Library.

July 2, 1919, letter to W.T. Smith from Rube Foster, National Baseball Library.

National Archives, Mid Atlantic Region, Philadelphia, PA (U.S. Bureau of the Census, Manuscript Schedules of Population, 1900, 1910, 1920).

November 15, 1922, letter to W.T. Smith from Rube Foster, National Baseball Library.

Philadelphia City Directories, 1910–1936.

U.S. Office of Personnel Management, official personnel folder and employee medical folder of Edward Bolden.

University Archives, University of Pennsylvania.

Note on Sources

Since African American sports coverage was notoriously incomplete, biased, and occasionally contradictory, an examination of several newspapers is often necessary to derive a full interpretation of a particular event. The ECL is well covered by the *Pittsburgh Courier*, *Philadelphia Tribune*, *New York Amsterdam News*, *Baltimore Afro-American*, as well as lesser papers such as *Washington Tribune*, *Norfolk Journal and Guide* and the *New York Age*. The *Chicago Defender*, *Kansas City Call*, *Cleveland Advocate*, *Chicago Whip*, *St. Louis Argus*, and *Indianapolis Freeman* contain superior coverage of the NNL and midwestern black baseball. White newspaper coverage varies from city to city, although local Philadelphia dailies published Hilldale box scores regularly. Secondary sources should be used with caution since several are poorly documented and factually unreliable.

Index